Catawba Valley Mississippian

Lionel Jones

CATAWBA VALLEY MISSISSIPPIAN

Ceramics, Chronology, and Catawba Indians

D A V I D   G.   M O O R E

*To Megan,
Thanks for your help
on the project. Come back
to visit and check us on
the web.
Best wishes,
Dave Moore*

The University of Alabama Press
Tuscaloosa and London

Typeface is Meridien

∞

The paper on which this book is printed meets the minimum requirements of
American National Standard for Information Science–Permanence of Paper for
Printed Library Materials, ANSI Z39.48-1984.

Library of Congress Cataloging-in-Publication Data

Moore, David G. (David Gilbert), 1951–
Catawba Valley Mississippian : ceramics, chronology, and
Catawba Indians / David G. Moore.
p.   cm.
Includes bibliographical references and index.
ISBN 0-8173-1163-7 (pbk. : alk. paper)
1. Catawba Indians—Antiquities. 2. Catawba Indians—History. 3. Catawba River
Valley (N.C. and S.C.)—Antiquities. 4. Yadkin River Valley (N.C.)—Antiquities.
5. Mississippian culture. I. Title.
E99.C24 M66 2002
975.74'501—dc21

2002006424

British Library Cataloguing-in-Publication Data available

Dedicated to the memory of
Roy S. Dickens, Jr.
Charles Carey
Tom Hargrove

Contents

Figures

Plates

Tables

Acknowledgments

This book represents a revision of my dissertation submitted to the University of North Carolina at Chapel Hill in 1999. I would like to thank my dissertation committee members, Vin Steponaitis, Carole Crumley, Janet Levy, Trawick Ward, and Steve Davis, for their guidance and support of my research. I especially appreciate the efforts that Vin Steponaitis made on my behalf. I would also like to thank Dick Yarnell for his support and especially for serving as the Chair of my committee following the death of Roy Dickens. Trawick Ward was my first mentor and I have benefited greatly from his friendship and all of his instruction, both in the field and out. At an earlier time, Trawick proposed to study Burke ceramics; I hope my work has done justice to his interests. Completion of the dissertation would not have been possible without the help and direction of Steve Davis. Over the years he provided advice, helped me at every stage on the computer, photographed pottery, and generally kept me on track. I cannot thank him enough.

I began the dissertation at the urging of the late Roy S. Dickens, Jr. Roy was fascinated by the work of Charles Hudson, Chester DePratter, and Marvin Smith on the routes of the sixteenth-century Spanish armies through the Southeast, and he encouraged me to use this new research to frame my investigations of the upper Catawba region. I enjoyed and was inspired by Roy's enthusiasm in our early discussions and I greatly miss his friendship. I was able to begin this research thanks to my supervisor, Tom Burke, who arranged a one-year leave-of-absence from my position at the Office of State Archaeology to conduct fieldwork and complete my course work at Chapel Hill.

The excavations of the McDowell and Berry sites were conducted from May to October 1986. I was helped by the kind and generous support of many Burke and McDowell County residents and organizations. Above all, I would like to thank James and Pat Berry, owners of the Berry site. Their wholehearted cooperation and the interest of the entire Berry family helped make the fieldwork more enjoyable and rewarding.

Financial support, equipment, and supplies for the field investigations were provided by the Research Laboratories of Archaeology at UNC-Chapel Hill, the North Carolina Office of State Archaeology, the Western Office of the Division of Archives and History, the Historic Burke Foundation, the Burke County Historical Society, Sigma Xi, the Huffman-Cornwell Foundation, Charles and Alice Carey, Dak Brinkley, Lowes, Inc., of Morganton, and the Catawba County Historical Society. The Historic Burke Foundation also allowed us to use the historic McDowell House at Quaker Meadows for our field camp. I especially wish to thank Millie Barbee, who served at that time as Executive Director of the Historic Burke Foundation, for her tireless assistance and unending good cheer. James Roach and the late Robert Rowe provided welcome support of my work at the McDowell site.

One of the greatest pleasures associated with this project was the opportunity to work with students and volunteers. Eight students from Western Piedmont Community College and three students from Western Carolina University enrolled in the archaeological field school and more than 70 volunteers participated in the excavations. Although I wish I could thank them all individually, several volunteers in particular deserve mention. Thanks to Willy Israel, Ed Treverton, Nell Murphy, Wayne Pitts, John Harris, Carl Myers, David Dyson, and Mike Patton, who volunteered an enormous amount of time and energy to the project. I also owe a great deal of thanks to Mary Ann Holm, who served as Assistant Field Director. The excavated materials were washed and cataloged by members of the Western Office Archaeology Volunteers including Willy Israel, Ed Treverton, Chris and Jack Sheridan, David and Katie Warren, and Dick Albyn.

I would like to thank Sam Phillips and Glen Bryson for permission to conduct the excavations at the McDowell site. Thanks to Charles and Alice Carey, Tom Stine, and Wayne Pitts for allowing me to use their personal pottery collections in my analysis. Larry Clark provided important assistance from Western Piedmont Community College. Thanks to Jim Krakker at the National Museum of Natural History in Washington, D.C., for his assistance with the Caldwell County collections.

Charles and Alice Carey are responsible for much of the ongoing interest in the archaeology of the upper Catawba region. The Careys worked for more than 30 years to build our knowledge of Catawba valley prehistory. Their efforts laid the foundation for the Upper Catawba Archaeology Project and Charles was also instrumental in supporting the magnetometer survey at the Berry site in 1997. Sadly, Charles passed away in 2000 and with his passing, North Carolina archaeology lost an important friend.

While writing the dissertation, I benefited tremendously from discussions with friends and colleagues including Mark Williams, Brett Riggs, Mark Mathis, Marvin Smith, Ken Robinson, Jane Eastman, Ann Tippett, Steve Watts, Mary Anne Holm, Dan Simpkins, Tom Hargrove, Linda Carnes-

McNaughton, Greg Waselkov, Stanley South, Russ Skowronek, Tom Whyte, Scott Ashcraft, and Larry Kimball. I wish to thank Charles Hudson for his interest and encouragement and I especially thank David Hally, Chester DePratter, and Chris Judge for their support. My association with Janet Levy and Alan May has been both enjoyable and rewarding. I look forward to many more years of fruitful work with these friends.

I am indebted to everyone at the North Carolina Office of State Archaeology and the Western Office of the North Carolina Division of Archives and History. I would never have completed my dissertation without their help (patience was their greatest virtue). A particular thanks to Steve Claggett for continual encouragement and for allowing me to take several extended leaves-of-absence, to Susan Myers for proofreading and general encouragement, to John Clauser and Dolores Hall, who usually had to cover for me while I was on leave, to John Mintz for site information, to Dee Nelms for being so efficient, and to Mark Mathis for help on the computer. At the Western Office, thanks to Diane Jones, Nick Lanier, John Beaver, John Horton, Jeff Futch, Clay Griffith, and Ron Holland, the best office manager one could ever hope for.

To my dear friends Bob and Jan Brunk—thank you for everything.

The University of Alabama Press staff guided me through the transition from dissertation to book and I thank them for their support and patience. I am indebted to copy editor Kathy Cummins, whose skills I greatly admire. I would like to thank Lynne Sullivan and Greg Waselkov, who reviewed the manuscript and whose comments and suggestions were extremely useful in the revision process.

Nick Lanier and Steve Davis provided the photographs of pottery and other artifacts.

While working on the book, I have received the support of many at Warren Wilson College. I would like to thank Sandra Hayslette, Laura Herman, Jim McGill, and David Harper for their assistance, advice, and support. I especially want to acknowledge the student Archaeology Crew— Megan Best, Isabel Salazar, Rachel Horn, Emily Dale, and Will Spoon— who had to tolerate me while I struggled with the demands of completing this volume. Megan Best also helped format the tables, Isabel Salazar helped edit figures, and Rachel Horn provided artwork for the book.

I am grateful to Chris Rodning and Robin Beck, who reviewed and commented on many of the revisions for this volume. Their advice and comments have greatly enhanced the final product and they were especially helpful in discouraging some of my most tortured prose. I also thank Chris for his many stimulating discussions and for his wonderful Chapel Hill hospitality. I wish to acknowledge Rob Beck for his key role in my research. He was responsible for the initial identification of the sixteenth-century Spanish artifacts from the Berry site, the discovery of which inspired both of us to continue on our paths. I cannot thank Rob enough for all of his encouragement.

And in the end, I thank my family for their love and support. Between the dissertation and the book, I've missed too much time with all of you; special thanks to Kaitlyn, Linda, Jason, and Ben.

Catawba Valley Mississippian

Introduction

From late December 1700 through late February 1701, the Englishman John Lawson traveled from the English settlement at Charles Town in present-day South Carolina to a plantation on the Pamlico River in present-day North Carolina. Lawson recorded numerous observations about plants and animals, the landscape, and the peoples he encountered (Lefler 1967). On his journey, Lawson passed through many settlements of Native Americans, including towns of the Esaw and Sugaree Indians located in the vicinity of the confluence of Sugar Creek and the Catawba River, near the present-day North Carolina–South Carolina state line. While among the Esaws, he and his companions spent one night at the house of the "Kadapau King." This reference to the Kadapau King is the earliest English-language reference to the Catawba Indians; prior to 1700, the history of the Catawba Indians is shrouded with uncertainty.

The origin of the name *Catawba* is not clear. The word *Katoba* appears on a map drawn by an unknown French cartographer sometime around 1697. This seems to be the earliest reference on a map to a group called "Catawba" (Speck 1939). However, the Bandera account of the second Juan Pardo expedition provides several references to a chief called "Orata Catapa," whom Pardo met somewhere in the vicinity of Charlotte, North Carolina (Hudson 1990:264). *Catapa* may represent the sixteenth-century form of *Catawba*.

The close association of the Catawba with Esaw and Sugaree Indians indicated in Lawson's account reflects what may be best described as a confederation of tribes (Hudson 1965). It was often the case in the late seventeenth and early eighteenth centuries that Virginia and South Carolina colonists referred to Indians of this region collectively as the Esaw or Ushery. According to Brown (1966:20), "Esaw and its variations are corruptions of the Catawba word iswa or eswa, meaning river. The river to them was Eswa-Taroa . . . interpreted as 'the Great River,' later known as the Catawba River." The name *Ushery* was a corruption of "iswa-here." Speck (1935:204) points out that "the historical proper names of the tribe have been, from the first (Lederer), variations of the term iswa, 'river (people),' as Esaw, Issa, Ushery and the like." He translates *Catawba* as a construction expressing the idea of "people upon the edge or bank of a river." However, it is probable that *Esaw* and *Catawba* originally distinguished two separate groups (cf. Baker 1972a, 1976; Hudson 1965; Merrell 1982).

By name and by tradition, the Catawba River valley and much of North Carolina's western Piedmont region are associated with the Catawba Indians despite the fact that late seventeenth- and early eighteenth-century accounts of the Esaw/Catawba Indians describe them as living primarily on the lower Catawba/Wateree River near the present North Carolina–South Carolina border (see Figure 1). Although there are seventeenth- and eighteenth-century ethnohistoric accounts of Indians in the North and South Carolina Piedmont, the lack of a well-documented eighteenth-century Native American population in North Carolina's Catawba valley has meant that Indian history in that area remains only within the hazy realm of tradition. As a result, the entire North Carolina Catawba valley is usually associated with the Catawba Indians.

In addition, the upper Catawba area is closely associated with the Cherokee Indians who inhabited the Blue Ridge Mountains to the west. According to legend (Mooney 1982:380–381), the Cherokees once occupied the region, but moved to the west after depleting it of game. Later, after conflicts with the Catawba Indians over possession of the region, the Cherokees made an agreement with the Catawbas to establish a neutral area between their respective territories. This neutral area was bounded on the west by the Broad River and on the east by the Catawba River. Late seventeenth- and early eighteenth-century accounts describe the Cherokees as located in the far-western mountains of North Carolina, the upper Savannah River, and east Tennessee—all locations well away from the Catawba valley. Clearly, the dual association of both the Cherokee and Catawba Indians with the upper Catawba River valley contributes to historical and archaeological confusion within the region. This factor, plus the dearth of documentary evidence, makes it difficult to link prehistoric and historic Native American populations in the Catawba valley, particularly in the upper and middle valley areas.

Little systematic research has been applied to the problems of Catawba Indian archaeology in either North or South Carolina and, in fact, the archaeological manifestation of the Catawba Indians in the Historic period remains poorly defined. Therefore, it is extremely difficult to identify the prehistoric antecedents of the Catawba. Despite the lack of substantive Catawba Indian archaeological research, the assumption has persisted, both implicitly and explicitly, that certain archaeological assemblages within North Carolina's Catawba and upper Yadkin river valleys represent late prehistoric and protohistoric period Catawba Indian material culture.

Without exception, these assumptions are based on ceramic characteris-

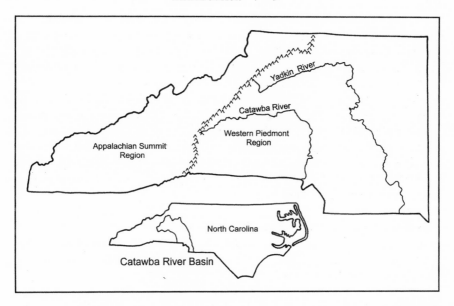

Figure 1. The Catawba River drainage in North Carolina.

tics. William H. Holmes (1903:143–144) was the first scholar to make the link between prehistoric and historic Catawba ceramics, noting that some of the pottery excavated from mounds along the upper Yadkin River in Caldwell County was similar to historic Catawba wares gathered between 1876 and 1886. Similarly, Coe (1952a:310) describes the presence of "Catawba trade sherds" on Dan River sites as an indication of Lamar influence on the Piedmont in the Historic period. The source of these trade sherds is uncertain; Coe does not indicate the specific Catawba Indian pottery to which he compared these sherds.

Coe has consistently referred to Catawba (Coe 1952b, 1964) and proto-historic Catawba (Coe 1983) ceramics in his discussions of archaeology in the lower and upper Catawba valley. Keel (1990) also suggests a seventeenth-century Catawba occupation at the Hardins site in Gaston County. Both Keel (1990:10) and Coe (1983:164) also describe Catawba-related ceramics on the upper Yadkin River. Keeler (1971) was the first to define the soapstone-tempered Burke pottery of the upper Catawba valley, and he further suggested that it was the product of protohistoric Catawba culture. Mathis (1979) has suggested that a protohistoric Catawba component is present at the Shuford (31CT115) site in Catawba County. Most recently, Wilson (1983, 1985) briefly discusses two Catawba valley sites (31ID31 and 31MK85) in terms of Catawba Indian ceramics and their relationships to the late prehistoric Pee Dee culture and to the protohistoric and historic period Siouan cultures of North Carolina's central Piedmont region.

Though it is rarely made explicit, each of these works relies on the observed similarity of select Catawba and Yadkin valley ceramic characteristics to a generalized "Catawba" pottery on the basis of form, style, and decoration. It is likely that some of the authors refer to late nineteenth-century Catawba Indian ceramics, but they may also have referred to eighteenth-century Catawba pottery. In any event, the prevailing impression in the archaeological literature is that prehistoric and protohistoric Catawba culture is represented throughout the entire Catawba valley and in parts of the upper Yadkin valley.

Two difficulties arise with these previous works. First, and most important, there has been no formal or systematic definition of Catawba Indian pottery recovered from documented eighteenth-century Catawba Indian archaeological sites. Obviously, the lack of documented historic period Catawba archaeological sites and/or phases hinders our ability to link Catawba River valley sites with Catawba Indian cultures (e.g., Levy et al. 1990). Second, little effort has been made to understand the cultural and temporal contexts in which the "Catawba-like" pottery is found.

The present study addresses these issues with two specific goals. My first goal is to outline a preliminary cultural chronology for the late Prehistoric and early Historic periods in North Carolina's Catawba River valley, through a regional analysis of ceramics from more than 300 sites. My analysis demonstrates a high degree of cultural continuity or homogeneity within the region during the late Prehistoric and Protohistoric periods. The analysis suggests that a large population of Catawba Valley Mississippian peoples occupied the Catawba valley well before Spanish armies entered the region. Site distribution data also suggest a substantial decline in the region's population at some point following Spanish contact. Second, this study outlines the historical process of Catawba Indian ethnogenesis. Despite the fact that reliable comparative data on the archaeology of the historic period Catawba Indians are still lacking, this study provides both ethnohistoric and archaeological support to earlier suggestions that ancestors of the historic period Catawba Indians occupied North Carolina's Catawba valley. It is also clear that further investigation of Catawba ethnogenesis requires a more complete examination of the sociopolitical nature of the late prehistoric Catawba valley groups that are often referred to as chiefdoms.

Chronology Building

Building a preliminary chronology for the late prehistoric and early historic period Catawba valley and western Piedmont involves stratigraphic evidence, radiocarbon dates, temporally diagnostic artifacts, and an analysis of the ceramic styles produced within the region. The project database consists of materials from a variety of sources. These include surface collections of potsherds from more than 300 sites surveyed by archaeologists at the Research Laboratories of Archaeology (RLA), University of North Carolina-Chapel Hill; surface collections gathered by amateur archaeologists; field notes about limited excavations by the RLA, the Schiele Museum of Natural History, and the University of North Carolina-Charlotte; and more extensive excavation data gathered during the 1986 Upper Catawba Archaeological Project, which I directed as a part of this study.

A ceramic attribute analysis was carried out to identify the range of ceramic variability within the study area. The analysis was adapted from the system developed at the RLA as a part of its extensive Piedmont Siouan archaeology project (see appendix D for more detailed discussion of the ceramic analysis). The attribute analysis enabled a comparison of broad categories of attributes over the entire range of collections. An attempt was also made to evaluate the distribution of attributes in terms of the previously identified Burke and Pisgah ceramic series (Dickens 1970, 1976; Keeler 1971). Two additional ceramic series, the McDowell and Cowans Ford series, were defined as a result of the analysis. The distribution of discrete ceramic attributes and the more general distribution of ceramic types provide the primary elements of material culture data on which the regional chronology is built.

Temporal parameters for this study were derived from radiocarbon determinations that dated archaeological features and artifact assemblages from seven excavated sites within the Catawba and Yadkin river valleys. These dates, along with limited stratigraphic evidence from several sites and comparisons with other regional chronologies, provided the means by which temporal assignments were made for the remaining surface sites and artifact (primarily ceramic) assemblages. In addition, the presence of European artifacts, including sixteenth-century Spanish artifacts from the Berry site, provided a convenient temporal marker for the Protohistoric period. This combination of temporal guides provided a more reliable means of dating the Catawba valley ceramics than has been possible in the past and enabled the construction of the regional cultural chronology presented in this study.

Determining the correct temporal placement of archaeological assemblages is one of the basic tasks of archaeology. Of course, this seemingly simple objective is often difficult to achieve. This study employs the *phase* as the basic temporal unit. The phase is the most commonly employed temporal unit in the Southeast today. Willey and Phillips (1958:22) defined the phase as "a basic archaeological unit possessing traits sufficiently characteristic to distinguish it from all other units similarly conceived, whether of the same or other cultures or civilizations, spatially limited to the order of magnitude of a locality or region and chronologically limited to a relatively brief interval of time." Such phases have been defined throughout North Carolina, but none have been proposed in the Catawba valley and surrounding western Piedmont region. To the west, in the Appalachian Summit region, Dickens (1970, 1976) and Keel (1972, 1976) have defined Woodland and Mississippian period phases, while in the central North Carolina Piedmont, Coe's (1964) pioneering phase chronology has been refined repeatedly (e.g., Simpkins 1985; Ward and Davis 1993; Wilson 1983). In many cases these phases have formal, spatial, and temporal dimensions. However, in some cases, phases are defined primarily on the distribution of a ceramic type or series that is believed to have a limited temporal span (e.g., Swannanoa, Pigeon phases).

Elsewhere, the practice of refining temporal units on the basis of ceramics has become a standard procedure (e.g., Anderson et al. 1986; DePratter and Judge 1990; Hally 1990, 1994; Williams and Shapiro 1990). As Williams (Williams and Shapiro 1990:18) states: "One of the greatest advances of the last 10 years has been the subdivision of Lamar into smaller units of time using pottery traits. The system adopted to implement this refinement is that of Phillips (1970), which consists of defining *phases* within the Lamar *period* as finer space-time units." Because the vast majority of Catawba valley pottery comprises Burke (Keeler 1971; Moore 1999) and Cowans Ford (Moore 1999) pottery types, which are regional variants of Lamar pottery, the present study relies heavily on Lamar cultural chronologies developed to the south of the Catawba valley. However, it should be stressed that the nature of the relationship between the Catawba peoples and other Lamar peoples is not entirely clear at this time. It is hoped that the new chronology will aid future research into the nature of the late prehistoric and early historic period Catawba cultures and their relationships with other peoples represented by sites and artifact assemblages identified by archaeologists as part of the Lamar tradition.

Catawba Ethnogenesis

The second goal of this study is to consider the course of Catawba Indian ethnogenesis. What is the earlier history of the people Lawson met on the Catawba River and did some Catawba ancestors occupy the Catawba valley in North Carolina prior to 1701? To answer these questions one must link archaeological sites and assemblages of fifteenth- and sixteenth-century populations with later populations known from ethnohistoric sources. This is a particularly difficult task with the Catawbas, whose past is inextricably entwined in the complex and incompletely understood history of the numerous Siouan-speaking native groups of the Carolinas. In fact, a full reconstruction of Catawba ethnogenesis is beyond the scope of this study. However, we are now able to propose a model of fifteenth- and sixteenth-century antecedents of the Catawbas/Esaws and can argue that the nucleus (or parts thereof) of the later Catawba confederacy occupied North Carolina's Catawba valley in the sixteenth century. This model is based on the new chronology and on the abundant ethnohistoric literature regarding the expeditions of Spanish armies under Hernando de Soto and Juan Pardo (Beck 1997b; DePratter et al. 1983; DePratter and Smith 1980; Hudson 1990, 1997; Hudson et al. 1984). In particular, new documentary (Beck 1997b; Worth 1994b) and archaeological evidence, in the form of Spanish artifacts recovered at the Berry site (31BK22), supports the presence of sixteenth-century Spaniards in the Catawba valley (Moore 1999; Moore and Beck 1994).

In her comprehensive treatment of the genesis of the historic Choctaw confederacy, Galloway (1995:5–6) describes the complexity of factors involved in understanding Choctaw prehistory, including demographic changes, changes in town locations, changes in sociopolitical organization, and changes in regional geopolitical relationships. Her work serves as a model for future investigations of Catawba origins, in which a similar complement of factors are likely to be integral to Catawba ethnogenesis and the formation of the Catawba confederacy.

Catawba Valley Chiefdoms

As early as 1965, the seventeenth-century Catawba were referred to as a "chiefdom occupying a strategic position in the southern Piedmont" (Hudson 1965:232–233). While Hudson's ideas about the Catawba have evolved since then (see Hudson 1990:ix–xi), so too have anthropological models of chiefdoms. Initially viewed in terms of function, evolutionary structure, and redistribution (Fried 1967; Oberg 1955; Service 1962), the chiefdom has been defined as a political entity characterized by different forms of hierarchical organization and leadership (Carneiro 1981; Earle 1987; Johnson and Earle 1987; Peebles and Kus 1977; Steponaitis 1978, 1991; Wright 1984). More recently, archaeological debates have concentrated on the political and ideological nature of chiefdoms (Anderson 1994b, 1996a, 1996b; Blitz 1999; DeMarrais et al. 1996; Drennan 1991; Earle 1991, 1997; Feinman 1991; Hally 1996; Milner and Schroeder 1999; Pauketat 1994; Spencer 1987, 1990, 1994).

Archaeologists in the southeastern United States have developed a large body of work describing the variation among Mississippian chiefdoms (Anderson 1994b, 1996a, 1996b, 1999; Blitz 1993, 1999; Brown 1966; DePratter 1983; Emerson 1997; Hally 1993, 1996; Hudson 1976; Knight 1990; Knight and Steponaitis 1998; Milner 1998; Muller 1997; Pauketat 1994; Peebles and Kus 1977; Scarry 1996, 1999; Steponaitis 1978, 1991; Welch 1991; Widmer 1988; Williams and Shapiro 1990). More specifically, researchers in the Southeast have discussed late prehistoric and protohistoric chiefdoms in the context of understanding the dramatic effect of European contact upon native southeastern societies in the sixteenth and seventeenth centuries (e.g., Anderson 1986, 1989, 1990a, 1990b, 1994a; DePratter

1983; Hudson 1965, 1970, 1976, 1997; Hudson and Tesser 1994; Larson 1971; Smith 1987; Smith and Kowalewski 1981; Thomas 1990). In fact, the present study developed out of research concerning sixteenth-century interaction between native chiefdoms and Spanish expeditions traveling through the Catawba/Wateree River valley of North and South Carolina (Anderson 1990a, 1990b, 1994a; Baker 1972a, 1974; Beck 1997a; Beck and Moore 2001; DePratter 1983; DePratter et al. 1983; Hudson 1990; Hudson et al. 1984; Levy et al. 1990). These works often view chiefdoms as ranked societies consisting of multicommunity political units (Anderson 1994a:7).

Though Catawba valley archaeology is still in its infancy, the present study not only advances the quantity of data available for consideration but also expands the nature of inquiry within the region. We are now able to relate Catawba valley societies (Beck and Moore 2001; Levy et al. 1990; Moore 1999) to the broader context of the late prehistoric Lamar polities that are described as chiefdoms on the basis of settlement patterns and the documentary evidence of sixteenth-century Spanish chroniclers (Hally 1994:167–172). However, it is not yet possible to evaluate different chiefdom models on the basis of the limited data from the Catawba valley.

In the meantime, I introduce a new term, *Catawba Valley Mississippians*, to refer to the people living in the Catawba valley from ca. A.D. 1100 to A.D. 1500. Catawba Valley Mississippian is derived from Ferguson's (1971) South Appalachian Mississippian, of which the Lamar phases are a part. I use it as a descriptive tool to distinguish the people of this time and region from the better-known North Carolina Piedmont Siouans and from other Lamar peoples, with the intention of developing a clearer picture of what and who the Catawba valley people were.

South Appalachian Mississippian is a geographical, temporal, and cultural framework for describing late prehistoric cultures in this broad region of the Southeast. Combining Holmes's (1903:130) South Appalachian province with its distinctive stamped ceramics and Griffin's (1967) temporal divisions, Ferguson (1971:243) sees South Appalachian Mississippian as "those cultural systems of the [South Appalachian] Province that were beginning to place a significant amount of emphasis on an agriculturally related economy and also beginning to pick up organizational and ideological characteristics, such as large villages and temple mound ceremonialism, consistent with agriculturally based economies." Ferguson created a framework of cultural units to combine related archaeological phases throughout the South Appalachian province; within that framework he examines the regional distribution of cultural traits, especially ceramic characteristics. The spread of Lamar style pottery reflected the evolution of a relatively homogeneous cultural landscape: "I do not see the expansion of the new and sophisticated Lamar style ceramics as associated with a drastic alteration of the cultural systems; rather I think the expansion of Lamar is representative of the close association that cultural constituents of South Appalachian Mississippian had developed" (Ferguson 1971:264).

As noted above, the relationships among Lamar polities remain an important research focus in the Catawba valley and surrounding areas of the Southeast. The preliminary chronology proposed in this book will form the foundation from which working hypotheses can be developed and discussed in the continuing effort to understand the history of late prehistoric and protohistoric chiefdoms in the Catawba valley.

Summary

North Carolina's Catawba River valley has been linked to the historic Catawba Indians by historical tradition and by presumed similarities between prehistoric ceramics and historic Catawba pottery. Until now, neither of these sources adequately accounted for such a linkage. The present study synthesizes both archaeological and ethnohistoric data to produce a preliminary cultural chronology of the late Prehistoric and early Historic periods in the Catawba River valley.

Chapter 1 presents a regional ethnohistory that examines the nature of the early eighteenth-century Catawba confederacy and uses the accounts of the sixteenth-century Pardo expeditions to link the prehistoric and historic eras in the Catawba/Wateree region. Chapters 2 through 4 lay the groundwork for the regional chronology; they present descriptions of excavated and surface-collected sites and focus on the ceramic assemblages from major sites (appendixes A–F provide more detail on the excavated sites and the ceramic analysis). The study area is divided into three regions on the basis of the geography of the Catawba and Yadkin river drainage systems and the intensity of archaeological investigations and available survey data. Chapter 2 addresses sites in the upper Catawba River valley, the Catawba headwaters region at the interface of the western Piedmont and the Blue Ridge Mountains. Archaeological investigations have been intermittent here, but the area has long been known for the presence of the unique soapstone-tempered Burke pottery. Chapter 3 moves to the nearby upper Yadkin River valley, which is best known for the late nineteenth-century excavations of the Nelson Mound and Triangle sites. Chapter 4 concerns sites of the middle and lower Catawba River valley. The middle valley consists of that portion of the river north of the Cowans Ford Dam, where an intensive archaeological survey was conducted in the early 1960s prior to the inundation of Lake Norman (almost no archaeological survey of the Catawba River valley has been conducted from the north end of Lake Norman to near Morganton in the upper valley region). The Catawba River south of Cowans Ford Dam, as well as the South Fork valley in Gaston County, make up the lower valley region in this study.

The new regional chronology is presented in chapter 5. Comparisons with a number of Lamar chronologies, radiocarbon dates, and the presence of European artifacts are all utilized to define late prehistoric and proto-historic period phases for the upper Yadkin valley and the upper, middle, and lower sections of the Catawba valley. Finally, the conclusion summarizes the new perspective on Catawba origins.

Catawba Valley Ethnohistory and Catawba Origins

1

John Lawson's visit with the "Kadapau King" was brief, but it is with his account that one usually begins the history of the Catawba Indians on the new Anglo-American frontier. Lawson clearly describes a group of apparently flourishing tribes—the Esaw, Sugaree, and Kadapau—in the vicinity of the confluence of Sugar Creek and the Catawba River. These tribes are the core groups of what became known over the next half century as the Catawba Nation (Figure 2). Charles Hudson (1965:75–76) suggests that the Catawba Nation or, more accurately, Catawba confederacy (i.e., the association of Esaws, Sugarees, Catawbas) had existed for several decades prior to 1701; it had developed in response to and was supported by their control of trade with the Virginia and Carolina colonies in the backcountry.

In 1701, Lawson viewed these people as distinctly named groups living in close proximity with one another. On the other hand, South Carolina colonial officials often referred to the Wateree/Catawba region Indians collectively as the Esaws (Merrell 1989:92–94). In fact, the Esaws were thought to be strong enough to pose a threat to the security of the Charles Town settlement. Hudson (1965), Wright (1981), and Merrell (1989) emphasize the extreme stress placed upon the interior tribes in the late seventeenth and early eighteenth centuries as a result of the competition between the Carolina and Virginia traders. The effects of that competition were compounded by the colonial efforts to reduce the perceived threat of the Indians upon the Charles Town settlement. In particular, the Carolinian tactics of favoring particular tribes in trade and of arming one Indian group against another, as well as the colonists' widespread slaving raids, wreaked havoc with native geopolitics on the colonial frontier.

These stresses culminated in the Yamasee War of 1715. Incensed by the actions of abusive traders, the Yamasees, Creeks, Choctaws, and some Cherokees initiated a concerted effort to attack and wipe out traders and plantations in the South Carolina backcountry. Early in the war a group of Catawbas, Cheraws, and Waterees killed a number of South Carolina traders. South Carolina ultimately repulsed the Indian offensive and crushed the Yamasees. In their effort to protect their new frontier, South Caro-

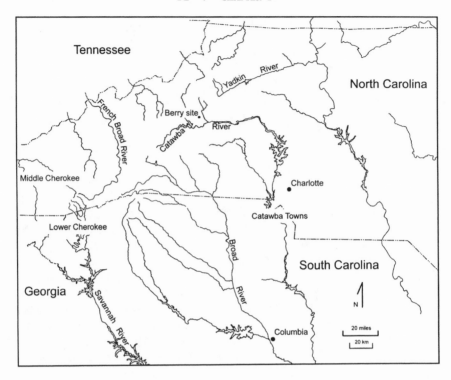

Figure 2. Location of eighteenth-century Catawba and Cherokee Indian territories.

lina forces were particularly ruthless with those Indians located closest to Charles Town; the Congarees, Santees, Sewees, Peedees, and Waxhaws suffered devastating losses (Hudson 1965:98). Survivors fled south into Florida or north to join the Catawbas, continuing the amalgamation of the Catawba confederation.

Despite having survived the Yamasee War, the peoples of the Wateree/ Catawba had entered a new period in their history, and the balance of power on the frontier had shifted. The Catawbas were no longer powerful trading partners with the colonies; Hudson (1965:98) describes them as a "colonial satellite, a military dependency whose affairs were shaped by the interests of various factions in the Colony of South Carolina." In addition, the Catawbas had become completely dependent upon the colonial trade and would necessarily accede to more and more colonial dictates (Merrell 1989:88–81).

Another glimpse of the early eighteenth-century Catawba world is revealed in the Catawba Deerskin Map presented to South Carolina Governor Francis Nicholson around 1721, probably by a Catawba headman (Waselkov 1989:322). The central towns represented on the map are those associated with the Catawba confederacy. Nasaw (later Nassaw) was the principal town of the Catawbas at this time and was closely surrounded by Nustie, Succa, and Sutterie. Waselkov (1989:323) describes Nustie as equivalent to Neustee, one of the six Catawba towns in 1754. According to Waselkov (1989:323), the Succas represent the group also known as Shoccories, Sughas, or Tansequas, and the Sutteries represent the Sugarees. Waselkov also points out that many of the other names on the map represent groups that were eventually assimilated by the Catawbas. These include the Charras (Saras or Cheraws), Saxippahas, Waterees, Casuies (Coosahs), Wasmisa (Waccamaws), and Wiapies.

This is a far cry from the numbers of towns implied by Lawson and, significantly, the term *Catawba* appears nowhere on the map; it was not a term used or recognized by the native people of the Catawba/Wateree River. On the other hand, prior to the Yamasee War, Anglo-Americans had referred to those people as Esaws, Catawbas, and Usherees, but "by 1715 even Esaw/Usheree disappeared, to emerge later as 'Nassaw,' a principal town of the 'Catawba' nation. Catawba itself had become the common term, though it remained unclear exactly what peoples this term included" (Merrell 1982:189). Merrell (1989:94–95) describes the continued usage of the term *Catawba* to the near exclusion of the other terms into the mid-eighteenth century, when colonials and Indians alike had adopted the convention "Catawba Nation" to refer to the amalgamation of the survivors of so many once discrete and independent peoples.

While it is clear from Lawson's account that the Catawba/Wateree groups seemed populous and secure at the turn of the century, by 1743 James Adair reported that the Catawbas had decreased to fewer than 400 warriors and these included remnant populations from 20 separate tribes (Adair in Mooney 1894:28). In other words, the confederacy had grown in terms of adopting even a wider number of groups, but their drastic loss of population reflected the results of disease, warfare, slaving activities, and colonial frontier politics. Figure 3 details the tribes considered to be part of the Catawba Nation in 1743. Hudson (1965:71) suggests that the linguistic diversity of the "Nation" reflects its history as a refuge; 20 different dialects were spoken among the "Catawbas," several of which were non-Siouan.

Indians of the Catawba Nation struggled through the eighteenth century in ever-decreasing numbers. In 1756 a map of the "Cuttahbaw Nation" shows six towns in the vicinity of Sugar Creek with a total of 204 "Men fit for Warr" (Merrell 1989:163). In 1763 the Catawbas were granted a reservation of 15 square miles in the vicinity of the confluence of Sugar Creek and the Catawba River, but at the end of the eighteenth century the Catawba Nation consisted of only about 100 Indians.

Following the end of the American Revolution and throughout the century the Catawbas were forced to protect their modest land holdings from economic losses and continued encroachment by Carolina settlers. Signifi-

---

Tribes comprising Catawba Nation (with other titles in parentheses).

Catawba proper (Issa, Iswa, Ushery, Ysa, Usi, Esau, Esaugh, Esaw)
Cheraws (Sara, Carrow, Saraw)
Sugarees (Sugari, Suttaree, Shuteree, Sittari, Sugaw, Sugar)
Waxhaws (Waxaw, Wisack, Wisacky, Weesock, Flatheads)
Congarees
Santees (Seretee, Setatee)
Pedees (Pee Dee)
Waterees (Watery, Watteree, Guatari)
Wateree-Chickenee ("Little Wateree")

Smaller tribes or refugees.

Shakori (Shaccoree)
Eno (Enoree)
Sissipahaws (Sauxpa, Sax:a:pax)
Keyauwees
Sewees
Waccamaws (Waggomans)
Woccons
Etiwaws (Eutaws)
Tutelos
Saponis (Sapony, Saponies)

Non-Siouans tribes also included.

Natchez, Coosahs, Yamassees

Figure 3. Eighteenth-century members of the Catawba Nation (from Brown 1966:3).

cantly, the late eighteenth century marks the time at which the Catawbas began to systematically barter their earthenware pottery to nearby white settlers. The trade in these wares grew to the point that by the early nineteenth century Catawba women bartered them as far away as Charleston (Merrell 1989:210–211). In 1826, just over 100 Catawbas lived in two towns, Newtown and Turkeyhead, located on either side of the river near Sugar Creek. However, by the Treaty of Nation Ford signed in 1840, the Catawbas agreed to cede their land to the State of South Carolina. In exchange, South Carolina would supply to the Catawbas a tract of land worth at least $5,000 in Haywood County, North Carolina, in order that the Catawbas would be able to live near the Cherokees. South Carolina did not comply with the terms of the agreement and no such tract was ever purchased. Though as many as 100 Catawbas ultimately moved into Cherokee territory in North Carolina, neither the Cherokees nor the State of North Carolina was party to the treaty and neither supported its terms (Merrell 1989:249–253). Unhappy among the Cherokees, many of the Catawbas wished to return to their homeland; over the years families left until only about a dozen remained among the Cherokees by 1852 (Hudson 1965: 135). In the late 1850s a reservation made up of approximately 630 acres of their original lands was given to the Catawbas to satisfy the terms of the Treaty of Nation Ford (Hudson 1965:134).

The Catawbas struggled through the latter half of the nineteenth century as a poor, isolated group whose self-identity as Indians became increasingly difficult to maintain within the social and political climate of the time. By the turn of the century, the Catawbas had lost much of their traditional culture and fewer than a dozen Catawbas spoke the language (Hudson 1965:152). However, much of their social identity was retained by the widespread adoption of the Mormon religion (Hudson 1965:152–157).

These issues of self-identity continued into the twentieth century and contributed to dissension over how the community should regard itself within the wider culture. Dissension peaked in the late 1950s when the Catawba tribe undertook a series of votes that culminated with a decision to divide their assets and terminate their status as a federally recognized tribe. Following negotiations with the Bureau of Indian Affairs, the Catawba tribe was formally terminated in 1962. The final tribal roll included 631 Catawbas (Hudson 1965:192).

Termination proved to be only a temporary solution, and in 1973 the Catawba reorganized as a nonprofit corporation. There followed continuous attempts to resolve long-standing disagreements with the State of South Carolina and the federal government. After lengthy negotiations, the Catawbas regained federal recognition in 1994.

Today, 300 years after Lawson's brief visit with the Kadapau King, more than 2,000 Catawba Indians live on reservation lands along the Wateree River around the towns of Catawba and Rock Hill, South Carolina—that is, in the same general vicinity in which Lawson encountered them. This apparent continuity masks the Catawba people's history of struggle as related above. Catawba Indian history reflects the profound changes that occurred among native Carolinian societies following the arrival of European explorers, traders, and settlers. Exploitative trade practices, warfare, disease, and colonial and federal politics resulted in the loss of native lands and sometimes caused catastrophic population losses. James Merrell (1989: 257–275) writes eloquently of these forces that tore the Catawba world to pieces, yet he also emphasizes the strength of the Catawba culture exemplified in stories, language, and especially the enduring ceramic tradition. These cultural elements are still alive in the contemporary Catawba community.

The Catawba language was an important aspect of Catawba self-identity well into the nineteenth century; however, among the already small population of Catawbas, the number of native speakers declined, and by the latter half of the nineteenth century, few native speakers remained. On the other hand, Merrell (1989:259) points out that some Catawba people carried on the use of Indian personal names until around 1900.

The Catawba language has been the source of much misunderstanding that derives primarily from the fact that the Catawba people comprised one of numerous Carolina Piedmont tribes identified by James Mooney (1894) as the Eastern Siouans. This identification, resulting in the association of the Catawbas with many small Piedmont groups who may or may not have spoken Siouan languages, has led to much confusion as to the relation of the Catawbas with other Siouan-speaking peoples (Hudson 1965:31–36). While the Catawba language is indeed a Siouan language, modern researchers are hampered by the fact that documentation of the language did not begin until the late nineteenth century, at which time few still spoke the language; linguistic data are therefore severely limited. The last known native Catawba speaker is believed to have died in the 1990s. Today, the Catawba tribe supports workshops and classes in the Catawba language as a part of the Catawba Cultural Preservation Project.

The Catawba Cultural Preservation Project also supports the active production of traditional pottery. This tradition has been a mark of Catawba identity for more than 200 years, from the eighteenth century when pottery production was an important economic means of survival to today when the work of master Catawba potters is recognized around the world. It is an unbroken tradition, a tangible connection to the past, and in succeeding chapters we shall see that it is a tradition that is well over 500 years old.

The foregoing is, of course, only the briefest survey of Catawba history. For a more comprehensive review of Catawba history, readers are referred to the works of Brown (1966), Hudson (1965, 1970), Baker (1972a), and Merrell (1989). The present study is more particularly concerned with the question of Catawba Indian origins. Who are the protohistoric ancestors of those people called Esaws, Kadapaus, and Sugarees, and where did they live in the fifteenth and sixteenth centuries? The following sections of this chapter explore the issue of Catawba origins, beginning with a more detailed consideration of Lawson's account that clearly sets the parameters for a look back into Catawba prehistory; it introduces some of the tribal elements that came to be known as the Catawba Nation. I then review ethnohistoric evidence about Native American inhabitants of North Carolina's Catawba and upper Yadkin valleys from the sixteenth through the late seventeenth centuries. Finally, I consider previous interpretations of Catawba origins and present a preliminary model that attempts to reconcile the protohistoric and historic period native geopolitics in the Catawba valley in North Carolina. I specifically address the question of whether there are likely linkages between the late prehistoric inhabitants of this region and the historic period Catawba Indians.

John Lawson's Journey, 1700–1701

John Lawson set out from Charles Town to explore the Carolina interior at the request of the Lords Proprietors in December 1700. His account of the journey (Lefler 1967) provides not only geographical data but also the most extensive descriptions to that time of the native inhabitants of the Carolina Piedmont. Lawson set off up the Santee/Wateree River, went into the lower Catawba valley, and then went northeast to the upper reaches of the Cape Fear and Neuse rivers, before finally turning east and passing through North Carolina's coastal plain on his return to the English settlement on the Pamlico River. Though his route carried him through the (presumed) heart of what had been the chiefdom of Cofitachequi, he did not mention that name. However, he visited Indians who in earlier years were believed to be associated with Cofitachequi. Lawson's account of his journey in the Wateree/Catawba area is summarized below.

Moving upriver on the Santee, Lawson first encountered the Sewee Indians, who are described as "formerly a large Nation, though now very much decreas'd" as a result of exposure to smallpox (Lefler 1967:17). The devastating effects of this disease are noted along the journey repeatedly by Lawson, who later stated, "Neither do I know any Savages that have traded with the English, but what have been great Losers by this Distemper [smallpox]." Two days' travel brought Lawson to the Santees, whose king is described as "the most absolute Indian Ruler in these Parts, although he is Head but of a small People" (Lefler 1967:27). Lawson then reached the Congaree town after five additional days' travel. This town is believed to have been in the vicinity of the confluence with the Wateree (Lefler 1967:33; Rights 1957:73). It was a small town of no more than a dozen houses, though Lawson described other settlements scattered along the Santee and another branch.

Lawson encountered the Wateree Chickanee Indians next, about 60 miles beyond the Congarees. These Indians were more numerous than the Congarees and were contrasted by their speech, the Waterees being Siouan speakers (Lefler 1967:39). Rights (1957:74) places them on the Wateree River near present-day Great Falls, South Carolina. Close to the Wateree were the Waxhaw Indians, believed to be located in the vicinity of Waxhaw Creek (Rights 1957:74). Notable here is the description of a "State-House," a building distinct from domestic structures and intended for use by chiefs (Lefler 1967:42–43). Lawson next passed through a Wisack (another term he uses for Waxhaw) town before reaching the Esaws. The Esaws comprised a "very large Nation containing many thousand people" (Lefler 1967:46). Once among them Lawson again commented on their abundance, describing their towns as "being very thick here-abouts" (Lefler 1967:49).

The Esaws usually are equated with either a part or the whole of the

Catawba people. However, after passing through many towns of the Sugaree Indians, in the vicinity of Sugar Creek, Lawson arrived at what he
calls the "Kadapau King's House" (Lefler 1967:49). This suggests that the
Kadapaus or Catawbas are in some respect distinct from the Esaws, or that
the name *Kadapau* already was being used as an inclusive term encompass-
ing both the Esaws and Sugarees. (I will argue on the basis of evidence
from the Pardo expeditions that they are recognized as separate groups in
the sixteenth century.) Here he met the Virginian trader John Stewart and
was surprised to find that their ultimate arrival had been announced more
than 20 days earlier. This location is believed to be in the vicinity of the
confluence of Sugar Creek and the Catawba River. Leaving here, Lawson
headed for the Sapona town by way of the Trading Path to Virginia (Rights
1957:77).

Although it is difficult to determine their exact locations, it is most likely
that the Esaw, Sugaree, and Kadapau towns Lawson visited were located
in the vicinity of the Catawba River and its tributaries (particularly Sugar
Creek) between present-day Charlotte, North Carolina, and Rock Hill,
South Carolina. Unfortunately, despite the references to numerous towns
associated with each of the "Nations," it is impossible to know the locations
of these towns. Whether any of them were located along the Catawba River
north of the Charlotte area is a question that can only be answered archaeologically.

Lawson's is the first English-language account to clearly name and locate the Catawba. For the next quarter century, the Esaws, Catawbas, and
Sugarees experienced the difficult and disruptive consequences of the colonial frontier expansion. The politics of trade and settlement, and the concern for protection from other Indians, were the major parameters of contact dynamics between Indians of the Carolina Piedmont and the South
Carolina and Virginia colonies.

Merrell (1989:46–47) points out that Lawson's descriptions of "Nations,"
"Kings," and other labels reflected the confusion with which Anglo-Americans regarded native societies. He states, "Nowhere was Anglo-American
blindness to the realities of native life more evident than in the names colonists came up with to identify Piedmont Indians" (Merrell 1989:47). He
goes on to describe how, at the close of the seventeenth century, colonists
of South Carolina distinguished the Westos, Savannahs, and other Indians
west of Charles Town, but merely lumped together those Indians located
toward the Virginia colony as "northern." They used the catch-all term
Esaw to refer to Indians living along the Catawba/Wateree River. In Virginia, the Indians of the Catawba/Wateree region were called "western"
Indians or Usheree (a corruption of Esaw with -*ri* suffix). "Neither colony
used a single term or said exactly what any of the names meant," writes
Merrell (1989:47).

John Lawson's journey revealed the limits to colonial comprehension. Esaws were there, a populous "nation"; but nearby were other "nations," each with its own territory, its own villages, its own "king." Lawson introduced *Catawbas* to Anglo-America, the term that, in time, would replace all others. For now however, the word was only one of many; like Western and Northern, Usheree and Esaw, it was neither consistently used nor clearly defined [Merrell 1989:48; original emphasis].

While Lawson and others on the Anglo-American frontier certainly misunderstood most of the complexity of native life and especially its political realities, it is also important to consider what Lawson's observations reveal about those realities. Misguided labels like Kings and Nations aside, he clearly described groups of settlements that were located at close proximity to one another along the Wateree/Catawba River. It is interesting that at first glance Lawson's description of the Kadapaus, the Esaws, and the Sugarees gives no hint to their respective past or future paths. Yet Lawson's account provides enough cultural and geographic detail that it forms the foundation of most histories of the Catawba people. Certainly, it sets the stage for interpretations of the historic period peoples called "Catawba." However, the Lawson account need not be viewed as a static, synchronic portrait. Merrell (1989:7) describes it as a looking glass to the future: "Lawson's journey, while offering a glimpse of the Carolina interior, also brought to light the elements that would shape Piedmont life over the next century." Yet Lawson is also a looking glass to the past, and I suggest that the Lawson account may help us understand the link between the history and prehistory of the Catawba people. This is accomplished with the recognition that Lawson visited peoples whose ancestors had experienced contact with Europeans nearly 150 years earlier.

Charles Hudson (1990) convincingly argues that sixteenth-century Spanish armies under Hernando de Soto and Juan Pardo traveled through the Wateree River valley in South Carolina and through the Catawba River valley in North Carolina. Along the way, they met with Indians and their leaders in more than a dozen towns, some of which were home to Siouan-speaking Indians. Thus, it is likely that the sixteenth-century ancestors of the Esaws and Catawbas occupied much of the far western Piedmont of North Carolina in the Catawba and upper Yadkin river valleys. Ethnohistoric evidence supporting these conclusions is presented below.

Sixteenth-Century Spanish Entradas

Sixteenth-century Spanish exploration and settlement in the southeastern United States profoundly affected the Native American population, although the degree of impact was undoubtedly greater in some areas than in others. The Indians of Florida, coastal Georgia, and South Carolina experienced the most sustained interaction with the Spanish, but Spanish influence was certainly felt in the interior, including Piedmont North Carolina. The degree to which Catawba valley populations were affected is uncertain, but by some accounts it may have been substantial, because researchers now propose that the armies of Hernando de Soto and Juan Pardo traveled through the region in the middle to late sixteenth century.

Four major accounts and one history compiled from interviews are available for the De Soto expedition (1539–1542), while five eyewitness accounts exist for the Pardo expeditions (1565–1568). These documents have served as the basis for numerous interpretations and reconstructions of the explorers' routes. The written accounts of the Spanish entradas provide an abundance of information regarding Indians with whom the Spanish interacted, but it is sometimes difficult to place the accounts in an accurate geographical setting.

This is particularly true for the De Soto route from Cofitachequi to Chiaha. The two major interpretations of this part of the route diverge considerably, one suggesting that De Soto traveled through the Savannah River valley (Swanton 1939) and the other arguing for the Catawba valley (Hudson et al. 1984). The exact path of De Soto's journey (and those of Juan Pardo, Narvaez, and other explorers) has been the subject of much discussion and debate (see particularly Boyd and Schroedl 1987; Brain 1985; DePratter et al. 1983, 1990; Eubanks 1989; Hudson 1997; Hudson and Smith 1990; Hudson et al. 1985, 1987; Larson 1990; Little and Curren 1990; Swanton 1939). Recent documentary (Beck 1997b; Worth 1994a, 1994b) and archaeological (Moore 1999; Moore and Beck 1994) evidence suggests that the route proposed by Charles Hudson and his colleagues is the correct one. It is not my purpose here to analyze the route controversy, but rather to examine the implications of the interpretation that Spaniards traveled through the Catawba valley.

Therefore, it is necessary to review briefly the current interpretations of the routes of sixteenth-century Spanish explorers Hernando de Soto and Juan Pardo. Charles Hudson, Chester DePratter, and Marvin Smith propose at least five locations in the greater Catawba River drainage at which De Soto (Hudson 1997; Hudson et al. 1984) or Pardo (DePratter et al. 1983; Hudson 1990) met with local Indians (Figure 4). Their research differs from that of their predecessors in that they worked from the longer and previously unavailable Bandera account to document the routes in a more systematic fashion than any researchers since Swanton. They charted Pardo's day-by-day progress on his second expedition, measured the direction and distance traveled each day, and also analyzed the geographic and cultural features mentioned in the account to establish the location reached at the end of each day.

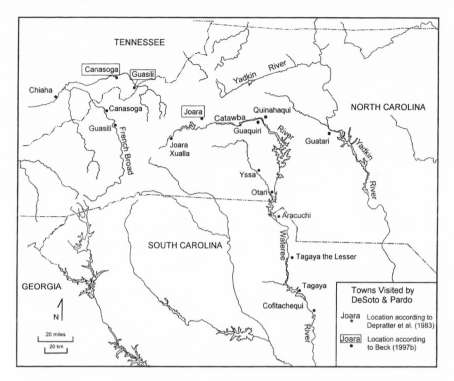

Figure 4. Indian towns visited by Hernando de Soto and/or Juan Pardo from Cofitachequi to Chiaha.

Using the abundant archaeological data that are available in some regions of the Southeast, they attempted to correlate known archaeological sites to the document locations wherever possible. They were also able to provide new locations for some of the towns on De Soto's route since Pardo apparently retraced a portion of the same trails and visited some of the same towns visited 26 years earlier by De Soto. According to these reconstructions, both De Soto and Pardo traveled through the Catawba valley. Few previous reconstructions of the De Soto or Pardo routes included the Catawba valley, although Brown (1966:7, 44) did propose that Pardo's site of Joara was located in the upper Catawba region in the vicinity of Pleasant Garden. However, the correlation of the Mulberry site in Camden, South Carolina, with the town of Cofitachequi (Baker 1974) provided the impetus for a major reorientation of the routes into the Catawba valley as opposed to the Savannah, Saluda, or Broad river valleys (see DePratter et al. 1983; Hudson et al. 1984). The following discussion draws from DePratter et al. (1983), Hudson (1990), and Beck (1997b) and follows Pardo's two trips into the interior, especially his route and activities from Cofitachequi to Cauchi, that is, from the Wateree to Catawba valleys and into the mountains of western North Carolina.

By the mid-sixteenth century, Spain had experienced little success at establishing viable settlements in the southeastern United States. Attempts at exploration and settlement by Panfilo de Narvaez (1528), Luca Vasquez de Ayllon (1526), Hernando de Soto (1538–1543), and Tristan de Luna (1559–1561) were disastrous. The threat of French success along the Atlantic coast spurred the Spanish to yet another attempt to secure the coast and interior north of La Florida. King Phillip II of Spain assigned the captain-general of the Indies fleet, Pedro Menendez de Aviles, the task of defeating the French and forming a Spanish colony in La Florida.

Menendez founded the settlement at St. Augustine in 1565, and in April 1566 founded his capital town, Santa Elena, at the modern-day site of Parris Island, South Carolina. At Santa Elena, Menendez ordered Captain Juan Pardo to explore the interior to find a route to Zacatecas, Mexico, over which the Spanish could transport their silver without threat from French and English ships.

Pardo left Santa Elena on December 1, 1566, headed north, and several days later arrived at the Indian town of Guiomae on the Congaree River. Continuing north along the Wateree, the expedition arrived at Canos, apparently the same town of Cofitachequi visited earlier by De Soto. The Spaniards followed the Wateree/Catawba north, coming to the towns of Tagaya, Tagaya the Lesser, and Yssa. Hudson (1990:25) locates Yssa on the South Fork of the Catawba River, in the vicinity of Lincolnton, North Carolina. Yssa is described as the home of a great chief; Pardo reportedly spoke to a large assembly gathered here. *Yssa* is most likely the sixteenth-century form of *Esaw* (Hudson 1990:187–188).

From Yssa, Pardo and his men traveled to Joara. Joara was apparently another important town, for many Indians were gathered there to meet Pardo. DePratter et al. (1983) first proposed the McDowell site (31MC41), near Marion on the Catawba River, as a likely location for Joara. Recent documentary and archaeological evidence suggests that the Berry site (31BK22), just north of Morganton, is a more likely candidate for the town of Joara (Beck 1997b; Moore and Beck 1994; Worth 1994a, 1994b; see below for discussion).

Unable to enter the nearby mountains because of snow, Pardo stayed at Joara for two weeks and had his men build a small outpost, christened Fort San Juan, which he left garrisoned with 30 men under the command of Sergeant Hernando Moyano de Morales. Pardo left with his remaining men and traveled east along the Catawba River to Quinahaqui, near present-day Catawba, North Carolina. From Quinahaqui, Pardo appears to have moved east, leaving the Catawba River, and two days later he arrived at Guatari, near present-day Salisbury, North Carolina. The Waterees, later located by Lawson just south of the Sugarees, are undoubtedly the descendants of the Guatari (Hudson 1990:187).

While at Quinahaqui, Pardo received word that a French attack on Santa Elena was imminent. He left for Santa Elena immediately, leaving one chaplain and four soldiers garrisoned at Quinahaqui; he traveled south to Otariyatiqui, near Charlotte, North Carolina, and then to Aracuchi, meeting his original path into the interior at Tagaya the Lesser. He arrived in Santa Elena with about 90 men on March 7, 1567.

No French attack materialized and, upon hearing of the excellent lands in the interior, Menendez ordered Pardo to undertake a second expedition to locate the best road to Zacatecas, to establish good relations with the Indians, and to take possession of the lands for the king of Spain. Menendez sent the scribe Juan de la Bandera to record all interactions with the Indians, as they were to become subjects of Spain.

In the meantime, Sergeant Moyano, in charge of the garrison at Joara, made several independent explorations. He traveled, probably in search of gold, with some of his men to a Chisca town, which he attacked. He also explored farther to the west and reached the town of Chiaha, where he awaited Pardo's return.

Pardo left Santa Elena the second time on September 1, 1567. Bandera maintained an account of each day's travel; therefore, the record of the towns visited (see Figure 4) and chiefs met is much more detailed than for the first expedition. Although the route differed slightly from that of the earlier expedition, the Spaniards once again reached the Wateree River valley and passed through Guiomae, Canos, Tagaya, and Tagaya the Lesser before reaching Gueça. Hudson (1990:34) places Gueça on the Wateree River, perhaps near Waxhaw Creek. Hudson (1990:187) also suggests that the Waxhaws, found in the same general location by Lawson, derived their name from the town of Gueça. Next, Pardo's army passed through Aracuchi and arrived in Otari. Otari, possibly in the vicinity of Charlotte, was located at the intersection with another important trail, and it was here that Pardo met two female caciques from Guatari, located to the northeast on the intersecting trail (Hudson 1990:35). From Otari, Pardo traveled to Quinahaqui and Guaquiri (near Hickory, North Carolina) and arrived at Joara on September 24, 1567. Upon arriving in Joara, Pardo received word that Indians had surrounded Moyano at Chiaha. Pardo then traveled into the mountains to the town of Cauchi and then on to Chiaha, which he reached on October 7.

Finding Moyano safe, Pardo planned to move south and west toward Zacatecas. However, upon reaching the town of Satapo, located on the Little Tennessee River near the confluence of Citico Creek, Pardo was warned of an ambush planned by the Indians to the south, and he decided to return to Joara, arriving on November 6, 1567. Pardo rested his men for two weeks, left 31 of his men garrisoned at Fort San Juan, and then began his return to Santa Elena, where he arrived on March 2, 1568.

Juan de la Bandera's report of the expedition provides a wealth of information about the Indians. It provides distances and directions between towns, names the Indian chiefs who met with Pardo at each town, and also lists the items traded by Pardo to the chiefs. It should be stressed, however, that in most cases it remains difficult to correlate the exact geography of Bandera's report to known sixteenth-century archaeological sites. Nonetheless, it is important to consider the proposed locations of a number of towns that are relevant to our interest in Catawba origins.

The location of the town of Joara is especially significant. Joara is likely the same town as De Soto's Xualla (DePratter et al. 1983:142; Hudson 1990:25). According to Bandera, Joara was located "at the foot of a range of mountains, surrounded by rivers" (DePratter et al. 1983:142); Ranjel described Xualla as "a village on a plain between two rivers near the mountains" (DePratter et al. 1983:142). DePratter et al. (1983:142) proposed the McDowell site (31MC41; see chapter 2 and appendix A) as Joara because its location on the Catawba River near Marion, North Carolina, fits the proposed route and because it was believed to date to the Protohistoric period.

However, recent investigations at the Berry site (31BK22), located in Burke County, North Carolina, have revealed a large number of sixteenth-century Spanish artifacts, the nature of which suggests that Berry may be a better location for the town of Joara (Beck 1997b; Moore and Beck 1994; Worth 1994a). Significantly, John Worth (1994b) has recently discovered a new account of the Pardo expeditions, written by Domingo de León, which supports the identification of the Berry site as Joara. Leon served under Pardo and participated in the expeditions as a soldier, notary, and interpreter. The León account is important because it provides details not found in other Pardo accounts, especially concerning the geography of the interior.

Worth finds León's location of Canos, or Cofitachequi, to be especially critical in correlating Pardo's route to the modern landscape. Canos is described as being located 40 leagues north of Santa Elena,

> on a river system that comprised two major branches that joined 30 leagues inland from the sea. An unnamed town at the junction of these rivers marked the beginning of population along the northwestern branch of the river, and towns were spaced at between half a league and a league apart. Canos was said to be 12 leagues upriver from this first town, and comprised a district stretching for 20 leagues in which the towns were more closely spaced, and on the eastern bank of the river [Worth 1994a:5].

Worth (1994a:6) argues that León's description of the river system and its chiefdoms "corresponds remarkably well to the Pardo route reconstructed by Charles Hudson and his colleagues." He especially feels that Leon's description of a river system with two major branches that both originate in the mountains and that join 30 leagues from the coast eliminates from consideration the Savannah River, long suggested as the setting for the main town of the chiefdom of Cofitachequi.

Having accepted the Hudson route as generally accurate (Worth 1994a:7), Worth then considers the Spanish artifacts from the Berry site. Initially reported by Moore and Beck (1994), and with subsequent discoveries, the assemblage of Spanish artifacts now consists of 12 Olive Jar sherds, 1 Caparra Blue Majolica jar fragment, 2 wrought-iron nails, 1 iron knife, 1 lead shot, 1 wrought iron buckle, 1 wrought staple, 1 unidentified wrought object, 1 lead sprue, 1 brass ball button, 1 brass clasp-knife plate, 1 rolled brass bead, and 2 glass beads (these artifacts are discussed in more detail in appendix B).

Sixteenth-century Spanish artifacts have been found in numerous contexts in the Southeast (Smith 1987), including at sites along the Hiwassee River in Clay and Cherokee counties, North Carolina (Rogers and Brown 1994; Skowronek 1991). Most of these artifacts have been described as trade items because they match the accounts of items given by Pardo and De Soto to the Indians. For instance, Hudson (1990:134–138) reports that Bandera's official record describes the following items as being traded to Indians on the second expedition: 126 iron chisels and wedges, 32 iron knives, 35 iron axes, 29 bead necklaces, 6 mirrors, gilded buttons, and pieces of Spanish cloth.

In fact, a specific record exists of items Pardo gave to the chiefs he met at Joara. As he was required to do at each transaction, Bandera recorded Pardo's actions at Joara: after Pardo received a satisfactory answer to his request for maize,

> the captain [Pardo], in view of the obedience of the cacique [chief], in addition to a little battle axe on a handle which previously he had given him in my presence, now he gave him an axe and for him and other caciques, his subjects, eight small long wedges like chisels and eight large knives, and a piece of satin and another of red taffeta [Bandera in Hudson 1990:265].

Several of the Berry site artifacts fit this pattern of trade or gift giving: the glass beads, the rolled brass bead, and the knife. The remaining items do not. Worth (1994b) has examined the documentary evidence of seven small Spanish military exploratory expeditions between 1597 and 1628, only one of which reached as far north as Cofitachequi. Fray Pedro de Chozas led one expedition from the Guale mission to the town of Ocute in 1597, carrying blankets, knives, fishhooks, scissors, glass beads, sickles, axes, and chisels for trade (Worth 1994b:117). Worth (1994b:120) also reports a list of planned trade items prepared for a follow-up expedition in 1600 that included "400 axes and four hundred hoes, one hundred sets [?] of butcher knives from Flanders, fifteen hundred *Reales* of large blue beads of glass and two hundred ordinary mirrors, [and] one hundred pairs of scissors."

Worth (1994a:1) describes only two mechanisms that can explain the presence of sixteenth-century Spanish artifacts at interior villages—trade or occupation. After a further review of likely sixteenth/seventeenth-century trade items, citing Smith (1987) and Waselkov (1989), Worth (1994a:9) states that there is "no hint that Spanish ceramics, lead shot, or iron nails ever entered into such a trade network, effectively eliminating such indirect trade as a probable mechanism by which these items arrived at the Berry site."

Finally, Worth (1994a:9–11) argues that olive jars, lead shot, and nails could easily have arrived at the Berry site as part of the garrison equipment carried by Pardo's troops. He suggests that these materials are associated with the Pardo expedition, rather than De Soto's, because while De Soto spent only one day at Joara, Pardo's men were there for more than nine months and built Fort San Juan. The construction of Fort San Juan could also account for the nails, always a scarce commodity in the Spanish colonies. In addition,

> Fort San Juan is the *only* site in the interior specifically noted to have been left with a supply of nails during the Juan Pardo expeditions. Based on Juan de la Bandera's account, none of the interior forts was left with nails, making Joara the principal location in the interior where archaeologists might expect to find 16th-century Spanish nails. This is not surprising, particularly considering the often extreme scarcity of forged iron nails in colonial Spanish Florida, even for Spaniards [Worth 1994a:10; italics in original].

Indeed, the potential for military supplies and occupational debris is striking. Hudson (1990:126–127) provides a list of supplies known to have been carried into the interior by Pardo's second expedition: 168 pounds of matchcord for harquebuses, 255 pounds of lead balls, 309 pounds of matchlock powder, 30 pounds of cannon powder, 85 pounds of biscuit (the first expedition carried 793 pounds of biscuit and 10 cheeses), 48.4 liters of wine (23.83 liters carried on the first expedition), 3 linen bags, 265 pairs of fiber sandals, and 178 pairs of shoes. When Pardo departed Joara, he left the following supplies with Moyano: 150 pounds of harquebus powder, 133 pounds of harquebus matchcord, 135 pounds of lead, 4 crossbows, 240 crossbow bolts, 3 shovels, 2 mattocks, and 2 picks (Hudson 1990:148).

In sum, Worth (1994a:11) suggests that the Spanish artifacts discovered at the Berry site are consistent with a mid-sixteenth-century Spanish occupation and particularly with a site like Joara where Fort San Juan was built. Since the Berry site is so close to the predicted location of Joara

(Berry is located about 25 miles east of the McDowell site) Worth argues that Berry is indeed the town of Joara.

Changing the location of Joara from the McDowell site to the Berry site has had other implications for students of the De Soto and Pardo routes. Beck (1997b:162) concurs with Worth's identification of Joara and has proposed revised routes for the De Soto, Moyano, and Pardo expeditions west of Joara in accordance with the new location. According to Hudson et al. (1984) De Soto traveled west from Joara, crossing the Swannanoa Gap and following the Swannanoa River to the French Broad River in the vicinity of present-day Asheville, North Carolina. He then traveled downriver to the confluence of the Nolichucky and the French Broad, where he entered the town of Chiaha, near present-day Dandridge, Tennessee. Beck (1997b:163–165) suggests that De Soto traveled north from Joara into the mountains, reaching the Toe River and then the Nolichucky River, and then proceeded west along the Nolichucky to Chiaha. Hudson (1997:480) supports the changes proposed by Beck.

Beck, on the basis of information in the Domingo de León account, also suggests changes in the Moyano and Pardo routes west of Joara. According to León, the towns destroyed in 1567 by Moyano were Maniatique and Guapere (Beck 1997b:165). Hudson (1990:87) has reported that Luisa Mendez described saltwater springs at the base of the mountains and claimed they were the only such springs in the land. Luisa Mendez was an Indian woman from the interior who married Juan de Ribas, a member of Pardo's company. Ribas, in testimony before Governor Canco in 1600, described her as the cacica of "Guanaytique" or "Manaytique" (Hudson 1990:190, 201).

From this testimony, Beck (1997b:166) argues that Maniatique was likely located on the South Fork of the Holston River near present-day Saltville, Virginia. Beck also places Guapere on the Watauga River in upper east Tennessee. Finally, Beck (1997b:167–168) suggests that when Pardo entered the mountains to meet with Moyano at Chiaha, he did not follow De Soto's earlier route but instead crossed the Swannanoa Gap, then crossed over the French Broad River to reach Cauchi, possibly located at the Garden Creek site (31HW1) on the Pigeon River near Canton, North Carolina. From there, he traveled north, back to the French Broad River and downstream to Chiaha.

Clearly, the ability to reliably locate a town such as Joara has many implications for future route research. However, the significance of this work lies not merely in revising locations but also in providing new perspectives on the interactions of aboriginal populations in the interior. In this case, Beck has linked Joara, in the upper Catawba valley, with Indians in the Saltville, Virginia, region by use of the 1751 Fry-Jefferson, 1770 Collet, and 1775 Mouzon maps that indicate an "Indian Path" extending from the upper Holston south to the upper Catawba and farther south to the Savannah River. Beck (1997b:166) cites Barber and Barfield (1992:2), who describe "the development of a chiefdom level society along the Holston River drainage powered by the extensive trade of salt for exotic wealth items." Noting that the De Soto accounts speak of the "Chisca" copper trade from this region, Beck (1997b:166) suggests "the inhabitants of Maniatique may have acted as middlemen, trading salt for native copper, then trading both copper and salt to Indians further south." Joara may have similarly exploited its location on this path to serve as a middleman for Indians farther to the south. Such access to exotic materials and possible control of their distribution may also have contributed to the regional significance that Joara appears to have held in the mid-sixteenth century (Beck and Moore 2001).

Given the current state of documentary and archaeological evidence, the location of Joara seems relatively certain. However, no such certainty exists for the locations of any of the other towns in the Catawba or Yadkin valleys that were visited by De Soto or Pardo. A similar uncertainty exists concerning the overall relationships of these towns to each other.

In some cases, the towns of the Catawba valley have been described as being part of or, to some degree, under the influence of the greater chiefdom of Cofitachequi (Anderson 1986; Baker 1974; Booker et al. 1992; DePratter 1983, 1989; Hudson 1986, 1987). However, DePratter (1994: 213) surveys these arguments and finds they are based on interpretations of conflicting sources of information from the De Soto and Pardo accounts. He suggests that the chiefdom of Cofitachequi extended to the north "only as far as the linguistic boundary at the present state line" (DePratter 1994:220).

The linguistic boundary has been defined by Booker et al. (1992) through an analysis of the names of towns and chiefs encountered by Pardo (and recorded by Bandera) on his second expedition. They suggest the languages spoken south of the town of Otari were Muskogean, and that Catawban languages were spoken at Otari, Catapa, Dudca, Guaquiri, Guatari, and Yssa (Booker et al. 1992:438–440). They are unable to determine the language affiliation for the town of Joara and suggest that while it could be Catawban or Iroquoian, it could also be Yuchi or an undocumented language isolate (Booker et al. 1992:425, 434).

The Pardo account indicates that a substantial population occupied North Carolina's Catawba valley in the mid-sixteenth century. According to Hudson (1990), Pardo visited six named towns in the region, as well as Guatari, located on the nearby Yadkin River. In addition, many native chiefs met with Pardo at Yssa and Joara, suggesting that other towns were also located in this region. Unfortunately, following the Pardo expeditions, there are no documented European incursions into the North Carolina Piedmont for nearly 100 years; thus, there are no clues as to the presence or absence of towns during this period. However, it is possible that Spanish exploration of the Piedmont continued after the fall of Pardo's forts in 1568. Hudson (1990:189–195) discusses the documentary evidence for gem-mining activities and argues that if mining occurred it began after 1602 and ended by 1700, given the increased influence in the Carolina interior by the Charles Town settlers.

Certainly, if mining enterprises were carried out in the North Carolina Piedmont, they were of such small scale that they have effectively been hidden from the historical record. It does seem plausible, however, that occasional, minor Spanish forays were launched to seek these rewards. If such forays occurred, it is also difficult to determine whether contact also took place between small mining parties and native populations and what impact these may have had on trade (both direct and indirect), disease transmission, and movements by Indians in response to such events.

Seventeenth Century

Although there are no documented eyewitness seventeenth-century accounts of the North Carolina Piedmont, there is an interesting second-hand account from Spanish coastal explorations. In 1605, Francisco Fernández de Ecija reconnoitered the Atlantic coast from St. Augustine to Cape Fear in advance of yet another attempt at settling the coast. In 1607 he set out again to investigate reports of English activity in the interior and sailed as far north as the vicinity of the reported English settlement of Jamestown (Hann 1986:1–2).

On the first trip he sailed up the River Jordan (Santee) and met two Indians, both natives of the town of Cayequa (Hann 1986:10). Upon being asked whether they had any knowledge of copper, gold, or silver sources, they replied that Indians "who came from the interior to their lands to barter for fish and salt and shellfish brought many chaguales of copper" (Hann 1986:10). When asked about a reported large mountain that shines and is bright, a reference to the crystalline mountain supposedly located by Pardo, the Indians replied that they had heard of such a place but had not been there and that only one of them had been on the path to the mountain as far as Guatari. They described the mountain as being close to a large town called Hoada, "which has many Indians and which is [on the] direct path to go to the mountain, and that the villages that are in between are Guatari and Coguan = Guandu-Guacoguayu = Hati = Guaca = Hati = Animache-Lasi-Guamr (?) = Pastuecoti -that by way of the said villages one goes on a direct path to the mountain" (Hann 1986:10).

Hann (1986:72) reports that while it is impossible to correlate the names of most of the towns with other towns known from the De Soto and Pardo accounts, Hoada is certainly Joara, and Guatari, while keeping its name, has shifted location from the Yadkin to the Catawba River. On his second voyage in 1607, Ecija returned to the Santee location, where he was met by many Indians to whom he gave knives and beads. Among the several chiefs he met was the chief from Guatari (Hann 1986:43).

Ecija's account is interesting for several reasons. It is clear that Joara still was occupied in 1605 and that it was still probably located near the mountains, but that the location of Guatari had possibly changed. Guatari was on the path to Joara, but there was no town reported between the two, suggesting that the area had fewer towns than at the time of Pardo (it is also possible that the informants were not completely accurate, having not been there themselves). Finally, if one assumes that the Guatari chief was one of the inland Indians who traded copper for salt, this might indicate a lack of salt from other sources, that is, from the Saltville vicinity. Perhaps there was less interaction at this time between Joara and Maniatique, or between Guatari and Joara, than there had been at the time of Pardo. Is it significant that no chief from Hoada was present to meet Ecija? Recall that Moyano participated with Indians from Joara in the attack on Chisca towns; perhaps this level of animosity between Joara and Maniatique existed at other times as well. There may have been no mutual exchange or cooperation between peoples in southwest Virginia and the upper Catawba/Yadkin region in 1605.

Regardless of Spanish activities, some researchers have argued that English traders had penetrated the Carolina Piedmont by the mid-1600s. Brown (1966:48–53) argues that Virginian traders may have been among the Catawbas by 1640 or 1650. She cites the fact that several traders (among them William Clayborne and Abraham Wood) were granted permission in 1652 to explore southwest of the James River in order to advance the fur trade. She also suggests that others had entered this area even earlier (Brown 1966:52). Alvord and Bidgood (1912:46–50) likewise suggest that travel south of the James River had occurred prior to the 1650s. Finally, citing William Byrd II's statement on the priority of Virginia's right to trade with the Cherokees over the rights of the new Georgia colony, Brown (1966:53) argues that the Virginia traders had established trade with the Cherokees before 1652 and that as a result, the trading route had passed through the Catawba region 20 years before the founding of Charles Town.

There is no documented evidence to support Brown's hypothesis of such early commerce, and yet there is no question that the people called the Westo were already intensively involved with the Virginia traders when the Englishman Henry Woodward first met them on the Savannah River in 1674 (Wright 1981:105). One can only guess to what degree the actions of this poorly known group accurately reflect the general availability of firearms and other trade items in the interior of Piedmont North Carolina during the last quarter of the seventeenth century.

It is extremely difficult to correlate any seventeenth-century accounts directly with the Catawba valley. The written account of John Lederer's travels in 1670 suggests that he was the first to describe the interior Piedmont of North Carolina, and he may have visited the Catawba region. However, his account is highly controversial and is not discussed in detail here since it cannot be used to document specific locations (see Wilson [1983] and Hudson [1990:184–185, 198–200] for excellent discussions of Lederer). It should be noted that Rights (1931, 1957) suggests Lederer generally traveled along the same path later followed by Lawson (though traveling in the opposite direction). In addition, while questioning whether Lederer actually made the trip himself, Hudson (1990:184) suggests that his information about the Carolina interior may have come from a knowledgeable Indian informant.

James Needam and Gabriel Arthur, 1673–1674

The sole seventeenth-century reference to the upper Catawba region might be found in the travels of James Needham and Gabriel Arthur in 1673–1674, as interpreted by Wilson (1983). With support from Virginia trader Abraham Wood, Needham and Arthur traveled into the southern mountains to extend Wood's trading territory. The description of their journey is contained in a letter written by Wood to John Richards in August 1674 (Davis 1990b). After one unsuccessful start from Fort Henry, Needham and Arthur embarked again on May 17, 1673. Wood reports that after one month they were joined by a group of Tomahitans. After stopping briefly at Occaneechi they continued west and passed through a Sitteree town before ascending the mountains.

Given Wilson's interpretation, it is necessary to consider this account in some detail. Alvord and Bidgood (1912) place the Sitteree town in the upper Yadkin while Rights (1957) equates the Sitterees with the Sugahs or Sugarees and places the town on the Trading Path near the confluence of Sugar Creek and the Catawba River in what is now York County, South Carolina. Wilson's interpretation of the physiographic references places the Sitteree town on the upper Catawba near Marion in McDowell County. The following discussion describes a number of inconsistencies that I believe argue against the head of the Catawba valley as a reliable location for Wood's Sitteree town.

The distance from Occaneechi to Sitteree is given as nine days. Sitteree was said to have been "the last towne of inhabitance and not any path further untill they came within two days jorney of ye Tomahitans" (Davis 1990b:33–34). There is no clear indication that any other towns were encountered after leaving Occaneechi, but it is possible that others encountered were not mentioned. It is impossible to know at what distance from Sitteree any other towns might have been located.

Leaving Sitteree, four days were required to reach the top of the mountains. It is difficult to determine what was meant by the "top" of the mountains, but the travelers appear to have crossed at a pass and descended into a less-mountainous terrain. An ascent of the Blue Ridge escarpment at any location is unlikely to require four days; if Sitteree was located near the head of the Catawba River as suggested by Wilson (1983), then four days of travel should have brought Needham and Arthur well into the mountains.

From the top of the mountains, their route crossed five rivers flowing to the northwest, and this portion of the trip was described thus: "when they travell upon ye plaines, from ye mountaines they goe downe, for severall dayes they see straged hills on theire right hand, as they judge two days journy from them, by this time they have lost all theire horses but one; not so much by ye badness of the way as by hard travel" (Davis 1990b:34). The total travel time from Sitteree to the Tomahitans was said to have been 15 days (Davis 1990b:34).

The description of travel upon the "plaines" and of "straged hills on theire right" suggests that they had crossed the Blue Ridge and were traveling southwest through the Ridge and Valley region of eastern Tennessee. (Note: an examination of seventeenth-century English lexicons failed to find any reference to *straged*.) Crossing the mountains in the vicinity of the Catawba River headwaters would have brought the travelers into the French Broad River valley. From this point, a mere two to four days' journey west would have brought them to the Cherokee Middle Towns on the Little Tennessee River; perhaps an additional three to four days would have been needed to reach the Overhill Towns. For comparison, in 1776, General Griffith Rutherford and more than 2,000 men and animals traveled from just west of Marion to the Middle Cherokee towns in six days, having covered only about 10 miles per day (Dickens 1967). However, this route requires an arduous crossing of numerous ridge systems to reach the Middle Towns. Nowhere along this route would one describe "plaines" and "straged hills" in only one direction. If, on the other hand, Needham and Arthur traveled north along the French Broad River they would have reached the Ridge and Valley region in a more circuitous route and may have proceeded to the Little Tennessee. Again, however, 15 days seems a lengthy time of passage. Assuming that the Tomahitan River was the Tellico or Little Tennessee River, it seems extremely unlikely that 15 days would be required to reach it from the upper Catawba area.

A final point concerns the statement that no path existed beyond Sitteree until they were two days away from the Tomahitans. This seems to imply a lack of commerce, transport, and communication between Sitteree and the Tomahitans. Yet one wonders how the accompanying Tomahitans guided Needham and Arthur. One would assume they returned by way of the same route they employed on their way to the Occaneechi. Perhaps not, though, considering that the Tomahitan chief was easily able to circumvent the Occaneechi after the attack on Arthur at Sarah (Davis 1990b:43). It appears that he was well acquainted with alternate routes to Fort Henry. However, the reported absence of a path beyond Sitteree also argues against the upper Catawba location since there was likely a trail of long standing that linked the French Broad River with the Catawba River by way of the Swannanoa Gap (Myer 1928).

Rights (1957:67–68) suggests that the route traveled by Needham and Arthur was the well-established Trading Path between the Occaneechi and the Catawba, the same path traveled three years earlier by Lederer. By his reckoning, Sitteree is most likely the capital Catawban town located near the confluence of Sugar Creek and the Catawba River. From there the party headed west and crossed the mountains near the headwaters of the Broad River. Although this route seems to better accommodate the 15 days of travel, it also is likely to have required passing through the Cherokee Middle Towns.

Wilson (1983:98) argues against Rights's route since there is no mention of any Indian group that would have been encountered had they been traveling on the Trading Path southwest of Eno Town. The same argument can be made for the route west from the Catawba River. It seems unlikely that no other Cherokee settlements were encountered in 15 days of travel; both Wilson's and Rights's routes make probable an early encounter with the Middle Cherokee settlements.

However, an approach to the Little Tennessee from the northeast seems more plausible with respect to the lack of settlements between Sitteree and the Tomahitans. Alvord and Bidgood (1912) place Sitteree on the upper Yadkin. It is possible that Sitteree was located near the foot of the Blue Ridge on the Yadkin River or one of its tributaries. A four-day westerly crossing of the mountains could realistically place one in the vicinity of the upper Nolichucky River or perhaps farther west in Tennessee. From here, a nine days' journey also seems more realistic to reach the Little Tennessee River. Or, the nine-day journey carried them to a location farther west and/or south. Any placement of Sitteree farther west than the upper Yadkin would further extend the location of the Tomahitans to the west. Following Rights's location for Sitteree, the Tomahitans might be located in the vicinity of Chattanooga.

Obviously, when the account is taken at face value, it is difficult to locate clearly the Sitteree town according to Wood's description of the Needham and Arthur route. If additional Indian towns were encountered but not noted (by Needham and Arthur or Wood) their locations would undoubtedly aid in establishing that of Sitteree. There is also the faint possibility that either Needham's or Wood's account was intentionally misleading in certain details to protect future interests. Nonetheless, it is difficult to argue for a Catawba valley location for Sitteree.

Wood's account of Gabriel Arthur's time with the Cherokees is important for the description of the raid on the Spanish mission 14 days to the south from the Cherokee town. This raid demonstrates the familiarity of the Cherokees with the Spanish settlements and the ease with which "commerce" may have occurred (this may also add support to a Tomahitan location much farther west or south than the Little Tennessee River). It seems likely that other Indians of the interior—including those of the Catawba valley—were also aware of the Spanish outposts of coastal Georgia and Florida.

Late Seventeenth Century

In the early years following the founding of Charles Town by the English in 1670, there is no direct documentation to demonstrate the effect of trade and, more important, slaving activities in the Catawba region. However, Wright (1981) argues that these activities severely affected native populations in most of the South Carolina interior. It seems highly likely that this pressure would have been felt directly or indirectly in the Catawba valley through either population losses or population increases by refugees. In any event, there seems to be tremendous potential for disorder in the Catawba valley as a result of slaving pressure from Charles Town.

It is difficult to glean any evidence of Indian populations in the western Piedmont between Pardo's visit and the eighteenth century. It is interesting that as early as 1670 the Trading Path connected Virginia with the Carolina interior tribes in an arc that seems to have passed near all the known tribes of the Piedmont (see Rights 1931). It is possible that there was no major trading path to the west (to the upper Yadkin or Catawba) because there was no population there by the late seventeenth century. However, it is also possible that no populations are documented there because they were scattered and small and were not located on the main trading path.

Other evidence indicates that the upper valley was much less populated if not completely depopulated by 1700. For example, a list of Indians fighting with the colonials in the Tuscarora War includes Essaws, Catabas, Sagarees, and others located in South Carolina and North Carolina. None of these groups (with the exception of Wilson's [1983] placement of the Suterees/Siterees in 1673) has ever been identified as living in the western Piedmont of North Carolina. It may be argued that any inhabitants of the upper Catawba region were well insulated from these events and felt no need to assist in the colonial effort. However, it must then be asked what enabled these groups to remain so insulated or isolated that they had no stake in events that affected the rest of the native population of the Carolinas.

More evidence of the lack of major towns in the seventeenth-century upper Catawba valley is a 1715 census of Indians prepared for Governor

Johnson of South Carolina (Rivers 1874:3). This census described those Indian Nations considered to be subject to the government of South Carolina and was compiled on the basis of the observations of the traders and travelers Thomas Nairne, John Wright, Price Hughes, and John Barnwell. Its importance cannot be overstated. The census figures do not represent casual or unconcerned estimates. The men responsible were interested in two things: trade and protection for the colonial settlements. It was in their self-interest to know the location and strength of potential trading partners or enemies. The account lists Indians from as far as 640 miles away from Charles Town. The Catawbas are listed as consisting of seven villages located 200 miles west-northwest. No other group is listed farther away in this direction. Therefore, it seems that if any substantial population were located in the upper Catawba area, the traders, who had been to the Cherokees and beyond, were unaware of them. It is possible there were groups living beyond the Catawbas who were known to the traders but were believed to be sufficiently buffered by the Catawbas (R. P. Stephen Davis, Jr., personal communication 1997), or it may also be that groups living farther northwest of the Catawbas may not have been considered to be subject to South Carolina. Given the potential for trade, concerns for potential threats to the safety of Charles Town, and the knowledge that the Cherokees could travel 14 days to attack Spanish settlements in Florida, it seems certain that the census would include people living on the upper Catawba if the traders knew of them. Thus, either people unknown to the traders lived in the upper valley (which seems unlikely) or this area had been depopulated by 1715.

The map presented by a Catawba headman to South Carolina Governor Francis Nicholson around 1721 (Waselkov 1989) provides further evidence about the lack of native population in the upper Catawba valley in the late 1600s and early 1700s. This map, painted on deerskin, consists of circles representing Indian groups connected by lines representing paths. Also represented are paths to Charles Town and Virginia. Waselkov (1989:300) points out that along with geographic information, social and political relationships are portrayed on the map with a "flexible, topological view of space." For instance, the Catawbas (Nasaws) occupy the largest circle at the center of the map in an attempt to reinforce their strategic position at the crossroads of trading paths (Waselkov 1989:303). It is clear that the deerskin map does not always reflect exact geographical relationships. However, it is obvious that general relationships are recognizable. There appears to be a central constellation of towns consisting of Indians known to be part of the Catawba amalgamation. Outside of this constellation, and connected by separate paths to both the Catawbas and Charles Town, are the Cherokees and Chickasaws. Waselkov (1989:324) suggests that despite the lack of scale in distance, most of the relative positions between groups and paths are accurate. Therefore, it is interesting to note that there is nothing in the entire area between Nasaw, the Cherokees, and Virginia. That is, the area north of Nasaw, west of the Occaneechi Trail, and east of the mountains is blank.

Admittedly, this line of evidence is circumstantial at best. There is no reason to believe that the limited ethnohistoric record accurately names and locates every Indian group that occupied the Carolina Piedmont between 1670 and 1830. And certainly the documented movements of certain groups and towns in the eighteenth century suggest that similar events may have gone unrecorded. However, I submit that there is a clear pattern (and there are clear limits) of colonial knowledge about the peoples of the interior and I think it unlikely that any large group occupied the western portion of the Catawba valley. I suggest the lack of ethnohistoric evidence truly reflects a relatively depopulated area in the middle and upper Catawba region in the late seventeenth century.

Despite that possibility, the region maintains its Catawba and Cherokee associations through the eighteenth century. The best example of this is found in the diary of Bishop August G. Spangenburg, who traveled into the upper Catawba valley in 1752 to survey land for a future Moravian settlement. While in the upper Catawba region he commented several times on the presence of both Catawba and Cherokee hunters (Saunders 1886). He further solidified the association of the area with both groups as follows: "As we believe it is the Lord's purpose to confer a blessing on the Catawba and Cherokee Indians—by means of the Brethren—we resolved to take up some land here" (Saunders 1886:6). Spangenburg assumed that the Moravian influence in this region would benefit both the Catawbas and the Cherokees. From such a belief it must be inferred that Spangenburg viewed the lands as Catawba and Cherokee "territory," despite encountering no Indian settlements except the remains of an "Indian Fort," possibly the remains of houses or a palisaded village that Spangenburg thought to be abandoned 50 years earlier (Saunders 1886:9). If Spangenburg's estimate of abandonment was accurate, it also suggests that this location, at least, was occupied in the late seventeenth century.

Catawba Origins: Migration

The previous sections have explored the idea that John Lawson's descriptions of the Esaws, Sugarees, and Kadapaus do not represent the earliest record of the Catawba Indians; ethnohistoric evidence from the Pardo expeditions suggests that protohistoric ancestors of these peoples lived in portions of North Carolina's western Piedmont. Before examining the archaeological evidence for these populations in the following chapters, it is useful to review earlier ideas about the origins of the Catawba Indians. The following discussion contrasts traditional with more recent models of early

Catawba history. I use the term *traditional* to refer to culture historical perspectives (e.g., Brown 1966; Mooney 1894; Speck 1939; Swanton 1946) that invoke migrations and generally ignore the ethnic complexity of the Catawba communities of the early eighteenth century. They tend to emphasize the spatial dimensions of Catawba culture and as such have had a major impact on the perception of Catawba valley prehistory. In contrast, more recent studies of the Catawbas (e.g., Baker 1972a, 1974, 1976; Hudson 1965, 1970; Merrell 1982, 1989) examine the sociopolitical complexity of the Catawbas, especially with respect to Catawba ethnic origins.

One of the earliest and most persistent stories concerning the origins of the Catawbas comes from Philip Edward Pearson's "Memoir of the Catawbas," written in 1842. Pearson was a lawyer and antiquarian who wrote the "Memoir" at the request of South Carolina's governor, James Henry Hammond (Brown 1966:28).

Pearson (Brown 1966:29–31) wrote that the Catawbas were a Canadian tribe who were driven from their homeland in 1650. They traveled south, staying in the Kentucky area before moving to their present land in 1660. Upon their arrival they fought a tremendous daylong battle with the Cherokees, who inhabited the area. The Catawbas were said to have possessed guns whereas the Cherokees did not; however, losses were devastating for both. It was said that the Cherokees lost 1,100 men and the Catawbas lost 1,000 men in the battle, which took place in the vicinity of Old Nation Ford. The following day, instead of resuming the battle, the Cherokees offered a settlement to the Catawbas, which established the Broad River as a boundary line for their lands and the country between the Broad and Catawba rivers as neutral ground.

Henry Schoolcraft (1853) relied on Pearson's account for his influential history of native North Americans. Schoolcraft went further to identify the Catawbas as the Eries, an Iroquoian tribe that had been forced southward by more powerful Iroquoian neighbors.

Mooney's (1894:69–70) *The Siouan Tribes of the East* refuted both Schoolcraft's identification of the Catawbas as the Eries and their purported travels and ridiculed the details of their alleged battle with the Cherokees according to Pearson's legend. Mooney did sustain the notion of Cherokee and Catawba conflict. He noted that upon their arrival in the Catawba region, the Catawbas struggled with the Cherokees, who claimed prior rights, and he agreed that the Broad River was established as a boundary between the two tribes. However, according to Mooney, this all occurred prior to 1567, when the Spanish found them in their historic territories. Mooney also made clear his version of their northern origins:

> The Catawba . . . had a tradition of a northern origin. All these statements and traditions concerning the eastern Siouan tribes, taken in

connection with what we know of the history and traditions of the western tribes of the same stock, seem to indicate the upper region of the Ohio—the Allegheny, Monongahela, and Kanawha country— as their original home, from which one branch crossed the mountains to the waters of Virginia and Carolina while the other followed along the Ohio, and the lakes toward the west. Linguistic evidence indicates that the eastern tribes of the Siouan family were established upon the Atlantic slope long before the western tribes of that stock had reached the plains [Mooney 1894:29].

Interestingly, Mooney was less consistent on the Catawbas in his later publication, *Myths of the Cherokee*. Here, in discussing the Catawbas' relationship with the Cherokees, Mooney cited no less a personage than Will Thomas, the legendary white chief of the Kituhwa Cherokees: "The Cherokee, according to the late Colonel Thomas, claim to have formerly occupied all the country about the head of the Catawba river, to below the present Morganton, until the game became scarce, when they retired to the west of the Blue ridge, and afterward 'loaned' the eastern territory to the Catawba" (Mooney 1982:380 [1900]).

Mooney followed this statement with the assertion that it "agrees pretty well" with the Catawba tradition of the battle recorded in Schoolcraft (i.e., the Pearson "Memoir" that he criticized earlier). He did qualify the legend. When introducing the story, he wrote that the Catawbas "are incorrectly represented as comparatively recent immigrants from the north" (Mooney 1982:380 [1900]). He then related the tale including the details of the battle, only replacing the numbers of warriors lost with "incredible loss on both sides." He completed his discussion with the statement that "the fact that one party had guns would bring this event within the early historic period" (Mooney 1982:381 [1900]). This sentence appears to contradict his earlier qualification of the date of the Catawba migration.

Mooney's ambiguity leaves the impression that the event did, indeed, occur in the early Historic period, despite his clear statement in 1894 about the presence of the Catawbas on the Catawba River prior to Spanish contact in the mid-sixteenth century. Regardless of the truth of the battle, there continues to be a consensus among scholars that the Catawbas and Cherokees did reach some kind of agreement about the boundaries of their respective homelands in the early Historic period.

The implication of the Pearson tradition is that the Cherokees preceded the Catawbas. In contrast, Swanton (1936) suggested that the Catawbas were once a larger cultural group who inhabited not only the foothills of the southern mountains but also the mountains themselves; they were forced from the mountains by the migrating Cherokees and moved to the territories in which the Spanish found them in the sixteenth century. Swanton had modified his view somewhat by 1946:

The De Soto and Pardo documents, particularly the latter, reveal the important fact that Siouan tribes of the Catawba division once occupied all of the present territory of South Carolina, and place names point to their occupancy of part of North Carolina . . . Partly as a result of Cherokee pressure and partly from their desire to withdraw from the Spaniards, some Catawba-speaking tribes later moved into central North Carolina [Swanton 1946:30].

Though he altered the geographical domain, Swanton still implied that the Catawba claims to their territories were at least as old as those of the Cherokees and he maintained that conflict with the Cherokees at least partially determined the location of Catawba territory in the Historic period.

Thus we see two general models describing Catawba origins in the Carolinas. First is the Pearson model positing a recent Catawba migration and ultimate conflict with the Cherokees, the resolution of which defined their historic territories. Second is the Swanton model, in which the Cherokees pressured the Catawbas out of their traditional territory. Ironically, Mooney's ambiguous account of the Pearson legend, I believe, has had the most long-lasting impact. The legend of the great battle is still very much alive (Brown 1966:34). This may be explained by the fact that the account is related in *Myths of the Cherokee,* a volume that is more widely read and cited in the general literature than is *The Siouan Tribes of the East.*

Although the Pearson "Memoir" has been criticized in the past (e.g., Speck 1939:405), the work has received very little specific critical attention. Recently, Delpino (1992) argued that the "Memoir" is less fact than fiction, based on gross misunderstandings and poor assumptions. One hopes that Delpino's work might, as she (Delpino 1992:88–89) suggests, put to rest Pearson's story of the Catawba origins.

Regardless of the mechanism by which they were claimed, the Catawba homelands are usually described as corresponding generally to the Catawba valley. Speck describes their historic period location as follows:

General consensus places the Catawba people from the earliest recorded times in the foothills of the southern Appalachian mountains, in the drainage area of Catawba River . . . and west to Broad River. North and south their range is given as lying entirely in the Piedmont level as far down the river as the fall-line at Camden S.C. [Speck 1939:404–405].

The Catawba region is also described by Rights (1957:128), though he states that their prehistoric territory was more extensive, reaching to the headwaters of the Catawba River: "The territory once claimed by the Catawba extended over the broad area drained by the Catawba River between Broad River and the Yadkin, and from the headwaters of the Catawba far down into South Carolina."

Brown (1966:34), in a discussion of the origin traditions, states that "it is also believed by some that the territory between the Catawba and the Broad rivers was practically uninhabited when the white man first came, and apparently both Catawbas and Cherokees used it as a neutral hunting ground."

Rights (1957:156) also cites Bishop Spangenburg's report in 1752 describing the territory west of Salem as "much frequented by the Catawbas and Cherokees, especially for hunting." Spangenburg found no Indian settlements, and it is impossible to determine whether the Catawbas and Cherokees viewed this territory as a neutral boundary region.

In summary, the migration models of Catawba history generally favor northerly origins. Although the period of migration to their historic territory is uncertain, those who describe the intertribal battle with guns would suggest it occurred after the sixteenth century. The histories generally identify a conflict with the Cherokees resulting either in a neutral boundary between the two tribes or in shifts in the locations of the tribes. And, apparently, this boundary area was unoccupied in the eighteenth century.

Sociopolitical Perspectives on Catawba History

Unfortunately, the foregoing migration models contribute little to an understanding of Catawba prehistory and the forces that contributed to their situation in 1700. Hudson (1965:34–37) has argued that Swanton's and Mooney's reliance on limited linguistic evidence was responsible for their development of the overall framework of the migration model. The linguistic framework is particularly misleading since it implies cultural similarities between the Catawbas and the larger body of "Eastern Siouans" (Hudson 1965:36).

Rather than rely on the Siouan migration model, Hudson initiated the use of the "hill tribes/southern chiefdoms" dichotomy to explain the development of eighteenth-century Catawba culture. He describes the cultural boundaries of the two kinds of societies as occurring along the Santee River drainage, which he describes as the homeland of the Catawba ancestors (Hudson 1965:51). Living in this contact niche, the Catawbas were culturally affiliated, Hudson feels, with the southern Piedmont chiefdoms rather than the northern and central Piedmont hill tribes (Hudson 1965:67). From Lawson's account, he cites the large population of the Wateree/Santee valley, the presence of town houses, and the cultural similarity of the Waxhaws and the Cherokee Indians as evidence of closer affiliation between Catawbas and the Mississippian chiefdoms to the south than between Catawbas and Siouan villages to the north (Hudson 1965:67–69).

In sum, Hudson (1965:232–233) views the seventeenth-century Catawbas as a "chiefdom occupying a strategic position in the southern piedmont." Evidence from the end of that century suggests that the Catawbas had "cultural affiliations with the Cherokee- and Muskogean-speaking chiefdoms to the south, and political affiliations with hill tribes in the northern piedmont." However, by the end of the seventeenth century, participation in the deerskin trade had made them dependent on Europeans for their economic vitality and reduced their autonomy. Hudson (1965: 233) views the ensuing cultural transition from effective trading middlemen to a group under the control of traders as a period of amorphous social structure.

Baker (1972a, 1974, 1976) expanded on Hudson's hill tribe/southern chiefdom dichotomy by explicitly searching for Catawba origins in sixteenth-century chiefdoms. Utilizing Spanish and English ethnohistoric accounts he describes the sixteenth-century Greater Chiefdom of Cofitachique as located on the Santee/Wateree River. Baker (1976:4–6) argues that Cofitachequi was a centralized chiefdom headed by a "paramount official," which controlled an extremely large territory. Baker (1976:8) also describes the chiefdom as a militaristic state that conquered and/or absorbed people of different ethnic and linguistic groups.

The nuclear culture forming the chiefdom was probably Muskogean, "descended from people who initially carried the seeds of South Appalachian Mississippian culture tradition into the Carolina subarea" (Baker 1976:7). As the chiefdom expanded its geographic range it could be described as being "composed of an unknown number of local polities or provinces of consistently diminishing levels of territorial extent" (Baker 1976:8).

Baker hypothesizes that the Catawbas were one of the Siouan hill tribes that were absorbed by the greater chiefdom, but he also expresses doubt as to whether the intrusive donor population of South Appalachian Mississippian culture actually incorporated or replaced the earlier hill tribes (Baker 1976:163). He summarizes the connection between the Catawbas and Cofitachequi as follows:

> [M]any of the peoples who eventually became known as Catawbas were linked together in what seems once to have been a northern division of the Greater Chiefdom of Cofitachique. This northern sociopolitical structure probably existed from some point in prehistory, was evident in the early eighteenth century, and remained viable longer than the lowland or southern division of the Greater Chiefdom. Other researchers have also indicated that the northern peoples were organized into a confederacy and Hudson specifically believed it was affiliated with the southern chiefdoms. This northern structure was known at different times under the general name of Ushery, Esaw, and Catawba [Baker 1976:155].

Until the early eighteenth century the pattern of occupation in the Wateree/ Catawba valley does not seem to have changed much from that predicted for the late precontact period and observed in the data from the very early Historic period. In this span of time individual peoples appear to have inhabited relatively discrete territories or provinces throughout the Santee/ Wateree/Catawba river valley. Eighteenth-century land claims suggest this northern or Catawba structure originally held territory extending from the .Pee Dee to the Broad River and from about the base of the Fall Zone to the Blue Ridge. Although Indians are at times known to have claimed more territory than they ever controlled, the Catawba land claims do correspond to the territory ascribed to peoples of the Greater Chiefdom in the accounts of the De Soto expedition and also conform to the South Appalachian Mississippian archaeological subarea noted by Ferguson (1971) and Reid (1967) and shown by Baker to correspond to the Greater Chiefdom's territorial limits as indicated in the historical accounts.

The division of the chiefdom into southern and northern groups is a key element in Baker's model of the development of Catawba culture. He believes that such a division existed well before the historic era and may have been based on "a division of [the chiefdom's] basic sociopolitical structure into Piedmont and Lowland elements" (Baker 1976:49). The division separated the Santees and other lowland groups from the Congarees and other groups located above the fall line (notwithstanding the fact that the Santees and Congarees were believed to be the core peoples of the chiefdom [Baker 1976:11–12]). Baker believes that the Carolinians first called the constellation of northern groups Esaws but that they relatively quickly became known as Catawbas. Virginian colonists knew both the northern constellation and the southern core Cofitachequis as Usherees (Baker 1976:53).

Baker argues that the Greater Chiefdom was able to maintain a centralized authority until the 1670s or 1680s when the combined pressures of Spanish and English contact, disease, and Westo Indian aggression proved to be too strong to withstand. Baker suggests that in the place of the centralized chiefdom authority colonial trade provided a new authority:

The very heart of the society was attacked by the disease and intensification of internecine competition, which accompanied introduction of the skin and slave trade within its borders. The viability of the *leading* province of Cofitachique was destroyed and its chieftain supposedly lost the ability to maintain his regional authority. The centralized structure of the Indian trade also seems to have offered an alternative to the indigenous structure of authority . . . Simply stated, the Indian peoples of South Carolina were led to focus their allegiance on Charles Town rather than on the native officials of Cofitachique . . .

The residue of the Greater Chiefdom included increasingly autono-
mous constituent polities [Baker 1976:9–10; my emphasis].

Under this model, the Indians of the northern constellation, including
the Congarees, Waxhaws, Catawbas, Esaws, Sugarees, and Cheraws, were
able to avoid the precipitous decline suffered by the southern division and
emerged as the major survivors ("residue") in the 1690s (Baker 1976:48–
49). Baker (1976:53) also suggests that the stresses suffered by the lowland
peoples ultimately led to their participation in the Yamasee War, an act that
effectively destroyed them, leaving the northern (or Catawba) constellation
to "emerge as the regionally dominant society and thereby form the nucleus of the Catawba Nation."

Baker (1976:24) proposes that the settlement pattern described by Lawson in 1701 probably resembled the general settlement pattern of the
Greater Chiefdom, albeit with some shrinkage of territory, with the upper
Catawba, Broad, Saluda, and Savannah rivers having been largely depopulated by the seventeenth century. Baker (1976:24–36) reviews Lawson's
account and attempts to identify cultural boundaries that also conform to
environmental boundaries. He places the Esaws on the Catawba River just
north of the confluence with Sugar Creek. The Catawbas are located north
of the Esaws with Nation Ford being the probable boundary between the
two. The Catawbas extend upriver somewhat north of Charlotte. The Sugarees are located along Sugar Creek. In sum, Baker views the development
of early eighteenth-century Catawba culture as a direct outgrowth of the
Greater Chiefdom of Cofitachequi.

Merrell's (1989) recent study views Catawba development somewhat
differently than the studies of Hudson and Baker. While he acknowledges
that the southern chiefdoms exerted some influence on the ancestors of the
Catawba people, he views these chiefdoms more in terms of a foreign
power unable to dictate freely over the neighboring Siouan hill tribes. He
also sees this as analogous to later interactions with Europeans:

Whether in English, Spanish or Muskogean, the words of the would-
be conquerors had little impact. During the sixteenth century, Cofitachiques apparently exercised some authority over settlements upriver,
but anyone with pretensions to ruling had to contend with the powerful political, economic, and ethnic localism dominating native existence. At best, the alien society's power was highly unstable. . . .
The Cofitachiques' influence beyond their immediate environs ebbed
and flowed; even at high tide, however, it must have had only a limited impact on the everyday lives of piedmont communities, communities which, of course, paid even less heed to Pardo's speeches and
Anglo-American calls for tribute [Merrell 1989:15].

Merrell does, however, agree that Catawba peoples may have owed some of their success to the chiefdom cultures. He suggests that while the southern cultures contributed to changing lifeways with the introduction of a more effective maize agriculture and new pottery styles, the interaction between such different peoples may have had more profound implications:

> [I]t may well have encouraged loosely structured communities in the highlands to develop more complex polities. Confrontation with powerful societies often compels those on the defensive to organize some means of meeting this new challenge . . . Perhaps, too, the peoples that came to be known as the Catawba Nation owed something to lessons learned over years of contact with Mississippian neighbors downriver. The eighteenth century Catawba nation could not match the size or scope of the sixteenth century Cofitachiques. Yet the willingness to incorporate many groups into a single entity is reminiscent of Mississippian practices, and it may be the Cofitachiques' greatest legacy [Merrell 1989:18].

Merrell's model differs, then, from Baker's in that he maintains a core Siouan culture for the Catawbas with the main effect of contact with neighboring chiefdoms being a potentially greater degree of political complexity. This may have allowed the Catawbas more flexibility to deal with the increasingly complex inter-Indian and colonial affairs necessitated after the mid-seventeenth century and the introduction of European trade.

Merrell has also shown that *Catawba* went through several transformations in meaning. Lawson was the first of the Englishmen to use the term, though in 1701 it referred only to one group out of many (keep in mind that the Spaniard Bandera used the term in 1568). It was neither consistently used nor, Merrell (1989:48) argues, consistently understood. However, by 1715 *Catawba* had replaced *Esaw* as the general term used by Carolinians to describe the Indians located in the vicinity of the confluence of Sugar Creek and the Catawba River (Merrell 1989:92–94). Finally, by the mid-eighteenth century, *Catawba* had come to mean the amalgamation of many Indian groups under the broader Catawba Nation.

Merrell believes that the location of the Catawbas on the trading paths was advantageous in that they were able to deal with both Virginia and Charles Town. He also credits their relative stability to the Catawbas' ability to remain generally neutral during the colonial trading wars between 1690 and 1710 (Merrell 1989:56). This placed the Catawbas in the position of having some control over trading access and also served as a motivation to maintain their position. Merrell suggests that their effort to attract remnant groups was a measure of self-interest, in that it removed potential competition. Those who joined the Catawbas often did so for protection not only from the Iroquois but also from the Catawbas themselves (Merrell 1989:104–105).

Discussion

Recent studies, particularly those by Hudson (1970) and Baker (1972a, 1974, 1976), have sought a more thorough understanding of the prehistoric cultural patterns that contributed to the cultural landscape of which the Catawba were a part in A.D. 1700. This has involved a consideration of the Catawba peoples with respect to both Piedmont Siouan and southern chiefdom cultures. In contrast, the earlier scholars viewed the Catawba cultural landscape at A.D. 1700 as a result of prehistoric Siouan migration and early historic period conflict with the Cherokees. It is especially important to note that the earlier migration models presumed that Siouan groups moved from one place to another as intact ethnic and political groups and presumably reconstituted themselves as such in their new settings; the more recent models suggest a more fluid interaction between people from Mississippian towns and Siouan villages.

Hudson, Baker, and Merrell stress the cultural (and potentially geographic) changes that are reflected in the usage by the colonials of the term *Catawba*. Although each describes the transitions in somewhat different terms, each recognizes three distinct phases: a town or group located near the confluence of the Catawba River and Sugar Creek in 1701; a referent for a larger group of ethnically diverse peoples living in the same vicinity ca. 1710–1730; and the Catawba Nation, a more extensive and inclusive amalgamation of peoples dating to the mid-eighteenth century. These distinctions highlight the inclusive nature of the term and are especially important to consider with respect to the potential relationship of precontact and protohistoric Catawba valley populations to the group named Catawba who, in the early 1700s, occupied a relatively restricted territory farther south along the river.

In sum, recent Catawba origin models emphasize the nature of the Cofitachequi chiefdom and the degree to which this chiefdom exercised control over its subject polities as driving forces in the ethnogenesis of the eighteenth-century Catawba. These models suggest that Catawba ancestors were either major constituents of the northern constellation of towns within Cofitachequi's domain or relatively independent Siouan-speaking tribes whose political culture developed within the context of interaction with the southern chiefdoms, especially Cofitachequi.

New research also addresses the internal complexity of Catawba valley polities. In their linguistic analysis of the written record of the Pardo expedition, Booker et al. (1992) construct sociograms from the names and titles of the chiefs who met with Pardo at each town. According to Hudson

(1990:61–63), Bandera recorded two native terms to describe the relative power of native chiefs. "Orata" referred to a lower-level cacique or chief. Apparently some orata may have held power over multiple communities. "Mico" also referred to a chief. However, whereas Pardo met with about 80 named oratas and perhaps 39 unnamed oratas, only three micos are named: Guatari Mico, Olamico, and Joara Mico. Each mico clearly had jurisdiction over multiple orata, unlike the vast majority of oratas (Hudson 1990:62). Bandera also defined a mico as a great lord and an orata as a minor lord. There was no recorded Indian name for the most powerful or paramount chief.

Thus Booker et al. (1992) use the names and titles of chiefs along with the locations of the towns at which they appear to hypothesize their linguistic affiliations and social relationships. Significantly, they see Joara as a multilingual chiefdom that integrated both Catawban and Iroquoian speakers. This possibly reflects the position of Joara in a trading location between Cherokees to the west, Siouans to the east and south, Muskogeans farther to the south, and possibly the Yuchi-speaking Chiscas to the north. Hudson (1990:87) suggests that the people of Joara traded salt from their advantageous location in the vicinity of major intersecting trails (see also Beck 1997b). Booker et al. (1992:434) also suggest that the title Joara Mico implies that the chief at Joara probably exercised power over the nearly 20 named chiefs who met Pardo there. While Joara Mico evidently enjoyed some degree of power over a relatively large number of orata, there are suggestions that such power was not fixed or stable and that, in fact, Joara Mico may have been seeking to extend the reach of his authority at the expense of Guatari Mico (Hudson 1990:91).

Although we cannot be certain as to the precise relations among the towns and leaders encountered, the documents do offer some provocative suggestions regarding the nature of political and social relations in the Carolina Piedmont. For example, both Yssa Orata and Catapa Orata were among the chiefs who met with Pardo on his first visit to Canos/Cofitachequi (Hudson 1990:74) and on another occasion they were together to meet Pardo at Quinahaqui (Hudson 1990:84). On yet another occasion in Joara, Pardo met with two Cataba (i.e., Catapa) Oratas and Yssa Chiquito Orata. Hudson suggests that the main town of Yssa was located near Lincolnton, North Carolina, and that Cataba Orata's town must have been located close by. Both Cataba Orata and Yssa Orata were Catawban speakers; *Yssa* is derived from the Catawban word *iswa*, meaning *river*, and Hudson (1990:75) believes the Yssa descendants are those people called Esaws in the early eighteenth century. Hudson (1990:75) notes that "there is no known etymology for *Cataba*, but it is clearly the same name as that used by contemporary Catawba Indians in South Carolina." It is impossible to ignore this sixteenth-century association in light of the clear association between Esaws and Catawbas in the early eighteenth century.

Levy et al. (1990) offer another viewpoint on the presumed sociopolitical relationships between the North Carolina Catawba valley towns and the
chiefdom of Cofitachequi and also on social relations within the Catawba
valley polities. They review the ethnographic and archaeological evidence
for the presumed North Carolina territories of the chiefdom of Cofitachequi
and find little compelling evidence that Cofitachequi controlled the Catawba
region. They (Levy et al. 1990:164) suggest that the Catawba region was
home to several small polities:

> [These] are probably affiliated with the main center of Cofitachequi
> but maintain a high degree of autonomy. These polities were not
> egalitarian; at least two kinds of stratification were present. First, the
> chief of Cofitachequi, in times of expanding influence, probably could
> require tribute, labor, and allegiance from much of the region. The
> De Soto documents hint that the early 1540s were such a period. Sec-
> ond, within the smaller polities, elite individuals probably had au-
> thority over a general population, both in the chief's town and in sur-
> rounding subsidiary communities, even when the influence of the
> elite at Cofitachequi was minimal. In fact, the influence of local chiefs
> may have expanded as the influence of the chief at Cofitachequi
> waned. This seems to have been the case at the time of the Pardo
> expeditions. We cannot, at this point, be more specific about the de-
> gree or organization of stratification within the region. In any case,
> the political situation in the Catawba-Wateree Valley in the four-
> teenth to sixteenth centuries was probably a shifting one.

Their model assumes that the location of Cofitachequi reported by De Soto
and Pardo was, indeed, in the area of Camden, South Carolina (Levy et
al. 1990:154–155), but suggests that the chiefdom was not necessarily a
monolithic structure that controlled the destiny of all polities within the
Catawba valley. This is essentially the position of DePratter (1994:220),
who suggests that the chiefdom of Cofitachequi never extended beyond the
linguistic boundary in the vicinity of the present-day state line.

The shifting nature of Catawba/Wateree valley politics is further reflected in the probable depopulation of most of the Catawba valley at some
point before the mid-seventeenth century. I believe that this depopulation occurred as the result of several factors, including the effects of Spanish diseases and the waning power of Cofitachequi. This depopulation was
accompanied by a coalescence of peoples farther to the south near the
North Carolina–South Carolina border. Why this location served as the area
of coalescence is uncertain. However, I do not consider it at all surprising
that Lawson encountered the descendants of Catawba valley peoples clustered in the lower Catawba valley. Both Merrell and Hudson argue that the
early eighteenth-century location of the Esaws/Catawbas reflected their

role in the colonial trade. I suggest that after the establishment of Charles Town in 1670 the people who had likely controlled trade through the Catawba valley for at least the past two centuries placed themselves in a position to take advantage of this new source of trade and also positioned themselves advantageously between the Carolina and Virginia traders.

Thus, I suggest that as a response to whatever other forces were acting on these populations, they pursued a strategy for their survival that had served them well in the past. Sometime, probably by the latter half of the seventeenth century, the upper Catawba valley in North Carolina was effectively depopulated. Siouan-speaking descendants of Mississippian chiefdoms established themselves on an old and well-known trading path with new partners and a new future. However, the future that seemed promising when seen through Lawson's eyes in 1701 would change quickly and dramatically for the worse over the next two decades.

The above discussion identifies a number of forces that contributed to Catawba ethnogenesis. First, sixteenth-century documentary sources describe Catawba-speaking peoples living throughout the entire Catawba River valley and in at least portions of the Yadkin River valley in North Carolina. In fact, according to the Pardo documents, only the southernmost towns of Catawban speakers were located in the vicinity of the early eighteenth-century Catawba towns. These people were organized in regional polities that engaged in long-distance trade and shifting political alliances; at least two towns, Joara and Guatari, appear to have exercised some degree of control over other towns. It is possible that Cofitachequi's declining authority in the seventeenth century contributed to a degree of instability among Catawba valley political relationships. However, the dynamics of political relations between the Siouan-speaking polities and the chiefdom of Cofitachequi are yet, and may forever remain, incompletely understood. The Catawba valley northwest of Charlotte appears to have been effectively depopulated by the mid-seventeenth century, with the result that in 1701 Lawson finds the Catawba towns located at the southern edge of their former territory. It is unclear to what degree population loss and/or population amalgamation contributed to the geographic shifts; however, depopulation did not result in wholesale loss of political identity because we see the eighteenth-century descendants of Catabas, Yssas, and Guataris in the Catawbas, Esaws, and Waterees.

We will see in the following chapters how the archaeological record contributes not only to our understanding of the sixteenth-century Catawba polities but also to that of their ancestors, the Catawba Valley Mississippians. It will become clear that we must revisit the Siouan hill tribes/ Mississippian chiefdom models and reconsider the relationship of the chiefdom of Cofitachequi to Catawba valley polities. Merrell regards Cofitachequi influence on the Catawbas as minor, but feels that the Catawbas may have derived a higher degree of political complexity from experience with Cofitachequi: "Perhaps, too, the peoples that came to be known as the Catawba Nation owed something to lessons learned over years of contact with Mississippian neighbors downriver" (Merrell 1989:18). In fact, rather than owing something to lessons learned from the south, I believe there is considerable evidence that the Catawba Nation included descendants of people who were Mississippian in their own right—the Catawba Valley Mississippians—and who, for at least several centuries, were indeed neighbors to and interacted with, Mississippian chiefdoms to the south.

Upper Catawba Valley Sites and Ceramics

2

This chapter presents an overview of the archaeology (post–A.D. 1000) of the upper Catawba River valley. The chapter begins with a review of previous research followed by brief descriptions of the Berry and McDowell sites, the two major excavated sites in the region, as well as descriptions of other significant upper valley sites (see Figure 5 for locations of sites discussed in this chapter). An overview of upper Catawba valley ceramics includes discussion of Berry and McDowell site ceramic assemblages and a discussion of the temporal and geographic contexts of Burke pottery. The chapter concludes with an overview of the late prehistoric and protohistoric period settlement pattern in the upper Catawba valley.

Previous Research

In general, upper Catawba valley archaeology reflects three historical trends in North Carolina archaeology: antiquarian investigation of mounds, professional research beginning in the 1960s, and cultural resource management activities since 1980. The antiquarian pursuits are the earliest investigations in the region and are associated with the energetic mound explorations of the late nineteenth century.

Cyrus Thomas (1887, 1891, 1894) and William Holmes (1903) mention at least nine mounds reported by James Mooney or J. Mason Spainhour to be located in McDowell, Burke, and Catawba counties (Table 1). Thomas investigated one of these mounds and Spainhour explored another. Four of these mounds have been tentatively identified in the North Carolina state site record as sites 31BK2 (also recorded as 31BK22), 31BK3, 31BK4, and 31BK17. Only at the Berry site (31BK22) has one of these purported mounds been verified.

Mound Exploration

Dr. James Mason Spainhour, a Morganton dentist, apparently investigated several mounds in Burke and Caldwell counties in the 1870s. These are reported in a Smithsonian Institution publication (Spainhour 1873) and in

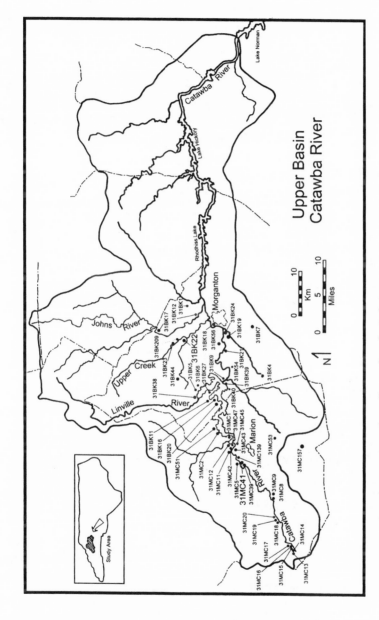

Figure 5. Location of upper Catawba valley archaeological sites.

Table 1. Mounds reported in the Catawba valley region by Cyrus Thomas

Catawba County

1. "Mound 2 miles from Catawba. Reported by J. D. Middleton" (Thomas 1891:153).
Note: This site is not confirmed.

McDowell County

2. "Large mound at old fort *[sic]* on south side of railroad, just east of the station, and about one-half a mile south of Mill Creek (i.e. the upper Catawba River). Probably 30 feet high. Perfect and unexplored. Reported by James Mooney" (Thomas 1891:156).
Note: Given the large outcroppings of bedrock at the base of this mound, it is unlikely to represent a mound but rather an isolated monadnock similar to the one adjacent to the McDowell site.

Burke County (all quotes are from Thomas [1891:151] unless indicated otherwise)

3. "Mound on (near) the west bank of John's River, 12 miles above Morganton. Several other mounds formerly existed in the same neighborhood. Explored and described by J. W. Spainhour."
Note: Designated 31BK3 in maps from Research Laboratories of Archaeology, this site has not been confirmed. It is possible that this description actually applies to 31BK17. It is apparently the site that Spainhour described as being on the Michaux farm.

4. "Mound on the west bank of John's River, 3 1/2 miles north of Morganton. Reported by James Mooney."
Note: This location is sometimes erroneously referred to as 31BK17. According to Rob Beck (personal communication 1997) this is a natural formation.

5. "Mound (about 15 feet high and unexplored) on the west bank of Upper Creek 8 miles north of Morganton."
Note: This is thought to be 31BK22 and 31BK2 -- the Berry site.

6. "Mound said to exist on the north side of a small branch of Silver Creek, on the road from Morganton to Brindletown."

7. "Mound on the north bank of Little Silver Creek, 8 miles southwest of Morganton."

8. "Mound on the north bank of Brindle or Hall Creek, 12 miles southwest of Morganton and about 3 miles from Brindletown. Reported by James Mooney."
Note: Designated as 31BK4 but the site has not been confirmed as a mound site.

9. "A conical mound 320 feet in circumference and 7 feet high, situated on the farm of Mrs. J. E. Collet, in the northern part of Burke County, was explored, but aside from the yellow sand and yellow clay of which it was chiefly composed, nothing was found in it except some remnants of charred straw and cane. These were scattered in small quantities through the sand" (Thomas 1894: 344).

speeches delivered by Spainhour in 1897 and 1899. Spainhour (1897:24) states in the 1897 speech that he "[took] out 188 skeletons and with them found a fine lot of implements of various kinds. The Smithsonian Institution . . . had a poor exhibit from North Carolina and I determined to make it equal, if not superior to that from any state, and was only satisfied when

Prof. Baird pronounced it such." The details of Spainhour's accounts are interesting on several points. First, Spainhour seems to be a reliable observer (although the apparently embellished account of the burials and mound in the 1897 speech seems to be a reinterpretation that is perhaps biased or colored by his Masonic philosophy of the time). Second, there are excavation details that provide structural information concerning the interments and the mounds.

Earthen mounds are significant features of the ancient landscapes of the upper Catawba valley and the nearby upper Yadkin River valley. Spainhour apparently investigated a mound on the Michaux Farm, probably the location of 31BK17. Spainhour's complete 1871 report to the Board of Regents of the Smithsonian Institution is presented below:

In a conversation with Mr. Michaux, of Burke County, North Carolina, on Indian curiosities, he informed me that there was an Indian mound on his farm, which was formerly of considerable height, but had gradually been plowed down; that several mounds in the neighborhood had been excavated, and nothing of interest found in them. I asked permission to examine this mound, which was granted, and upon investigation the following interesting facts were revealed. Upon reaching the place I sharpened a stick four or five feet in length, and ran it down in the earth at several places, and finally struck a stone about eighteen inches below the surface, which, upon digging down, was found to be about eighteen inches long and sixteen inches wide, and from two to three inches in thickness, the corners rounded. It rested on solid earth and had been smoothed on top.

I then made an excavation in the south of the mound, and soon struck another stone, which upon examination proved to be in front of the remains of a human skeleton in a sitting posture; the bones of the fingers of the right hand had been resting on the stone. Near the hand was a small stone about five inches long, resembling a tomahawk or Indian hatchet. Upon a further examination, many of the bones were found, though in a very decomposed condition, and upon exposure to the air they soon crumbled to pieces. The heads of the bones, a considerable portion of the skull, jaw-bones, teeth, neck-bones, and the vertebra were in their proper places. Though the weight of the earth above them had driven them down, yet the frame was perfect, and the bones of the head were slightly inclined toward the east. Around the neck were found coarse beads that seemed to be of some substance resembling chalk. A small lump of red paint, about the size of an egg, was found near the right side of this skeleton. From my knowledge of anatomy, the sutures of the skull would indicate the subject to have been twenty-five or twenty-eight years of age. The top of the skull was about twelve inches below the mark of the plow.

I made further excavation in the west part of this mound and found another skeleton similar to the first, in a sitting posture, facing the last. A stone was on the right, on which the right hand had been resting, and on this was a tomahawk which had been about seven inches in length, broken into two pieces, and much better finished than the first. Beads were also on the neck of this one, but were much smaller and of finer quality than those on the neck of the first; the material, however, seemed to be the same. A much larger amount of paint was found by the side of this than the first. The bones indicated a person of larger frame, and I think of about fifty years of age. Everything about this one had the appearance of superiority over the first. The top of the skull was about six inches below the mark of the plow.

I continued the examination, and rather diligent search found nothing at the north part of the mound but on reaching the east side found another skeleton in the same posture as the others, facing the west. On the right side of this was a stone on which the right hand had been resting, and on the stone was also a tomahawk about eight inches in length, broken into three pieces, much smoother and of finer material than the others. Beads were also found on the neck of this, but much smaller and finer than on those of the others, as well as a large amount of paint. The bones would indicate a person of forty years of age; the top of the skull had been moved by the plow.

There was no appearance of hair discovered; besides, the principal bones were also entirely decomposed, and crumbled when handled; these two circumstances, coupled with the fact that the farm on which this mound was found was the first settled in that county, the date of the . . . first deed running back about one hundred and fifty years, (the land still belonging to descendants of the same family that first occupied), would prove beyond doubt that it is very old.

The mound was situated due east and west, in size about nine by six feet, the line being distinctly marked by difference in color of soil. It was dug in rich black loam, and filled with white or yellow sand, but contiguous to the skeleton was a dark-colored earth, and so decidedly different was this from all surrounding in quality and smell, that the lines of the bodies could be readily traced. The decomposed earth, which had been flesh, was similar in odor to that of clotted blood, and would adhere in lumps when compressed in the hands [Spainhour 1873].

Spainhour's 1899 speech details his excavation of three burials from a mound located on Johns River north of Morganton. This appears to be the same excavation described above. Spainhour (1899:53–56) describes the placement of the three skeletons seated on clearly defined steps within the mound. Each was accompanied by a bead necklace, a celt, and a piece of "red paint" (hematite?). Although Spainhour concluded from his observations that the Indian burials were interred with Masonic rites, his account is more significant because of his description of the mound itself. He says the mound was

> shaped differently from any of the others that I have found, as they are generally circular. The earth had been removed to a depth of about five feet, except at the center, south, east and west, where some had been left. In length the excavation from east to west was 12 to 14 feet and from north to south nine to ten feet in width [Spainhour 1899:52].

Spainhour explains:

> It was a custom among the Indians to make the excavation for burials, then place the bodies in the position they desired them to occupy, and fill the entire space with white or yellow sand taken from beneath the water of the stream. With this sand they filled the grave to a level and then placed the earth that had been excavated, making a mound over the grave. Our rapid mountain streams often overflow and the loose mounds wash away, and it is difficult to find the Indian mounds and burials [Spainhour 1899:57].

Both of these accounts perhaps provide some insight into the interpretations and observations of the late nineteenth-century antiquarians and scientists who pursued the prehistoric Indians. Several points must be mentioned. First is Spainhour's description of the mound. The first paragraph quoted above bears a striking resemblance to descriptions of excavations of the Nelson Mound and Triangle in adjacent Caldwell County (Thomas 1894; these sites are discussed in chapter 3). There have been no mound excavations in this region since the late nineteenth century and, unfortunately, these descriptions bear little resemblance to those of mounds excavated in the nearby Appalachian Summit region at the Garden Creek site (Dickens 1976; Keel 1976), the Peachtree site (Setzler and Jennings 1941), and the Coweeta Creek site (Egloff 1971).

As far as is known, mounds in the mountain region were substructure mounds with buildings placed on their summits. They sometimes served for contemporary and/or later intrusive interments. It is likely that most of their use occurred during the late Prehistoric and Protohistoric periods, although some of these southern Appalachian mounds were initially constructed as earthlodges during the late Woodland period.

In contrast, Spainhour seems to describe mounds that were built solely for interment of individuals or small numbers of individuals. It should be noted, however, that at this time few investigators understood the difference between burial mounds and substructure mounds. It is likely that Spainhour would have been unable to conceive a purpose for mound building other than for burial. Neither he nor other excavators ever investigated village burial contexts (or the villages themselves) that may have been associated with the mounds.

Recent Investigations

Despite the presence of mounds, little professional work was conducted in the upper Catawba region until the 1960s. One exception was a small salvage excavation in 1940 by Joffre Coe at 31BK1 (see Figure 5 for location), where a number of features were exposed by flooding. The ceramics (now termed Burke series) recovered from this site were believed, at the time, to represent those of early historic period Catawba Indians (Joffre Coe, personal communication 1986; Keeler 1971).

The 1960s saw the start of systematic professional work in the Catawba region as a number of large, professionally directed site surveys were conducted by the Research Laboratories of Anthropology (UNC-Chapel Hill). The first of these, the Cowans Ford Reservoir (Lake Norman) project, undertaken between 1960 and 1962, identified more than 400 sites in Catawba, Iredell, Lincoln, and Mecklenburg counties. Most of these were subsequently inundated (this project is discussed in chapter 4).

Roy S. Dickens, Jr., and Robert Keeler conducted additional surveys in McDowell and Burke counties in the late 1960s and early 1970s. Dickens (1970, 1976) identified Pisgah ceramics from a number of sites along the Catawba River in McDowell County. Keeler (1971) identified 40 sites in McDowell and Burke counties and provided the first comprehensive study of the ceramics of the upper Catawba River valley. He defined the Burke ceramic series and discussed the possibility that it was ancestral to historic Catawba pottery. He also noted that a significant blending of Burke and Pisgah ceramic attributes occurred at the McDowell site (31MC41) near Marion in McDowell County. At the time, the McDowell site appeared to be located at the western edge of the distribution of the Burke series and on the eastern limits of the Pisgah series distribution.

The co-occurrence of the two ceramic series, as well as the presence of a small earthen mound, stimulated further interest in the McDowell site, and test excavations were conducted there in 1977 (Ward 1977). A permanent grid was established and a total of 500 ft^2 was excavated to below the plow zone. Four features and portions of two possible posthole patterns were observed. A brief test excavation conducted by Mars Hill College (Eblen 1981) also revealed postholes in two 5-ft excavation units. As mentioned in chapter 1, the McDowell site has been proposed as the location of the sixteenth-century town of Joara/Xualla (DePratter et al. 1983).

During the past 20 years a number of archaeological sites have been added to the state's site files for the study area. These have resulted from a variety of CRM-related projects and more recent surveys funded by National Parks Service Historic Preservation grants. In addition, U.S. Forest Service surveys have located more than 50 sites since the late 1970s. Finally, a number of sites have been recently recorded by avocational archaeologists. However, with the exception of those mentioned below, few of these investigations produced evidence of late prehistoric or protohistoric sites.

There are several Burke County investigations that are relevant to this study. The first is a survey of 58 sites (Clark 1976). Site boundaries were not determined and no artifact collections were maintained; however, the descriptions of the sites and the artifacts are consistent with the findings of Keeler (1971). Also, a brief archaeological field school was conducted at 31BK18, though no records of this work are presently available (Larry Clark, personal communication 1986).

A salvage investigation occurred in 1980 on the grounds of a North Carolina State Forest nursery where grading for planting preparation disturbed the remains of a burial. This site, 31BK56, has never been fully evaluated, but monitoring of the 1980 disturbance revealed the possibility of some remaining midden and features, though most of the site was apparently graded away (Mathis 1980; Ward 1980a, 1980b). It was impossible to determine the nature of the original burial context, but two shell gorgets were recovered from the burial prior to the arrival of archaeologists. One is a Citico gorget; the second has not been documented.

More recently, a limited survey project in McDowell County identified more than 30 sites and conducted test excavations at three sites (Robinson 1990). Several of the sites from this survey are discussed below. Finally, excavations were conducted in 1986 at the McDowell site (31MC41) and the Berry site (31BK22) as part of the Upper Catawba Archaeological Project (Moore 1987, 1999). Details of this work are presented below and in appendixes A and B.

Burke Pottery

Although there have been relatively few archaeological investigations in the Catawba River valley, all have consistently focused on pottery. Woodland period and Mississippian period ceramics have been reported, but it is primarily the late prehistoric Pisgah and Burke ceramic series that have been discussed in any detail. In his major work on the Pisgah phase, Dickens (1976:188) briefly mentions Pisgah and Pisgah-like ceramics (some featuring soapstone temper) at the McDowell site (31MC41) and several other sites at the head of the Catawba River in McDowell County. These Pisgah sites within the upper Catawba valley are thought to reflect the eastern boundary of the Pisgah phase (Dickens 1976:188–190). The soapstone-tempered pottery was thought by Dickens to represent pottery produced by the protohistoric Catawba Indians:

Easily recognized because of their steatite temper were 38 sherds with plain or complicated stamped surface finish which belong to an as yet unidentified ceramic series which may be the product of the proto-historic Catawba tribe (Joffre Coe, personal communication) . . . Sites producing this pottery in quantity are found on the Catawba River in Burke and Caldwell Counties, immediately east of the mountains [Dickens 1970:58].

The soapstone-tempered ware is defined as the Burke pottery series in Robert Keeler's (1971) survey of the upper Catawba valley. During the survey Keeler identified 52 sites in McDowell County and 24 sites in Burke County. Most of the sites are concentrated on the Catawba River floodplain and amateur artifact collectors originally identified many of them. The survey methodology entailed surface collecting all recorded sites. Site size was not recorded systematically nor was subsurface testing conducted to identify potential intact deposits.

The survey identified sites with Archaic, Woodland, and late prehistoric components; however, it is the late prehistoric sites that are relevant to this study. For this period, Keeler notes the presence of Pisgah pottery and an associated crushed quartz–tempered pottery in McDowell County. He also notes the occurrence in Burke County of another late prehistoric pottery tempered with soapstone and often exhibiting burnished or complicated-stamped surface finishes. The abundance of soapstone-tempered pottery from the Burke County sites prompted him to define a new ceramic series: the Burke series.

Keeler (1971:40) points out the clear similarities of the Burke series with Lamar pottery of Georgia, but does not attempt to explain any possible relationship between the two potteries. Similarly, he feels that stamp designs, rim treatments, and vessel forms of the Burke series and the historic Catawba ceramics closely resemble historic Cherokee Qualla pottery. However, according to Keeler (1971:41), "the question of relationship between the Catawba and the Cherokee areas remains open."

Upper Catawba Valley Archaeological Sites

This section presents an overview of those upper Catawba valley sites for which testing or excavation information is available. It also includes those surface-collected sites with large ceramic assemblages (see Figure 5 for locations of sites discussed).

McDowell Site

The McDowell site (31MC41) is located on the floodplain of the Catawba River west of Marion in McDowell County. It covers an area of three to four acres and includes a low rise about 100 ft in diameter and less than

2 ft in height that has generally been interpreted as the remnant of an earthen substructure mound (Ward 1977:5).

Robert Keeler and Charles Carey first reported the McDowell site in 1971. Keeler (1971) discusses the site's ceramic assemblage, which features both Pisgah and Burke ceramics. Dickens (1976:188) also notes the presence of Pisgah ceramics in the extreme upper Catawba valley and describes this area as representing the easternmost limit of the distribution of Pisgah pottery.

Several investigations have been undertaken at the McDowell site. In 1977 test excavations were conducted at the site by archaeologists from the Research Laboratories of Anthropology (Ward 1977). Charcoal from Feature 3 yielded a corrected radiocarbon age of A.D. 1458 ± 75 (Boyd 1986a:67).

The McDowell site received further notice as the likely location of the town of Xualla or Joara, visited by Hernando de Soto in 1539 and again in 1566 by Juan Pardo (DePratter et al. 1983; Hudson et al. 1984). The selection of the McDowell site as the location of Joara rested principally on the fact that it was the best-known site with a possible protohistoric occupation in the area determined by route reconstruction. More recent studies of documentary (Beck 1997b; Worth 1994a, 1994b) and archaeological (Moore 1999; Moore and Beck 1994) evidence suggest that Joara is located at the Berry site (31BK22; see below) rather than the McDowell site.

As a result of the citation in the De Soto and Pardo research and the late radiocarbon date, the McDowell site was investigated further during the Upper Catawba Archaeological Project in 1986 (Levy et al. 1990; Moore 1987, 1999). More complete descriptions of the 1977 and 1986 excavations are presented in appendix A. During the excavations, plow zone was removed from a total of 3,010 ft^2, divided among five blocks. Block A (750 ft^2), excavated in 1977, contained 28 postholes and four features. The postholes included portions of a possible house structure (Structure 1) and a palisade running east-west across the trench (Ward 1977:6–8).

Four blocks were excavated in 1986. Block B (900 ft^2) included seven features along with numerous postholes. One row of postholes appeared to be a possible extension of the palisade running east-west from Block A, and a second posthole pattern represents a probable domestic structure.

Block C (660 ft^2) was located just northeast of the putative mound. Most of this block consisted of a large feature, more than 24 ft in diameter. This feature included a central core of dark loamy soil with concentrations of burned soils, ash, charcoal, and burned timbers. Two bands of mottled brown soil, each about 2 ft wide, surrounded the dark core. The overall size of the feature cannot be determined since it extended beyond the edges of the excavation block. The feature probably represents a burned structure. Given its large size (perhaps as large as 30–40 ft in diameter) and its possible association with the mound, it may represent a public building.

Block D consisted of a single 100-ft^2 unit placed on the mound, and a 600-ft^2 block (E) was located 200 ft south of the mound.

Berry Site

The Berry site (31BK22) is located on Upper Creek, a tributary of the Catawba River, about eight miles north of Morganton in Burke County. The site is situated on the extreme northeast margin of a 200-acre alluvial bottomland formed by the confluence of Upper Creek and Irish Creek. It is named for the Berry family, property owners of the site and its surroundings for four generations.

The Berry site was first identified in Cyrus Thomas's 1891 report, where it is described as "Mound on the west Bank of Upper Creek 8 miles north of Morganton (about 15 feet high and unexplored)" (Thomas 1891:151). The mound and surrounding site were regularly plowed and in 1964 the mound was bulldozed by the landowner, leaving a low rise about 2 ft above the level of the surrounding field.

Charles Carey and Robert Keeler recorded the site in the state site files in 1970, noting that earlier it had been designated BK2 on the basis of the mound report in Thomas (1891). However, the site was renumbered 31BK22 because of the uncertainty of the earlier identification. At a later date the mound was identified on the site form as a "refuse mound" because of the high concentration of artifacts, charcoal, and faunal remains found on the surface of the mound. The entire site covers as much as 12 acres, as is apparent from the extent of surface artifacts.

The Berry site was selected for excavation in 1986 because of its relatively large size, the presence of the mound, and surface indications of abundant artifactual, floral, and faunal remains. The site was especially important because of the overwhelming presence of Burke ceramics, and it was hoped that test excavations would yield productive chronological information regarding the age of the Burke ceramic series.

Two areas, designated A and B, were selected for excavation. The first (A) totaled 700 ft^2 and was placed across the mound from west to east and revealed basket-loaded fill beneath the plow zone. The second excavation unit (Area B) was located about 50 ft south of the mound and totaled 1,300 ft^2. The stratigraphy in this area was deep and more complex than on top of the mound. Four zones were encountered, each representing different formation processes. Eighteen features were identified. Twelve features and two burials were excavated. A more complete description of the Berry site excavation is presented in appendix B.

Unfortunately, very little can be said about site structure on the basis of the 1986 excavations at the Berry site. A portion of a circular structure is represented by postholes immediately north and east of Burial 1. Clearly the density of postholes in excavation Area B suggests that additional structures were located adjacent to the mound.

Little else can be said of overall village structure including the number or arrangement of domestic structures or public structures or the presence of palisades, a plaza, or any other features. However, Beck (1997a) has shown that the Berry site may be as large as 12 acres. He bases this estimate on the results of a systematic surface collection. The density of artifacts (gathered from 25-m² units), primarily potsherds, was relatively consistent across these 12 acres, although lower densities were found southwest of the mound. However, the density of the three collection units that included the mound was 10 times higher than the average collection unit density. This is probably a function of the fact that midden soils were used to build the mound and these same soils have been spread around the mound by plowing.

More than 20 sixteenth-century Spanish artifacts have been recovered from the Berry site (Moore and Beck 1994; see appendix B for complete description and discussion). These include Olive Jar fragments, majolica, nails, and lead shot. These are items not normally traded by the Spanish to Indians and their presence at the site lends support to the hypothesis that the Berry site is the location of the town of Joara, where Juan Pardo built and garrisoned Fort San Juan (Beck 1997b; Worth 1994a).

Investigations are continuing at the Berry site. A proton-magnetometer survey revealed the presence of at least three large anomalies believed to represent burned structures (Hargrove and Beck 2001). Excavations conducted by the Warren Wilson College archaeological field school confirmed that at least one of these anomalies is a burned square structure approximately 8 m in diameter (Moore and Rodning 2001). Future investigations will aim to determine the nature of this structure and the other anomalies revealed by the magnetometer survey.

31BK17

Site 31BK17 is located in a large bend of Johns River about four miles northeast of the Berry site. It is described as one of the largest sites in the region, covering perhaps as much as 50 acres (Clark 1976:56). It may also be the location of one of the mounds (Michaux Farm or vicinity) described in J. Mason Spainhour's (1873) report to the Board of Regents of the Smithsonian Institution. Obviously, this site should be considered extremely significant, but no modern investigations have been conducted there and there are reports of vandalism on the site. It is likely that this site and the Berry site represent the two largest sites in the Upper Creek/Johns River drainage area. Despite the lack of information regarding the nature of the site, a large assemblage of pottery was available for study from the Carey collection.

31BK1

Site 31BK1 is located on Bristol Creek, a branch of Lower Creek, which is a small tributary of the Catawba River. While Bristol and Lower creeks are substantially smaller streams than Upper Creek and Johns River, they both

Plate 1. Burke Incised cazuela bowl from 31BK1.

feature relatively large bottomlands, particularly along their upper reaches. These settings are similar to that of the Berry site in that they represent the last large bottoms before the uplands. Site 31BK1 is located in one of these final large bottomland settings.

Unfortunately, little is known about the site except that Joffre Coe conducted a salvage excavation there following a major flood in 1941 (Joffre Coe, personal communication 1986). The flooding exposed a number of features that were subsequently excavated. There is no report on the work except for notes on artifact bags and in the artifact catalog. A sketch on one bag shows the relative locations of the excavated features; it is unclear whether these were the only features observed or merely the only features excavated. Five features (described as "pits" in the catalog) were excavated. Although information regarding the pits themselves is absent, they are presented below in terms of their contents.

Feature 1 contained charred wood fragments and a few animal bones, a single chipped stone artifact, and 37 potsherds (28 of which are from a single vessel). Feature 2 contained charcoal and 13 potsherds. The record for Feature 3 is unclear as the catalog lists "pit #3 and #5" and lists 50 potsherds all from a single Burke Incised vessel (Plate 1). Feature 4 contained charcoal, 19 fragments of animal bone, several stone tools, and 95 potsherds. Feature 5 contained a much larger artifactual assemblage. It included numerous charcoal fragments, 252 pieces of animal bone, 6 shells,

11 stone tools, a ceramic disk, and 151 potsherds. The pottery consisted overwhelmingly of Burke types.

Edwards Tree Nursery Site

The Edwards Tree Nursery site (31BK18) is located on a large alluvial terrace of the Catawba River, just west of the confluence of Warrior Fork with the Catawba. Collectors recognize the Nursery as one of the largest sites in the area; it probably covers in excess of five acres. No excavations have been conducted at this site; Robert Keeler and Charles Carey gathered the ceramics in surface collections.

Pitts Site

The Pitts site (31BK209) is located on Upper Creek about one mile north of the Berry site in the first large opening of bottoms above the Berry site. The floodplain is more constricted here, being less than 100 acres in extent. The site is situated immediately adjacent to the creek and covers about one to two acres on the basis of the surface scatter of artifacts. Wayne Pitts gathered the surface collection analyzed here. The collection includes a wide range of materials including flakes, projectile points, and other lithic tools. The Pitts site ceramics show interesting patterns of Burke and Pisgah attributes. Unfortunately, before this site could be further investigated, the property changed ownership and it has since been destroyed by the construction of a small golf course.

Tyler-Loughridge Site

The Tyler-Loughridge site (31MC139) is the only excavated site in the upper valley whose major component dates to the Woodland period. The site was recorded and investigated during a McDowell County survey project in 1989 (Robinson 1996). The site is located north of Marion on the Catawba River, just over one mile east of the McDowell site. It is situated on the margin of a large alluvial bottom 500 meters from the river on a nearly level toe of a steep hillside. The site covers about six acres and consists of a large Connestee phase component as well as a smaller Pisgah phase component. Although the majority of artifacts from this site fall outside the primary period of concern, the site is significant for overall temporal and settlement information. Its large ceramic assemblage is composed almost entirely of Woodland period Connestee pottery with the exception of a small Pisgah assemblage recovered from a single feature context (see appendix C for a brief discussion of Connestee pottery from this site).

The following description of the excavation results is summarized from Robinson (1996:60–95). Two blocks were excavated: Block A (180 m²) was placed on the north (front) edge of the site and contained numerous postholes and features from the Connestee occupation; Block B (27 m²) was placed on the southern (back) edge of the site and contained evidence of the Pisgah occupation. The plow zone was removed from each unit in a single level approximately 20 cm deep. Postholes and features were prominent in the red-orange clay subsoil beneath the plow zone.

The Connestee component in Block A is represented by postholes, features, and abundant artifacts. Two partial structures were identified as well as 23 features representing 6 distinct feature types. The feature types include large cooking pits (3), circular storage pits with straight-sided walls (3), medium to small circular pits (10), oval pits (2), burned areas (4), and a rectangular pit (1). Many of the features contained abundant charred ethnobotanical remains as well as lithic artifacts and pottery. Lithic artifacts consisted primarily of flakes of clear crystal quartz.

Four radiocarbon dates were obtained from features within the Connestee component. Feature 20-1 was a large cobble-lined pit that contained abundant charcoal, 20 lithic flakes, 2 cores, 1 utilized flake, 1 scraper, and 337 sherds, all of which were Connestee types. The calibrated date has three intercepts, A.D. 253, 304, and 314 (Beta-32925), with a calibrated 1-sigma range of A.D. 137–402.

The second feature (20-2) was a circular storage pit 1 m in diameter and 60 cm deep. The fill contained charcoal, 20 lithic artifacts, and 209 ceramic sherds, all of the Connestee type. The calibrated date for this feature (Beta-32926) also has three intercepts, A.D. 347, 360, and 374. The age range at 1 sigma is A.D. 249–419. Both of these dates and age ranges are consistent with early Middle Woodland Connestee phase dates in the Appalachian Summit region (Keel 1976; Robinson et al. 1996).

Additional radiocarbon dates were obtained for Features 7-41, a rock-filled cooking pit, and 21-2 (Robinson 1996:147; Robinson et al. 1996). The radiocarbon age for Feature 7-41 (Beta-69799) is 1280 ± 60 B.P. Calibration yields three intercepts of A.D. 821, 840, and 860 and a 2-sigma range of A.D. 727–891. The radiocarbon age for Feature 21-2 (Beta-69800) is 1200 ± 80 B.P. Calibration yields a date of A.D. 888 and a 1-sigma range of A.D. 782–984.

Block B included a single circular feature (102-1) nearly 1.4 m in diameter and .4 m deep. This basin-shaped pit contained an abundance of charred nutshell and wood fragments. Numerous flakes and two small triangular projectile points were recovered from the fill. Rectilinear complicated-stamped and plain Pisgah-like sherds and a single Burke type sherd were also recovered. The charred nutshell yielded a radiocarbon determination of 970 ± 70 B.P. (Beta-32927). The calibrated mean is A.D. 1028 and the age range at 1 sigma is A.D. 999–1164. This is consistent with early Pisgah phase dates in the Appalachian Summit (Dickens 1976; Moore 1981; but cf. Boyd 1986a:89–90) as well as the earlier date from Structure 3 at the McDowell site.

The artifactual evidence, particularly the ceramics, and the radiocarbon dates are consistent with a three-component occupation of the Tyler-

Loughridge site. The Connestee component is represented by a small village with multiple structures dating to the third or fourth century A.D. and to the eighth century A.D. The Pisgah component is restricted in size and may represent the location of an occasional residence or a limited-use ceremonial/ritual structure such as a sweat lodge or menstrual hut (Robinson 1996:116). The occupation dates to the early Pisgah phase around the eleventh century A.D. and it is possible that the site was contemporary with an early occupation of the McDowell site.

Lewis Site

The Lewis site (31MC157) is located in southern McDowell County on Rock Creek near its confluence with the Second Broad River. The site is actually within the Broad River drainage just south of the Catawba River; very little of the Broad River drainage has been surveyed for archaeological sites and few ceramic-bearing sites have been recorded in the North Carolina portion of the drainage. Rock Creek is a very small stream and the site, which covers less than one acre, is situated along a narrow floodplain that slopes slightly up to the base of the surrounding ridge. Limited shovel testing at the site has not revealed intact features beneath the plow zone (Robin Beck, Kenneth Robinson, personal communication 1989).

Interestingly, the Lewis site assemblage contains neither Pisgah nor Burke pottery, but instead consists primarily (39.8 percent) of what would be described elsewhere as Napier-like or Etowah complicated-stamped types (Wauchope 1966). No other site in the region has displayed more than one or two sherds of these types. It is uncertain what this site represents, but the lack of local pottery and the occurrence of pottery types usually associated with north Georgia sites suggests that it may be an example of early Mississippian site-unit intrusion of people from the north Georgia area or the presence of those people in the area for trading purposes. Such potential migration has often been dismissed when the process of "Mississippianization" (Smith 1984) is considered. However, I suggest that it is unwise to deny the possibility of any degree of migration or exploration (Moore 1986). The Lewis site may reflect the activities of more southerly Lamar peoples as they explored the upper Catawba region.

Overview of Upper Valley Ceramics

A total of 13,514 potsherds from upper valley sites were analyzed in this study. The total includes 10,513 sherds from 23 Burke County sites and 3,001 sherds from 25 McDowell County sites. Most of the ceramic variability from these upper valley sites is attributable to the Pisgah (Dickens 1970, 1976), Burke (Keeler 1971), McDowell, and Cowans Ford ceramic series. A very small percentage is attributable to earlier Woodland period ceramic types.

The occurrence of Pisgah and Burke pottery at the McDowell site and the "blending" of Pisgah and Burke attributes there has been well documented (Dickens 1970; Keeler 1971; Ward 1977). My analysis confirms this pattern but also reveals that the co-occurrence of Pisgah and Burke attributes is widespread within McDowell County or west of the Linville River (Figure 5), whereas east of the Linville River in Burke County, ceramic assemblages comprise nearly exclusively Burke types and few Pisgah sherds are present. In addition, the analysis identifies two additional patterns of variation reflecting two new ceramic series: McDowell and Cowans Ford.

McDowell Site

The range of variation west of the Linville River is exemplified by that found at the McDowell site (Tables 2–4). The McDowell site is the largest site recorded west of the Linville River and it accounted for nearly one-half of the analyzed potsherds from McDowell County (see appendix C for upper valley site assemblages). Previous researchers have described a variety of ceramic types from the McDowell site. Sand-, quartz-, and grit-tempered wares are associated with Pisgah series pottery (Keeler 1971), whereas the soapstone-tempered wares represent the Burke series (Dickens 1976:188; Keeler 1971). Ward (1977:9) suggests that some of the sand-tempered sherds were similar to "proto-historic Catawba pottery." Beyond the presence of multiple temper groups, each of these authors has also remarked on the "blending" of Burke and Pisgah ceramics.

Keeler (1971) provides the most detailed description of McDowell County ceramics, including those from the McDowell site:

In McDowell County there is a large proportion of Pisgah pottery and pottery exhibiting Pisgah-like features. This is generally accompanied by a fairly well made ceramic with crushed quartz temper. The sand-tempered Pisgah and the crushed quartz tempered pottery blend into one another quite effectively until it is almost impossible to distinguish between the two. The crushed quartz tempered pottery is found in several surface treatments. Complicated stamped designs are indistinct, but appear to be somewhat larger and coarser than Pisgah. They are, however, no[t] so large and sloppy as those found on Burke Complicated Stamped, a steatite tempered ceramic type [Keeler 1971:29].

Keeler also describes the blending of Pisgah and Burke attributes:

In McDowell County, Burke [soapstone-tempered] ceramics are found on the surface with pottery which bears strong resemblance to the

Table 2. Summary of McDowell site potsherds by temper and other selected attributes

Temper*	Soapstone					Sand				Quartz			Grit		
Temper Size	Fine	Med.	Coarse	Plus**	Total	Fine	Med.	Coarse	Total	Fine	Med.	Total	F/M	Coarse	Total
Exterior Surface															
Curv Comp St	10	35	·	5	50	1	15	33	49	·	4	4	117	1	118
Rect Comp St	8	27	·	·	35	·	2	10	12	·	·	0	28	·	28
Comp St Indet	12	31	1	5	49	1	10	26	37	1	3	4	105	·	105
Large Curv Comp St	·	2	·	·	2	·	·	·	0	·	·	0	1	·	1
Simple St	·	·	·	·	0	·	·	8	8	·	·	0	2	·	2
Pisgah Rect Comp St	5	19	1	2	27	2	2	8	12	1	2	3	76	·	76
Indet St Linear	4	9	·	1	14	1	8	13	22	2	·	2	24	·	24
Smoothed-Over Comp St	4	17	1	·	22	·	4	19	23	·	1	1	42	·	42
Burnished	15	31	·	·	46	7	17	26	50	4	·	4	58	1	59
Corncob Impressed	·	·	·	·	0	·	·	·	0	·	·	0	1	·	1
Plain/Smoothed	19	37	·	4	60	7	55	62	124	3	1	4	122	1	123
Check Stamped	1	2	·	2	5	·	·	·	0	·	·	0	1	·	1
Cord Marked	5	7	·	1	13	·	2	4	6	1	·	1	5	·	5
Fabric Impressed	1	·	·	·	1	·	·	1	1	·	·	0	2	·	2
Net Impressed	·	1	·	1	2	·	2	2	4	·	·	0	3	·	3
Brushed	·	·	·	·	0	·	·	·	0	·	·	0	2	·	2
Indeterminate	10	45	·	5	60	1	24	35	60	·	3	3	81	1	82
Total	94	263	3	26	386	20	141	247	408	12	14	26	670	4	674
Interior Surface															
Burnished	11	16	·	5	32	11	45	83	139	2	3	5	225	2	227
Plain/Smoothed	15	65	3	19	102	9	85	150	244	10	11	21	419	2	421
Scraped	·	4	·	2	6	·	1	3	4	·	·	0	12	·	12
Indeterminate	·	·	·	·	0	·	10	11	21	·	·	0	14	·	14
Total	26	85	3	26	140	20	141	247	408	12	14	26	670	4	674
Thickness															
<6 mm	7	4	·	2	13	5	43	41	89	2	2	4	51	1	52
6-8 mm	14	37	·	10	61	13	78	143	234	10	9	19	372	·	372
>8 mm	5	44	3	12	64	2	17	57	76	·	3	3	243	3	246
Total	26	85	3	24	138	20	138	241	399	12	14	26	666	4	670
Rim Form															
Applique	·	·	·	·	0	·	·	2	2	·	·	0	4	·	4
Collar	·	2	·	2	4	·	·	2	2	·	·	0	25	·	25
Folded	·	·	·	·	0	·	·	2	2	·	·	0	·	·	·
Thickened	·	·	·	1	1	·	·	1	1	·	·	0	4	·	4
Unmodified	3	2	·	1	6	2	14	18	34	·	·	0	23	·	23
Total	3	4	0	4	11	2	14	25	41	0	0	0	56	0	56

* Table 2 does not include 4 sherds for which temper was indeterminate.

** Indicates mixed temper size; see Appendix C.

late prehistoric Cherokee pottery termed Pisgah . . . Rims exhibiting a sort of collaring and decorated with a pattern of hachure indentations are found rather than the Burke incised or folded rims found a little further east. The steatite tempering is present along-side sand and crushed quartz and the Pisgah-like hachured rims occur on sherds with all three kinds of temper [Keeler 1971:40].

Table 3. Summary of McDowell site potsherds by exterior surface treatment and other selected attributes

Exterior Surface / Attribute / Attribute State	Curv Comp St	Rect Comp St	Comp St Indet	Large Curv Comp St	Simple Stamped	Indet St Linear	Pisgah Rect Comp St	Smoothed-Over Comp St	Burnished	Corncob Impressed	Plain/Smoothed	Check Stamped	Cord Marked	Fabric Impressed	Net Impressed	Brushed	Indeterminate	Total
Temper																		
Soapstone (F)	10	8	12	·	·	4	5	4	15	·	19	1	5	1	·	·	10	94
Soapstone (M)	35	27	31	2	·	9	19	17	31	·	37	2	7	·	1	·	45	263
Soapstone (C)	·	1	2	·	·	·	·	·	·	·	·	·	·	·	·	·	·	3
Soapstone (In)	5	·	5	·	·	1	2	·	·	·	4	2	1	·	1	·	5	26
Sand (F)	1	·	1	·	·	1	2	·	7	·	7	·	·	·	·	·	1	20
Sand (M)	15	2	10	·	·	8	2	4	17	·	55	·	2	·	2	·	24	141
Sand (C)	33	10	26	·	8	13	8	19	26	·	62	·	4	1	2	·	35	247
Quartz (F)	·	·	1	·	·	2	1	·	4	·	3	·	1	·	·	·	·	12
Quartz (M)	4	·	3	·	·	·	2	1	·	·	1	·	·	·	·	·	3	14
Grit (F/M)	1	28	105	1	2	24	76	42	58	1	122	1	5	2	3	2	81	554
Grit (C)	117	·	·	·	·	·	·	·	1	·	1	·	·	·	·	·	1	120
Misc./Ind.	1	·	·	·	·	·	·	·	1	·	2	·	·	·	·	·	·	4
Total	222	76	196	3	10	62	117	87	160	1	313	6	25	4	9	2	205	1498
Interior Surface																		
Burnished	66	38	45	2	·	20	34	46	119	1	51	2	6	3	3	1	49	486
Plain/Smoothed	140	32	142	·	10	39	76	38	33	·	252	4	18	1	5	·	133	923
Scraped	10	6	7	1	·	2	3	3	6	·	5	·	1	·	·	1	6	51
Thickness																		
<6 mm	13	3	20	·	1	9	6	12	20	·	46	·	4	·	3	·	21	158
6-8 mm	113	42	103	·	1	36	55	47	88	1	158	1	12	2	4	·	89	752
>8 mm	95	31	72	3	8	16	56	28	51	·	106	5	9	2	2	2	89	575
Rim Form																		
Applique	·	·	·	·	·	·	·	·	1	·	3	·	·	·	·	·	3	7
Collar	3	2	2	·	·	1	3	·	1	·	7	·	·	·	·	·	15	34
Folded	1	·	·	·	·	·	·	·	·	·	·	·	·	·	·	·	1	2
Thickened	·	2	2	·	·	·	1	·	·	·	1	·	·	·	·	·	·	6
Unmodified	4	2	5	·	2	2	4	·	14	·	22	·	·	·	1	1	13	70
Lip Form																		
Flat	7	3	5	·	2	2	4	·	11	·	16	·	·	·	1	1	17	69
Rounded	·	2	3	·	·	1	1	·	4	·	12	·	·	·	·	·	9	32

F, Fine; M, medium; C, coarse; In, inclusions.

The attribute analysis of the McDowell site ceramics more clearly revealed the patterns of blending that previous researchers have noted. The analyzed potsherds from the McDowell site were recovered from Features 1 through 4 (n = 224) excavated in 1977 (Ward 1977), from two undisturbed levels of mound fill and two levels associated with Structure 3 from the 1986 excavation units (n = 1,034; excavations described in appendix A), and from the Carey surface collections (n = 240). The following overview of the site ceramic assemblage is based primarily on Table 2, a summary of the assemblage by temper groups; Table 3, a summary of the assemblage by exterior surface treatment; and Table 4, which correlates

Table 4. Frequency of decoration attributes for selected exterior surface treatments on McDowell site potsherds

Decoration / Decoration Location	Punctation	Burke Incised	Incised Misc.	Finger-pinched	Notched	Smooth/Burnish	Complicated St.	Scraped	Fillets	Rosette/Node	Total
Curvilinear Comp. St.											
Collar	1	..	..	..	..	..	1	..	..	..	2
Lower Edge/Scallop	..	..	..	1	..	..	..	..	..	..	1
Total	1	0	0	1	0	0	1	0	0	0	3
Rectilinear Comp. St.											
Collar	1	..	..	..	..	..	1	..	..	..	2
Lip	..	..	..	..	..	1	..	..	..	..	1
Exterior Edge Lip	2	..	..	..	..	..	..	..	..	..	2
Just Below Lip	..	1	..	..	..	..	..	..	..	..	1
Total	3	1	0	0	0	1	1	0	0	0	6
Burnished											
Rim	..	1	..	..	..	..	..	..	..	..	1
Applique/Thickened	..	..	..	1	..	..	..	..	..	..	1
Collar	..	..	..	..	..	1	..	..	..	..	1
Total	0	1	0	1	0	1	0	0	0	0	3
Plain/Smoothed											
Applique/Thickened	..	..	..	..	2	..	..	..	..	..	2
Collar	5	..	..	..	..	..	..	..	..	..	5
Lip	..	..	..	..	..	1	..	..	..	..	1
Exterior Edge Lip	..	..	..	..	1	..	..	..	..	..	1
Just Below Lip	..	..	..	..	..	..	..	..	1	2	3
Total	5	0	0	0	3	1	0	0	1	2	12
Comp. St. Indeterminate											
Rim	..	..	..	..	..	1	..	..	..	..	1
Collar	2	..	..	..	..	..	..	..	..	..	2
Lip	1	..	..	..	..	1	..	..	..	..	2
Total	3	0	0	0	0	2	0	0	0	0	5
Pisgah Rectilinear Comp. St.											
Rim	2	..	..	..	..	..	..	..	..	..	2
Collar	3	..	..	..	..	..	..	..	..	..	3
Lip	..	..	1	..	..	..	..	..	..	..	1
Total	5	0	1	0	0	0	0	0	0	0	6
Indeterminate											
Rim	1	..	..	..	..	1	..	..	..	..	2
Applique/Thickened	..	..	..	..	2	..	..	..	..	..	2
Collar	10	..	1	..	..	..	2	....	....	..	13
Lower Edge/Scallop	1	..	..	..	..	..	..	..	..	..	1
Exterior Edge Lip	..	..	..	..	2	..	..	..	..	..	2
Neck	..	..	..	..	..	..	..	1	..	..	1
Total	12	0	1	0	4	1	2	1	0	0	21

type and location of decoration with exterior surface. The tables make clear the extent to which Burke and Pisgah ceramic attributes are mixed.

The McDowell site ceramics exhibit three major temper classes as previously described (Table 2). Most of the sherds are tempered with grit (n = 674; 45.1 percent) and with few exceptions the remainder are tempered with sand (n = 408; 27.3 percent) or soapstone (n = 386; 25.8 percent). A very few (n = 26; 1.7 percent) are tempered with crushed quartz.

The grit-tempered sherds include a wide variety of exterior surface treatments including the following (percentage of identifiable surfaces unless otherwise specified): complicated stamped (55.3 percent), linear stamped (4.3 percent; it is likely that at least some of these represent fragments of rectilinear complicated-stamped sherds), plain smoothed or smoothed-over complicated stamped (27.9 percent), and burnished (10.0 percent). Minority surface treatments (2.3 percent) include cob impressed, cord marked, check stamped, fabric impressed, net impressed, and brushed.

Grit-tempered, complicated-stamped sherds include curvilinear complicated motifs (36.3 percent), rectilinear motifs identical to those defined for Pisgah Rectilinear Stamped pottery (23.2 percent; Dickens 1976:174–177), indeterminate rectilinear complicated designs (8.5 percent), and small sherds for which the possibility of a curvilinear design could not be discounted (32.0 percent). However, most of this latter category probably represents fragments of Pisgah or other rectilinear complicated-stamped patterns. Significantly, the curvilinear stamped patterns are consistent with designs found on Burke complicated-stamped pottery and not with those described for Pisgah Curvilinear Complicated Stamped sherds (Dickens 1976:183–185) (Plate 2). Most grit-tempered sherds (with the exception of the curvilinear complicated-stamped sherds) conform to Pisgah type pottery.

Vessel and rim form data are not numerous; most rims are small and are usually broken just below the rim or collar, making it difficult to determine overall vessel characteristics. However, nearly one-half (n = 25; 44.6 percent) of all rims are collared, a form characteristic of Pisgah types. A small number (n = 4) feature appliqued rim strips or are otherwise thickened.

The second-largest temper class is sand, which represents 27.2 percent of the assemblage. Identifiable surface treatments among sand-tempered sherds are as follows: 31.5 percent complicated stamped, 8.6 percent linear stamped (it is likely that at least some of these represent fragments of rectilinear complicated-stamped sherds); 42.2 percent plain smoothed or smoothed-over complicated stamped; 14.4 percent burnished; and 3.1 percent minorities including cob impressed, cord marked, check stamped, fabric impressed, and net impressed.

Sand-tempered, complicated-stamped sherds include 44.5 percent curvilinear complicated motifs, 10.9 percent rectilinear Pisgah-like motifs, 10.9 percent rectilinear complicated designs, and 33.6 percent designs that are indeterminate. Again, most of the latter two categories probably represent fragments of Pisgah rectilinear complicated-stamped patterns. On the other hand, the curvilinear stamps are more consistent with designs found on Burke complicated-stamped pottery.

In typological terms, the sand-tempered sherds appear to include at least some Pisgah types; this includes sherds with rectilinear or specific Pisgah

Plate 2. Grit-tempered pottery from the McDowell site. *a–f*, Pisgah Complicated Stamped; *g–k*, McDowell Complicated Stamped.

exterior surface treatments along with some of the plain and minority surface treatment (cord marked, fabric and net impressed) sherds. Some of the plain and minority surface treatment sherds are very small and have a more friable paste; they are quite distinctive in comparison with the later Pisgah and Burke types and appear to be an earlier Woodland ceramic.

The remainder of the sand-tempered sherds do not fit established types for this area. Since they consist of curvilinear and burnished surfaces, they should perhaps be considered as the westernmost examples of Cowans Ford pottery (see below and chapter 4 for more detailed description).

Soapstone tempering represents the third-largest temper class (25.8 percent; n = 386). Identifiable surface treatments among soapstone-tempered sherds are as follows: 49.9 percent complicated stamped; 4.3 percent linear stamped (it is likely that at least some of these represent fragments of rectilinear complicated-stamped sherds); 25.1 percent plain smoothed or smoothed-over complicated stamped; 14.1 percent burnished; and 6.4 percent minorities including cob impressed, cord marked, check stamped, fabric impressed, and net impressed.

Soapstone-tempered, complicated-stamped sherds include 32.3 percent curvilinear complicated motifs, 16.8 percent rectilinear Pisgah-like motifs,

Plate 3. Soapstone-tempered Pisgah Rectilinear Complicated Stamped pottery from the McDowell site.

21.7 percent rectilinear complicated designs, and 30.4 percent designs that are indeterminate. Most of the latter two categories probably represent fragments of Pisgah complicated-stamped patterns. And again, the curvilinear stamps are consistent with designs found on Burke complicated-stamped pottery (Plate 3). Soapstone-tempered sherds are generally 6 to 8 mm thick and have smooth, plain interior surfaces. Vessel form information is incomplete, but it is clear that Pisgah collared and thickened rims are relatively common.

Typologically, most of the soapstone-tempered sherds are appropriately termed Burke sherds, with the exception being those sherds with Pisgah Rectilinear Complicated Stamped exterior surface treatments. In addition, it is likely that most of the rectilinear and indeterminate exterior surfaces represent Pisgah designs and should therefore be classified as Pisgah. The Pisgah type explicitly includes soapstone temper in some cases (Dickens 1976).

The final temper class is crushed quartz (n = 28; 1.9 percent). As a group, this small class does not stand out as being significantly different from the other temper classes in any characteristics. Typologically, I suggest that the grit-tempered burnished and curvilinear complicated-stamped sherds should be classified as McDowell type pottery (H. Trawick Ward, personal communication 1992) and that the sand-tempered burnished and curvilinear complicated-stamped sherds should be typed as Cowans Ford pottery (see appendix C for formal type descriptions). It is then possible to describe the McDowell assemblage as follows:

A. Pisgah series (consisting of sherds tempered with sand, quartz, grit, or soapstone). Types include rectilinear complicated stamped, plain, cord marked, check stamped, fabric impressed, and net impressed.
B. Burke series (soapstone tempered). Types include complicated stamped (primarily curvilinear though including some non-Pisgah rectilinear designs), plain, burnished, cord marked, check stamped, fabric impressed, and net impressed.
C. McDowell (grit tempered). Types include curvilinear complicated stamped and burnished. I have not developed a formal series description. These sherds are, for all practical purposes, identical to Burke except for the temper.
D. Cowans Ford series (sand tempered; formal description in appendix C). This series consists of the sherds that Ward (1977:9) recognized as being hard and thin and perhaps related to protohistoric Catawba pottery (more will be said about these wares in chapter 5). Types include complicated stamped, burnished, and plain.
E. There are also a small number of sand-, grit-, and quartz-tempered sherds that do not easily fit any of the typologies. These sherds are plain, cord marked, fabric impressed, or net impressed with generally friable paste. They probably represent earlier Woodland period ceramics.

While typological labels allow us to characterize these ceramics as a group, they tend to obscure the "blending" phenomenon that has always been the focus of attention. In fact, if one were to rely strictly on these typologies for analytical purposes, it would be difficult to assign types to some sherds. This is particularly true for soapstone-tempered plain, cord-marked, and check-stamped sherds, which could conceivably fit both Burke and Pisgah types as I have defined them. As always, the utility of typological or attribute analysis will depend on the goals of the research questions being asked.

In summary, late prehistoric and protohistoric period sites from the extreme upper Catawba River valley in McDowell County tend to be characterized by mixed ceramic assemblages. The McDowell site, one of the largest late prehistoric to protohistoric period sites in the region, is the best example. Its ceramics reflect types from four different series: Pisgah, Burke, McDowell, and Cowans Ford. The ceramic diversity seen at this site is replicated at most other sites in the area.

Burke Ceramics in the Upper Catawba Valley

While the extreme upper Catawba valley is characterized by sites with mixed assemblages of Pisgah, McDowell, Cowans Ford, and Burke pottery, those sites located east of the Linville River exhibit predominately Burke series pottery. The Burke series was defined by Keeler (1971) and is characterized by the use of crushed soapstone temper. Burke pottery is a regional variant of the Lamar pottery tradition found throughout much of the Southeast (Hally 1994; Williams and Shapiro 1990; a complete series description is presented in appendix C). Burke pottery is made with a medium-fine to fine paste and the ware is well fired, hard, and durable. The soapstone temper particles normally range in size from small flakes to chunks as large as 6 to 8 mm that vary in color (gold, red, orange, silver, grey) and texture (soft and dense, soft and platy, hard and compact). The quantity of temper also varies widely and sand or crushed quartz was occasionally mixed with the soapstone temper.

Few intact vessels have been recovered; therefore, there is little information on the vessel assemblage, but vessel forms seem to consist primarily of cazuela bowls and open-mouthed jars. The cazuela bowls usually possess a Lamar incised rim decoration. Jar rims include plain or folded rims that often are decorated with finger pinching, punctation, or notching.

Exterior surface finishes include three major techniques: complicated stamped (62 percent of all upper valley assemblages), burnished plain (16 percent), and plain (19 percent). Both curvilinear and rectilinear patterns occur among the complicated-stamped surfaces, but curvilinear patterns far outnumber the rectilinear and include spirals or concentric circles joined by fields of arcs or straight lines; figure eights and filfot crosses are rare. Minority surface finishes include check stamped, simple stamped, and brushed. Interior surfaces range from smoothed to highly burnished.

Keeler (1971:39) originally observed several patterns in paste and temper distribution: (1) paste tended to be more fine from west to east; (2) where sand was present as temper the trend was toward less and finer sand from west to east; and (3) the density of the soapstone temper diminished from west to east. These observations seemed to indicate a spatial shift from west to east (downriver) toward a finer paste with less temper. Keeler felt that this trend (as well as the concomitant trend toward increased burnishing) reflected a link between the late prehistoric Burke series and the historic period Catawba ceramics found on the lower Catawba/Wateree River. The present analysis was unable to confirm these spatial patterns; however, later discussion will show that it is very likely that the plain and burnished wares are related to historic Catawba wares.

The Berry site assemblage (Tables 5 and 6) is the largest sample (n = 3,692) of pottery from sites in the upper valley. The Berry ceramic assemblage exhibits the widest range of variation among those sites located east

Table 5. Summary of Berry site potsherds by temper and other selected attributes

Temper	Soapstone					Sand				Quartz					Grit
Temper Size	Fine	Med.	Coarse Plus*			Fine	Med.	Coarse		Fine	Med.	Coarse Plus*			
	#	#	#	#	Total	#	#	#	Total	#	#	#	#	Total	Total
Exterior Surface															
Curv Comp St	356	528	13	80	977	.	5	4	9	2	.	.	1	3	3
Rect Comp St	7	32	.	6	45	.	.	.	.	.	.	.	.	.	1
Comp St Indet	87	84	2	43	216	1	5	2	8	2	.	.	.	2	3
Large Curv Comp St	.	4	.	.	4	.	2	.	2	.	.	.	.	.	.
Simple St	2	.	.	1	3	.	.	2	2	.	.	.	.	.	1
Pisgah Rect Comp St	5	14	1	2	22	.	.	.	.	.	.	.	.	.	.
Etowah Rect Comp St	.	.	.	1	1	.	.	.	.	.	.	.	.	.	.
Indet St Linear	32	20	.	9	61	.	2	2	4	.	.	.	1	1	8
Smoothed-Over Comp St	40	58	1	8	107	.	.	1	1	.	.	.	1	1	2
Burnished	290	243	1	71	605	8	41	30	79	7	1	1	2	11	19
Corncob Impressed	2	9	.	3	14	.	2	1	3	1	.	.	.	1	1
Plain/Smoothed	163	141	2	74	380	4	52	81	137	15	48	1	4	68	89
Check Stamped	2	2	.	1	5	.	.	.	.	.	.	.	.	.	.
Cord Marked	12	6	.	7	25	1	3	16	20	8	8	2	.	18	32
Fabric Impressed	.	2	.	.	2	1	.	15	16	4	12	1	1	18	20
Net Impressed	6	7	.	3	16	.	2	.	2	.	1	.	.	1	2
Brushed	4	4	.	2	10	1	1	7	9	6	2	.	.	8	5
Indeterminate	181	211	6	51	449	5	19	29	53	7	7	.	.	14	31
Total	1189	1365	26	362	2942	21	134	190	345	52	79	5	10	146	217
Interior Surface															
Burnished	694	622	9	164	1489	11	54	37	102	12	3	1	1	17	33
Plain/Smoothed	448	666	17	178	1309	8	75	122	205	25	67	5	8	105	157
Scraped	37	53	0	16	106	0	0	22	22	13	9	0	0	22	22
Indeter.	10	23	0	4	37	2	5	6	13	2	0	0	0	2	3
Total	1189	1364	26	362	2941	21	134	187	342	52	79	6	9	146	215
Thickness															
<6 mm	404	225	1	94	724	11	69	55	135	20	19	1	1	41	36
6-8 mm	642	809	11	203	1665	7	56	110	173	25	50	3	9	87	154
>8 mm	130	309	14	59	512	1	6	20	27	5	10	1	1	17	20
Total	1176	1343	26	356	2901	19	131	185	335	50	79	5	11	145	210
Rim Form															
Applique	3	3	0	0	6	0	0	0	0	0	0	0	0	0	1
Collar	3	2	0	0	5	0	0	0	0	0	0	0	0	0	0
Folded	22	13	0	6	41	0	0	1	1	0	0	0	0	0	0
Thickened	5	7	0	2	14	0	0	0	0	0	0	0	0	0	0
Unmodified	112	43	0	27	182	1	21	15	37	5	4	0	2	11	23
Total	145	68	0	35	248	1	21	16	38	5	4	0	2	11	24
Vessel Form															
Carinated Bowl	12	3	0	1	16	0	1	1	2	0	0	0	1	1	0
Hemisphere Bowl	1	0	0	0	1	0	0	0	0	0	0	0	1	1	0
Everted-Rim Jar	47	23	0	10	80	0	5	3	8	1	0	0	0	1	5
Str. Sided Jar	14	8	0	1	23	0	2	4	6	2	3	0	0	5	8
Total	74	34	0	12	120	0	8	8	16	3	3	0	2	8	13

* Indicates mixed temper size; see Appendix C.

of the Linville River (most of Burke County). Descriptions of several other Burke County site ceramic assemblages are presented in appendix C.

The Berry site (31BK22) is likely a multicomponent site but, as will be shown, the ceramic assemblage is quite homogeneous (Tables 5 and 6). Although soapstone tempering is most common (79.7 percent), sand (9.3 percent), grit (5.9 percent), crushed quartz (3.9 percent), hornblende (.6 percent), and shell (.1 percent) temper also occur. The grit-tempered (n = 217), hornblende-tempered (n = 23), and quartz-tempered (n = 147) sherds from the Berry site do not fit established ceramic types in the Pied-

Table 6. Summary of Berry site potsherds by exterior surface treatment and other selected attributes

Exterior Surface / Attribute / Attribute State	Curv Comp St	Rect Comp St	Comp St Indet	Large Curv Comp St	Simple Stamped	Pisgah Rect Comp St	Napier/Etowah Comp St	Indet St Linear	Smoothed-Over Comp St	Burnished	Corncob Impressed	Plain/Smoothed	Check Stamped	Cord Marked	Fabric Impressed	Net Impressed	Brushed	Indeterminate	Total
Temper																			
Soapstone (F)	356	7	87	.	2	5	.	32	40	290	2	163	2	12	.	6	4	181	1189
Soapstone (M)	528	32	84	4	.	14	.	20	58	243	9	141	2	6	2	7	4	211	1365
Soapstone (C)	13	.	2	.	.	1	.	.	1	1	.	2	.	.	.	.	.	6	26
Soapstone (In)	80	6	43	.	1	2	1	9	8	71	3	74	1	7	.	3	2	51	362
Sand (F)	.	.	1	.	.	.	.	.	.	8	.	4	.	1	1	.	1	5	21
Sand (M)	5	.	5	2	.	.	.	2	.	41	2	52	.	3	.	2	1	19	134
Sand (C)	4	.	2	.	2	.	.	2	1	30	1	81	.	16	15	.	7	29	190
Quartz (F)	2	.	2	.	.	.	.	.	.	7	1	15	.	8	4	.	6	7	52
Quartz (M)	.	.	.	.	.	.	.	.	1	.	.	48	.	8	12	1	2	7	79
Quartz (C)	.	.	.	.	.	.	.	.	1	.	.	1	.	2	1	.	.	.	5
Quartz (In)	2	.	.	.	.	.	.	1	1	2	.	4	.	.	1	.	.	.	11
Hornblende	.	.	.	.	1	.	.	.	1	.	.	12	.	4	2	.	1	2	23
Grit (F/M)	3	1	3	.	1	.	.	8	2	19	1	86	.	30	19	2	5	30	210
Grit (C)	.	.	.	.	.	.	.	.	.	.	.	3	.	2	1	.	.	1	7
Shell	.	.	.	.	.	.	.	.	.	1	.	1	.	1	.	.	.	.	3
Misc./Ind.	2	.	2	.	.	.	.	.	.	2	.	2	.	1	1	.	.	5	15
Total	995	46	231	6	7	22	1	74	112	717	19	689	5	101	59	21	33	554	3692
Interior Surface																			
Burnished	539	14	104	6	1	7	1	31	48	560	3	142	.	19	.	4	5	165	1649
Plain smoothed	406	24	115	.	5	11	.	39	61	138	15	508	3	68	45	13	11	346	1808
Scraped	39	6	11	.	1	4	.	4	2	11	1	25	2	13	10	4	17	24	174
Thickness																			
<6 mm	207	3	34	.	1	.	1	17	25	295	4	223	.	20	5	6	12	95	948
6-8 mm	625	26	137	5	5	13	.	44	63	340	11	373	3	67	45	13	17	314	2101
>8 mm	154	15	59	1	1	9	.	13	23	73	4	81	2	13	9	2	4	121	584
Rim Form																			
Applique	.	.	.	.	.	.	.	.	.	1	.	.	.	.	.	.	.	6	7
Collar	1	.	.	.	.	.	.	.	.	1	.	.	.	.	.	.	.	2	4
Folded	9	.	1	.	.	.	.	1	.	4	.	3	.	.	.	.	.	26	44
Thickened	2	.	.	.	.	.	.	.	.	2	1	1	.	.	.	.	.	9	15
Unmodified	17	2	13	.	.	2	.	1	7	79	1	52	1	6	2	1	5	66	255
Lip Form																			
Flat	22	.	13	.	.	2	.	1	5	63	2	39	1	4	.	1	3	93	249
Rounded	5	1	1	.	.	.	.	1	2	21	.	14	.	2	.	.	2	21	70

F, Fine; M, medium; C, coarse; In, inclusions.

mont or nearby Appalachian Summit regions. These sherds are usually plain, with minority amounts of cord-marked, fabric-impressed, or burnished sherds. Vessel rims, though uncommon, are almost always unmodified. Though difficult to type, the burnished, grit-tempered sherds fit the McDowell series, described above, and some of the quartz-tempered sherds appear similar to Woodland period Yadkin series (Coe 1964) or late Woodland Uwharrie series (Coe 1952b:307–308) ceramics.

Plate 4. Burke curvilinear complicated-stamped potsherds from the Berry site.

Plate 5. Burke curvilinear complicated-stamped potsherds from the Berry site.

The sand-tempered sherds (n = 345) are primarily plain and smoothed (46.9 percent of sherds with identifiable exterior surface treatment), though burnishing (27.0 percent) occurs in large numbers, followed in frequency by curvilinear and linear stamped (8.6 percent), cord marked (6.8 percent), fabric impressed (5.5 percent), brushed (3.2 percent), corncob impressed (1.0 percent), net impressed (.7 percent), and smoothed-over complicated stamped (.3 percent). Sand-tempered sherds tend to be thinner than the grit- and quartz-tempered wares, with 40 percent having a thickness of less than 6 mm. Vessel forms include straight-sided and everted-rim jars and carinated bowls. Rims are unmodified with the exception of one folded rim. These sand-tempered sherds do not fit established types such as Badin (Coe 1964:28–29), Haw River (Ward and Davis 1993:65–67), Dan River (Coe and Lewis 1952), or Pee Dee (Reid 1967); these sherds are best considered Cowans Ford pottery. Cowans Ford pottery bears a strong resemblance to protohistoric and historic period Caraway ceramics (Coe 1964:34, 1995:160–166). Caraway pottery was defined at the Poole site, thought to be the location of the Keyauwee town visited by John Lawson in 1701 (Rights 1957). The relationship between Cowans Ford and Caraway pottery will be explored further in chapter 4.

The remainder of the Berry assemblage (Table 5) consists of soapstone-tempered sherds (n = 2,942), which represent examples of the Burke series as defined by Keeler (1971:31–37). Exterior surface treatments include complicated stamped (49.8 percent of identified sherds), burnished (24.3 percent), plain (15.2 percent), smoothed-over complicated stamped (4.3 percent), simple or linear stamped (2.6 percent), cob impressed (.6 percent), check stamped (.2 percent), cord marked (1.0 percent), fabric impressed (.1 percent), net impressed (.6 percent), and brushed (.4 percent). Twenty-two (.9 percent) soapstone-tempered sherds feature clear Pisgah type (Dickens 1976) rectilinear complicated-stamped motifs.

It is usually difficult to define the design elements on curvilinear complicated-stamped sherds. The motifs are large and often lightly applied, smoothed over, or eroded. Most designs include combinations of whole or partial spirals or concentric circles joined by fields of arcs or straight lines; or sometimes curvilinear elements surround diamond or square motifs (Plates 4 and 5). Formal figure eights or filfot crosses are rare (cf. Keeler 1971:34). Although Keeler (1971) originally characterized Burke stamps as "large and sloppy," this description is misleading. The stamps are large but well made and only occasionally appear "sloppy," perhaps from being applied to a vessel surface while it was still damp.

No complete vessels were recovered during the site excavation, but identifiable vessel forms include straight-sided jars (19.2 percent), everted-rim jars (66.7 percent), hemisphere bowls (.8 percent), and carinated bowls (13.3 percent). A small intact Burke vessel was recovered by the Berry fam-

Plate 6. Burke type rim sherds, unmodified rim form, from the Berry site. *a, b, e, g,* Notched lips; *c, f,* no decoration; *d,* Burke Burnished with drilled hole; *g, h, j,* Burke Incised; *i,* miscellaneous incised.

ily from the mound area when it was graded. This vessel is a constricted-neck jar with folded rim and a plain exterior surface treatment.

Within the collected assemblage, most rims are unmodified (73.4 percent), but 22.1 percent are folded or thickened and 2.4 percent feature an appliqued strip beneath the rim (Plates 6 and 7). Jar rims are often decorated with a wide variety of notching, punctation, and pinching. Carinated bowls are often incised between the shoulder and rim. The incised patterns are similar to those found on other Lamar Incised vessels and most often include three to five parallel horizontal lines that usually incorporate scrolls or loops at regular intervals around the vessel rim. Incising is usually executed in clean, firm lines between 1 and 2 mm wide. Carinated shoulders also exhibit a variety of punctations; these may occur on otherwise undecorated vessels, but often occur in combination with Lamar Incised decorations.

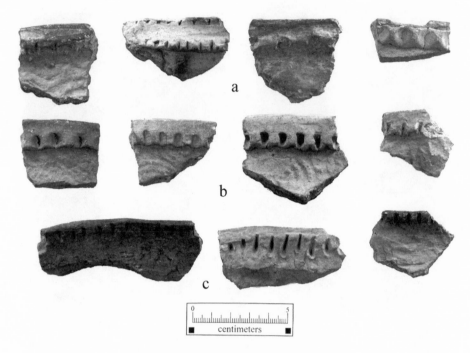

Plate 7. Burke type rim sherds (appliqued, folded, and thickened rim forms) from the Berry site. *a*, Rims with appliqued strip with notching or finger-pinching; *b*, folded rims punctated along the bottom edge of the rim fold; *c*, thickened (manner uncertain) rims with punctations.

A comparison of the Berry ceramic assemblage with ceramics from other Burke assemblages reveals very few differences among them. However, several deserve some mention. Assemblages from 31BK1, 31BK17, 31BK18, and 31BK12 (see appendix C) are similar to that of the Berry site, but vary in the relative frequencies of different attributes such as exterior surface treatment. The Pitts site (31BK209; see appendix C) is most dissimilar, with a significantly lower percentage of Burke sherds (65 percent) overall and a higher percentage of Pisgah sherds (35 percent; compare Plates 8 and 9). Plain exterior surface treatments are most common, with only a low frequency of curvilinear complicated-stamped and burnished exteriors. The combined frequency of Pisgah complicated-stamped and linear-stamped sherds is the highest (5.2 percent) among all Burke County sites. It is possible that assemblages featuring low percentages of curvilinear complicated-stamped and burnished exterior surfaces, combined with the presence of Pisgah rectilinear complicated stamped, occur earlier than as-

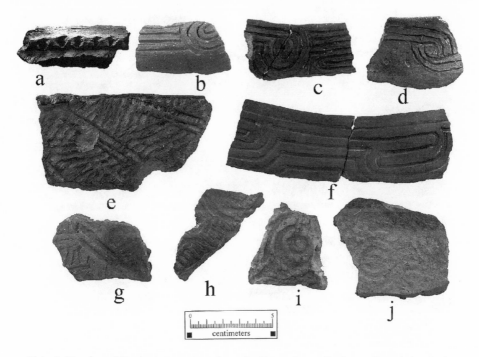

Plate 8. Pisgah and Burke type pottery from the Berry site. *a*, Burke appliqued rim; *b–d*, *f*, Burke Incised; *e*, *g*, Pisgah Rectilinear Complicated Stamped; *h–j*, Burke Complicated Stamped.

semblages featuring high percentages of curvilinear complicated-stamped and burnished exterior surfaces. It must be kept in mind that few of these assemblages represent single-component occupations.

Another site that may exhibit ceramic temporal variation is 31BK1, where the ceramics (Plates 1, 10, and 11) are nearly exclusively Burke series pottery with little variety. This is not entirely unexpected since the ceramics are derived from only five features. It is unknown whether these features (and the pottery from them) are representative of the site as a whole. Curvilinear complicated-stamped (54.3 percent of identified surface treatment states) and burnished exterior surfaces (35.0 percent) predominate and such sherds almost always feature burnished interiors (87.1 percent). Overall, adding indeterminate complicated stamped (5.5 percent) and plain (3.5 percent) brings the common group of complicated stamped, burnished, and plain to 98.3 percent of the identified assemblage. The assemblage is nearly as homogeneous when temper is considered in association with exterior surface treatment; complicated-stamped, burnished, and plain soapstone-tempered sherds comprise 90.3 percent of the assem-

Plate 9. Pisgah and Burke type pottery from the Pitts site. *a, b, e,* Pisgah Rectilinear Complicated Stamped; *b, c, d,* Pisgah rim sherds; *f, g,* Pisgah Check Stamp; *h–k,* Burke Complicated Stamped.

blage. The remaining sherds consist of grit-tempered, complicated-stamped sherds that can be called McDowell type, as well as what are probably earlier, grit-tempered, Uwharrie type (Coe 1964) sherds, as seen in Plate 11.

Interestingly, though a relatively large number of rims are present (n = 51), only one is folded (Plate 12); the remainder are unmodified. The preponderance of unmodified rims may reflect temporal variation, but it may also reflect the small sample of the site from which these sherds came. Vessel forms are not well represented, but at least three forms are present: a hemisphere bowl with everted lip, a tall jar with slightly constricted neck, and carinated or cazuela forms. The latter are most common. Burke Incised decorations usually occur on the carinated vessels and occasionally occur on constricted-neck jars (see Plate 13). Examples include three- to five-line motifs with the incised line 1 to 1.5 mm in width and a design field of 25 to 35 mm that usually covers at least one-half of the area between the shoulder and the rim.

A comparison of the Berry site ceramics with those of the two larg-

Plate 10. Burke pottery from 31BK1. *a, b,* Burke Complicated Stamped with folded rim (*a*) and unmodified rim form (*b*); *c, d,* Burke Incised with three lines; *e,* effigy rim sherd.

Plate 11. Grit-tempered potsherds from 31BK1. *a–g*, McDowell Complicated Stamped sherds; *h*, Uwharrie cord-marked sherd.

est surface-collected sites (31BK17 and 31BK18) revealed little variation among them. The assemblages appear to vary most in the relative frequencies of Burke Complicated Stamped, Burke Burnished, and Burke Plain/ Smoothed types; this sort of variation may prove to be temporally significant in the future. However, it is perhaps useful to compare the frequencies of Burke Incised in more detail.

Plate 12. Burke curvilinear complicated-stamped rim sherd with folded rim from the Berry site.

Plate 13. Burke Incised constricted-neck jar from 31BK17.

Table 7. Frequency of Burke Incised potsherds from 31BK17, 31BK18, and the Berry site

Burke Incised sherds	n	% of Total Sherds						
31BK17	212	6.4						
31BK18	64	3.4						
Berry site	119	2.4						
No. of incised lines	3	4	5	6	7	8	9	
	%	%	%	%	%	%	%	n
31BK17	31.7	43.7	19.0	3.5	2.1	0.0	0.0	142
31BK18	30.0	45.0	20.0	0.0	0.0	5.0	0.0	20
Berry site	36.0	41.3	10.7	4.0	1.3	1.3	1.3	72

Table 7 shows the relative frequency of Burke Incised sherds at the three sites in the upper valley that have large samples: 31BK17, 31BK18, and 31BK22. It also shows the numbers of lines included in the design. These should be treated as conservative figures since many sherds broke along the incised lines. Therefore, the figure within each category should be viewed as "at least" the number represented. (Note: The number of sherds in Table 7 includes additional surface collections from 31BK17 received after the attribute analysis was completed; these were analyzed for surface treatment and decoration only.)

The number of incised lines in Lamar decorations has been determined to be temporally significant (Hally 1994) in Georgia (Smith and Williams 1990) and South Carolina (DePratter and Judge 1990). Designs with two to four lines are usually dated to the mid-fifteenth to early sixteenth century whereas those with more than four lines are dated to the early to late sixteenth century (see Plates 14 and 15), and those with many (>6–8) thin lines date to the late sixteenth to seventeenth century (Smith and Williams 1990:61). As shown in Table 7, there is little difference in the frequencies of incised lines among the three sites.

There are also limited data on the specific types of design elements. Burke Incised features only two general design motifs: rows of horizontal lines linking scrolled loops and horizontal lines linking bracketed U or tear-drop shapes. There is some variation within these two motifs and it is likely that additional motifs will be identified when larger sherd and vessel assemblages are available. Unfortunately, the most common design element present in currently available collections is the band of horizontal lines connecting the curvilinear elements. However, the figures for identifiable curvilinear elements are interesting.

At the Berry site, 13 of 66 Lamar Incised sherds are identified as "looped" or "bracketed": 61.5 percent of the recognizable motifs are loops and 38.5

Plate 14. Burke Incised pottery from 31BK17.

Plate 15. Burke Incised pottery from the Berry site.

percent are brackets. At site 31BK17, 74 looped and bracketed examples are identified out of 119 Lamar Incised sherds. At this site, the frequencies are reversed, as loops represent 25.7 percent and brackets represent 74.3 percent of the identifiable incised motifs. It is possible that the percentage differences represent a temporal phenomenon, but without larger samples and better functional and contextual evidence it is impossible to discount explanations involving such variables as vessel form and use.

To summarize, it is difficult to extract temporally sensitive patterns from the attribute analysis. This is at least partially the result of sampling problems since there is only one site, Berry, with a variety of excavated contexts; the majority of other assemblages are made up of surface collections. Some general observations are in order, however. First, it seems likely that the assemblage at the Pitts site reflects a relatively early date, perhaps early to middle fourteenth century, as evidenced by the greater than usual frequency of Pisgah rectilinear stamped and the relatively low frequencies of Burke Complicated Stamped and Burnished types. Second, the prevalence of Burke Burnished and Burke Incised is also likely to reflect later assemblages dating from the mid-fifteenth into the early seventeenth century: perhaps 31BK17 is later than the Berry site—this is a working hypothesis based primarily on the greater occurrence of incised carinated vessels and their associated design patterns. In addition, it is likely that rim forms change through time, with the addition of appliqued strips below the lip along with folded punctated rims probably in the fifteenth century. Clearly, little more can be said without better-dated ceramic contexts.

Dating Upper Catawba Valley Ceramics

The preceding sections have described some of the variability within the Burke ceramic series and between the Burke, Pisgah, McDowell, and Cowans Ford series. I have suggested that some of the variability reflects temporal differences, but lack of contextual data makes it difficult to evaluate these suggestions. This section considers the ceramics from the McDowell and Berry sites with respect to site contexts and radiocarbon dates.

At the McDowell site, blending of Burke and Pisgah ceramic traits is accompanied by additional variation reflected by the presence of McDowell and Cowans Ford types. Unfortunately, there is little site contextual data to help determine whether some of this variation and blending represents the ceramics of temporally distinct occupations. However, before one can attempt to explain the phenomenon, it is important to provide an explicit description of the attributes that demonstrate this blending of several ceramic types.

This blending is visible in patterns of association of temper, surface treatments, rim form, and decoration attributes within the Pisgah and Burke ceramic series. This is primarily exemplified by the occurrence of typical Pisgah exterior surface treatments (rectilinear stamps) and Pisgah rim forms (thickened or collared) on soapstone-tempered (Burke) pottery. In addition, the assemblage is further blended by the presence of sherds that do not fit either series definition but exhibit characteristics of both; that is, sand-, quartz-, or grit-tempered (Pisgah) sherds occur with burnished and curvilinear complicated-stamped surfaces (Burke). Is this blending a function of temporal variation or does it result from other sources? Unfortunately, we have little supporting temporal data for the McDowell site; there is no internal site stratigraphy and few feature contexts have been recovered. However, there are two radiocarbon dates from the site and one radiocarbon date from the Tyler-Loughridge site (31MC139) that can be considered.

The radiocarbon dates from the McDowell site were obtained from Feature 3 and a burned timber in Structure 3. Wood charcoal from Feature 3 yielded a calibrated date of A.D. 1441 (GX 11057; Boyd 1986a:67). The second date, from a timber in Structure 3, is earlier, with a radiocarbon assay of 890 ± 50 B.P. (Beta-21818) and a calibrated date of A.D. 1158. At 1 sigma there is a 40-percent probability of an age range from A.D. 1041–1094 and a 35-percent probability of an age range from A.D. 1151–1195. At 2 sigma there is a 98-percent probability of an age range from A.D. 1023–1229.

The Tyler-Loughridge site, less than 1.5 miles from McDowell, is primarily middle to late Woodland, but also has a small Pisgah phase component (Robinson 1996). Excavation of Feature 102-1 yielded a calibrated date (Beta-32927) of A.D. 1028 with a 1-sigma range of A.D. 999–1164 and a 2-sigma range of A.D. 894–1227. The feature contents included Pisgah Complicated Stamped, Pisgah Plain, and Pisgah Check Stamped types and one soapstone-tempered Burke sherd. Unfortunately, the exterior surface treatment of the Burke sherd is not distinct; it could be punctated or stamped and is slightly smoothed over. In any event, this date overlaps with the earlier date from the McDowell site.

In his discussion of the radiocarbon dates for soapstone-tempered pottery in upper east Tennessee and at the McDowell site, Boyd (1986a:85) states that "soapstone-tempered ceramics are considered Protohistoric because of their late radiocarbon dates and their comparability to historic ceramics of the Catawba Indians." He (Boyd 1986a:91–92) further confirms this assessment by considering the distribution of soapstone-tempered sherds at the Ward site, along the upper Watauga River in North Carolina, and at sites in the Watauga Reservoir and along the upper Nolichucky in Tennessee. In each case he describes their tentative associations with Burke and protohistoric Catawba ceramics (see also Boyd 1986b:61, 173, 179).

Clearly Boyd feels that the later date for the McDowell site is consistent given the ceramics there. Boyd did not analyze the ceramics from the McDowell site and does not consider whether the characteristic "blending" is temporally significant. He feels secure in considering all of the soapstone pottery (Pisgah types included) as late. Obviously, the fifteenth-century date falls within the range generally accepted for the Pisgah phase (Dickens 1976; Moore 1981). I also consider this date to be a reliable date. But what does it mean with respect to the entire ceramic assemblage and the occupation of the McDowell site? In my opinion, the ceramic assemblage at the McDowell site is primarily a late assemblage. It is significant that the distribution of Pisgah type sherds at the McDowell site is quite dissimilar from that of other described Pisgah assemblages, the best examples being from the Warren Wilson (Dickens 1976:173, 192), Garden Creek (Dickens 1976), and Brunk sites (Moore 1981:46–47). Each of these assemblages consists of more than 75 percent rectilinear complicated-stamped sherds. Check stamping occurs on 15 percent to more than 20 percent of the sherds and plain sherds comprise less than 3 percent of the sherd assemblages from Garden Creek and Warren Wilson. In contrast, at the McDowell site, rectilinear stamping is a major component, but occurs on less than 50 percent of the overall assemblage. Check stamping is almost nonexistent and plain surfaces account for around 20 percent of the assemblage.

I believe the Pisgah ceramics at the McDowell site represent a late Pisgah assemblage. They occur at the site with similarly late Burke, McDowell, and sand-tempered Cowans Ford wares (see chapters 4 and 5 for further discussion of dating these ceramics). It is likely that further excavation data and a refinement of the ceramic analysis will allow distinctions between an earlier and later assemblage at the site, but at present I believe that the site was occupied ca. A.D. 1450–1550.

It is also necessary to consider the earlier radiocarbon date for the site. One option is merely to assume it to be an unreliable date. However, it is clearly within an appropriate Pisgah period framework. It also nearly matches the date for the feature with Pisgah ceramics at the nearby Tyler-Loughridge site. The Pisgah ceramics from the dated feature there are more like the Pisgah assemblages from Warren Wilson and the Brunk site than they are like the McDowell assemblage. Were the single Burke sherd from the Tyler-Loughridge site absent, I would argue that this assemblage is obviously earlier than the McDowell material on the basis of the radiocarbon date. However, the presence of the Burke sherd might suggest that the date is too early. Perhaps the presence of the Burke sherd should suggest that some soapstone pottery was being made earlier. If that were the case, it could also be present at the McDowell site in the twelfth to thirteenth century. Finally, it is also possible that the presence of the Burke sherd is the result of a mixed context.

In any event, the early date at the McDowell site might be accurate, but I am unable to say what ceramics were present at that time other than to suggest that the assemblage would probably have greater amounts of Pisgah rectilinear stamped pottery and less Burke complicated-stamped, plain, and burnished pottery. Perhaps future excavations will identify assemblages like this from feature contexts, especially features associated with Structure 3.

The Berry site offers somewhat more potential to discover temporally diagnostic ceramic variability within the contexts of features and stratigraphic levels, but, unfortunately, these do not provide a great deal of help (see appendix C for discussion). In general, there is some indication that an earlier period at the Berry site may be represented by an assemblage that includes a larger percentage of quartz- and sand-tempered wares of predominately plain and minority surface treatments with a smaller quantity of complicated stamped and burnished sherds. The later period probably consisted of Burke pottery and sand-tempered wares (Cowans Ford) with complicated-stamped, plain, and burnished surfaces and Burke Incised vessels. It is possible that these patterns may represent minor temporal distinctions between the four temper groups, but it is likely that all four were produced at relatively the same times at the site (see Boyd 1986a:87–93 for discussion of the wide range of temper variability on late prehistoric and protohistoric sites).

In general, the contextual data also support the idea that the Berry assemblage is relatively homogeneous. Despite the presence of four major temper classes or wares, it is unclear whether these represent one or more functional, temporal, or other factors. In any case, each of the three non-soapstone-tempered wares exhibits some degree of similarity to the Burke ceramics. Given the relative homogeneity of the ceramic assemblage, it appears unlikely that we can derive much in terms of intrasite chronology. However, what of the overall chronological placement of these ceramics and the Berry site? Two radiocarbon dates have been obtained at the site, both from feature contexts and one of which was obtained from a direct association with Burke ceramics. The first yielded a radiocarbon age of 500 ± 60 B.P. (Beta-21816) with a calibrated age of A.D. 1422. A second correction yields a single-sigma age range with a 78-percent probability for A.D. 1391–1446. The second sample yielded a radiocarbon age of 520 ± 50 B.P. (Beta-21817) with a calibrated age of A.D. 1415. A second correction for this date yields a 75-percent probability for the age range A.D. 1392–1435.

The two dates are nearly congruent, with an overlapping single-sigma age range of A.D. 1392–1435. Although Keeler (1971:39–41) does not describe an explicit age range for Burke ceramics, he compares the series with late prehistoric, protohistoric, and early historic ceramics; that is, Pisgah ceramics from the mountains of North Carolina, Nolichucky and Dallas ceramics from east Tennessee, and Lamar pottery from Georgia. He also notes the similarity of Burke ceramics to historic period Qualla ceramics in the North Carolina mountains. The radiocarbon dates firmly support this general late prehistoric placement for Burke pottery.

However, it is my impression that much of the Berry site ceramic assemblage dates to a somewhat later time than indicated by the radiocarbon dates, perhaps as late as the late sixteenth or early seventeenth century. Boyd (1986a:137–138) also provides support for protohistoric use of soapstone-tempered Burke ceramics by their associations with European artifacts in sites in upper east Tennessee. Obviously, at the Berry site the presence of the iron knife in Burial 1 and the association of middle to late sixteenth-century Spanish artifacts offer some support for this dating.

Without better stratigraphic data and more radiocarbon dates, it is difficult to attempt to date the Berry site with more precision. However, the temporal range of Burke ceramics and sites will be considered further over the next three chapters.

Geographic Distribution of Burke Ceramics

It is now clear that the geographic range of Burke ceramics is greater than originally reported (Keeler 1971:37–38). However, the core area of distribution (see Figure 6) remains within the upper Catawba valley in Burke County. Sites along the Upper Creek/Warrior Fork and Mulberry Creek/Johns River tributary drainages exhibit the highest frequencies (50–99 percent of total assemblages) of Burke ceramics. A similarly high frequency occurs in the nearby upper Yadkin valley in Caldwell County's Happy Valley community (see chapter 3) and there is a lower frequency downriver in Wilkes County. Additional sites with Burke ceramics are found west of Morganton in Burke County to just west of Marion in McDowell County.

Unfortunately, survey coverage is still not extensive in the upper Catawba valley and only a total of 28 sites with Burke ceramics were analyzed in this study. However, Robinson (1996:41) reports three new sites in McDowell County that have at least one Burke sherd present and Beck's (1997a) recent survey of Upper Creek/Warrior Fork identified 24 new sites with Burke ceramics. All of the new sites are much smaller than the Berry site. The discussion below takes into account the new total of 55 Burke components in the upper Catawba valley.

Somewhat unexpectedly, we also find Burke ceramics at a total of 62 additional sites along the middle Catawba river valley, principally in the Lake Norman reservoir, where Cowans Ford pottery is most common (see chapter 4). However, in most cases (n = 47; 75.8 percent), the Burke ceramics make up less than 5 percent of the Lake Norman sites' ceramic assemblages, and at only two (3.2 percent) sites do they make up more than 50 percent of the total assemblage. This contrasts with 30 (58.8 percent) sites in the upper valley (not including Caldwell County) with assemblages greater than 50 percent Burke. Clearly, the Burke range is more extensive than previously known, but the core area remains the same.

The distribution of Burke ceramics extends south along the Catawba River into Mecklenburg and Gaston counties, where they are found in small numbers at a few sites. For example, they are found at the Belk Farm site (31MK85; n = 5, .9 percent) and at the Hardins site (31GS29; n = 1, .8 percent) (Keel 1990:11).

To the north of the upper Catawba/Yadkin region, ceramics that have been called Burke or Burke-like are also found on the Nolichucky River (Keeler 1971) and Watauga River (Figure 6) in Carter and Johnson counties in northeastern Tennessee (Boyd 1986b:60–68). Boyd reports the presence of nearly 200 soapstone-tempered potsherds from surface and feature contexts at 11 sites located within the Watauga Reservoir. He relates these

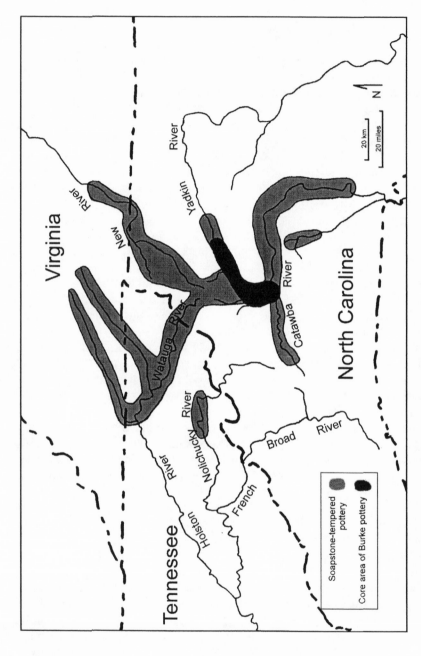

Figure 6. Geographic range of Burke series and other soapstone-tempered pottery.

ceramics to both Pisgah and Burke ceramics because of the association of soapstone tempering with plain and burnished surface treatments (Burke-like) as well as with Pisgah rectilinear complicated-stamped surface treatments and Pisgah collared rims (Boyd 1986b:61–64). In addition, Boyd (1986b:63) finds soapstone-tempered net-impressed sherds (comparable to Smyth types) that are identical to Dan River types save for the temper material. He describes the soapstone-tempered sherds as a "true ceramic series (contemporaneous surface treatments on sherds of the same temper)" (Boyd 1986b:60) and dates them to the late Prehistoric and Protohistoric periods on the basis of a radiocarbon date of A.D. 1562 from site 40JN89 (Boyd 1986b:61, 173).

In other words, the soapstone-tempered ceramics from the Watauga Reservoir evidence ceramic attributes from Burke, Pisgah, Dan River, and Smyth pottery types. This phenomenon of intra-assemblage mixed type attributes occurs elsewhere in association with soapstone tempering.

I believe that a potentially useful distinction may be made between the distribution of soapstone-tempered pottery and the distribution of diagnostic Burke series pottery. It is clear that there are numerous examples of groups of sites where soapstone tempering seems to have been incorporated within local ceramic traditions. This seems to be the case in the Watauga Reservoir, where Burke types appear but are also associated with soapstone-tempered sherds with other type characteristics.

This is also the case in the westernmost part of Virginia, where the local late prehistoric ceramic traditions feature primarily net-impressed, plain, and scraped surface treatments on sand-tempered, shell-tempered, and limestone-tempered wares. The soapstone-tempered Smyth sherds occur infrequently, yet they feature the same surface treatments (Holland 1970: 78–80).

Though they are soapstone tempered, Smyth sherds bear little resemblance to Burke pottery. Holland dates the series to ca. A.D. 1200–1400 and defines three types: Net and Knot Roughened, Plain, and Scraped. Paste characteristics are similar to those of Burke, the body being hard and well made, but Holland (1970:68) notes that the sherds do not ring when dropped. Finally, although Smyth sherds appear on 28 sites along the North and South Forks of the Holston and along the New River, they account for less than 5 percent of all assemblages except for one in which they make up nearly 35 percent.

This pattern continues in the New River valley of North Carolina, where Smyth pottery also occurs. Here, however, it is the second-largest ceramic group, making up around 20 percent of the collections (about 400 sherds from 70 sites). Surface treatments are usually net impressed or plain and smoothed, along with smaller quantities of brushed and simple stamped (Mathis and Moore 1984:66).

Another related example occurs at the Ward site (31WT22) on the Watauga River in Watauga County, North Carolina. This is a large palisaded village that is believed to date from the fourteenth to seventeenth century A.D. (Ayers et al. 1980; Loucks 1982). The ceramics are primarily net impressed and plain with some Pisgah rectilinear stamping and many Pisgah-style collared rims. Temper is either crushed rock or soapstone.

This pattern is also found in Wilkes County, on the Yadkin River, downstream of the Happy Valley sites in Caldwell County. We will see that Burke ceramics constitute the predominant ceramics of the Happy Valley sites. Idol (1996:3) describes the Porter (31WK6) and Jones (31WK33) site ceramics as "dominated" by soapstone temper. However, the Porter assemblage is characterized by net-impressed surface treatments whereas the Jones assemblage is dominated by plain and complicated-stamped soapstone-tempered pottery (Idol 1996:4). Three other sites, downstream from the Porter site, have small frequencies of soapstone-tempered pottery: two of the sites feature net-impressed sherds, and the third features plain and complicated-stamped sherds. Idol (1996) explains the degree of mixed ceramic attributes as the result of competition between lineages within sites.

To summarize, Burke ceramics are found in the largest quantities in the upper Catawba valley along Warrior Fork and Johns River north of Morganton in Burke County, as well as in the nearby upper Yadkin valley of Caldwell County. Burke pottery is found in smaller quantities west of Morganton on the Catawba and at much lower frequencies in the middle and lower Catawba River valley. Finally, Burke ceramics are found in small numbers along the Watauga River in upper east Tennessee.

We also find a corresponding, and possibly related, distribution of soapstone-tempered ceramics surrounding the core area of Burke distribution (Figure 6). This occurs to the west, as Pisgah attributes appear on soapstone-tempered sherds; to the north (Watauga River in North Carolina and Tennessee), where Pisgah and Dan River attributes occur on soapstone-tempered pottery; and to the northeast (Yadkin River below Caldwell County), where Dan River attributes occur on soapstone-tempered sherds.

Upper Catawba Valley Settlement Pattern

Understanding the geographic and temporal range of the aforementioned ceramic types helps in identifying chronological relationships between sites and in reconstructing settlement patterns in the upper Catawba valley. It is difficult to describe settlement patterns for a large region from such a small sample of sites. Most of the sites in this study were recorded in opportunistic surveys, which focused on previously known sites. They tend to be located in the larger floodplain settings along the Catawba River and several of its larger tributaries, locations that are undoubtedly related to the distribution of reliable and productive agricultural soils (see Ward 1965).

The opportunistic nature of site discovery obviously leaves much potential for bias in location, site density, and other characteristics necessary to understand settlement patterns. Fortunately, there are now new data that suggest a great deal more potential for understanding settlement patterns in the upper Catawba valley. Prior to a 1996 probabilistic survey there were only three sites with Burke pottery recorded in the Upper Creek/Warrior Fork drainages in Burke County (31BK22, 31BK23, 31BK209); however, this recent survey recorded 24 new sites in this watershed with Burke ceramic components (Beck 1997a).

The Upper Creek/Warrior Fork watershed includes a mixed physiography, as these streams flow through the Blue Ridge Mountains and the Piedmont Foothills before reaching the Piedmont and eventually draining into the Catawba River at Morganton, North Carolina (Beck 1997a:13). Beck (1997a:16–17) divided the watershed into four strata, Piedmont Uplands, Piedmont Floodplains, Mountain Uplands, and Mountain Floodplains, and attempted to conduct a random sample of 20 percent of each stratum. Although field conditions and logistical considerations prevented a strict adherence to the random 20 percent sample, Beck (1997a:23–24) was able to survey 27 percent (210.3 ha) of the Piedmont Floodplains and 16 percent (410.6 ha) of the Piedmont Uplands strata. A total of 57 new sites were recorded, 16 of which were located in the Piedmont Uplands and 41 of which were located in the Piedmont Floodplains. All of the 24 new Burke sites (see Figure 7) were located in the Piedmont Floodplains stratum (Beck 1997a:26). Though unable to survey the two mountain strata, Beck (1997a:27) points out that while more than 200 sites have been recorded in Burke County in the surrounding mountainous Pisgah National Forest lands, a total of five Burke potsherds have been found on two sites there.

Thus, perhaps not unexpectedly, Beck's survey results confirm the association of these late prehistoric sites with floodplain locations. In fact, since all but one of the Burke sites was located on one of two soil types, Toccoa sandy loam and Riverview loam, which constitute 58.5 percent of all Piedmont Floodplain soils, Beck (1997a:30) feels that these soil types are the best predictors of Burke sites. However, Beck's results are more surprising and significant when site size and distribution are considered.

Beck (1997a:31) was able to establish reliable site boundaries for 21 Burke sites (this total includes the three previously recorded sites but not six small sites that Beck recorded). On the basis of site size Beck (1997a:31) identified 11 fourth-order sites (<.5 ha; 17 if the six sites with poor boundaries are included), 7 third-order sites (.8–2.0 ha), 2 second-order sites (2.7–2.8 ha), and 1 first-order site, the Berry site, which covers 4.9 ha. He (Beck 1997a:35) also points out that the Berry site, the largest site and the single mound site, is within 250 meters of being halfway between the point where Upper Creek enters the Piedmont and the point where Warrior Fork empties into the Catawba River.

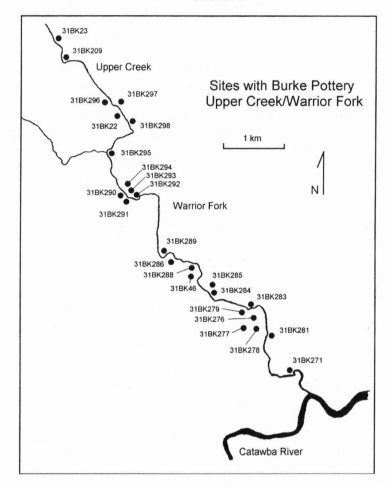

Figure 7. Location of sites with Burke pottery on Upper Creek and Warrior Fork in Burke County (after Beck 1997a). Figure includes sites recorded by Beck as well as previously recorded sites.

Beck (1997a:37) summarizes the Burke settlement pattern along Upper Creek and Warrior Fork as consisting of

one large, single mound, First Order site, Berry, with at least nine large, non-mound, Second and Third Order settlements distributed at very regular intervals along the stream; the Third Order sites seem to occur in pairs, while the larger, Second Order sites seem to be un-paired. Finally, a substantial number of very small, Fourth Order sites surround, and are distributed between, settlements of the larger three size classes. In contrast to these larger sites, there appears to be little regularity to the distribution of Fourth Order sites.

He (Beck 1997a:39) further characterizes this settlement pattern as reflecting a settlement system that consists of one large, nucleated mound center with several associated large, nucleated non-mound sites, and numerous small, dispersed homesteads.

Beck's findings are extremely important, because they allow us for the first time to view Burke sites within the context of a regional settlement system. It is unclear whether this system is replicated throughout the region; certainly mound distribution is not even. However, this survey makes clear the need for probabilistic sampling throughout the region.

Summary

The accumulated data derived from investigations over the past 25 years help to shed light on settlement patterns, ceramic distributions, and chronology in the upper Catawba River valley. It is clear that the previously described Pisgah and Burke pottery series account for most of the late prehistoric and protohistoric period ceramic variability of the upper Catawba valley. Pisgah pottery is most common at the extreme western end of the valley, whereas attributes of Burke series pottery such as curvilinear complicated-stamped and burnished exteriors, jars exhibiting folded and appliqued rims, and Burke Incised bowls occur with more frequency downstream.

The overall predominance of the Burke series is striking. As mentioned above, the similarities of this series to the more southern Lamar ceramics have been well noted. What this study makes clear is that the region features this type of pottery nearly to the exclusion of other ceramics known for the late Prehistoric and early Historic periods in the North Carolina Piedmont. There is little ceramic evidence of influences by Siouan peoples making Dan River pottery, nor is there evidence of influence from the Pee Dee culture in the late Prehistoric period. Nor is there much evidence for the practices of brushing, check stamping, and simple stamping that are seen in the late prehistoric and protohistoric central and northern Piedmont region. The following chapter shows that ceramics from the nearby upper Yadkin River valley show a similar pattern in the abundance of Burke pottery. However, in chapter 4 we will see a slightly different pattern in ceramic assemblages from sites farther downstream in the middle and lower Catawba valley.

Upper Yadkin Valley Sites and Ceramics

3

In Caldwell County, the upper Yadkin River rises on the eastern flank of the Blue Ridge Mountains. The river flows northeast at the foot of the mountains to form a valley nearly 20 miles long before turning east and then south to flow through the North Carolina Piedmont. The northeast-trending Yadkin valley is the region described here (see Figure 8 for locations of sites discussed in this chapter). Little systematic archaeological work had been conducted in the region until recently (Idol 1995, 1996; Kimball et al. 1996). However, one site, 31CW8, was excavated by Richard Polhemus in 1964 (Polhemus n.d.) and, of course, the mound excavations conducted in the valley in the nineteenth century are well known as the result of Cyrus Thomas's mound exploration reports (Thomas 1887, 1894).

The upper Yadkin River valley and the Catawba River valley are strikingly similar with respect to the presence of earthen mounds and an abundance of soapstone-tempered Burke ceramics. The presence of Burke ceramics is particularly striking. The previous chapter described the heavy concentration of Burke ceramics in Burke County along the upper tributaries of the Catawba River. Soapstone-tempered pottery has also been reported from southwest Virginia (Holland 1970:67–68), upper east Tennessee on the Nolichucky and Watauga rivers (Boyd 1986a, 1986b), and at the Ward site (Senior 1981) on the Watauga River in North Carolina. Soapstone-tempered pottery is also found in the middle Catawba and lower Catawba valley areas (see chapter 4). However, outside of Burke County, the upper Yadkin River valley in Caldwell and Wilkes counties is the only locale where soapstone-tempered Burke series pottery occurs on numerous sites, sometimes almost to the exclusion of other types.

William H. Holmes (1903) was the first to write about the upper Yadkin valley pottery. His (Holmes 1903:144) descriptions of the pottery excavated from the Nelson Mound and Triangle and the Davenport Jones Mound in Caldwell County led him to observe that this pottery reflected influence from the north, west, and south, but that it was from the latter direction that the major influence was felt. Holmes (1903:143–144) also noted the pottery bore "evidence of recentness, and in cases, of relationship to mod-

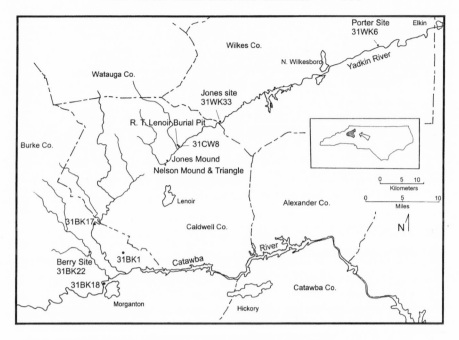

Figure 8. Location of archaeological sites in the upper Yadkin River valley.

ern ware." By modern ware, Holmes was referring to historic Catawba pottery made in the 1880s. This was the first statement describing what we now call Burke pottery and its obvious similarities to the Lamar ceramics in Georgia and to historic Catawba pottery.

It is also important to note that the distance from 31BK17 to the Nelson Mound site is less than 15 miles and there is a direct link between the Catawba and Yadkin valleys through Mulberry Creek, a large creek that drains from just south of Happy Valley (the community name for the mound locale) to its confluence with Johns River just above 31BK17. This is also the vicinity of the mound explored by Dr. James Mason Spainhour on the Michaux Farm (chapter 2), and Thomas (1891:153) reported two mounds near the confluence of Mulberry Creek with Johns River and two more mounds in the Collettsville vicinity. Though none of these mounds has been identified, it is known from collectors that large sites are found in this area, and collectors also report sites on Mulberry Creek with soapstone-tempered pottery (Figure 8 illustrates the proximity of the major Upper Creek and Johns River sites with the upper Yadkin valley sites).

Given the proximity of the upper Yadkin River to the upper Catawba River tributaries, and the occurrence of multiple mound sites and Burke pottery in each area, it seems likely that the sites in the upper Yadkin valley are related in some manner to the sites along Johns River and Upper Creek in Burke County. A review of the eighteenth-century investigations in the light of and along with data from more recent work in the upper Yadkin valley is relevant to understanding potential relationships between the two areas.

The investigations reported by Thomas (1887, 1891, 1894) were actually carried out in 1882 by John P. Rogan, apparently often assisted by Spainhour. The excavated sites included the T. F. Nelson Mound (31CW1) and the T. F. Nelson Triangle (31CW2), the W. Davenport Jones Mound (31CW4), and the R. T. Lenoir Burial Pit (31CW5). The remainder of this chapter compares and discusses the descriptions by Thomas (1887, 1894) and those from more recent investigations by Polhemus (n.d.), Kimball et al. (1996), and Idol (1995, 1996). Also, I include descriptions of artifacts recovered during the nineteenth-century investigations, since they have not previously been well documented. I examined these artifacts at the National Museum of Natural History, Washington, D.C., and they are described in more detail in appendix F.

Early Mound Exploration

In his *Catalogue of Prehistoric Works,* Thomas (1891:152) described 17 mounds in Caldwell County, the largest number for any North Carolina county. Aside from the sites described in the 1887 (Figure 9) and 1894 publications, none of these mound sites has been confirmed. It is possible that being low mounds they have been obliterated by 150 years of plowing. It is also possible that many, if not most, of the locations reported were not actually mounds. Nonetheless, it cannot be denied that the upper Yadkin valley featured an unusual complex of mounds or mound-like features.

The published summaries of the excavations carried out at several of the sites (Thomas 1887, 1894) describe large geometrically shaped pits and low mound areas with various numbers of individuals interred within the pits. The skeletal remains often were accompanied by large numbers of artifacts, including shell gorgets, ceramic vessels, and, in two cases, metal objects. As discussed in chapter 2, the descriptions of these mounds bear little resemblance to descriptions of platform or substructure mounds excavated in the nearby Appalachian Summit region at the Garden Creek site (Dickens 1970, 1976; Keel 1972, 1976), the Peachtree site (Setzler and Jennings 1941), and the Coweeta Creek site (Egloff 1971). In contrast, the Caldwell County sites may represent interment facilities. In addition, the quantities of "exotic" artifacts in the form of European metal implements, shell masks, shell gorgets, spatulate axes, shell beads, copper, and mica plates suggest elite burials.

The descriptions of these sites (Thomas 1887, 1894) suggest that they and several others in the area represent burial mounds or large burial pits. Such a characterization is anomalous since there is no evidence of burial

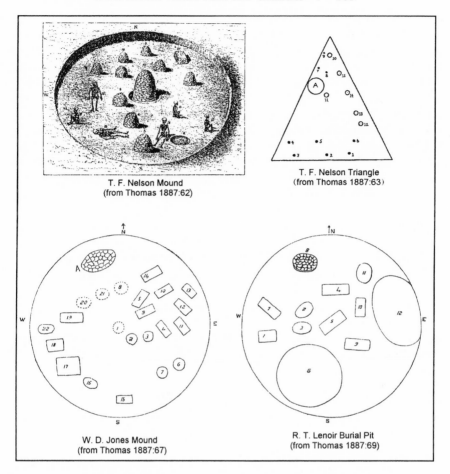

T. F. Nelson Mound
(from Thomas 1887:62)

T. F. Nelson Triangle
(from Thomas 1887:63)

W. D. Jones Mound
(from Thomas 1887:67)

R. T. Lenoir Burial Pit
(from Thomas 1887:69)

Figure 9. Illustrations of Caldwell County excavated sites reported in Cyrus Thomas, *Burial Mounds of the Northern Sections of the United States.*

mounds elsewhere in western North Carolina. Joffre Coe (personal communication 1990) has pointed out that the Yadkin River floodplain is extremely rocky here (and today is a major source of construction gravel and rock). He suggests that (1) the Nelson site burials were merely interred within a village context; (2) the Nelson mound was no more than a natural landform (reported as only 18 inches high); and (3) the Nelson Triangle was an artifact of the investigative techniques. He suggests that the burials "walled" with stone were merely interred in an extremely rocky soil matrix. Although we are unable to determine any other details of the Yadkin "mounds," I believe that it is unwise to dismiss these accounts from the upper Yadkin valley as mere misinterpretations by the excavator. Mound construction occurred at the nearby Berry site in Burke County, and it seems probable that at least some of the reported structures on the Yadkin are, in fact, mounds.

Thomas clearly distinguishes two types of sites: the T. F. Nelson and W. D. Jones "mound" sites and the T. F. Nelson Triangle and R. T. Lenoir "burial pits." Aside from their shapes, however, the four sites are remarkably similar. The W. D. Jones Mound is identical to the Nelson Mound in size and in its subterranean aspect. Whereas the Nelson Mound and the W. D. Jones Mound have a slight surface mounding, the R. T. Lenoir Burial Pit and the Nelson Triangle lack surface mounding. All four sites appear to have subterranean components about 3 feet deep that were clear to the investigators, and the burials seem to occur at or near the floor of the subterranean component. If we can attribute any level of accuracy to the excavation descriptions, it seems possible that these four sites represent subterranean interment facilities rather than platform or substructure mounds (possibly even earthlodge or other semisubterranean constructions that were subsequently abandoned, used for multiple interments, and then filled).

It is possible that we will never fully understand the nature of the Caldwell mounds, but current efforts by Appalachian State University's Laboratories of Archaeological Science (Kimball et al. 1996) to identify the locations of the investigated sites may yield more information about them in the future (see below).

T. F. Nelson Mound

The T. F. Nelson Mound is described as follows (Thomas 1887:61–63; also see Figure 9):

> This mound, so insignificant in appearance as scarcely to attract any notice was located on the farm of Rev. T. F. Nelson, in Caldwell county, North Carolina, on the bottom land of the Yadkin, about 100 yards from the riverbank. It was almost a true circle in outline, 38 feet in diameter, but not exceeding at any point 18 inches in height. The thorough excavation made, revealed the fact that the builders of the mound had first dug a circular pit, with perpendicular margin, to the depth of 3 feet, and 38 feet in diameter, then deposited their dead in the manner hereafter shown, some in stone cists and others unenclosed, and afterwards covered them over, raising a slight mound above the pit.

Sixteen burials were located within the pit. Ten burials were found within stone vaults, including one said to be placed vertically on its feet; the remainder are illustrated in both extended and "sitting" positions. The burials were accompanied by a wide variety of artifacts including plates of cut mica, polished celts, stone discoidals, a pitted stone, and soapstone pipes.

Several significant details may hold clues to how the Nelson Mound functioned. First, within the pit, there appears to be intentional structuring of individual burials by the use of stone cairns. Second, the burials are distributed relatively evenly across the pit. Third, Burial 1 seems to hold a central position within the pit and is, in itself, a remarkable burial. This burial is described as follows (Thomas 1887:61–62):

> No. 1 is a stone grave or vault standing exactly in the center of the pit. In this case a small circular hole, a little over three feet in diameter and extending down 3 feet below the bottom of the large pit, had been dug, the body or skeleton placed perpendicularly on its feet, and the wall built up around it from the bottom of the hole, converging, after a height of 4 feet was reached, so as to be covered at the top by a single soapstone rock of moderate size . . . Although the bones were much decayed, yet they were retained in position by the dirt which filled the vault, an indication that the flesh had been removed before the burial and the vault filled with dirt as it was built up.

These details suggest that the use of space within the pit was orderly, planned, and may represent a single episode of multiple interments (although intermittent single interments could also be orderly and planned).

However, Thomas (1894:335) also describes the legs of Skeleton 16 as being extended upon a bed of burned earth, and he then mentions two unusual locations, A and B, within the pit and describes further evidence for burning:

> At A was a considerable quantity of black paint in little lumps, which appear to have been molded in the hull of some nut. B indicates a cubical mass of waterworn bowlders built up solidly and symmetrically, 24 inches long, 18 inches wide, and 18 inches high, showing no indications of fire, without ashes or bones on or around it.
>
> On the contrary, the stones built around the bodies bore more or less evidence of fire, having been blackened by smoke in places, and the earth immediately around them was considerably hardened by baking. The bones of the skeletons also showed indications of heat. Scattered throughout the mound were small pieces of pottery and charcoal.

These descriptions convey an impression of repetitive interments with ritual fires. It is possible that locations A and B represent preparation stations within this mortuary facility. Preparation may have involved defleshing in some cases, application of paint or pigment, arrangement of cairns, and ritual firing after completion of the cairns.

T. F. Nelson Triangle

The T. F. Nelson Triangle (Figure 9), located 75 yards south of the mound, is described as follows:

> It is not a mound, but simply a burial pit in the form of a triangle, the two longest sides each 48 feet and the (southern) base 32 feet, in which the bodies and accompanying articles were deposited and then covered over, but not heaped up into a mound; or if so, it had subsequently settled until on a level with the natural surface of the ground . . . The depth of the original excavation, the lines of which could be distinctly traced, varied from 2½ to 3 feet [Thomas 1887:63].

Burials 1 through 9 were single extended burials whereas Burials 10 through 15 were placed within stone vaults similar to those at the adjacent mound. Burials 11 and 14 consisted of two individuals each. Interestingly, the only artifacts associated with Burials 1 through 15 were a broken pipe (Burial 2) and two polished celts (Burials 5 and 9).

In dramatic contrast to the individual and dual burials was a mass interment at location A, where investigators found the remains of 10 or more skeletons, all of which were believed to have been buried at one time. One individual, characterized by Thomas (1887:64) as "the 'old chief'(?), or principal personage of the group," was surrounded by the other individuals and by an extraordinary inventory of artifacts.

> Under his head was a large engraved shell gorget; around his neck were a number of large sized shell beads, evidently the remains of a necklace; at the sides of the head, near the ears, were five elongate copper beads, or rather small cylinders, varying in length from one and a quarter to four and a half inches, part of the leather thong on which the smaller were strung yet remaining in them. These were made of thin pieces of copper cut into strips and then rolled together so that the edges meet in a straight joint on one side. The plate out of which they were made was as smooth and even in thickness as though it had been rolled.
>
> A piece of copper was also at his breast. His arms were partially extended, his hands resting about a foot from his head. Around each wrist were the remains of a bracelet composed of copper and shell beads, alternating . . .
>
> At his right hand were four iron specimens, much corroded but still showing the form. Two of them were of uniform thickness, one not sharpened at the ends or edges, the other slightly sharpened at

one end, 3 to 3½ inches long, 1 to 1½ inches broad, and about a quarter of an inch thick. . . . Another is 5 inches long, slightly tapering in width from one and an eighth to seven-eighths of an inch, both edges sharp; it is apparently part of the blade of a long, slender, cutting or thrusting weapon of some kind, as a sword, dagger, or knife. The other specimen is part of a round awl-shaped implement, a small part of the bone handle in which it was fixed yet remaining attached to it.

Under his left hand was another engraved shell, the concave surface upward and filled with beads of all sizes.

Around and over the skeleton of this chief personage, with their heads near his, were nine other skeletons. Under the heads of two of these were two engraved shells. Scattered over and between the ten skeletons of the group were numerous polished celts, discoidal stones, copper arrow-points, plates of mica, lumps of paint, black lead, etc. [Thomas 1887:65–66].

Unfortunately, during my examination of the excavated materials housed at the National Museum of Natural History (NMNH), I found that the artifacts from the Nelson Mound and Nelson Triangle sites were probably all cataloged as "Nelson Mound." However, I was able to confirm that the published artifact lists are reliable.

The best-known artifacts from these sites are, of course, the metal implements. The items I observed included an iron celt and a portion of an iron blade (Plate 16). The celt is nearly identical to the one illustrated in Thomas (1887:65, fig. 30, and 1894:337, fig. 211). It is undoubtedly the second of the two iron celts described as being at the right hand of the principal skeleton of Group A in the Nelson Triangle. The iron blade is probably a portion of the blade illustrated by Thomas (1887:65, fig. 31, and 1894:337, fig. 212). (Note: I saw no other European trade items in the collection labeled as Nelson Mound; however, because of ongoing moving of collections it was not possible to see every box from Caldwell County. The catalog lists only one additional metal artifact—a brass button without the eye.)

Four Citico shell gorgets (Plate 17), eight chunkey stones, and one spatulate celt (Plate 18, *right*) were also present, along with a large quantity of pottery. Pottery included three complete (or reconstructed) vessels, one of which was a small Burke Incised carinated bowl.

The collection also included a total of 208 potsherds. Of these, 187 (89.9 percent) are Burke sherds, 7 (3.4 percent) are sand-tempered plain or burnished sherds that are probably Cowans Ford, 2 (.9 percent) are Pisgah and Dan River sherds, and 12 (5.8 percent) are grit- or quartz-tempered fabric-impressed and cord-marked Woodland period sherds. One other lot of ceramics is listed in the catalog for the Nelson Mound, but I was unable to find it.

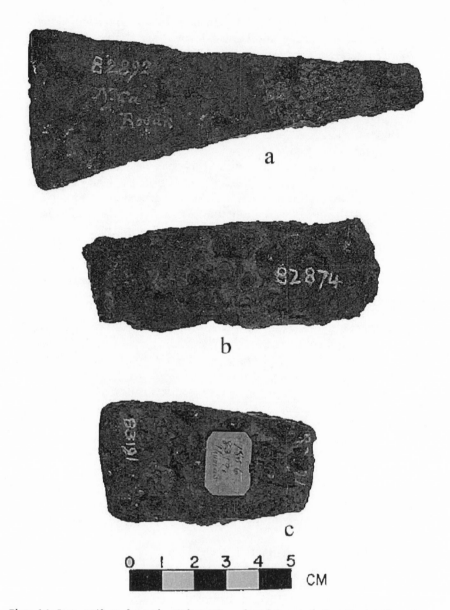

Plate 16. Iron artifacts from the Nelson Mound and Lenoir Indian Burial Place site, NMNH collection. *a,* Catalog #82892, Nelson Mound; *b,* Catalog #82874, Nelson Mound; *c,* Catalog #83191, Lenoir Indian Burial Place.

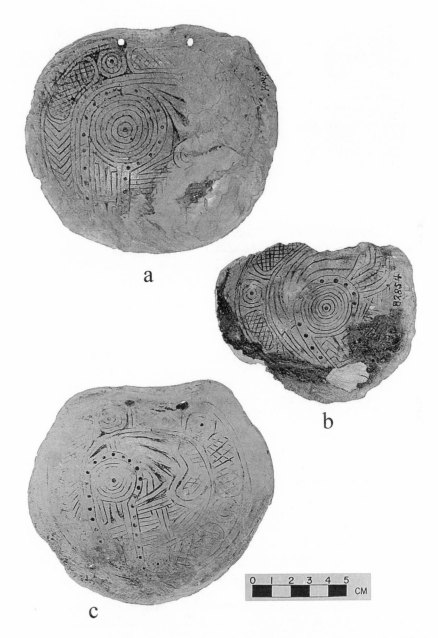

Plate 17. Citico-style shell gorgets from the NMNH collection. *a*, Catalog #82853, Nelson Mound; *b*, Catalog #82854, Nelson Mound; *c*, Catalog #83174, Lenoir Indian Burial Place.

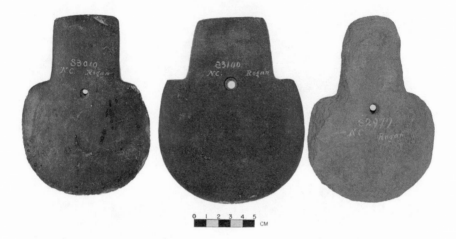

Plate 18. Spatulate celts from the NMNH collection. *Left,* Catalog #83010, W. Davenport Jones Mound; *middle,* Catalog #83100, W. Davenport Jones Mound; *right,* Catalog #82979, Nelson Mound.

W. Davenport Jones Mound

The W. Davenport Jones Mound (Thomas 1894:338–342) was located two miles east of Patterson on the north bank of the Yadkin River. It was described as being associated with a village site 200 yards away, though there is no description of investigation of the village. This mound was similar to the Nelson Mound, being 32 feet in diameter and about 1 foot high (Figure 9).

> This mound was found upon investigation to cover a circular pit of the same diameter and 3 feet deep, the margin and bottom being so well defined as to leave no doubt as to the limits of the pit; in fact the bottom, which was of clay, had been baked hard by fire to the depth of 2 or 3 inches. The pit was filled with soil and loose yellow clay similar to the surface soil around the mound covering twenty-six skeletons and one stone heap . . . Some of the skeletons were inclosed in vaults formed of cobble stones [Thomas 1894:338–339].

Burials 1, 8, 20, and 21 consisted of individuals in stone vaults; the remainder had no stone enclosures. Most of the burials were accompanied by artifacts, including numerous stone celts, shell, and copper beads. Burials 17 and 18 included four and two skeletons, respectively, and none were accompanied by artifacts.

The pit also included a boulder platform, remarkably similar to the one in the Nelson Mound, which Thomas (1887:68) described as follows: "A

Plate 19. Burke ceramic vessels from the W. Davenport Jones Mound, NMNH collection. *Top,* Catalog #83008, 31.6 cm tall; *bottom,* Catalog #83007, 27.8 cm tall.

solid oval-shaped mass of bowlders, 33 inches long, 22 inches wide, and 24 inches high, resting on the bottom of the pit. No ashes or other indications of fire about it."

The artifacts I viewed from the Jones Mound included five whole or partial Burke vessels (Plates 19 and 20). These include one straight-sided cup, a bowl with an effigy figure on the rim, a Burke Incised carinated bowl, and two constricted-neck jars. In addition, the collection included 169 potsherds of which 163 (96.4 percent) are Burke type sherds, 1 (.6 percent) is a Smyth net-impressed sherd, and 5 (2.9 percent) are untyped sand- or grit-tempered sherds.

Plate 20. Burke ceramic vessels from the W. Davenport Jones Mound, NMNH collection. *Top,* Catalog #83201, partial carinated vessel; *bottom,* Catalog #83009, 42.4 cm wide.

Additional artifacts included two spatulate celts (Plate 18, *left* and *middle*), one shell mask (Plate 21), and four shell gorgets (Plate 22, *a,* probable Citico style).

R. T. Lenoir Burial Pit

The R. T. Lenoir Burial Pit site was described as being nearly a mile west of Fort Defiance, about 200 yards from Buffalo Creek approximately one-half mile above its confluence with the Yadkin River (Thomas 1887:68). The site is described as

Plate 21. Shell masks from the NMNH collection. *Left,* Catalog #83166, W. Davenport Jones Mound site; *right,* Catalog #83179, Fort Defiance/Lenoir Indian Burial Place site.

a circular burial pit, similar to those already described, but without any rounding up of the surface . . . The pit, which is 27 feet in diameter and about 3½ feet deep, is almost a perfect circle, and well marked, the margin, which is nearly perpendicular, and the bottom being easily traced. The dirt, in this case, as in the other, was all thrown out [Thomas 1887:68].

This burial pit is similar in many ways to the three previously described (Figure 9). However, the Lenoir pit is somewhat different from the others in that there were no stone cairns. There was, however, a boulder pile:

No. 8. An irregular layer of water-worn stones, about 4 feet square. On top was a bed of charcoal 3 or 4 inches thick, on and partially imbedded in which were three skeletons, but showing no indications of having been in the fire. Scattered over these were discoidal stones, one small, saucer-shaped dish, shells (of which one is engraved), pipes, shell beads, and pieces of pottery [Thomas 1887:70].

In addition, Thomas describes the presence of an apparent in situ cremation:

Plate 22. Shell gorgets from the NMNH collection. *a*, Catalog #83166, W. Davenport Jones Mound site, possibly a variant of Citico style; *b*, Catalog #83172, Fort Defiance/Lenoir Indian Burial Place site, Citico style; *c*, Catalog #83173, Fort Defiance/Lenoir Indian Burial Place site, Citico style; *d*, Catalog #82856, Nelson Mound site, Citico style.

No. 1. A bed of charred or rather burnt bones, occupying a space 3 feet long, 2 feet wide, and about 1 foot deep. The bones were so thoroughly burned that it was impossible to determine whether they were human or animal. Beneath this bed the yellow sand was baked to the depth of 2 or 3 inches. Under the bones was an uncharred shell gorget [Thomas 1887:68–69].

The description of the burned bones and the underlying baked sand supports the idea that this was an in situ cremation, but the presence of the unburned shell gorget complicates this interpretation. It is possible that the gorget was placed beneath the bones after cremation. It is also possible that the gorget was placed on a previously burned and cleaned location and, subsequently, the charred remains from that cremation (along with others, perhaps) were placed on top of the gorget.

The Lenoir Pit contained the skeletal remains of at least 55 individuals, 7 of which were buried alone and the remainder of which were buried in groups of 3 (Burials 8 and 9), 25 (Burial 6), and 17 (Burial 12) individuals. Most of the burials were accompanied by artifacts such as stone celts and shell beads. The 2 large mass graves included large quantities of artifacts. Burial No. 6 was described as

> a communal grave, containing at least twenty-five skeletons, in two tiers, buried without any apparent regularity as to direction or relative position. Thirteen of the twenty-five were "flat-heads," that is "the heads running back and compressed in front."
>
> Scattered through this grave, between and above the skeletons, were polished celts, discoidal stones, shells, mica, galena, fragments of pottery, and one whole pot. Around the neck and wrists of some of the skeletons were also shell beads. There may have been more than twenty-five individuals buried here, this, however, being the number of skulls observed [Thomas 1887:70].

This description suggests a possible corporate burial episode. There is no discernible central figure and it appears that the artifacts may have been scattered among the skeletons rather than placed with individuals. Finally, the observation that there may have been more than 25 individuals here opens the possibility that this was a secondary interment, possibly resulting in mixed or absent skeletal parts.

Burial 12 is notable for two features, the presence of two children and the observation that seven individuals were "flat-heads." Included in this burial were six clay vessels, shell beads, polished celts, discoidal stones, and paint.

The artifacts from this site are listed in the NMNH catalog as "Fort Defiance/Lenoir Indian Burial Place." This collection includes one "iron wedge" (Plate 16, *bottom*) that is nearly identical to the wedge from the T. F. Nelson Triangle illustrated by Thomas (1894:337, fig. 211); however, his report makes no mention of a similar wedge from the R. T. Lenoir Burial Pit. Given the previously described problems with the catalog numbers and proveniences, it is possible that the wedge illustrated in Plate 16 is actually the one from the T. F. Nelson Triangle.

Seven complete or reconstructed ceramic vessels are present in the collection (Plates 23 and 24). They include five constricted-neck jars and two open bowls (one with slightly in-slanting rim). At least six are Burke series vessels and the seventh, with a corncob-impressed exterior surface, may also be Burke.

Two probable weeping-eye shell masks (Plate 21) and six shell gorgets (Plate 22) are also present.

Plate 23. Burke ceramic vessels from the R. T. Lenoir Burial Pit, NMNH collection. *Top,* Catalog #83200, soapstone tempered, curvilinear complicated stamped, 30.5 cm tall; *bottom,* Catalog #83199, soapstone tempered, curvilinear complicated stamped, 33.7 cm tall.

Discussion: Caldwell County Artifacts in NMNH Collection

Unfortunately, analysis of the artifacts reported from the Happy Valley sites is hampered by the lack of reliable contextual data. The published reports describe associated artifacts, but although the cataloged material at the NMNH includes the same classes of artifacts as are described in the reports,

Plate 24. Burke ceramic vessels from the R. T. Lenoir Burial Pit, NMNH collection. *Top,* Catalog #83183, soapstone tempered, burnished with corncob impressing, 24.1 cm tall; *bottom,* Catalog #83184, sand tempered (?), corncob impressed, 30.5 cm tall.

the numbers of artifacts do not always correspond. This in itself would be a minor problem except that the cataloged material is not cataloged by context, that is, by numbered burial association, but merely by site name. And, unfortunately, the catalog site names do not exactly correspond to the reported site names.

The NMNH catalog for Caldwell County lists six proveniences (Table 8): Nelson Mound, Jones Mound, Fort Defiance/Lenoir Indian Burial Place,

Table 8. Artifacts from NMNH catalog for Caldwell County sites

Sites / Artifact Class	Nelson Mound	W. D. Jones Mound	Fort Defiance	Lenoir Mound	Caldwell County*
Artifact Class	n	n	n	n	n
Ceramic vessel	2	7	9	.	1
Ceramic sherds**	4	5	.	.	.
Ceramic beads**	1	.	1	.	.
Shell gorget	3	8	8	.	.
Shell hairpin, pin	2	1	.	.	.
Shell mask	.	.	2	.	.
Shell bead**	4	2	1	1	.
Shell cup	.	1	1	.	1
Shell, misc.	1	1	2	.	.
Mica plates**	2	1	1	.	.
Carved figure	1	.	.	.	.
Copper bead**	4	.	1	.	.
Copper strip, ornament	1	1	.	.	.
Metal button	1	.	.	.	.
Iron celt	1	.	.	.	.
Iron wedge	.	.	1	.	.
Iron blade	1	.	.	.	.
Stone discoidal	23	8	9	.	2
Clay pipe	.	2	8	6	.
Stone pipe	2	7	13	10	2
Celt	25	23	28	.	3
Spatulate celt	1	2	.	.	.
Grooved axe	1	2	.	.	1
Stone chisel	2	.	.	.	.
Stone hoe	.	.	.	.	2
Chipped stone projectile point**	6	5	1	.	9
Misc. stone tools	.	1	1	.	5
Stone pendant	.	.	.	.	2
Ceremonial stone	.	.	.	.	1
Soapstone vessel	1	.	.	.	1
Worked soapstone	.	3	1	.	.
Hammerstone	1	1	.	.	6
Mortar, pestle	1	1	.	.	2
Graphite, hematite	3	.	.	.	1
Paint or pigment**	4	3	4	.	.
Clay, unfired?**	.	2	.	.	.
Pebbles**	.	.	.	.	.
Charred nuts**	1	1	.	.	.

* Spainhour donated artifacts from various locations entered as
"Lenoir" and "Caldwell County."
** Occurrence of catalog numbers rather than numbers of artifacts.

Lenoir Mound, Caldwell County, and Lenoir (the latter two undoubtedly include multiple locations). The most obvious problem with the cataloged proveniences is that the catalog does not distinguish between the Nelson Mound and Nelson Triangle sites, but refers only to Nelson Mound. I have had to assume, then, that the catalog term "Nelson Mound" includes both the Mound and the Triangle sites, particularly since the metal artifacts described from the Triangle (Thomas 1894:337) are cataloged as "Nelson Mound."

In addition, I believe that the catalog provenience "Fort Defiance/Lenoir Indian Burial Place" refers to the R. T. Lenoir Burial Pit since it is described as being just one mile west of Fort Defiance (Thomas 1887:68–70). Finally, I believe that "Lenoir Mound" refers to the site now identified as the Broyhill-Dillard site (Kimball et al. 1996:37). A photograph of this site taken by Stanley South in the 1950s identifies the site as "Indian Mound in Caldwell Co. in large bottom-land owned by Mr. Walter Lenoir's heirs (photo on file at the Research Laboratories of Anthropology, UNC-Chapel Hill)." The mound is less than one-quarter mile from the presumed location of the Lenoir Burial Pit (Kimball et al. 1996:42–43), thus suggesting that the mound and the pit were both located on Lenoir property.

Given the contextual problems, can these artifacts provide useful information? I believe it is still appropriate to examine these artifacts as potential temporal indicators and to consider the significance of the entire assemblage. Many of the artifacts detailed above are relatively good temporal markers. Foremost among those considered to be temporally diagnostic, of course, are the iron implements. No other European trade items are described in the published accounts, and only one other, labeled "metal button without the eye" (NMNH Cat. #A082870), is listed in the artifact catalog. DePratter and Smith (1980:71) note that Juan Pardo traded iron chisels, wedges, axes, and knives with southeastern "chiefs," "commanders," and "principal men." Smith (1987:27) has argued that in the sixteenth century these rare items usually accompanied the recipient to the grave as markers of elite status.

Unfortunately, these iron objects are often difficult to date on the basis of form alone (Smith 1987:35–36). At the very least, we can acknowledge that the "iron wedge" (Plate 16; Cat. #83191) appears to be almost identical in form and size to the iron celts from a probable sixteenth-century context at the King site in Georgia. And while I cannot argue undeniably that these implements were obtained directly from sixteenth-century Spaniards, there is evidence that sixteenth-century Spaniards were in the vicinity of Happy Valley while at the Berry site (Beck 1997b; Moore and Beck 1994; Worth 1994a, 1994b).

The spatulate axe is thought to indicate high status for the individual with whom it is buried (Hatch 1975:132–133). The ceremonial axe form dates from A.D. 1360–1610 (Smith 1987:101). Other researchers suggest that, in Alabama, "perforated spatulate axes have consistently been recovered from sites yielding sixteenth century European artifacts" (Little and Curren 1990:185). However, Keel (1990:15) discounts the idea that the perforated axe form represents a priori evidence for sixteenth-century occupation.

At the least, it can be said that these sites evidence numerous examples of Burke ceramics, spatulate celts, and Citico gorgets, all of which can be dated from the fifteenth to seventeenth century. Also, no other European trade items were reported from any of the more than 150 combined burials at the four sites. If these sites were occupied into the seventeenth or early eighteenth century, we should expect to find a wider variety of trade materials, especially glass beads, from English colonial sources in Virginia and Carolina. It is possible that relatively crude recovery methods of the late 1800s may have obscured the presence of small to moderate quantities of glass beads. It seems unlikely that they would have missed large quantities associated with burials. Therefore, while the other sites may be earlier, I suggest that the presence of the iron implements supports an associated interment period of about A.D. 1542–1700, and most likely from A.D. 1542–1600, for the Nelson Mound (assuming that all of the interments are roughly contemporary).

It seems quite clear from the quantity and type of artifacts present that these sites are mortuary facilities for individuals of special status, probably chiefly elites. It is difficult at this point to know what the four sites represent; they are currently anomalies, the presence of which leads to numerous questions. Is each site a sequential mortuary facility where individuals or groups were placed over a period of time or were all the burials contemporaneous? Are the different sites contemporary with each other, and how long were these sites in use? Are any or all of them mass graves associated with sixteenth-and/or seventeenth-century epidemic disease? How are these sites related to local non-mound sites and local hierarchy or social organization? How are these sites related to the nearby mound sites found on Johns River and Upper Creek? Is there a regional level of chiefly hierarchy involved?

Little more than the above can be said about these sites and their significance without more reliable information about their actual contextual associations.

Current Research

There is one Happy Valley site, 31CW8, for which good contextual data are available. The site, recorded and tested in 1964, is located near the confluence of Buffalo Creek and the Yadkin River, where the surrounding bottomland totals nearly 500 acres (Polhemus n.d.). Large quantities of lithic flakes, stone tools, potsherds, animal bone, and ethnobotanical remains were recovered from nine excavation units and seven features (Kimball et al. 1996; Polhemus n.d.).

Ceramics from Features 2 and 3 were the only portion of the ceramic collection accessible for my analysis (Table 9). Many of the sherds are from two vessels (Plates 25 and 26) although at least seven vessels are represented. Therefore, the relative frequencies shown in Table 9 are not com-

Table 9. Summary of 31CW8 potsherds by exterior surface treatment and other selected attributes

Exterior Surface Attribute Attribute State	Curv Comp St	Comp St Indet	Large Curv Comp St	Smoothed-Over Comp St	Burnished	Plain Smoothed	Cord Marked	Fabric Impressed	Brushed	Indeterminate	Total
Temper											Total
Soapstone (F)	7	.	.	5	9	2	.	.	.	.	23
Soapstone (M)	23	1	25	20	48	4	.	.	.	3	124
Soapstone (C)	2	.	5	24	11	1	.	.	1	.	44
Sand (M)	.	.	.	.	.	.	1	.	.	.	1
Sand (C)	.	.	.	.	.	.	.	1	.	.	1
Total	32	1	30	49	68	7	1	1	1	3	193
Interior Surface											
Burnished	26	.	24	30	64	.	.	.	.	1	145
Plain/Smoothed	5	1	.	13	1	7	.	1	.	2	30
Scraped	1	.	6	6	1	.	1	.	1	.	16
Thickness											
<6 mm	12	.	1	15	33	.	1	.	.	.	62
6-8 mm	20	1	28	30	31	4	.	1	1	1	117
>8 mm	.	.	1	4	3	3	.	.	.	2	13
Rim Form											
Applique	6	.	6	.	1	.	.	.	.	1	14
Folded	.	.	.	6	9	.	.	.	.	.	15
Unmodified	.	.	.	.	2	.	.	.	.	.	2
Lip Form											
Flat	6	.	5	3	6	.	.	.	.	.	20
Rounded	.	.	.	3	6	.	.	.	.	1	10

F, Fine; *M*, medium; *C*, coarse.

parable with those of most of the other assemblages I analyzed. However, it is clear that this is an assemblage of Burke pottery. It is primarily (92.7 percent) soapstone-tempered, curvilinear complicated-stamped, burnished, and smoothed-over complicated-stamped pottery. It is interesting that the assemblage includes a high percentage of the large curvilinear complicated-stamped designs (Plate 26) and numerous folded or appliqued rims that are 15 mm or greater in width. These are thought to be "late" (post A.D. 1550) characteristics of ceramic assemblages in the Wateree valley of South Carolina (DePratter and Judge 1990).

No modern investigations have been conducted at the sites reported by

Plate 25. Burke Burnished jar from the Broyhill-Dillard site.

Thomas. In fact, there has been some uncertainty about their exact locations, which are known only by the descriptions provided by Thomas,
which in turn are extremely difficult to correlate to the modern landscape
and property ownership in the valley. In 1995, archaeologists from the Appalachian State University Laboratories of Archaeological Science began a
research project to survey the upper Yadkin River valley and to relocate
and evaluate the sites reported by Thomas and Polhemus (Kimball et al.
1996). The results of their preliminary work are summarized here.

Kimball et al. (1996:28) were unable to conduct investigations at 31CW1
and were thus unable to verify the recorded location of 31CW1 as the T. F.
Nelson Mound and Triangle site. Nor were they able to verify the site of
31CW5, the R. T. Lenoir Burial Pit (Kimball et al. 1996:42–43). However,

Plate 26. Burke Complicated Stamped vessel from the Broyhill-Dillard site.

in each case, the investigators feel some degree of confidence about their general location.

The relocation and evaluation of 31CW8, tested by Polhemus in 1964, proved to be more successful. The site is now referred to as the Broyhill-Dillard site (Kimball et al. 1996:37) and is probably the site referred to by the NMNH catalog as "Lenoir Mound" (see above). The site location, while appearing to be similar to a large flat-topped ceremonial mound, is, in fact, a natural mound approximately 200 by 300 feet (Kimball et al. 1996:42). Test excavations revealed midden deposits, nine features, numerous postholes, and the location of one of Polhemus's test units (Kimball et al. 1996:39–40). Numerous late eighteenth-century artifacts were recovered during the investigation. These are not associated with the Native American occupation, but instead reflect the presence of William Lenoir's log cabin built in 1782 prior to the completion of Fort Defiance in 1792 (Kimball et al. 1996:41–42).

One radiocarbon date was obtained at the Broyhill-Dillard site (Larry Kimball, personal communication 1997). The date (Beta-97657) has calibrated intercepts of A.D. 1535, 1545, and 1635 with a 1-sigma range of A.D. 1475–1655. This date lends further credence to the late age of Burke ceramics and also supports the assumption of a Spanish origin for the metal objects recovered from the Nelson Mound and Triangle.

Burke pottery was the predominant pottery type identified during the recent upper Yadkin valley survey, making up 40.0 percent of the assemblage at 31CW3, 17.9 percent at 31CW3-West, 67.6 percent at the Melton

II site, and 85.4 percent at the Broyhill-Dillard site (Kimball et al. 1996:appendix C). The extremely high frequency at Broyhill-Dillard is nearly as high as that recorded in my earlier analysis (92.7 percent) of the Polhemus collection.

Thus, recent investigations in the extreme upper Yadkin valley have been partially successful at locating sites from the earlier mound explorations. They also confirm the presence of large quantities of Burke series pottery in the area. It is also important to note the work by Wake Forest University archaeologists at the nearby Jones (31WK33) and Porter (31WK6) sites, located downriver about 5 miles and 25 miles, respectively, from the Broyhill-Dillard site. Soapstone-tempered pottery predominates at each of these sites (Idol 1995:2); however, at the Porter site the soapstone-tempered potsherds appear primarily to represent the Smyth series, whereas at the Jones site they are primarily Burke series sherds. Two uncalibrated radiocarbon dates have been obtained for the Jones site: 510 ± 80 B.P. (A.D. 1440; Beta-84449) and 400 ± 60 B.P. (A.D. 1550; Beta-84450). Both Idol (1995, 1996) and Rogers (1993) have discussed the soapstone-tempered pottery in the upper Yadkin valley with respect to social relationships between Yadkin valley tribes and Catawba valley chiefdoms.

Summary

Certainly, there is much we would wish to know about the fascinating upper Yadkin valley archaeological sites. What is clear is that several of these sites feature subterranean mortuary facilities that may suggest elaborate preparation of elite burials. It is uncertain whether these facilities represent burial mounds, earthlodges, or low platform mounds, but on the basis of the reported evidence they reflect a high degree of cultural activity directed toward construction of mortuary facilities for elite individuals. It is also possible that non-elite individuals are present in the mass burials, perhaps suggesting sacrifice or death as the result of epidemic disease (see Kimball et al. 1996:30).

While the size and scope of these burial facilities is unique to the upper Yadkin valley, recall that Spainhour (1873, 1899) describes similar subterranean features and probable elite burials at nearby locations in Burke County. In addition, Burke pottery predominates at sites in the upper Yadkin valley, as it does on the sites in the Upper Creek/Johns River drainages. Sites in both areas date to the fifteenth and sixteenth centuries on the basis of the presence of Spanish artifacts and late prehistoric period radiocarbon dates. Considering these factors in light of the geographic proximity of the two areas, it appears that late prehistoric peoples at sites such as Berry, Michaux Farm, and 31BK17 in the Upper Creek/Johns River drainages were closely affiliated with peoples at the upper Yadkin valley sites in Caldwell County.

Middle and Lower Catawba Valley
Sites and Ceramics

4

This chapter examines the sites and ceramics from the middle and lower portion of the Catawba valley. This area is crucial to an understanding of any potential relationship between the protohistoric upper valley peoples and the Catawba peoples located in the lower valley in the eighteenth century. In particular, the ceramics from this area are compared with Burke ceramics of the upper valley to determine whether any spatial link exists between historic Catawba pottery and the Burke ceramics, which have been described as ancestral to them.

Previous Research

Archaeological data from the middle and lower Catawba region suffer from the same limitations we have seen in the upper valley—uneven survey coverage and limited excavations. Investigation along the main stem of the Catawba River has obviously been limited since the inundation of Lake Norman, Mountain Island Lake, and Lake Wylie. Those parts of the valley that are not under water have been subjected to tremendous development pressure over the past 30 years, and unfortunately, without mounds to investigate, the region received none of the early attention accorded to the upper Catawba and Yadkin river valleys.

During the 1960s, archaeologists from the Research Laboratories of Anthropology (RLA) at UNC-Chapel Hill conducted an extensive survey of sites in the Cowans Ford Reservoir (Lake Norman). RLA archaeologists also conducted salvage excavations at the Belk Farm site (31MK85) in 1964 and at the Hardins site (31GS29) in 1966 (Figure 10). However, no report was written for the Cowans Ford survey, the Hardins site work was not reported until 1990 (Keel 1990), and no report is available for the work at the Belk Farm site.

Beginning in the 1970s, cultural resource legislation led to a small but steady increase in site information as surveys were conducted for utility construction, highway construction, and industrial and residential development. However, these surveys were usually limited in scope, and with

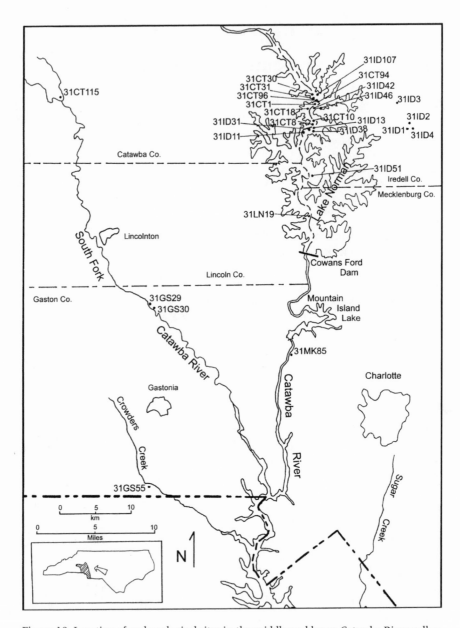

Figure 10. Location of archaeological sites in the middle and lower Catawba River valley.

very few exceptions, usually recorded lithic scatter sites with an occasional piece of pottery. One exception was the survey for the new location of U.S. Highway 321 in Gaston, Lincoln, and Catawba counties (McCabe et al. 1978). Some of the survey covered the small valley associated with Henry Fork and Jacob Fork, tributaries of the South Fork Catawba River. Numerous ceramic-bearing sites, including the Shuford site (31CT115), were recorded during this survey.

In the 1980s, while small-scale cultural resource surveys continued, more extensive research including survey and excavation was undertaken for the greater Catawba valley region by archaeologists from the Schiele Museum of Natural History and the University of North Carolina at Charlotte. This work included a reconnaissance survey of Gaston County (May 1985, 1988) and excavations at the Crowders Creek site (31GS55) and the Hardins II site (31GS30) (Levy and May 1987; May 1988, 1989). One result of this work was a better awareness of the distribution of late prehistoric sites, which were found usually on the main stem of the South Fork. Study of these late sites was linked with the work reported here in the upper and middle Catawba region (Levy et al. 1990).

The general lack of late sites outside of the main stem of the Catawba and South Fork Catawba rivers has been confirmed by additional cultural resource surveys of the 1990s. When located, these late sites tend to be small temporary sites. For example, Abbott and Sanborn (1996) recorded 28 sites and 21 isolated finds on their survey of N.C. Highway 16 in Gaston, Lincoln, and Catawba counties. Among these, five Mississippian period sites and five Mississippian or Woodland period sites were identified (Abbott and Sanborn 1996:155–156). Each was small and no site had more than 13 sherds. Abbott and Sanborn refer to the sites as "field camps," an appropriate contrast to the larger sites found along the Catawba and South Fork rivers.

The middle valley sites described in this chapter are primarily from the Cowans Ford Reservoir, the major exception being the Shuford site (31CT115) (Figure 10). The lower valley discussion is limited to the Belk Farm (31MK85) and Hardins (31GS29) sites in the 1960s and the more recent testing of the Hardins II (31GS30) site and the Crowders Creek site (31GS55) by archaeologists from the Schiele Museum of Natural History and the University of North Carolina at Charlotte. Figure 10 shows the middle and lower Catawba Valley region and the sites mentioned in the text.

Cowans Ford Reservoir Survey

The Duke Power Company began construction of the Cowans Ford Dam in 1959. Students under the direction of Joffre Coe at the Research Laboratories of Anthropology at UNC-Chapel Hill surveyed the Cowans Ford

Reservoir from 1960 to 1962. When completed in 1963, the impoundment extended nearly 34 river miles on the Catawba River, creating Lake Norman, which covers 35,510 acres in Catawba, Iredell, Lincoln, and Mecklenburg counties.

There is no written project report and very little documentation exists of survey activities by the RLA. Joffre Coe (personal communication 1988) has described the survey as having been carried out "on weekends and on the side between other jobs." That seems unlikely, however, since the scope of the survey was so large. At least eight individuals took part in the survey over a two-year period; more than 300 sites were recorded, and test excavations were conducted on at least 10 of these sites. The extant survey information includes site forms, burial forms, field site maps, notations on field bags of collected samples, and daily reports from testing activities at the following sites: 31ID38 and 31ID31 (7/13/61 through 8/30/61) and 31CT10 (12/6/61 through 12/8/61).

The collected artifacts were cataloged and catalog entries appear to correspond to the field bag notations. The catalog lists surface collections as well as excavated test pits, excavations of features exposed by bulldozer cuts, and collections of materials exposed by bulldozer cuts. It appears that most of the survey took place in open fields or pastures, but, in some cases, survey occurred after clearing of brush or trees. In almost all cases in which the term *trench* is used in the notes, it refers to bulldozer cuts as opposed to archaeologically excavated trenches. This seems to be borne out by the field maps, which provide notations such as "Trenches 10' wide, 75' long" (31CT30). These maps are very carefully rendered and were apparently created with a transit or plane table and alidade; however, it is not clear to what extent the trenches were cleaned or how they were observed to identify features and postholes.

In addition, a reservoir map was prepared that shows the location and size of each site. This information is invaluable since it provides a glimpse of general settlement patterns. However, it is not possible to determine whether the site sizes as mapped actually reflect the size of the sites; without documentation of the survey methods it is difficult to evaluate the comparability of the artifact collections with recorded site size or anything else. Clearly the data gathered from the Cowans Ford survey represent a somewhat problematic database. Though there can be much gained by a review of the site and artifact collections, it will be apparent to the reader that the unrealized potential of this survey project is of tragic proportions. The following is a brief description of middle Catawba valley sites for which any level of documentation beyond site location is available.

Low Site

The Low site (31ID31), now inundated by Lake Norman, is located in Iredell County on the east bank of the Catawba River in the vicinity of

Sherrill's Ford. Sherrill's Ford is named for Adam Sherrill, one of the earliest settlers west of the Catawba River, who first crossed the river here in 1747. It is likely that the ford was well used for centuries by native Catawba valley peoples; numerous sites are recorded in its vicinity.

Based on the survey maps, the Low site appears to be located on a terrace or low ridge toe slope just above the floodplain. A surface collection and limited test excavations took place. The site form states the following: "This site has been excavated. The concentration of pottery is located about 3' down. Pot clusters have been uncovered. This site has given us a good sample of prehistoric Catawba pottery" (RLA site files).

According to Wilson (1983:297), large sherds and a few broken pots were first observed in a washed-out bulldozer cut. Nine excavation squares were placed adjacent to the bulldozed cut. Stratigraphy in the excavated units is described inconsistently, but on the basis of notes and profile drawings, Zone I describes a dark brown soil level immediately beneath the plow zone and Zone II refers to the humus level, also called "Black Soil." Zone III is "Grey Soil," apparently a sandy subsoil, and the lowest level is labeled "Red-Brown Sand." Most artifacts come from Zones II and III. Artifacts are also reported from four additional generic contexts: surface, overburden, plowed soil, and old humus.

The cataloged artifacts include 12 projectile points (1 identified as Yadkin), 1 chipped stone fragment, 1 hammerstone, 2 grinding stones, 1 clay pipe, 10 flakes, 2 half-bricks, 3,006 potsherds, and 1 small ceramic vessel. It should be noted that my analysis of the Cowans Ford collections focused only on the ceramics. I examined the pottery from every cataloged context, but I did not examine the other curated materials. Sadly, the Low site represents the best-documented site in the reservoir survey. The following descriptions constitute all that is known of the other tested sites.

31CT8

Site 31CT8 is located in Catawba County across the Catawba River from the Low site. According to the site form, a test pit measuring 4 × 4 × 3 ft was excavated and a "large amount of shell, bone, potsherds, and other pit refuse" was removed. The catalog entry consists of a single "test pit" context.

31CT10

Site 31CT10 is located on the Catawba River just upstream of 31CT8. The site form states that a 3-ft-deep test pit was excavated and this is described as having three zones: river sand, light-brown sand, and dark-brown or black (this zone is presumably the one referred to as a possible midden). The catalog includes two contexts only: "Test pit, midden" and "Test pit, plowed soil."

31CT30

The site form shows site 31CT30 on a small rise adjacent to the Catawba River floodplain. It was apparently recorded on July 18, 1961, and excavated in one day on July 12, 1962. A notation on the site form says "Now underwater" and "burials found." Most of the information about this site comes from a field map that shows the rise with contour lines, and a notation of "500'" appears to represent the size of the area marked by the 730-ft contour line. This may or may not indicate the site limits. Three bulldozer trenches 10 ft wide and 75 ft long were cut at right angles to the river and a note on the map says they were "started about center of mound." This is the only reference I found to a mound. The map shows 23 postholes in Trench 3. Trench 1 shows 30 postholes, plus a "Bone pit" and a "shell pit," both of which appear to be slightly larger than the postholes. No clear structures are indicated by the postholes, but there are several potential lines of posts indicated in Trench 1. Trench 2 includes five postholes and five burials. Burial forms indicate that fragmentary skeletal remains were found in five burials, but there are no further data regarding the burials.

The catalog includes ceramics from the following contexts: "Burial 1 fill," "Burial 2 fill," "Burial 3 fill," "Burial 4–5 fill," and "Trench 1 pit #1." The catalog lists 35 potsherds from excavated contexts and 2,220 from surface collection. Unfortunately, the vast majority of the surface materials were probably broken by the bulldozer and were too small for analysis; my analyzed sample consisted of only 194 sherds (it is also possible that some sherds were missing from the collection).

31CT31

The catalog lists ceramics for site 31CT31 from a "pit in bulldozer run."

31CT94

The catalog lists three contexts for 31CT94: Trench #1, Trench #2, and Trench #3.

31CT94A

The catalog for site 31CT94A lists a single context: sand fill over humus. There is no recorded site with this number in the RLA site files. Therefore, it is likely that this represents a portion of site 31CT94. However, I have treated it separately since it was collected separately. It may represent a distinct component of 31CT94.

31CT96

The site form indicates that site 31CT96 was recorded on June 6, 1962, and is located at the foot of a low terrace about 500 ft west of the Catawba River. The site may extend as far as 1,000 ft parallel to the river. The feature forms and map indicate that the site was excavated on July 11 and 12, 1962, by Joffre Coe and one assistant.

The site map shows seven bulldozer trenches running generally parallel to the river; the trenches range from 80 to 1,000 ft in length. Numerous postholes are scattered throughout the trenches; they include Feature 2, described as a stockade wall consisting of a row of postholes nearly 25 ft long. Three of the remaining features are described as pits, one is called a burned-out stump, and one is referred to as a corn pit. Feature 1 appears to be a roughly circular pit, 6 ft in diameter, that included projectile points, pipe fragments, a pottery disk, flakes, daub, and 177 potsherds.

31ID38

The catalog describes three excavation squares for site 31ID38, each with two levels beneath the plow zone. It is uncertain whether these levels are arbitrary levels or represent some soil condition or horizons.

31ID107

Two excavation units are listed in the catalog for site 31ID107, both apparently only plow zone excavations.

Shuford Site

The Shuford site (31CT115) is not a part of the Cowans Ford survey; its location in a large alluvial bottom, where Jacob Fork and Henry Fork join to form the South Fork of the Catawba River, is less than 20 miles west of Lake Norman. The site was identified during the survey for the construction of U.S. Highway 321 in Catawba County (McCabe et al. 1978). Shovel tests revealed a midden that contained large potsherds as well as abundant charcoal (McCabe et al. 1978:74–76).

Additional testing was conducted in 1979 with the excavation of "one 1 × 2 meter test unit, two 50 × 50 cm units, and 11 3-inch auger holes" (Mathis 1979:3). The presence of a midden zone at a depth of 30 to 55 cm was confirmed in two of the three units. Beneath the midden level, the largest unit also revealed 14 post molds and one shallow basin-shaped feature that contained charred corncobs and an abundance of soapstone-tempered complicated-stamped ceramics (Mathis 1979:3). The charred cobs were submitted for a radiocarbon date, but unfortunately the date was modern, postdating 1950. It is uncertain why the date is so late; the cobs are aboriginal. Mathis (1979:15) described the pottery as representative of the Burke type of pottery defined in the upper Catawba valley. He also suggests that the homogeneity of the ceramics argues for a single occupational component. Unfortunately, the ceramic collection was not available for my analysis.

The Shuford site was investigated again during the Upper Catawba Archaeological Project in 1986. Three 10-x-10-ft units were excavated (plow

Table 10. Ceramic assemblage sizes for sites in the Cowans Ford Reservoir
Survey

No. of sherds	<10	10-25	26-50	51-100	>100	Total
County						
Catawba	37	20	10	3	8	78
Iredell	36	14	11	5	11	77
Lincoln	22	6	4	1	1	34
Mecklenburg	24	5	1	4	1	35

zone removed by backhoe) and a few postholes were identified at the subsoil level in each unit. No other features were identified. This investigation
produced little additional artifactual material.

Middle Valley Ceramics

The attribute analysis was conducted on pottery from 224 Cowans Ford
Reservoir survey sites (Table 10). The majority of the pottery was gathered
in surface collections. Very few of the tested sites yielded significant quantities of ceramics from features or other stratigraphic contexts, and the analysis
of assemblages from sites with stratigraphic contexts (e.g., 31ID31, 31CT10)
yielded no useful indications of variability within the assemblages. Thus,
for discussion purposes, all of the survey collections are treated as surface
collections. As a result, the following discussion of the ceramics from the
middle valley sites is extremely limited in scope. Nonetheless, the attribute
analysis revealed several significant patterns of ceramic variability within
the reservoir area, the most significant of which is the widespread occurrence of Cowans Ford series pottery (described below and in appendix C).

Cowans Ford Pottery

The Cowans Ford ceramic series (Moore 1999) consists of thin, sand-tempered and fine quartz–tempered sherds with primarily plain/smoothed,
burnished, complicated-stamped, and corncob-impressed exterior surfaces
(Plates 27 and 28). Some sherds also exhibit net-impressed or brushed exterior surfaces. Vessels include restricted-neck jars that often feature folded
or appliqued rim strips. Carinated bowls are also present. Cowans Ford pottery is similar to Burke series pottery; it is another regional variant of Lamar pottery and is thought to date to ca. A.D. 1350–1700.

In many respects Cowans Ford ceramics resemble Caraway pottery (Coe
1964:33–35, 1995:160–65; Coe and Lewis 1952; Ward and Davis 1999:
137). Caraway is described as a thin, hard, sand-tempered ware that is
usually plain or burnished and may also be brushed, net impressed, corncob impressed, or stamped with concentric circles (Coe 1995:160). Coe

Plate 27. Cowans Ford Plain/Smoothed tall cazuela-form cup from the Low site.

(1964:33) dates this pottery to A.D. 1700 at the Doerschuk site and refers to these sherds as the "culmination of the Badin-Yadkin-Uwharrie-Dan River tradition, which incorporated . . . certain elements of Pee Dee influence." More recently, Coe (1995:160–165) describes Caraway pottery at the Poole site, probably the location of the historic Keyauwee town visited by John Lawson in 1701. Noting the presence of Lamar appliqued rims and incising on Caraway pottery, Coe (1995:164) states that it is "essentially the style of Early Historic Catawba pottery most commonly found in the Catawba River area," and he further characterizes Lamar as a style of pottery that spread through the Southeast around the beginning of the Historic period. Others argue that while some Caraway types may date to the early eighteenth century, "Caraway phase ceramics represent types spanning some 300 years and most seem to date to around the beginning of the

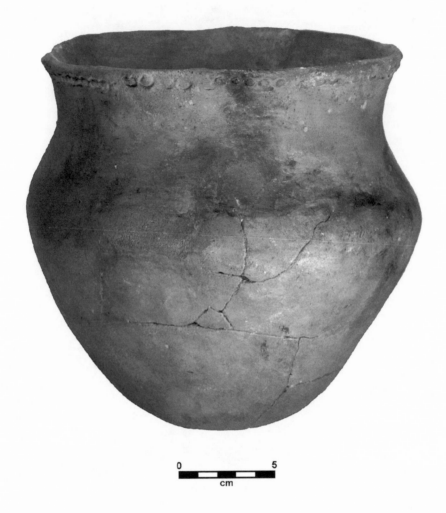

Plate 28. Cowans Ford Burnished jar with "pseudo-nodes" from the Low site.

sixteenth century" (Ward and Davis 1999:137). The following discussion of Cowans Ford pottery provides clear support for the latter view.

Despite the seeming similarities between Cowans Ford and Caraway pottery and the proximity of their distribution in the Yadkin/Pee Dee region, I formulated the new ceramic series—Cowans Ford—to describe the sand- and fine quartz–tempered, plain, burnished, and complicated-stamped pottery of the middle Catawba valley. Several factors contributed to this decision. First, no formal Caraway type description had ever been published and none of the brief descriptions mentioned the presence of the fine crushed-quartz temper that was so common in the Lake Norman pottery.

More important, the Caraway pottery type had been used to characterize early historic period Catawba valley pottery (Coe 1995:164). Rather than assume that this attribution, based on observations on pottery from outside the Catawba valley, was correct, I felt that it was important to establish a formal type description of pottery that had reliable geographic and temporal parameters within the Catawba valley. I believe that the following discussion will establish those parameters clearly and will also offer a somewhat different perspective by which we may view the Caraway type.

Low Site Ceramics

The RLA catalog lists 3,006 potsherds for the Low site. However, 629 sherds were reported from one context, "bottom of post in bulldozer gully," and these sherds were not found in the collections. In addition several hundred sherds were spalled or split longitudinally and 955 were smaller than one-half inch and therefore not analyzed. Nonetheless, the remaining 1,188 sherds represent the largest analyzed ceramic assemblage from the Cowans Ford survey. The Low site ceramic assemblage is typical of many of the large middle Catawba valley sites.

The Low site ceramics (Table 11) are tempered primarily with crushed quartz (48.6 percent) and sand (45.6 percent); a small percentage of sherds are tempered with soapstone (4.9 percent) and feldspar or granite (.8 percent). The quartz-tempered wares include two distinctive subgroups: fine quartz sized less than 2 mm and medium quartz sized 2 to 4 mm. The medium quartz–tempered (and, less frequently, coarse quartz–tempered) sherds tend to be thicker (>6 mm), with fabric-marked, cord-marked, and plain exterior surfaces and occasionally scraped interiors. The medium quartz–tempered sherds represent Woodland ceramics of the Badin, Yadkin, and Uwharrie types found throughout the Piedmont region (Coe 1964; Ward and Davis 1999). The fine quartz–tempered sherds represent Cowans Ford type sherds.

Fine quartz–tempered sherds (representing 35.5 percent of the assemblage) are quite distinct from coarse quartz–tempered sherds. Fine quartz–tempered sherds tend to be thinner and have plain, burnished, or complicated-stamped surfaces. In all respects they are similar to the sand-tempered sherds (45.6 percent of the assemblage); in fact, it is sometimes difficult to distinguish coarse sand from the fine quartz. These sand- or fine quartz–tempered sherds are complicated stamped (17.9 percent), plain/smoothed (28.7 percent), burnished (25.9 percent), or corncob impressed (23.5 percent). Net-impressed, fabric-impressed, and brushed sherds are also pres-

Table 11. Summary of Low site potsherds by exterior surface treatment and other selected attributes

Exterior Surface **Attribute** Attribute State	Curv Comp St	Rect Comp St	Comp St Indet	Large Curv Comp St	Large Rect Comp St	Indet St Linear	Smoothed-Over Comp St	Burnished	Corncob Impressed	Plain/Smoothed	Fabric Impressed	Net Impressed	Brushed	Indeterminate	Total
Temper															
Soapstone (F)	1	.	.	.	.	.	.	13	.	.	.	.	.	.	14
Soapstone (M)	1	.	.	.	.	.	.	30	3	11	.	.	.	.	45
Sand (F)	.	.	.	.	.	.	.	19	5	.	.	.	.	1	25
Sand (M)	22	1	.	.	.	.	1	116	59	100	.	10	6	23	338
Sand (C)	40	1	1	2	.	1	.	15	35	55	1	2	.	26	179
Quartz (F)	44	.	3	43	2	.	2	81	110	100	2	8	2	25	422
Quartz (M)	2	.	.	.	.	.	.	3	10	13	.	1	.	6	35
Quartz & grog	7	.	5	10	.	4	.	.	.	1	.	20	.	.	47
Quartz (In)	.	.	.	9	.	.	.	.	1	.	.	62	.	1	73
Feldspar (F)	.	.	.	.	.	.	.	.	.	1	.	.	.	.	1
Granite	.	.	.	.	.	.	.	.	.	2	1	.	6	.	9
Total	117	2	9	64	2	5	3	277	223	283	4	103	14	82	1188
Interior Surface															
Burnished	39	1	5	60	2	4	2	241	101	67	.	48	2	27	599
Plain smoothed	77	1	4	4	.	1	1	30	121	215	1	53	5	52	565
Scraped	.	.	.	.	.	.	.	.	1	1	3	.	7	1	13
Thickness															
<6 mm	35	2	1	.	.	1	.	74	7	37	1	1	1	22	182
6-8 mm	65	.	6	54	.	3	3	166	137	214	2	65	10	46	771
>8 mm	16	.	2	10	2	1	.	31	79	33	1	32	3	12	222
Rim Form															
Applique	.	.	.	2	.	.	.	2	.	.	.	.	.	1	5
Thickened	.	.	.	.	.	.	.	3	.	.	.	.	.	6	9
Unmodified	10	1	1	3	.	.	.	31	11	25	.	.	.	14	96
Lip Form															
Flat	8	.	1	3	.	.	.	24	10	18	.	.	.	.	64
Rounded	2	.	.	2	.	.	.	13	1	7	.	.	.	.	25

F, Fine; *M*, medium; *C*, coarse; *In*, inclusions.

ent, though they make up only 3.5 percent of this assemblage. The preponderance of the sand- and fine quartz–tempered Cowans Ford pottery is not unique to the Low site, but is found throughout the reservoir.

Decoration on the Low site Cowans Ford pottery is generally similar to that found on Burke pottery. This includes punctations and notching on the lip of unmodified jar rims and on appliqued jar rims. Punctations also appear on the shoulder of plain and burnished carinated vessels. However, Cowans Ford pottery differs from Burke pottery in one surprising fashion;

Plate 29. Cowans Ford vessels from the Low site and the NMNH collection. *Top,* Cowans Ford Plain/Smoothed bowl with incised decoration, RLA accession #1041p2 & 1041p4; *bottom,* globular jar with eccentric incising, 31.7 cm tall, NMNH accession #388120.

no Lamar incised designs comparable to those on Burke Incised sherds were recorded in the Low assemblage and, in fact, very few were recorded in the entire middle Catawba area. Rarely, non-Lamar incised decorations appeared; the best example is illustrated in Plate 29 (*top*). This partially reconstructed bowl exhibits two lightly incised parallel lines that cover

Plate 30. Cowans Ford vessels from the NMNH collection. *Top,* Cowans Ford Incised vessel, coarse sand temper, tall (38.0 cm) cazuela form, NMNH accession #387747, "Mound N. Carolina" and "Curtis Coll." written on vessel; *bottom,* Cowans Ford Complicated Stamped (large spiral design), constricted-neck jar with punctated appliqued rim strip, 35.5 cm tall, NMNH accession #388119.

nearly the entire vessel with an unusual eccentric pattern that is unlike anything else I observed in the entire study.

Remarkably, I encountered two other unique Cowans Ford vessels in the collection of the National Museum of Natural History, Washington, D.C. While examining the museum's collection of Caldwell County vessels, I found three vessels that were identified as coming from Iredell County, North Carolina (Plates 29 and 30). The globular jar illustrated in Plate 29 is as unusual as the Low site vessel shown in the same plate, but the incising style is somewhat reminiscent of that on the other incised vessel. The source of this vessel within Iredell County is unknown, but it would not surprise me if it had been found at the Low site. Plate 30 illustrates the other two vessels from Iredell County. The top vessel is unique for the region; not only does it exhibit the Lamar style incising so infrequent in the middle valley, but also the incising covers the entire vessel. The accession information on this vessel included the following notation: "Mound N. Carolina" and "Curtis Coll." It is possible that this vessel came from an individual (Curtis?) residing in Iredell County. If the vessel was found in Iredell County, it may have come from 31ID31, but I am unaware of any "mound" in Iredell County. I suggest a more likely source of this vessel would be from the upper Catawba valley or upper Yadkin valley. The third Iredell County vessel (Plate 30, *bottom*) in the National Museum of Natural History collection is a typical Cowans Ford Complicated Stamped jar with a punctated folded rim.

While the Low site ceramic assemblage consists primarily of Cowans Ford pottery, other wares reflect additional middle Catawba valley ceramic patterns. A sizable minority (13.0 percent) of Low sherds are tempered with larger quartz particles. These sherds include a sizable number with complicated stamping (28.5 percent, n = 37), with smaller amounts of burnished (2.3 percent, n = 3) and plain/smooth (10.8 percent, n = 14) surfaces. I associate these sherds with Cowans Ford ceramics and note that over half (51.3 percent) of the complicated-stamped sherds feature the late, large, sloppy designs. However, most of this group consists of net-impressed (63.8 percent) and cob-impressed (8.5 percent) sherds. These sherds are likely to be early Dan River type ceramics (Ward and Davis 1999:106) and may mark an earlier component at the site.

Finally, the presence of a small number of feldspar-(n = 1) and granite-tempered (n = 9) sherds also reflects temporal variation. Sherds tempered with these materials as well as hornblende are found in greater quantities at other sites in the reservoir (see below). Granite and hornblende are always associated with larger sherd thickness, more scraped interiors, and plain, fabric-impressed, cord-marked, and brushed exterior surfaces. These sherds may be related to the Uwharrie type (Coe 1964). Fine feldspar–tempered sherds tend to have the same associations as Cowans Ford series sherds.

To summarize the Low site ceramics, the vast majority (84.7 percent) are sand- or fine quartz–tempered Cowans Ford type sherds. It is clear there is little difference in the frequency of exterior surface treatments between sherds tempered with sand or fine quartz. Burnished, plain/

smoothed, corncob-impressed, and complicated-stamped exterior surfaces predominate and these four surface treatments represent the major types of the Cowans Ford series.

The Low site ceramics also include Burke ceramic types. The relative frequencies of Cowans Ford Plain/Smoothed, Burnished, and Complicated Stamped pottery suggest that potters at the Low site participated in the same ceramic tradition (i.e., Lamar style vessel forms and exterior surface treatments) as did the Burke potters. The difference between the series lies in temper type, and the sand and quartz temper in the middle Catawba valley likely represents the influence of the sand- and quartz-tempered wares of the central Piedmont Woodland tradition. This influence is also reflected in the high frequency of net impressing, corncob impressing, and brushing among the Cowans Ford pottery. The latter exterior surface treatments are nearly absent from the upper valley Burke ceramics. Their presence in the middle valley suggests some influence from, or interaction with, the Dan River ceramic tradition commonly found to the north and east in the Yadkin River valley (Woodall 1984) and throughout the north-central Piedmont (Coe and Lewis 1952; Wilson 1983). It is likely that this pattern of influence reflects a thirteenth- to fourteenth-century component at Low. A later component at Low is suggested by the presence of a relatively high percentage (5.1 percent of the Cowans Ford pottery) of sherds with large "exploded" or sloppy curvilinear complicated stamps thought to postdate A.D. 1500 (DePratter and Judge 1990). Plate 31 illustrates one example of the "exploded" curvilinear designs. It is possible that this design is derived from an earlier filfot cross design.

Discussion

Cowans Ford ceramics are found throughout the reservoir. Other sites with large pottery assemblages that are similar to that of the Low site include 31CT1, 31CT10, 31CT18, 31CT94, 31CT94A, 31ID11, 31ID42, 31ID46, 31ID51, and 31LN19. Some of these assemblages feature curvilinear complicated stamped frequencies of more than 20 percent, a figure that resembles frequencies in the upper valley region.

However, even among these assemblages there tends to be a wider distribution of minority surface finishes than were observed generally in the upper Catawba valley Burke pottery assemblages. Cob-impressed, brushed, cord-marked, simple-stamped, and fabric- and net-impressed surface finishes occur consistently in the middle valley. These patterns reflect the typological and temporal diversity of the Cowans Ford region, which includes varying frequencies of Dan River–like pottery and Cowans Ford and Burke ceramics, as well as earlier Woodland wares. It is difficult to try to sort these patterns on the basis of what are essentially surface collections, some of which we can assume represent multiple temporal components. However, there appear to be at least three patterns of ceramic diversity that can be

Plate 31. Late-style Cowans Ford complicated Stamped potsherd.

described with respect to the entire range of Lake Norman ceramic assemblages. The following discussion is based on sites with ceramic assemblages greater than 100 sherds.

The first pattern occurs in ceramic assemblages that feature high percentages of medium or coarse quartz or granite temper associated with fabric-impressed, cord-marked, brushed, or net-impressed exterior surfaces. Net impressing generally begins with the Uwharrie phase (A.D. 800–1200), whereas sherds with the former treatments are generally recognized as early and middle Woodland ceramics that resemble Badin and Yadkin series pottery (Coe 1964). They are present in small numbers on many sites, but occur in significant numbers at sites 31ID1, 31ID2 (Table 12), 31ID4 (appendix C), and 31ID38 (appendix C). The assemblages showing this particular pattern also include relatively low frequencies (six assemblages <6.6 percent) of Cowans Ford Complicated Stamped and Burnished. These sites are believed to represent primarily Woodland period components. The Cowans Ford pottery represents post–A.D. 1350 occupation.

The second pattern is the most common and consists of assemblages that

Table 12. Summary of 31ID2 potsherds by exterior surface treatment and other selected attributes

Exterior Surface Attribute Attribute State	Simple St	Burnished	Corncob Impressed	Plain/Smoothed	Check Stamped	Cord Marked	Fabric Impressed	Net Impressed	Brushed	Indeterminate	Total
Temper											
Soapstone (F)	.	.	.	3	.	.	.	.	.	.	3
Soapstone (M)	.	.	.	5	.	.	.	.	1	.	6
Sand (F)	.	.	4	13	.	5	.	.	5	4	31
Sand (M)	.	1	5	77	.	55	1	1	41	17	198
Sand (C)	1	2	5	50	1	15	4	.	18	12	108
Quartz (F)	1	.	9	54	.	14	3	.	14	18	113
Quartz (M)	.	.	.	6	.	2	1	.	1	.	10
Granite	.	.	.	11	.	1	2	.	2	1	17
Feldspar (F)	.	.	.	23	3	.	.	1	1	2	30
Total	2	3	23	242	4	92	11	2	83	54	516
Interior Surface											
Burnished	.	2	2	8	.	.	.	.	2	.	14
Plain/Smoothed	2	1	19	210	4	44	11	2	36	41	370
Scraped	.	.	2	24	.	48	.	.	45	13	132
Thickness											
<6 mm	.	1	3	17	.	11	2	1	8	4	47
6-8 mm	1	2	20	156	2	62	4	.	59	29	335
>8 mm	1	.	.	62	2	19	5	1	16	21	127
Rim Form											
Unmodified	.	2	4	36	.	15	2	1	11	17	88
Lip Form											
Flat	.	1	2	21	.	13	1	.	9	13	60
Rounded	.	.	2	14	.	2	1	1	1	4	25

F, Fine; M, medium; C, coarse.

are usually 30 to 55 percent Cowans Ford Complicated Stamped and Burnished. Cowans Ford Plain/Smoothed also accounts for 20 to 55 percent of the assemblage. Minority surface treatments are present in lower frequencies (2–15 percent of the assemblage) and most of these are on sherds with scraped interiors. Many of these can be associated with Dan River ceramic types and a smaller number with Uwharrie types. This pattern primarily reflects varying relative frequencies of Cowans Ford and Dan River–like ceramics along with small quantities (<10 percent) of Burke ceramics. This pattern is seen at sites 31CT1 (Table 13), 31CT10 (appendix C), 31CT18

Table 13. Summary of 31CT1 potsherds by exterior surface treatment and other selected attributes

Exterior Surface	Curv Comp St	Rect Comp St	Comp St Indet	Large Curv Comp St	Simple Stamped	Indet St Linear	Burnished	Corncob Impressed	Plain/Smoothed	Check Stamped	Cord Marked	Fabric Impressed	Net Impressed	Brushed	Indeterminate	Total
Attribute																
Attribute State																
Temper																**Total**
Soapstone (F)	.	.	1	.	.	.	.	.	3	.	2	.	.	.	2	8
Soapstone (M)	3	.	4	.	.	.	1	.	5	.	.	.	1	.	1	15
Soapstone (In)	9	.	5	.	.	.	1	.	5	.	.	.	.	.	3	23
Sand (F)	3	1	3	.	.	.	1	1	6	.	.	.	.	.	3	18
Sand (M)	29	1	20	.	.	5	6	1	47	.	3	.	2	3	21	138
Sand (C)	12	.	9	.	.	1	.	1	20	.	1	1	.	2	17	64
Quartz (F)	76	.	16	1	4	6	15	7	90	.	3	6	4	8	67	303
Quartz (M)	.	.	.	.	.	.	.	1	1	1	1	.	.	1	.	5
Feldspar (F)	12	.	6	1	.	1	.	.	15	.	.	.	.	.	6	41
Feldspar (C)	1	.	.	.	.	.	.	.	3	.	.	.	.	.	.	4
Total	145	2	64	2	4	13	24	11	195	1	10	7	7	14	120	619
Interior Surface																
Burnished	18	.	8	1	1	.	16	.	10	1	3	.	.	1	8	67
Plain/Smoothed	125	2	55	1	2	12	8	9	184	.	6	6	6	10	108	534
Scraped	.	.	1	.	1	.	.	2	1	.	.	1	1	3	3	13
Thickness																
<6 mm	34	.	15	.	.	8	8	3	56	.	1	1	2	2	25	155
6-8 mm	97	2	36	1	4	2	14	6	114	1	8	3	4	8	69	369
>8 mm	12	.	13	1	.	2	2	2	25	.	.	3	1	4	18	83
Rim Form																
Applique	.	.	.	.	.	.	.	.	1	.	.	.	.	.	.	1
Folded	.	.	.	.	.	.	.	.	.	.	1	.	.	.	7	8
Thickened	.	.	.	.	.	.	.	.	.	.	.	.	.	.	4	4
Unmodified	.	.	2	.	.	.	2	1	12	.	.	1	.	1	6	25
Lip Form																
Flat	.	.	2	.	.	.	2	.	9	.	1	.	.	1	9	24
Rounded	.	.	.	.	.	.	.	1	4	.	.	1	.	.	6	12

F, Fine; *M*, medium; *C*, coarse; *In*, inclusions.

(Table 14), 31CT94 (appendix C), 31CT96 (appendix C), 31ID11, 31ID31, 31ID46, and 31LN19. It is likely that this variation reflects the presence of multiple components on these sites. Those sites whose assemblages include higher frequencies of Dan River pottery are thought to date to ca. A.D. 1000–1450 (Ward and Davis 1993:185, 197, 1999:105). Those sites with assemblages featuring higher percentages of Cowans Ford pottery are thought to postdate A.D. 1350. The presence of Burke pottery likely reflects components dating into the sixteenth century.

On the basis of the relative degree of influences from interaction with people making Dan River ceramics on the Yadkin and Dan River drainages (it should be stressed that the overall frequency of these attributes is rela-

Table 14. Summary of 31CT18 potsherds by exterior surface treatment and other selected attributes

Exterior Surface	Curv Comp St	Rect Comp St	Comp St Indet	Large Curv Comp St	Simple Stamped	Smoothed-Over Comp St	Burnished	Corncob Impressed	Plain/Smoothed	Cord Marked	Fabric Impressed	Net Impressed	Brushed	Indeterminate	Total
Attribute															
Attribute State															
Temper															**Total**
Soapstone (F)	10		2	.	1	.	4	.	7	1	.	.	1	1	27
Soapstone (M)	8	1	2	.	.	.	.	.	2	.	.	.	.	1	14
Soapstone plus*	2	1	2	.	.	1	4	.	7	.	.	.	.	2	19
Sand (F)	4	3	6	.	.	.	4	.	10	2	1	1	.	4	35
Sand (M)	35	.	16	.	.	.	4	1	40	1	.	2	2	19	120
Sand (C)	24	.	2	1	1	1	19	.	34	2	2	6	4	21	117
Quartz (F)	33	.	7	2	1	.	14	2	37	.	4	1	5	14	120
Quartz (M)	2	.	.	.	.	.	.	.	5	1	1	1	1	2	13
Quartz (C)	.	.	.	.	.	.	.	.	.	.	1	.	.	.	1
Grit (F/M)	5	.	.	.	.	.	.	.	1	.	.	.	.	.	6
Misc./Ind.	.	.	1	.	.	.	.	.	.	.	.	.	.	.	1
Total	123	5	38	3	3	2	49	3	143	7	9	11	13	64	473
Interior Surface															
Burnished	19	2	6	1	.	.	36	.	27	2	.	2	3	8	106
Plain/smoothed	102	3	31	2	3	2	13	3	112	4	6	8	4	51	344
Scraped	2	.	.	.	.	.	.	.	4	1	3	.	6	5	21
Thickness															
<6 mm	19	1	7	.	1	1	18	.	56	4	2	4	5	22	140
6-8 mm	81	3	21	2	1	.	27	1	74	2	6	2	7	32	259
>8 mm	23	1	9	1	1	1	4	2	13	1	1	4	1	7	69
Rim Form															
Applique	.	.	1	.	.	.	.	.	.	.	.	.	.	.	1
Folded	1	.	.	.	.	.	.	.	.	.	.	.	.	3	4
Thickened	.	.	.	.	.	.	.	.	1	.	.	.	.	1	2
Unmodified	5	.	.	.	.	.	3	.	10	1	.	.	.	7	26
Lip Form															
Flat	4	.	1	.	.	.	2	.	8	1	.	.	.	6	22
Rounded	2	.	.	.	.	.	1	.	3	.	.	.	.	1	7

F, Fine; *M*, medium; *C*, coarse.

* Indicates mixed temper size; see Appendix C.

tively rare), I think it likely that middle Catawba valley sites dating from the eleventh to thirteenth century should feature ceramics consisting of sand- and fine quartz–tempered sherds with predominantly plain exterior surfaces and small numbers of net-impressed, cord-marked, and brushed exterior surfaces, some of which feature scraped interior surfaces as well. This earlier pattern can be seen in the ceramics from 31CT30, 31ID3 (Table

Table 15. Summary of 31ID3 potsherds by exterior surface treatment and other selected attributes

Exterior Surface Attribute Attribute State	Curv Comp St	Comp St Indet	Corncob Impressed	Plain/Smoothed	Cord Marked	Net Impressed	Brushed	Indeterminate	Total
Temper									**Total**
Soapstone (In)	·	·	·	1	·	·	·	·	1
Sand (F)	·	·	1	3	1	·	1	·	6
Sand (M)	1	1	·	10	13	1	6	7	39
Sand (C)	·	·	·	8	14	·	3	4	29
Quartz (F)	·	·	·	12	13	·	1	10	36
Quartz (M)	·	·	·	1	·	·	·	2	3
Total	1	1	1	35	41	1	11	23	114
Interior Surface									
Plain/Smoothed	1	1	1	32	30	1	3	21	90
Scraped	·	·	·	3	11	·	8	2	24
Thickness									
<6 mm	·	·	·	7	8	·	1	4	20
6-8 mm	1	1	1	23	28	1	8	16	79
>8 mm	·	·	·	5	5	·	2	3	15
Rim Form									
Unmodified	·	·	1	2	1	·	·	2	6
Lip Form									
Flat	·	·	·	2	1	·	·	2	5
Rounded	·	·	1	·	·	·	·	·	1

F, Fine; *M*, medium; *C*, coarse; *In*, inclusions.

15), 31ID13, and 31ID107 (Table 16), where Cowans Ford Complicated Stamped and Burnished combined represent less than 10 percent of the assemblage. By the fourteenth century Cowans Ford Complicated Stamped and Burnished appear in small numbers, but their frequency increases in the later centuries.

The third and final assemblage pattern is seen at relatively few sites. These assemblages feature very high frequencies of Cowans Ford Complicated Stamped and Burnished (>55 percent), relatively low frequencies of Cowans Ford Plain/Smoothed, and low frequencies of the minority surface treatments. Notably, whereas most assemblages include rare occurrences of the large, "exploded" curvilinear and rectilinear complicated-stamped designs, in two assemblages they account for 8.8 percent and 40.8 percent of the total. This pattern is seen at sites 31CT94A (Plate 32; Table 17) and

Table 16. Summary of 31ID107 potsherds by exterior surface treatment and other selected attributes

Exterior Surface Attribute Attribute State	Curv Comp St	Comp St Indet	Large Curve Comp St	Indet St Linear	Burnished	Corncob Impressed	Plain/Smoothed	Cord Marked	Fabric Impressed	Net Impressed	Brushed	Indeterminate	Total
Temper													
Soapstone (F)	.	1	.	.	2	.	2	.	.	.	.	1	6
Soapstone (M)	2	.	.	.	1	.	.	.	.	.	.	.	3
Soapstone (In)	.	.	.	.	.	.	1	.	.	.	.	6	7
Sand (F)	.	.	.	.	2	.	.	1	.	.	.	13	16
Sand (M)	1	1	3	.	1	1	31	86	3	5	30	.	162
Sand (C)	1	.	.	.	2	.	23	73	5	.	18	.	122
Quartz (F)	1	.	1	1	3	2	11	54	5	.	9	8	95
Quartz (M)	.	.	.	.	.	.	1	1	1	.	1	1	5
Feldspar (F)	.	.	.	.	.	.	3	1	.	.	1	.	5
Total	5	2	4	1	11	3	72	216	14	5	59	29	421
Interior Surface													
Burnished	.	.	2	.	8	.	2	93	.	.	.	.	105
Plain/Smoothed	5	2	2	.	3	2	64	123	3	2	17	23	246
Scraped	.	.	.	1	.	1	6	.	11	3	42	4	68
Thickness													
<6 mm	1	.	.	.	4	.	14	30	2	1	7	2	61
6-8 mm	3	1	4	1	7	2	48	152	9	3	46	22	298
>8 mm	1	1	.	.	.	1	10	34	3	1	6	4	61
Rim Form													
Unmodified	.	.	.	.	.	.	8	9	1	.	5	2	25
Lip Form													
Flat	.	.	.	.	.	.	3	2	1	.	2	1	9
Rounded	.	.	.	.	.	.	5	7	.	.	3	2	17

F, Fine; *M*, medium; *C*, coarse; *In*, inclusions.

31ID51 (Table 18) and likely represents sixteenth- to seventeenth-century components. The lack of examples of Lamar incising in the middle valley also suggests that fewer sites are located in the middle valley region in the sixteenth and seventeenth centuries.

Obviously, it is difficult to support these hypothesized temporal patterns (especially considering that many of the sites have multiple components). However, it is likely that most of the diversity present in the Cowans Ford sand- and fine quartz–tempered wares dates to the fourteenth to sixteenth

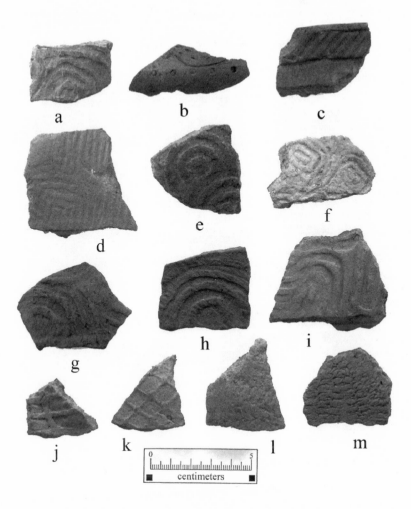

Plate 32. Cowans Ford potsherds from 31CT94A. *a, d–i,* Cowans Ford Complicated Stamped (*a, g, h, i* are late examples); *b,* Cowans Ford Burnished with incised decoration; *c,* Cowans Ford Plain/Smoothed with appliqued rim; *j, k,* check stamped; *l, m,* cob impressed.

centuries and the minor influences from Dan River ceramics reflect earlier components.

Finally, the Shuford site (31CT115) ceramics represent a pattern unlike that of any of the other middle valley sites. In fact, the Shuford site is located midway between Burke County and Lake Norman and its ceramics are much more like an upper valley Burke assemblage (Table 19). The Shu-

Table 17. Summary of 31CT94A potsherds by exterior surface treatment and other selected attributes

Exterior Surface Attribute Attribute State	Curv Comp St	Rect Comp St	Comp St Indet	Large Curv Comp St	Large Rect Comp St	Indet St Linear	Smoothed-Over Comp St	Burnished	Corncob Impressed	Plain/Smoothed	Check Stamped	Cord Marked	Fabric Impressed	Net Impressed	Brushed	Indeterminate	Total
Temper																	
Soapstone (F)	2	.	.	.	.	.	.	1	1	.	.	.	.	.	.	.	4
Soapstone (M)	3	.	.	.	.	.	.	.	.	.	.	.	.	.	.	.	3
Soapstone plus*	5	1	.	.	.	1	.	1	.	1	1	.	.	.	.	.	10
Sand (F)	.	.	.	1	.	1	1	3	1	2	.	.	.	.	2	2	13
Sand (M)	31	1	5	8	2	3	2	21	4	29	.	2	.	.	2	7	117
Sand (C)	16	3	6	5	.	.	.	10	3	20	1	1	1	.	5	11	82
Quartz (F)	9	.	1	6	.	2	5	13	6	11	.	.	1	1	.	2	57
Quartz (M)	1	.	.	.	.	.	.	1	.	1	.	2	.	.	1	.	6
Feldspar (F)	5	1	.	.	.	1	1	1	1	4	.	1	.	.	.	.	14
Total	72	6	12	20	2	7	10	51	15	68	2	6	2	1	10	22	306
Interior Surface																	
Burnished	19	3	4	10	2	4	7	35	3	17	1	3	.	1	4	4	117
Plain/Smoothed	52	3	8	10	.	3	4	15	12	51	2	.	.	.	3	18	181
Scraped	.	.	.	.	.	.	.	.	.	.	.	3	2	.	3	.	8
Thickness																	
<6 mm	25	1	2	2	.	5	2	21	1	22	.	4	2	1	4	8	100
6-8 mm	44	4	7	15	2	1	7	25	12	38	3	1	.	.	6	12	177
>8 mm	3	1	3	3	.	1	2	4	2	8	.	1	.	.	.	2	30
Rim Form																	
Folded	.	.	.	.	.	.	.	.	.	1	.	.	.	.	.	1	2
Thickened	.	.	.	.	.	.	.	.	.	.	.	.	.	.	.	4	4
Unmodified	2	1	.	1	.	1	.	6	2	8	.	.	.	.	.	3	24
Lip Form																	
Flat	2	1	.	1	.	.	.	6	1	9	.	.	.	.	.	6	26
Rounded	.	.	.	.	.	1	.	.	1	.	.	.	.	.	.	2	4

F, Fine; M, medium; C, coarse.

* Indicates mixed temper size; see Appendix C.

ford site assemblage is 59.8 percent Burke ceramics and 31.7 percent Cowans Ford ceramics. Complicated-stamped exterior surfaces predominate within both series, followed by plain, burnished, and cord-marked sherds. Fabric-impressed, brushed, net-impressed, and cob-impressed sherds are also represented. The cord-marked sherds are very similar to fine cord-marked sherds found more commonly at sites in the lower valley and thought to perhaps date to the seventeenth century. It is uncertain why the frequency of Burke ceramics is so great at the Shuford site compared with sites in the Lake Norman area. Because of the lack of systematic surveyed areas in Catawba County, it is impossible to know whether this site is an anomaly. It is possible that the presence of such large quantities of Burke

Table 18. Summary of 31ID51 potsherds by exterior surface treatment and other selected attributes

Exterior Surface Attribute Attribute State	Curv Comp St	Rect Comp St	Large Curv Comp St	Large Rect Comp St	Burnished	Corncob Impressed	Plain/Smoothed	Indeterminate	Total
Temper									
Sand (M)	8	2	.	.	.	5	2	.	17
Sand (C)	4	.	16	15	2	7	2	1	47
Quartz (F)	.	.	.	.	.	.	1	.	1
Total	12	2	16	15	2	12	5	1	65
Interior Surface									
Burnished	3	1	15	14	1	1	1	.	36
Plain/Smoothed	9	1	1	1	1	11	4	1	29
Thickness									
<6 mm	2	.	.	.	1	1	1	.	5
6-8 mm	6	2	5	1	1	10	3	.	28
>8 mm	4	.	11	14	.	1	1	.	31
Rim Form									
Folded	.	.	1	10	.	.	1	.	12
Unmodified	.	.	1	.	1	.	.	.	2
Lip Form									
Flat	.	.	2	10	1	.	1	.	14

F, Fine; *M*, medium; *C*, coarse.

ceramics here argues for some type of closer direct contact between this site and the upper Catawba sites in Burke County. If so, it may also reflect a sixteenth-century occupation.

Wilson's (1983:315) description of a small sample of Low site sherds suggests that most of the assemblage attributes are derived from Pee Dee pottery:

> The presence of burnished and complicated stamped surfaces, cazuela and hemispherical bowl forms, the use of circular reed punctations to create "pseudo-nodes," and applique rim strips, all illustrate the direct influences that emanated from the Pee Dee, and Pee Dee related, culture (cf. Reid 1965, 1967) of the Wateree River in South Carolina, and the Little River section of the Pee Dee River in south-central North Carolina.

Table 19. Summary of Shuford site potsherds by exterior surface treatment and other selected attributes

Exterior Surface Attribute Attribute State	Curv Comp St	Rect Comp St	Comp St Indet	Large Curv Comp St	Indet St Linear	Smoothed-Over Comp St	Burnished	Corncob Impressed	Plain/Smoothed	Cord Marked	Fabric Impressed	Net Impressed	Brushed	Indeterminate	Total
Temper															
Soapstone (F)	4	2	1	1	1	1	10	·	2	1	·	·	·	4	27
Soapstone (M)	27	·	7	·	·	1	3	3	8	3	1	1	5	13	72
Soapstone (In)	3	·	6	·	·	1	3	·	12	7	2	·	·	4	38
Sand (M)	13	·	1	·	·	·	4	·	8	4	2	·	·	2	34
Sand (C)	4	·	2	·	·	3	3	·	15	2	·	·	·	4	33
Quartz (F)	2	·	·	·	·	·	·	·	1	1	1	·	·	3	8
Quartz (M)	·	·	1	·	·	1	1	·	1	2	7	·	·	1	14
Quartz (C)	·	·	·	·	·	·	·	·	·	·	·	·	·	2	2
Grit (F/M)	·	·	·	·	·	·	·	·	1	·	·	·	·	·	1
Total	53	2	18	1	1	7	24	3	48	20	13	1	5	33	229
Interior Surface															
Burnished	19	·	4	1	·	2	16	·	15	14	·	·	·	7	78
Plain/Smoothed	31	2	10	·	·	3	7	·	33	3	5	1	1	17	113
Scraped	3	·	4	·	1	1	1	3	·	3	8	·	4	8	36
Thickness															
<6 mm	8	·	2	·	1	·	10	·	14	·	1	·	·	5	41
6-8 mm	39	2	8	1	·	4	12	·	28	19	8	1	3	18	143
>8 mm	6	·	8	·	·	2	2	3	6	1	4	·	2	9	43
Rim Form															
Folded	3	·	·	·	1	·	·	·	·	1	·	·	·	2	7
Thickened	·	·	·	1	·	·	·	·	·	·	·	·	·	·	1
Unmodified	1	·	·	·	·	·	2	·	2	3	2	·	1	3	14
Lip Form															
Flat	3	·	·	1	·	·	1	·	1	4	1	·	·	6	17
Rounded	1	·	·	·	1	·	1	·	·	·	1	·	1	·	5

F, Fine; M, medium; C, coarse; In, inclusions.

A more appropriate interpretation is now possible for the Low site ceramics. The analysis of the entire Lake Norman collection demonstrates the regionwide distribution of Cowans Ford ceramics and the obvious similarity of this series to the Burke series in the upper Catawba valley. The complicated-stamped motifs of the Low site assemblage, and of Cowans Ford pottery in general, resemble the motifs of the Burke series as opposed to the complicated-stamped motifs of the Pee Dee series. Pee Dee Complicated Stamped pottery includes the filfot cross, concentric circles, barred circles, nested diamonds, nested blocks, split-diamond, herringbone, and arc-angle designs (Coe 1995:153; Reid 1967:70). Of these, only concentric circles are commonly found on Cowans Ford and Burke pottery. Although a few examples of the filfot cross/scroll were observed, the overwhelming majority of Cowans Ford designs consist of spirals and concentric circles joined by arcs and rays. These appear to represent a complicated stamping style that developed within the Catawba valley.

A comparison of Pee Dee pottery from the Town Creek site with Cowans Ford pottery from the Catawba valley is instructive. Pee Dee Complicated Stamped sherds accounted for 70 percent of the Town Creek sherds (Reid 1967:80). Burnished or polished sherds accounted for nearly 14 percent, but plain sherds accounted for only 2 percent (Reid 1967:80). This pattern is quite distinct from the Catawba valley pattern in which many Cowans Ford assemblages include 30 to 60 percent plain or burnished sherds. Finally, though there are examples of Pee Dee pottery attributes present at the Low site, particularly the circular reed punctations, these are few (n = 6). The majority of surface treatments, vessel forms, and decoration attributes are more similar to the Burke series than to Pee Dee.

The Catawba valley complicated-stamped, plain, and burnished Burke and Cowans Ford wares do not result from Pee Dee influence. They are related to Pee Dee, but only in the same sense as fingers of a hand. The Catawba valley and the Pee Dee region represent separate and independent expressions of Lamar styles in the Piedmont of North Carolina. In the Catawba region, the expansion of a Lamar style pottery began at least during the fourteenth century A.D. and very possibly one to two centuries earlier.

Lower Valley Archaeological Sites

Archaeological investigations in the lower Catawba valley south of Lake Norman are limited and only a very few lower valley ceramic assemblages were available for the present study. Aside from salvage investigations at the Hardins and Belk Farm sites, little professional archaeological work occurred in this region until the 1980s. The following is not a comprehensive discussion, but illustrates a degree of continuity in ceramic patterning between the middle and lower Catawba valley areas. The last part of this chapter considers recent investigations of the presumed locations of two eighteenth-century sites in the Wateree valley that may shed some light on ceramic assemblage characteristics for the early historic period Catawbas.

Hardins Site

The Hardins site (31GS29) is located on the north side of the South Fork River between the communities of Hardins and High Shoals in Gaston County (see Figure 10 for the locations of sites mentioned in the text). The South Fork River is the largest tributary of the Catawba River in the lower valley. Archaeologists from the RLA conducted investigations at the Hardins site in 1966 (Keel 1990). The work was limited to a brief salvage excavation that resulted from the accidental discovery of human burials during earth-moving operations. Two burials and three features were excavated. Each of the burials contained the flexed remains of a single child accompanied by grave goods. Burial 1 was accompanied by "two ceremonial axes, a celt, shell beads, a shell pendant, and a piece of mica," and Burial 2 was accompanied by a ceremonial axe and a stone discoidal (Keel 1990:3–4).

This ceremonial axe type has been dated from A.D. 1360–1610 (Smith 1987:101), though others suggest that it may date to somewhat earlier periods as well (Keel 1990:10, 15–16). Perforated spatulate axes, in particular, "have consistently been recovered from sites yielding sixteenth century European artifacts" (Little and Curren 1990:185). Keel (1990:15) suggests that a mid-fifteenth to early-sixteenth-century date is more appropriate for the specimens at the Hardins site. Some researchers suggest that ceremonial or spatulate axes indicate high status for the individuals with whom they are buried (Hatch 1975:132–133). Their presence, along with other high-status artifacts in burials at the Dallas site, may reflect the burial of chiefly elites (Hatch 1975:134–135), but it is not clear how that interpretation may apply to the Hardins burials.

The excavated features contained faunal and ethnobotanical material (no microscopic analysis reported), a small number of stone tools, and pottery described as an early form of "emerging Catawba ceramics" (Keel 1990:10), a thin and hard, well-made sand-tempered ware. The reported pottery is sand tempered (with occasional crushed quartz) and includes 115 sherds with identifiable surface treatments, 108 of which are complicated stamped, plain, or burnished. One soapstone-tempered, simple-stamped sherd is reported. It is likely that this pottery is equivalent to, if not the same as, Cowans Ford pottery.

Hardins II Site

The Hardins II site (31GS30) is located nearly one-half mile south of 31GS29 on the west and east banks of the South Fork River. This site was recorded in 1965 and described as "protohistoric Catawba" (RLA site files). The site was originally recorded only on the east bank of the South Fork. Apparently, prior to the 1940 flood, the river cut to the southwest and flowed around this large site. During the flood, the river overran a partially excavated modern ditch, cutting the site in half and permanently altering the location of the river. Thus, although found on both sides of the river today, the site was originally contiguous and located entirely on the east side of the river.

Archaeologists from UNC-Charlotte and the Schiele Museum of Natural History investigated the portion of the site located now on the west side of the river with limited test excavations from 1985 to 1987 (Levy and May 1987; May 1988). This is obviously a large site, but structural information is limited to two incomplete circular patterns of postholes; however, more than 50 features and nearly 100 postholes have been recorded.

May (1988:25) describes the ceramics as including about 50 percent complicated-stamped sherds, "in the general South Appalachian tradition," and states that plain, burnished, and cob-impressed sherds each make up about 10 percent of the assemblage. Though I did not formally analyze this material, it appears to be equivalent to Cowans Ford pottery.

Five radiocarbon dates are available for the Hardins II site (May 1988; also Eastman 1994a:51–52, 1994b:45–46). Four of the five dated feature contexts included complicated-stamped, burnished, or plain pottery. Three of the dates have calibrated fifteenth-century intercepts, whereas the other two have calibrated thirteenth-century intercepts. Without more analysis I am unable to judge whether the two sets of dates reflect two temporal components. However, the earlier dates might support an argument for the presence of complicated stamping in the lower Catawba region prior to the fourteenth century.

Crowders Creek Site

The Crowders Creek site (31GS55) is located in southeast Gaston County on Crowders Creek, a tributary of the Catawba River (Levy et al. 1990; May 1989; Pace 1986). The site is situated on an alluvial terrace and covers an area of approximately 2.5 hectares. The Gaston County Archaeological Society first investigated the site in 1983 and the subsequent discovery of a burial was reported to the North Carolina Office of State Archaeology (Moore 1983). Archaeologists with the Schiele Museum of Natural History and UNC-Charlotte conducted systematic investigations of the Crowders Creek site in 1985 and 1986 (May 1987, 1989; May and Pace n.d.). Shovel testing and mechanical stripping were employed to remove the plow zone from more than 180 m^2 of the site. Three burials, 34 features, and 102 postholes were recorded, and 30 features were excavated (May 1989:38). Features contained substantial quantities of ethnobotanical and faunal remains and pottery.

May (1989:35) indicates that the ceramics are tempered with crushed quartz (7.1 percent), medium sand (65.5 percent), and grit (27.7 percent). Surface treatments on sand-tempered sherds are smoothed plain (63.2 percent), burnished plain (10.6 percent), and complicated stamped (14.7 percent), along with minor amounts of cord marked, fabric impressed, brushed, check stamped, and simple stamped (total 8.9 percent). This pottery is also similar to the Cowans Ford pottery in the Lake Norman reservoir. It is possible that a more complete comparison will reveal some differences in paste and temper characteristics; for instance, the Gaston County sherds seem to contain less temper than the Lake Norman sherds.

Three radiocarbon dates are available for the Crowders Creek site (May 1989:40–42). Features 12, 13, and 39 produced uncorrected dates ranging from A.D. 1350–1600. Features 12 and 13 include conjoining pottery fragments and their corrected date ranges overlap at 1 sigma from A.D. 1329–1419 (Eastman 1994b:44). The third date (Feature 39) has three calibrated intercepts: A.D. 1515, 1591, and 1621. May's interpretation of a mid-fourteenth- to mid-fifteenth-century date for these features seems well supported. However, I would suggest that the corrected intercepts for Feature 39 may reflect a sixteenth-century component as well.

Belk Farm Site

The Belk Farm site (31MK85) is located on the east side of the Catawba River, north of Charlotte. The site was apparently discovered and vandalized after topsoil was removed from a portion of the site. With the report of vandalism, archaeologists from the RLA worked at the site for one weekend in the fall of 1964. No report was written and Wilson's (1983) description remains the only published account of the work. Wilson (1983:455) terms this site the "Bell" Farm site; however, the property is owned by the Belk family and it is likely that "Bell" is erroneous. Wilson (1983:455) describes the site as follows:

> Two ten foot, three five foot, and three irregularly shaped test squares were excavated at the site. Little information on the stratigraphy encountered exists. The soil was described as sandy loam. Two features were uncovered and removed. One of these appears to have been a large, elongated shallow basin that resembles the "roasting pits" found at the two Historic Period Dan River sites. Recovered from the features were 102 glass trade beads, 354 potsherds, clay pipe fragments, animal bone, acorn and hickory shell/meat, burnt cane, carbonized peach pit, a bone awl, flakes, and a small triangular chipped stone projectile point. From the square excavations and surface collection, an additional 193 potsherds were found, along with four glass trade beads, a brass bangle, clay pipe fragments, animal bone, and flakes. The presence of a large number of glass trade beads, the brass bangle, and the peach pit, places this site well within the Historic period. The exact dating can not be determined, but the late seventeenth or early eighteenth century represents an excellent approximation.

Linda Carnes-McNaughton (personal communication 1990) examined the trade beads from the Belk Farm site and reached a similar conclusion, citing the similarity of the beads to those found on late protohistoric sites ca. 1680–1710 in the North Carolina Piedmont.

The Belk Farm site ceramics (Table 20) are nearly exclusively (96.1 percent) sand- and fine quartz–tempered Cowans Ford pottery and the assemblage is similar to many in Lake Norman. Cowans Ford types include com-

Table 20. Summary of Belk Farm site potsherds by exterior surface treatment and other selected attributes

Exterior Surface	Curv Comp St	Rect Comp St	Comp St Indet	Large Curv Comp St	Large Rect Comp St	Indet St Linear	Smoothed-Over Comp St	Burnished	Corncob Impressed	Plain/Smoothed	Check Stamped	Cord Marked	Net Impressed	Brushed	Indeterminate	Total
Attribute																
Attribute State																
Temper																
Soapstone (F)	·	·	·	·	·	·	·	1	·	·	·	·	·	·	1	2
Soapstone (M)	·	·	2	·	·	·	·	·	·	1	·	·	·	·	·	3
Sand (F)	25	1	·	5	·	·	4	23	3	31	·	13	·	·	6	111
Sand (M)	74	1	2	4	·	2	1	19	40	60	·	23	1	6	14	247
Sand (C)	46	1	4	4	2	1	8	5	3	40	1	8	·	2	6	131
Quartz (F)	4	·	1	·	·	·	·	4	1	9	·	8	·	·	2	29
Quartz (M)	·	·	1	·	·	·	·	·	·	·	·	·	·	·	·	1
Quartz (In)	8	·	·	·	·	·	·	·	·	·	·	·	·	·	·	8
Feldspar (F)	·	1	·	·	·	·	·	1	·	·5	·	·	·	·	·	7
Total	157	4	10	13	2	3	13	53	47	146	1	52	1	8	29	539
Interior Surface																
Burnished	82	2	4	7	1	·	7	44	35	33	1	28	·	2	5	251
Plain/Smoothed	75	2	6	6	1	3	6	9	12	111	·	24	1	6	24	286
Thickness																
<6 mm	53	·	4	3	1	1	7	23	3	62	·	20	1	3	15	196
6-8 mm	100	4	4	10	1	1	5	29	40	73	1	26	·	4	13	311
>8 mm	4	·	2	·	·	1	1	1	4	9	·	6	·	1	·	29
Rim Form																
Folded	1	·	2	·	·	·	·	·	5	1	·	·	·	·	3	12
Thickened	·	·	·	·	·	·	·	·	·	·	·	·	·	·	1	1
Unmodified	·	·	·	·	·	1	·	6	1	10	·	·	·	·	1	19
Lip Form																
Flat	1	·	2	·	·	1	·	6	6	7	·	·	·	·	4	27
Rounded	·	·	·	·	·	·	·	·	·	4	·	·	·	·	3	7

F, Fine; *M*, medium; *C*, coarse; *In*, inclusions.

plicated stamped (35.5 percent), burnished (10.4 percent), plain/smooth (28.6 percent), and cob impressed (9.6 percent). Fifteen sherds (3.1 percent) exhibit the late large rectilinear and curvilinear complicated-stamped designs (see Plate 33 to compare "early" and "late" curvilinear-complicated stamped designs). Check-stamped (n = 1), net-impressed (n = 1), and brushed (n = 6) exterior surfaces also occur.

Cord marking is relatively common (10.0 percent) and these sherds stand out as unlike most cord-marked sherds seen in the collections. These sherds (also found at 31MK5 and at the Shuford site) are hard and thin and feature even impressions of extremely fine (1 mm or less) S-twist cords

Plate 33. Cowans Ford Complicated Stamped vessel fragments from the Belk Farm site. *Left,* "Early" curvilinear design; *right,* "late" curvilinear design.

across the vessel. The cords, wrapped on a paddle, were always applied in parallel lines 1 to 2 mm apart. There is occasional cross-stamping or diagonal stamping, but it is always evenly and neatly applied. Vessel interiors are smoothed or burnished: complicated-stamped, burnished, and cob-impressed sherds are usually burnished whereas plain sherds are usually smoothed. Rim forms show a variety of everted-rim jars as well as carinated bowls, and a large percentage (41.9 percent; n = 13) of rims are folded or thickened.

The preponderance of Cowans Ford ceramics argues for a fifteenth- to sixteenth-century date for the Belk Farm assemblage. However, the historic European artifacts support a later date, ca. 1680–1710. Despite the range differences, I suggest that no discrepancy exists. The Cowans Ford ceramics are dated only by similarities with the Burke series. Burke series ceramics are associated with fifteenth- to seventeenth-century radiocarbon dates, middle to late sixteenth-century Spanish ceramics at the Berry site, and metal artifacts of possible sixteenth- to seventeenth-century dates at the Nelson Mound. We cannot be sure when production of Burke ceramics ceases, but, obviously, Cowans Ford ceramics are produced into the early eighteenth century at least at the Belk Farm site. Keel (1990:16) suggests that the site was not occupied until the early seventeenth century, and while an early seventeenth-century occupation cannot be ruled out, an early eighteenth-century occupation seems certain.

Wilson (1983:472–473) analyzed only a small sample of pottery from the Belk Farm site and noted that it was difficult to document changes in ceramic attributes in the Catawba valley as thoroughly as had been done for the Dan River region. However, he felt that a comparison of the Belk Farm assemblage with the Low site assemblage showed the following:

> Overt Pee Dee influences noted . . . from 31ID41 [sic; should be 31ID31] [disappear] by the Historic period . . . Lasting Pee Dee influences can be seen in the presence of burnished and complicated stamped surface finishes, and, by inference, hemispherical and cazuela bowl forms . . . Rim folds, not present at 31ID41 [sic], replace applique strip decorations as a rim treatment in [the Belk Farm assemblage] [Wilson 1983:472–473].

Although my analysis of the entire collections from 31ID31 and 31MK85 generally confirmed Wilson's observations of attribute frequencies, my interpretation of the assemblages is somewhat different. As argued earlier, I believe that the Low site assemblage reflects an "in situ" Catawba valley ceramic tradition (albeit a form of Lamar ceramics), rather than the influence of Pee Dee ceramics. However, I agree that the Belk Farm assemblage is later than the Low site assemblage, based on the rim forms (folded rims as opposed to appliqued or thickened rims at the Low site) and on the obvious presence of European artifacts.

Summary

Pottery from middle and lower Catawba valley archaeological sites includes relatively small quantities of Middle and Late Woodland types and much larger quantities of late prehistoric and early historic period Cowans Ford ceramics. In addition, many sites feature sand-, grit-, quartz-, and granite-tempered sherds with plain, cord-marked, net-impressed, and brushed exterior surfaces. I have made no attempt to identify these by type, but suggest they represent local Catawba valley ceramics of the late Prehistoric period ca. A.D. 1000–1300. They may also reflect influence by potters of the north-central Piedmont Dan River phase.

Cowans Ford Complicated Stamped, Burnished, and Plain/Smoothed are nearly identical to their upper valley Burke counterparts except for the unique soapstone temper of the Burke series. In fact, small quantities of Burke ceramics are found associated with Cowans Ford ceramics throughout the middle valley region. However, Cowans Ford Corncob Impressed has no real correlate in the Burke series, and the presence of this type is believed to reflect interaction with the Dan River series with its common usage of cob impressing.

Also, there is a much greater frequency of the large, "exploded" complicated-stamped designs among Cowans Ford assemblages. These designs do occur in Burke assemblages, but they are rare, and they are usually associated with wide punctated or notched appliqued rims. These ceramics are thought to postdate the early sixteenth century and it is possible that they may ultimately warrant their own type distinctions with better contextual support.

In any event, Cowans Ford ceramics are associated with seventeenth-century European trade materials at the Belk Farm site, making it clear that the complicated stamping tradition lasts that late in the lower Catawba valley at least.

The Belk Farm site is believed to represent a historic Catawba Indian occupation and as such represents the only link joining a prehistoric ceramic tradition now documented for the entire Catawba valley with ceramics used by the historic Catawba peoples. However, it must be stressed that the ethnic identification is based solely on the proximity of the Belk Farm site to the documented early eighteenth-century Catawba villages located farther south on the river.

Late eighteenth- to twentieth-century Catawba pottery making has been documented by Baker (1972b), Fewkes (1944), and Harrington (1908). These sources emphasize that this late Catawba pottery comprises a hard, burnished ware. It now seems likely that this is a tradition of several centuries' duration, its antecedents being Burke and Cowans Ford Burnished pottery made as early as the fourteenth century.

Caution is still warranted, however, when making the link between Cowans Ford and Burke ceramics and the historic period Catawba peoples. Of all the citations pointing to the similarity of Burke ceramics (Boyd 1986a; Coe 1983; Keel 1976; Ward 1977) or of the Hardins or Belk Farm ceramics (Keel 1990) with protohistoric Catawba ceramics, none actually states where the link is demonstrated. Fewkes (1944) makes the most explicit statements after viewing materials at the University of North Carolina identified as having come from historic Catawba sites. He says, "The sherds show close resemblance to the modern ware in forms, surface finish, color, the *flat* bottom, and construction technique" (Fewkes 1944:108; italics in original).

Yet, even Fewkes (1944:71) writes:

The recent archaeological fieldwork of the University of North Carolina, under the direction of Joffre L. Coe, has helped to identify several historic sites. Among them are early eighteenth century locations, long since abandoned, which reliable sources ascribe to the

Catawba. The pottery found at such sites includes mottled polished ware which in construction, surfacing, and firing closely resembles the modern Catawba product.

The sites to which Fewkes refers are unknown, but it is possible that Coe conducted surface collections at several York County, South Carolina, sites and used these as the basis for the comparisons (R. P. Steven Davis, Jr., personal communication 1996).

Clearly, formal comprehensive analysis of pottery from well-documented eighteenth-century Catawba towns will ease the dilemma we currently face in understanding the possible relationship between protohistoric period Catawba valley pottery and historic period pottery associated with Catawba peoples. Ongoing investigations in York and Lancaster counties, South Carolina, appear to hold great potential to contribute to a resolution. The Spratt's Bottom site (38YK3) is named for Thomas Spratt, who according to legend became the first legal tenant of the Catawba Nation in 1761 (Merrell 1989:209). The site is located on the Catawba River just outside Rock Hill, South Carolina. Archaeological investigations of the Spratt's Bottom site from 1991 to 1993 have yielded radiocarbon dates and a preliminary ceramic analysis (May and Tippett 2000).

Testing was conducted in northern and southern portions of the site and more than 1,500 potsherds were recovered for analysis. Most of the pottery was recovered from plow zone and feature contexts in the northern portion of the site; less than 10 percent of the pottery was recovered from the southern portion. Two radiocarbon dates were obtained from features in the northern site portion: the first is an uncorrected ninth-century A.D. date and the second is an uncorrected twelfth-century A.D. date (May and Tippett 2000:12). The southern portion of the site is dated to the eighteenth century on the basis of the presence of several hundred glass beads, kaolin pipe stem fragments, and metal fragments including a pistol or rifle trigger piece. The beads consist primarily of small white, black, and blue drawn beads similar to Kidd and Kidd's (1970) Type IIA2 beads. Also present are black- or brown-bodied beads with multiple white stripes similar to Type IIB1 (Kidd and Kidd 1970) and several "Cornaline D'Alleppo" beads. The bead assemblage likely dates from A.D. 1670–1760 (May and Tippett 2000:13). An analysis of more than 39 pipe stem fragments yielded an age range from A.D. 1710–1750 with individual fragments that probably date to ca. A.D. 1680 and after 1758.

Pottery from the two site areas is similar and includes sherds with plain smoothed, burnished, brushed, incised, cord-marked, and complicated-stamped exterior surface treatments. Interestingly, plain and burnished exterior surfaces account for 39 percent of the assemblage from the southern portion of the site and 26 percent of the assemblage from the northern portion. May and Tippett (2000:15–16) note that high percentages of plain and burnished pottery were also present at the Crowders Creek and Hardins II sites and that these traits were present in North Carolina's lower Catawba valley in the late Prehistoric period. Indeed, we have seen above that the Catawba valley plain and burnished vessel tradition may have begun as early as the fourteenth century A.D.

The Spratt's Bottom site cannot be correlated with any specific eighteenth-century town location, nor can it be determined what specific group or groups, whether Catawbas, Esaws, Cheraws, Sugarees, or others, may be represented at this site. However, this investigation is extremely significant since it provides the first glimpse of ceramics and other artifacts from an archaeological site that is located in the heart of the area associated with early- to mid-eighteenth-century Catawba Indians. Continued investigations at Spratt's Bottom and other sites within the traditional Catawba Reservation lands will be essential to locate historically documented towns and more clearly define the characteristics of eighteenth-century pottery produced by peoples of the Catawba confederacy.

The next chapter summarizes the Catawba valley ceramic patterns described in this and the previous chapters to develop a preliminary chronology of the late prehistoric and early historic Catawba valley.

Late Prehistoric and Early Historic Period Catawba Valley Chronology

5

The preceding chapters have demonstrated that the sand- or soapstone-tempered, complicated-stamped, plain, and burnished pottery of the upper Catawba River valley are, in fact, representative of the late prehistoric and protohistoric pottery of the entire Catawba valley and the extreme upper Yadkin River valley in North Carolina. The Catawba valley ceramic assemblages are quite distinct from most North Carolina Piedmont ceramics and are more similar to Lamar and Pee Dee ceramics to the south and Qualla ceramics to the west. While these affinities have been noted before (Coe 1952a; Keeler 1971; Wilson 1983), there has been no attempt to create an integrated regional chronology for the Catawba valley based on the ceramics or other data.

This chapter describes the preliminary chronology for the late Prehistoric and early Historic periods in the Catawba valley and western Piedmont. The chronology is based on the ceramic analysis presented in the preceding chapters, radiocarbon dates, and the occurrence of temporally diagnostic artifacts. In this chapter I first consider other regional chronologies and then review the radiocarbon dates associated with Burke and Cowans Ford ceramics. Finally, the Catawba valley chronology is presented and discussed with respect to the model of Catawba ethnogenesis outlined at the conclusion of chapter 1.

Because of the overwhelming preponderance of the Burke and Cowans Ford ceramics throughout the region, this chronology is developed within the framework of other Lamar phase chronologies (Williams and Shapiro 1990). However, as the preceding chapters have shown, we are still limited in our ability to define or date archaeological phases in the Catawba valley. A few small excavations provide a minimum of information about site structure and material culture. Ceramics from surface collections still make up the largest quantity of data for the region.

Keeping in mind potential problems arising from the use of surface collections as temporal units (Phillips 1970:3–4), I do not intend to establish narrow temporal phase limits. Further refinement of the chronology will require additional excavations to provide radiocarbon dates and to define more temporally diagnostic ceramic assemblages, as well as to detail other aspects of material culture and settlement systems. However, comparisons of other regional chronologies, combined with the small but increasing numbers of radiocarbon dates for the late Prehistoric period, make it possible to date the Catawba valley ceramics more reliably than in the past and provide the first step to establishing a useful regional cultural chronology.

North Carolina Piedmont Phases

It should be clear from chapters 2, 3, and 4 that the Catawba valley ceramics are quite distinct from the ceramics generally found on the central North Carolina Piedmont. While it appears that during the Woodland period small quantities of Piedmont types such as Badin, Yadkin, and Uwharrie were present, such is not the case for the late Prehistoric and Historic periods. During these periods the Catawba valley pottery tradition was quite distinct from that of the well-known Piedmont Siouan tradition.

Therefore, the regional chronologies established for the central Piedmont (Coe 1964; Coe and Lewis 1952; Davis and Ward 1991; Ward 1983; Ward and Davis 1993; Wilson 1983) are not useful guides to framing the Catawba valley chronology. Similarly, the central Yadkin valley ceramic tradition is firmly a part of the greater Yadkin-Uwharrie-Dan River continuum (Marshall 1988:1). However, before leaving any consideration of the Piedmont ceramics, it is important to look at some of the ways in which Catawba valley ceramics have been viewed and compared with the general Piedmont pattern in the late Prehistoric period (Dan River phase) and the Historic period.

The Dan River pottery series is characterized by sand-tempered, net-impressed pottery. Plain surface treatments are also common and cob-impressed decoration is an important minority type (Coe and Lewis 1952: 1–4). The series was first defined as "the ceramic complex of the Sara Indians in the Dan River area along the Virginia–North Carolina boundary between 1625–1675" (Coe and Lewis 1952:1). Extensive work on the Siouan Project has led researchers to place the Dan River phase several centuries earlier, ca. A.D. 1000–1450 (Ward and Davis 1993:418–419, 1999: 105–106).

Dan River Net Impressed sherds occur in very small numbers in the Catawba valley. Net impressing does occur throughout the valley, however, and I feel that its presence reflects a minor Dan River influence in this area between A.D. 1200 and A.D. 1400. Similarly, Dan River Corncob Impressed, Plain, and Cord Marked sherds occur in small numbers. However, it should be remembered that all three of these surface treatments occur within the Burke and Cowans Ford series.

Wilson (1983:315) states very clearly that late prehistoric period Catawba River ceramics are markedly different from those of the Dan River region. He also attributes a wide range of ceramic attributes in the two areas to influences from the Pee Dee culture. Although Wilson's observations were based only on an analysis of pottery from 31ID31, this study has fully confirmed his evaluation of the respective ceramic traditions. However, his interpretation of cultural influences will be discussed more fully below.

Wilson (1983:490) observes a closer similarity between the two areas in the Protohistoric period. He describes the Oldtown series as the "end-product of the changes within the ceramics of the Dan River Ware from the Protohistoric period through the late 1600s." By the time of the late Protohistoric and early Historic periods, complicated incised decorations are common within the Oldtown series and there is an increase in non-fingertip punctations as decoration, as well as the appearance of cazuela and hemisphere bowl vessel forms.

Davis and Ward (1989:11–15, 1991; also Ward and Davis 1993:418–426) present further refinements of the Piedmont chronology (Ward and Davis 1993:408). They date the Dan River phase to A.D. 1000–1450. This is followed by the protohistoric and historic Saratown phase. The Saratown phase is divided into three subphases (Ward and Davis 1993:419–426): Early Saratown (A.D. 1450–1620), Middle Saratown (A.D. 1620–1670), and Late Saratown (A.D. 1670–1710).

Early Saratown phase pottery is characterized by the Oldtown series (Wilson 1983:386–413). Early Saratown phase ceramic vessel assemblages from the William Kluttz and the Early Upper Saratown sites are primarily smoothed or burnished, with net impressed also well represented (Ward and Davis 1993:421). Simple-stamped and complicated-stamped exterior surface treatments are also present. Ward and Davis (1993:421) also re-mark on the change in vessel forms with the appearance of cazuela and hemispherical bowls:

> Both of these are new vessel forms within the Dan River drainage and, along with the presence of burnishing, carved-paddle stamping, and new decorative techniques employing fillet applique strips, reflect an introduction of new pottery styles, probably from the Catawba drainage to the south. The fact that net impressing continued to be a predominant method of surface treatment suggests that these new styles blended with the indigenous Dan River pottery-making tradi-tion to form the Oldtown series.

The late prehistoric chronology for the Eno, Flat, and Haw river drain-ages is summarized from Ward and Davis (1993:407–416). The late pre-historic Haw River phase dates to A.D. 1000–1400. The pottery of the early

Haw River phase is viewed as a late form of the Uwharrie series, whereas later Haw River phase pottery is characterized by the Haw River series (Ward and Davis 1993:408).

The succeeding Hillsboro phase is dated to A.D. 1400–1600. Hillsboro ceramics include smoothed bowls, simple-stamped jars, and checked-stamped jars, along with new cazuela bowl and carinated jar vessel forms.

The Historic period is represented by the Mitchum (A.D. 1600–1670), Jenrette (A.D. 1600–1680), and Fredricks (A.D. 1680–1710) phases. These phases are attributed to the historic Sissipahaw, Shakori, and Occaneechi Indians, respectively (Davis and Ward 1991:44–45).

Fredricks phase pottery from the Fredricks site is generally tempered with sand or fine crushed feldspar. Exterior surface treatments include check stamped, plain, and brushed (Davis 1987:214). Mitchum phase pottery from the Mitchum site is similar, with sand or fine crushed feldspar temper and plain, simple-stamped, or brushed exterior surfaces (Davis 1987:214).

The late prehistoric and early historic period Catawba valley ceramics represent a tradition unlike the general North Carolina Siouan ceramics of those periods. However, it is likely that the north-central Piedmont region is influenced by the Catawba valley ceramic tradition as seen in the Oldtown and Hillsboro series. Therefore, the existing Piedmont chronologies are of little direct use in establishing more chronological refinement for the Catawba region. In fact, the converse has already occurred. Ceramic attributes ascribed to the Catawba valley directly (Davis 1987; Davis and Ward 1991) or to the Pee Dee via the Catawba valley (Wilson 1983)—i.e., folded rims, complicated stamping, and plain and burnished and incised cazuela bowls—have been used as protohistoric markers within the general Piedmont Siouan chronology. Today, the chronology established by Ward and Davis (1993) confirms the relative temporal relationship of the Catawba patterns. However, though the Piedmont chronologies have become increasingly sophisticated, and show quite clearly the regional influence from the Catawba, they are of little utility in establishing firm chronologies within the Catawba valley itself. Therefore, I turn next to a discussion of regional Lamar phases.

Lamar Phases

We have seen that, traditionally, the Catawba valley wares have been compared with Lamar ceramics found to the south. Therefore, in order to make more useful chronological comparisons, Lamar ceramics are discussed below in the context of regional chronologies from Georgia, the Appalachian Summit region, the Pee Dee River valley, the Savannah River valley, and the Wateree River valley.

The term *Lamar* is derived from the Lamar site in Macon, Georgia. Hally's (1994:144–151) recent overview of Lamar culture provides a comprehensive review of the history of Lamar studies, the Lamar pottery complex, and regional Lamar ceramic variation and chronologies. Hally summarizes the temporally diagnostic features of the pottery complex as follows:

> Lamar Complicated Stamped, with its distinctive thickened and pinched/punctated rim, appears in the archaeological record during the latter half of the 14th century. Lamar Incised does not appear for another 100 years, but with relatively few exceptions the two types co-occur throughout the area . . . into the seventeenth century. Plain-surfaced pottery is also common . . . and along with Lamar Complicated Stamped and Lamar Incised is one of the three basic types constituting the Lamar pottery complex [Hally 1994:145].

Hally also reviews temporal phase distinctions based on temporally diagnostic ceramic attributes. These include "the presence/absence of Lamar Incised; changes in the motifs characteristic of Lamar Incised; stylistic changes in the way these motifs are portrayed; changes in the motifs characteristic of Lamar Complicated Stamped; and changes in the form of thickened jar rims" (Hally 1994:147). According to Hally (1994:147), these changes "occur in the same relative order and are roughly contemporaneous throughout the Lamar area" (Anderson et al. 1986; DePratter and Judge 1990; Hally 1979; Hally and Rudolph 1986; Rudolph 1986; Smith 1981; Williams 1984; Williams and Shapiro 1990).

The following summary of ceramic attributes from the Early Lamar (A.D. 1350–1450), Middle Lamar (A.D. 1450–1550), and Late Lamar (A.D. 1550–1800) phases is based on Hally's (1994) overview and the multi-authored chapter "Phase Characteristics" in Williams and Shapiro (1990). The characteristics are presented in some detail since few chronologies have made their ceramic attributes so explicit. It will be clear that there is a great correspondence with Catawba valley ceramic attributes. Table 21 provides detailed ceramic characteristics for selected Lamar phases.

Hally (1994:147) characterizes Early, Middle, and Late Lamar ceramics as follows:

> Early Lamar pottery is best known from the Rembert, Duvall, Little Egypt, and Irene phases. Lamar Incised is absent or very uncommon and is characterized by a limited number of simple designs executed in two or three broad lines. Complicated stamping is fairly well executed although motifs may be difficult to identify. Filfot cross, figure-9, and figure-8 are common motifs. Temper is fine and uniform in size. Jar rims are decorated with either large individually molded

Table 21. Ceramic attributes for selected early, middle, and late Lamar phases

---

Rembert phase A.D. 1300-1450 Upper Savannah River

1. Lamar Complicated Stamped accounts for 50 percent. Motifs include concentric circles, figure eights, figure nines, filfot cross, line block.

2. Lamar Incised accounts for less than 1 percent. Motifs include simple broad line designs with two or three parallel lines encircling bowl rims, with pendant festoons and loops.

3. Lamar Plain accounts for 34 percent; Lamar Burnished Plain accounts for 8 percent and Lamar Coarse Plain accounts for 6 percent.

4. Minority surface treatments (1 percent each) include check stamping, cob impressing, and cord marking.

5. Jar rims are (a) unmodified and decorated by cane punctations or rosettes, and (b) thickened and decorated with punches, notches, or cane punctations.

Little Egypt phase A.D. 1400-1500 Upper Coosa River

1. Lamar Complicated Stamped accounts for 10 percent. Motifs include filfot cross, concentric circles, figure eights, and nested rectangles. Rectilinear motifs are slightly more common than curvilinear motifs.

2. Lamar Incised accounts for less than 1 percent. Motifs include simple broad line designs with two or three parallel lines encircling bowl rims, interrupted by pendant festoons and loops.

3. Narrow forms of folded and pinched rims are present.

4. Simple stamping is present.

Tugalo phase A.D. 1450-1600 Upper Savannah River

1. Lamar Complicated Stamped accounts for 62 percent. Motifs are difficult to identify but include concentric circles and figure-nine.

2. Lamar Incised accounts for 8 percent. Motifs have more than two or three lines and include concentric circles, ovals with brackets, and line-filled triangles.

3. Lamar Plain accounts for 12 percent. Lamar Coarse Plain accounts for 16 percent. Lamar Burnished Plain accounts for 1 percent.

4. Rims of jars are thickened and decorated with pinches, notches, and cane punctations at the bottom of the rim.

Estatoe phase A.D. 1650-1750 Upper Savannah River

1. Lamar Complicated Stamped accounts for 68 percent. Motifs difficult to identify but include concentric crosses, line block, concentric circles, figure nine, keyhole.

2. Lamar Incised accounts for 4 percent. Check stamping accounts for 6 percent. Lamar Plain accounts for 11 percent. Lamar Coarse Plain accounts for 7 percent. Lamar Burnished Plain accounts for 4 percent.

Note: All attributes selected from Hally 1990:43, 53-54, with minor changes.

nodes or narrow thickened strips that are notched, punctated, or pinched.

Middle Lamar pottery is best known from the Barnett, Dyer, Tugalo, and Cowerts phases. Lamar Incised is common and characterized by a greater variety of more complex designs that are carried out with narrower lines and a greater number of lines. Temper particles are large and often protrude through the vessel surface. Complicated stamping is generally poorly executed. Motifs are large, overstamped, and frequently lightly impressed. Jar rims are usually thickened by the addition of a strip or by folding. The width of the thickened rim is greater and modification is predominately pinching along the lower edge of the rim.

Late Lamar pottery is best known from the Bell, Ocmulgee Fields, Estatoe, and Atasi phases. Incising is present in most phases with lines continuing to decrease in width and increase in number. Incising disappears, however, in the Appalachian portion of North and South Carolina, Piedmont South Carolina, and northern Georgia. Complicated stamping continues in most phases but is replaced by brushing in the lower Chattahoochee, Coosa, and Tallapoosa drainages. Check stamping becomes common in the Appalachian portion of North and South Carolina, Piedmont South Carolina, and northern Georgia. Thickened jar rims continue to increase in width, and new forms— rolled, "L"-shaped, and filleted strip—appear in the Appalachian area [Hally 1986].

The Catawba valley assemblages (Burke and Cowans Ford types) include many of the attributes described for Early Lamar phases. Complicated stamping is common and sherds with this surface treatment often occur in large numbers. In general, the filfot cross, figure eight, and figure nine are relatively infrequent and, in contrast to the Little Egypt phase, rectilinear designs are usually uncommon. Lamar style incising with two to four lines occurs on less than one percent of Burke and Cowans Ford Plain/Smoothed and Burnished sherds at numerous sites. Also, plain and burnished surfaces account for large portions of most assemblages. Finally, many sites include narrow to medium width (10–15 mm) folded or thickened jar rims.

However, the Catawba valley assemblages bear even more similarities with the Middle Lamar phases, especially the Tugalo phase. Burke Complicated Stamped accounts for as much as 50 to 60 percent of the assemblage on most of the sites where it occurs in large numbers and Cowans Ford Complicated Stamped accounts for 40 to 50 percent at many sites. In both cases, curvilinear designs far outnumber rectilinear, and many of the motifs have large elements. Lamar style incising occurs at numerous sites, accounting for 2 to 6 percent of the assemblage. However, designs are limited to the loops and brackets and although they occur with four to nine lines, these are less common than two- or three-line designs. Also, numerous examples of the wide (17–20 mm) folded/thickened jar rims occur.

Finally, Catawba valley assemblages have less in common with Late Lamar phases such as Estatoe. It is possible to identify late ceramic attributes such as very wide folded rims and concentric-cross complicated stamps, but these are rare. Also, the highly complex, many-lined, incised designs from phases like Bell (Smith and Williams 1990:61–62), Cowerts, and Ocmulgee Fields (Williams 1990:64) are absent. It is also significant that Appalachian-region attributes such as check stamping and the L-shaped or filleted rim are very rare.

While there is a close similarity of Burke and Cowans Ford ceramics to general Lamar characteristics, these similarities are strikingly close for the Middle Lamar Tugalo phase. It is important now to compare the Burke and Cowans Ford types with regional Lamar pottery that is closer to the Catawba Valley; i.e., the Wateree, Pee Dee, and Appalachian Summit areas.

Wateree River

Because the Wateree River phases were established on the same river system just to the south of the study area, I initially expected to find considerable similarities between the Wateree ceramics and those upriver on the Catawba. This expectation was also predicated on the developing models of the geographical expanse of the chiefdom of Cofitachequi. In fact, there was less similarity between these areas than there was for the Tugalo phase pottery. The dissimilarity is clear in the following examination of the Wateree ceramic chronology (Table 22). The chronology is summarized from DePratter and Judge (1990).

I must repeat the caution that the Catawba River assemblages are primarily surface collections and I assume them to represent mixed temporal periods; hence the concentration on attributes rather than assemblage frequencies. The Wateree chronology is also based primarily on surface collections, and for this reason I think it is likely that the phase characteristics and temporal boundaries will be altered as more pottery from excavated sites is analyzed.

Burke and Cowans Ford assemblages are similar to the Wateree valley assemblages in the overall presence of complicated-stamped and plain exterior surfaces as well as the presence of Lamar style incising. However, the details of the distributions of attributes make the Wateree chronology of surprisingly little utility upriver on the Catawba. This appears to be true for two basic reasons. First, the upper and middle Catawba valley assemblages contain very little rectilinear (including Etowah related styles) complicated-stamped pottery such as the line block common to the Adamson and Town Creek phases. The filfot cross is also much less prevalent on the Catawba. Second, the segmented appliqued strips that figure so prominently in the Wateree chronology are virtually absent from the Catawba; punctated appliqued strips occur, but in much smaller numbers.

Interestingly, the attributes that are most similar are those listed for the Daniels phase (A.D. 1550–1675). Though such sherds are few in number, wide thickened rims, thick vessel walls, and "exploded" stamping are present, especially in the middle and lower Catawba valley. These are believed to represent late attributes and their presence on the Wateree and the lower to middle Catawba may be related to the presence of protohistoric Catawba Indians (or Catawba related; see chapter 6). These attributes are noticeably present at 31MK85, 31LN19, and 31ID51.

To summarize, the Wateree chronology shows some similarity with the

Table 22. Ceramic attributes for Wateree valley phases

Belmont Neck phase A.D. 1200–1250 (Etowah)
1. Complicated stamped accounts for 43 percent. Motifs mostly concentric circles and undefined concentric curvilinear forms; Etowah cross-bar diamond present but rare.
2. Incising is absent.
3. Plain accounts for 31 percent; Burnished plain accounts for 9 percent.
4. Simple rims account for 86 percent.
5. Notched rims account for 7 percent.

Adamson phase A.D. 1250–1300 (Savannah)
1. Complicated stamped accounts for 23 percent; motifs are primarily filfot cross and line block.
2. Plain accounts for 45 percent; Burnished plain accounts for 14 percent.
3. Rim forms include simple (53 percent), notched (13 percent), punctations below lip (13 percent), and rosettes (3 percent).

Town Creek phase A.D. 1300–1350 (Lamar)
1. Complicated stamped accounts for 30 percent; motifs are mostly filfot cross and line block.
2. Plain accounts for 30 percent; Burnished plain accounts for 19 percent.
3. Rim forms include simple (43 percent), segmented applique strips (17 percent), punctated applique strips (13 percent), rosettes (8 percent), and nodes (4.5 percent).

McDowell phase A.D. 1350–1450 (Lamar)
1. Complicated stamping accounts for 45 percent; filfot cross predominates; stamping is bolder and motifs larger.

Mulberry phase A.D. 1450–1550 (Lamar)
1. Complicated stamping is present.
2. Lamar-like incising is present.
3. Segmented or punctated applique strips are present.
4. Vertical ticks present on vessel shoulders.

Daniels phase A.D. 1550–1675 (Lamar)
1. Sloppy "exploded" stamping present.
2. Wide applique rim strips.
3. Thick vessel walls are present.

Note: All attributes selected from DePratter and Judge 1990:56–58, with minor changes.

Catawba assemblages, but except for the late Daniels phase it offers little that is helpful for establishing or confirming the Catawba sequence.

Pee Dee Phases

The Pee Dee culture was one of the first protohistoric archaeological cultures described in the North Carolina Piedmont (Coe 1952a:308–309). It has been viewed traditionally as an intrusive culture that established itself in the Pee Dee valley in the early Protohistoric period. However, recent research at the Leak (31RH1) and Teal (31AN1) sites provided an abundance of new radiocarbon dates for a more developed chronology (Oliver 1992).

The Town Creek Pee Dee pottery was originally thought to date to the Protohistoric period ca. A.D. 1550–1650 (Coe 1952b). Reid (1967) expanded the chronology to A.D. 1450–1650. Dickens (1976:198) provides four radiocarbon dates from Town Creek ranging from the twelfth to fifteenth centuries A.D., suggesting a longer, and earlier, lifespan for Pee Dee culture.

In fact, Mountjoy (1989:15–19) suggested even earlier temporal contexts for Pee Dee ceramics. He cites three eleventh- and twelfth-century dates from the Payne site. The two earlier dates (A.D. 1040 ± 60 and A.D. 1090 ± 70) were obtained from features that included Pee Dee and Uwharrie pottery. The later date (A.D. 1130 ± 70) was obtained from a feature that contained a few pieces of pottery thought to postdate Pee Dee.

In his discussion of the Town Creek dates, Mountjoy (1989:18) states:

It appears significant that the earliest radiocarbon date from Town Creek comes from premound humus and that this humus layer contained a higher frequency of Pee Dee complicated stamp pottery than the overlying deposits formed by mound construction and use (Reid 1967:57). This earliest date from Town Creek overlaps on its early end the two dates on Pee Dee pottery from the Payne site, and raises the possibility that the intrusion of people responsible for the Pee Dee pottery in south central North Carolina occurred in the period A.D. 980–1160. Furthermore, it also is possible that this intrusion was not accomplished by first establishing a political and religious center at Town Creek and radiating out from that base. Instead, there may have been an initial population expansion into south central North Carolina and then 100 years or so later the Town Creek site was turned into a ceremonial center to serve an already fairly large resident population.

Mountjoy's interpretation of Pee Dee origins appears to be compatible with the idea discussed in the previous chapter that Pee Dee culture and Catawba Valley Mississippian culture expanded into the Piedmont of North Carolina in unison.

DePratter and Judge (1990) have also presented a slightly modified view of Pee Dee chronology. Their work on the Wateree valley ceramics confirms the similarity of Pee Dee material to other Lamar ceramics in the Wateree valley. However, they tend to date this material in the Savannah culture Adamson phase (A.D. 1250–1300) and the Lamar culture Town Creek phase (A.D. 1300–1350). These dates seem consistent with those of Mountjoy and place the Pee Dee ceramics within the general Lamar chronology (Williams and Shapiro 1990).

Finally, Oliver (1992) has proposed further changes in the Pee Dee chronology. His model is consistent with both Mountjoy's and DePratter and Judge's interpretations, as it affirms a much earlier date for the origins of Pee Dee culture. Oliver (1992:240) defines the Teal phase (A.D. 950–1200) as "a time of exploration, frontier settlement, and developing ceremonialism by early Pee Dee, or perhaps 'pre-Pee Dee,' populations. These people, and their associated culture, represented the northernmost extension of an expanding chiefdom that traced its roots through coastal South Carolina and Georgia."

Teal phase pottery includes complicated-stamped, plain, fine cordmarked, and simple-stamped vessels (Oliver 1992:240). The Town Creek phase (A.D. 1200–1400) evolved from the Teal phase and is characterized by plain pottery, filfot cross complicated-stamped pottery, and textile-impressed pottery (Oliver 1992:247). The Leak phase (A.D. 1400–1600) is characterized by complicated stamping, plain finishes, filfot cross decoration, and textile-impressed pottery (Oliver 1992:145).

Previous researchers have cited the influence of Pee Dee ceramics on the late prehistoric ceramics of the Dan, Yadkin, and Catawba river valleys (Wilson 1983). For the Catawba valley, at least, I believe that influence was minimal and, as Ward and Davis (1993) suggest, it is more likely that Lamar style ceramic attributes appear in the north-central Piedmont as a result of influence from the Catawba valley as opposed to the Pee Dee region.

Reid's (1967) original statement on Pee Dee pottery from the Town Creek site mound was the first comprehensive description for Pee Dee pottery in North Carolina. In general, Reid (1967:3) observed that the Town Creek ceramic assemblage included 71 percent complicated-stamped pottery. Although complete designs are difficult to define, he provided the following percentages (of total sample) of identifiable complicated-stamp designs (Reid 1967:4–6): concentric circles, 6.7 percent; filfot cross, 5.6 percent; herringbone, 2.0 percent; quartered circles, 1.8 percent; arc-angle (unique to Pee Dee), 1.6 percent; split diamond, .5 percent; and line block, .1 percent. Oliver (1992) observed some change from these overall distributions with respect to the frequencies at the Leak and Teal sites.

These figures show little similarity with the Catawba valley complicated-stamped patterns, which tend to be large concentric circles joined by angled and straight lines. Filfot cross and scroll designs are present in small numbers, but the remaining patterns are absent in the Catawba assemblages. Perhaps most significantly, incised cazuela bowls are not present in the Pee Dee pottery. One similarity in complicated-stamped designs between the two regions is illustrated in a photograph of a sherd labeled as "undefined curvilinear stamp" (Reid 1967:plate V), but the frequency of this design is unknown. Finally, Reid (1967:4) notes the Pee Dee complicated-stamped sherds rarely show the impression of wood grain, a characteristic he says is common in the Qualla ceramics in the mountains. This is also common among Burke and Cowans Ford ceramics and may be another temporal indicator of later ceramics.

Appalachian Summit Phases

The final region to be examined is the southern Appalachian Mountains. The late prehistoric Pisgah phase (A.D. 1000–1550) and historic Qualla phase (A.D. 1550–1800) are well defined in the mountains of western North Carolina (Dickens 1970, 1976; Egloff 1967; Keel 1972, 1976). However, since their formulation there has been little temporal refinement within the phases. As described in the previous chapter, Pisgah ceramics have a prominent but restricted distribution in the upper Catawba valley. On the basis of stylistic characteristics, most of the upper Catawba Pisgah ceramics appear to date to the late Pisgah phase, ca. A.D. 1300–1500 (Dickens 1976:177–178).

The Qualla phase represents the culture of the protohistoric and historic Cherokee Indians and is dated to ca. A.D. 1450–Removal (Dickens 1976:14–15; Keel 1976:214–216). Qualla ceramics are defined by Egloff (1967:34):

> The [Qualla] series possesses the basic attributes of the Lamar style horizon: folded finger impressed rim fillets; large, sloppy, carved stamps, and bold incising. The complicated-stamped motifs illustrating Lamar Complicated Stamped exhibit a greater degree of regularity and symmetrical design than is found on Qualla Complicated Stamped . . . The same holds true with the incised cazuela bowls, though to a lesser degree. Incising accompanied by reed punctations, which is common upon Lamar Bold incised vessels, was absent in the material analyzed. These differences are very striking and have led to the definition of the Qualla Series as a distinctive ceramic complex.

There has been no further published analysis of Qualla ceramics in western North Carolina, but a brief examination of Egloff's summary of Qualla types shows that the major similarity with the Catawba valley assemblages is found in the high frequency of complicated-stamped pottery.

Egloff (1967:35–36, 72) summarizes the Qualla ceramics as follows:

1. Complicated Stamped, smoothed over complicated stamped, and roughened complicated stamped account for 75 percent of total sherds. Most common motifs are concentric loops and circles; some concentric squares, wavy lines, and zigzags.
2. Qualla Plain accounts for 5 percent; never more than 17 percent at any site.
3. Qualla Check Stamped accounts for 3 percent; not more than 5 percent at any site.

4. Qualla Burnished accounts for 1 percent; never more than 6 percent at any site.
5. Qualla Cord Marked accounts for 1 percent.
6. Qualla Corncob Impressed accounts for less than 1 percent (only 9 sherds were identified).
7. Incised sherds accounted for 3 percent.

Egloff's collections were also primarily surface collections and are subject to the same cautions expressed above. In fact, Hally (1994:147) feels that the series encompasses a great period of time: "The Qualla ceramic series, as defined by Egloff (1967) for the Appalachian area almost certainly spans three to four centuries, although most of the pottery Egloff illustrates in his thesis dates to the late Lamar period."

A more recent Qualla phase chronology includes an early, yet unrecognized, Qualla phase ca. A.D. 1000–1450, a Middle Qualla phase from A.D. 1450–1700, and a Late Qualla phase from A.D. 1700–1838 (Ward and Davis 1999:178–183, 267–270).

Middle Qualla phase pottery is characterized by constricted-neck jars often decorated with notched appliqued strips just beneath the rim (Ward and Davis 1999:181). Carinated bowls with a wide variety of incised decorations are also present. The incised designs are thought to be most similar to incised designs found on Tugalo phase Lamar ceramics from north Georgia (Ward and Davis 1999:181). Vessel surfaces are usually stamped and include concentric circle, figure nine, parallel undulating line, chevron, and herringbone designs (Ward and Davis 1999:181). Minority surface treatments include burnishing, check stamping, and cord marking (Ward and Davis 1999:182–183).

Late Qualla phase pottery is described as changing only gradually from Middle Qualla phase pottery (Ward and Davis 1999:267–270). Curvilinear complicated-stamped designs become more popular than rectilinear designs and the stamping becomes somewhat more bold and crude. The frequency of incised decorations and burnished exterior surfaces decreases while that of cord marking and corncob impressing increases (Ward and Davis 1999:267–270).

Qualla pottery closely resembles the Burke pottery series. Middle Qualla phase pottery and Burke pottery are particularly similar to Middle Lamar Tugalo phase ceramics. However, it should also be clear that the specific complicated-stamped designs executed on the respective ceramics vary considerably, as do the relative frequencies of complicated-stamped designs and plain and burnished surface treatments. The Burke and Cowans Ford series are quite dissimilar from the Qualla series with a greater frequency of curvilinear complicated-stamped motifs, a higher frequency of Lamar style incising and plain surface types, and a complete absence of check stamping.

Catawba Valley Phases

I fully expect that continued research will demonstrate that the general course of temporal changes found throughout the Lamar region (Hally 1994) is repeated in the Catawba valley. As Hally also points out, the periods of origin and rates of change may be somewhat different. Nonetheless, it is clear that most of the chronologically diagnostic characteristics of the Burke and Cowans Ford pottery support a middle and late Lamar time frame. However, it is also important that the Catawba valley ceramics be temporally grounded in the Catawba valley. As will be seen in this section, the radiometric data for the Catawba valley and related areas also support a middle and late Lamar time frame for the Burke and Cowans Ford ceramics.

Radiocarbon Dates

Recent investigations have provided 12 radiocarbon dates (Table 23) from four Catawba valley sites: the Berry (31BK22) and McDowell (31MC41) sites in the upper valley and the Crowders Creek (31GS55) and Hardins II (31GS30) sites in the lower valley region. It is unfortunate that no dates are available for middle valley sites; it would be particularly helpful to have additional dates from sites such as 31ID31, 31CT1, 31CT115, and 31LN19. However, there are several additional dates from contexts associated with Burke and other soapstone-tempered pottery that can also provide temporal data for our use. These include dates from 31CW8 (Kimball et al. 1996), 31WK33 (Idol 1995), 31WT22 (Senior 1981; Boyd 1986a), and 40JN89 in upper east Tennessee (Boyd 1986b).

Five radiocarbon dates are directly associated with definite Burke ceramic assemblages. These include two dates from the Berry site (31BK22), two from the Jones site (31WK33), and one from the Broyhill-Dillard site (31CW8). There are also six dates associated with assemblages that include Burke types or related soapstone-tempered sherds. These include two dates from the Ward site (31WT22), one date from 40JN89, two dates from the McDowell site (31MC41), and one from the Tyler-Loughridge site (31MC139).

The two earliest of these are from the nearby McDowell and Tyler-Loughridge sites. It is likely that they represent Pisgah components or components with early Burke pottery. The second date from the McDowell site and the early date from the Ward site overlap at 1 sigma in the fourteenth and fifteenth centuries, whereas the second date from the Ward site and the date from 40JN89 overlap at 1 sigma from the mid–fifteenth century to the early seventeenth century.

Thus it seems clear that there are now solid radiometric data to support a range of production of Burke ceramics from at least as early as the fourteenth century to at least as late as the sixteenth century. The radiometric

Table 23. Calibrated radiocarbon dates for the Catawba valley and other related areas

Site and Context	Sample No.	Uncalibrated Age (years B.P.)	Lower Limits		Calibrated Dates (A.D.) Intercepts	Upper Limits	
			2	1		1	2
Tyler-Loughridge (31MC139), Fea. 102-1	Beta-32927	970+/-70	894	999	1028	1164	1227
McDowell (31MC41), Structure A	Beta-21818	890+/-50	1019	1041	1168	1226	1279
Hardins II (31GS30), Fea. 12c	Beta-23587	860+/-80	1013	1043	1214	1277	1296
Hardins II (31GS30), Fea. 24	Beta-20947	770+/-100	1028	1183	1278	1301	1405
Crowders Creek (31GS55), Fea. 13	Beta-13287	600+/-70	1280	1298	1328, 1333, 1395	1419	1445
Ward (31WT22), Fea. 21	UGa-683	555+/-90	1282	1305	1406	1441	1614
Hardins II (31GS30), Fea. 20	Beta-20946	540+/-60	1298	1322	1410	1438	1472
Crowders Creek (31GS55), Fea. 12	Beta-20945	520+/-70	1299	1329	1421	1446	1613
Berry (31BK22), Fea. 8	Beta-21817	520+/-50	1307	1400	1421	1441	1473
Hardins II (31GS30), Fea. 15	Beta-23089	520+/-80	1294	1323	1421	1448	1623
Berry (31BK22), Fea. 13	Beta-21816	500+/-60	1308	1403	1431	1448	1614
McDowell (31MC41), Fea. 3	GX-11057	460+/-75	1321	1412	1441	1480	1638
Hardins II (31GS30), Fea. 19	Beta-23088	430+/-80	1325	1422	1449	1625	1654
40JN89, Fea. 1 (Boyd 1986b)	GX-10244	350+/-130		1422	1562	1702	
Crowders Creek (31GS55), Smudge Pit	Beta-13917	350+/-50	1438	1461	1516, 1591, 1621	1644	1663
Broyhill Mound (31CW8), Fea. 3	Beta-97657	320+/-70	1440	1475	1535, 1545, 1635	1655	1675
Ward (31WT22), Fea. 21	UGa-684	310+/-165	1306	1436	1638	1954	1955
Jones (31WK33) (Idol 1995)	Beta-84449	510+/-80*					
Jones (31WK33) (Idol 1995)	Beta-84450	400+/-60*					

All dates as reported in Eastman (1994a, 1994b) unless otherwise noted.
*Uncorrected.

Table 24. Chronological framework for the Catawba and upper Yadkin valley in the late Prehistoric and early Historic periods

Region Archaeological Phase	Estimated Time Range	Source of Radiocarbon Date	Calibrated Intercepts (A.D.)
Upper Catawba River			
Pitts phase	**A.D. 1200-1400**	Berry (31BK22), Fea. 8	1421
Burke phase	**A.D. 1400-1600**	Berry (31BK22), Fea. 13	1431
Pleasant Garden phase	**A.D. 1400-1600**	McDowell (31MC41)	1441
Happy Valley phase	**A.D. 1600-1700**	Broyhill Mound (31CW8)	1535, 1545, 1635
Upper Yadkin River			
Burke phase	**A.D. 1400-1600**	Jones (31WK33)	1440*
Elkin phase	**A.D. 1400-1600**	Jones (31WK33)	1550*
Happy Valley phase	**A.D. 1600-1700**	Broyhill Mound (31CW8)	1535, 1545, 1635
Middle Catawba River			
Low phase	**A.D. 1400-1600**		
Iredell phase	**A.D. 1600-1725**		
Lower Catawba River			
Belk Farm phase	**A.D. 1680-1725**		

* Not calibrated.

dates appear to cluster in three groups (Table 23). The first grouping shows that each of the four Catawba valley sites appears to have a component dating from the early to mid–fifteenth century. This includes three dates from 31GS30, both dates from the Berry site, and one date each from the McDowell site and the Crowders Creek site. This would correlate well with the proposed contemporaneity of the Burke and Cowans Ford ceramic series pottery.

One date from 31GS55 is late fifteenth to early seventeenth century (corrected at 1 sigma). Considered at 1 sigma, two additional sites, 31GS30 and 31MC41, range into the sixteenth century. It should be noted that for this date from 31MC41 (GX 11057), Boyd (1986a:67) provides additional corrections of A.D. 1458 and A.D. 1434 ± 75. Finally, two dates from 31GS30, one date from 31GS55, and one date from 31MC41 range from the twelfth to fourteenth centuries. These dates may support the presence of multiple components at the McDowell site, the Hardins site, and the Crowders Creek site. The Berry site dates are extremely close and, when viewed alone, they argue for a single component at the site (although I believe additional work will demonstrate that to be incorrect). I fully expect that future radiocarbon dates will help date additional phases prior to the fourteenth century, just as those reported by Mountjoy (1989) and Oliver (1992) did in the Pee Dee region.

The preceding discussion has reviewed the regional chronologies that are relevant to the Catawba valley assemblages. This chapter concludes with the formulation of preliminary phases for the Catawba valley and the upper Yadkin River valley (Table 24; Figures 11 and 12). These phases have been developed with respect to the occurrence of temporally diagnostic Lamar ceramic attributes from dated contexts when possible, and otherwise

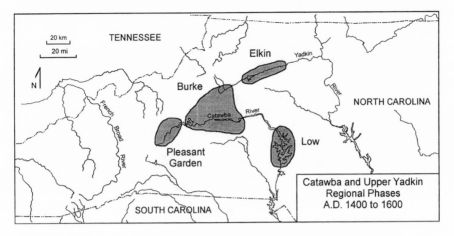

Figure 11. Location of Catawba and Yadkin valley phases, A.D. 1400 to 1600.

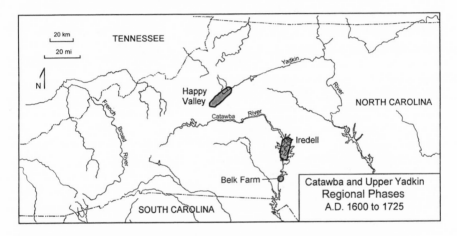

Figure 12. Location of Catawba and Yadkin valley phases, A.D. 1600 to 1725.

the formulation relies on the distribution of temporally significant ceramic attributes and historic European artifacts. It should be made clear that the omission of named phases for earlier periods in the middle and lower valley regions does not imply a lack of occupation. I have only attempted to define phases in those areas that I feel are clearly supported by current data.

Upper Catawba Valley Phases

Pitts Phase

The Pitts phase (A.D. 1200–1400) is named for the Pitts site, 31BK209, and is defined solely on the basis of the ceramic assemblage there. The Pitts site assemblage is predominately plain/smoothed and complicated-stamped Burke series pottery. However, the frequency of curvilinear complicated-stamped motifs is very low, and rectilinear complicated-stamped and Pisgah motifs are relatively well represented. Also, Burke Burnished is present in relatively low numbers and Burke Corncob Impressed is absent. Burke Incised sherds are rare (n = 3); their low frequency does not necessarily support a thirteenth- to fourteenth-century date, but these three sherds also provide the only definite examples of carinated or hemisphere bowls in the assemblage. These vessel forms occur more commonly in the fourteenth century. The lack of carinated vessels here, especially in contrast to their high frequency at the nearby Berry site, argues for an earlier date for the Pitts site assemblage.

It is difficult to identify additional temporal components from the mixed ceramic assemblages available for sites in the Upper Creek drainage; however, I expect that a component will be identified at the Berry site. I suggest that a coeval phase should be established for the extreme upper Catawba valley where Pisgah assemblages predominate (with few McDowell type sherds represented). However, I have not been able to determine how these assemblages are characterized. Future work at sites like the McDowell and Tyler-Loughridge sites should clarify this situation.

Pleasant Garden Phase

The Pleasant Garden phase (A.D. 1400–1600) is named for the early colonial settlement near the McDowell site (31MC41) in McDowell County, and it is defined by the late prehistoric component at the McDowell site. Pleasant Garden phase sites are found on the upper Catawba River in McDowell County. The phase dates are provisional, but are based on the occurrence of Burke, Pisgah, and McDowell ceramics, a calibrated radiocarbon date of A.D. 1441 (Table 23), and a possible fragment of sixteenth-century Spanish chain mail (appendix A). A second calibrated date of A.D. 1168 reflects an earlier Pisgah occupation at the McDowell site.

The Pleasant Garden phase is characterized by the presence of both Pisgah and Burke ceramics and a blending of their respective attributes of surface treatment, temper, and form. The Pisgah pottery is primarily rectilinear complicated stamped and plain with soapstone, grit, and coarse sand temper, and the Burke pottery is primarily curvilinear complicated stamped, plain, and burnished with soapstone and sand temper. Grit-tempered McDowell Complicated Stamped and Burnished pottery also occur.

The Pleasant Garden phase component at the McDowell site consists of a palisaded village with a probable substructure platform mound. At least one Pisgah style structure has been identified as a domestic structure. In addition, a possible public structure has been identified.

Burke Phase

The Burke phase (A.D. 1400–1600) is named for the predominance of Burke series pottery on sites on Upper Creek and Johns River in Burke County and in the Happy Valley area of the upper Yadkin River valley in Caldwell County.

The major known Burke phase component is present at the Berry site (31BK22; appendix B) located on Upper Creek in Burke County. The ceramic assemblage from the Berry site is nearly exclusively Burke series pottery. Two radiocarbon dates from the Berry site provide a solid fifteenth-century site context. However, the ceramic attributes and sixteenth-century Spanish artifacts support a middle to late sixteenth-century occupation as well. The high frequency of curvilinear complicated stamping, carinated bowls with Lamar incising, and medium to wide thickened and punctated jar rims is most similar to Tugalo phase (A.D. 1450–1600) pottery in the upper Savannah River (Anderson et al. 1986; Hally 1990, 1994).

The Berry site is a large town with a substructure platform mound. Mound construction is assumed to occur in the Burke phase but, unfortunately, no further structural information is available. Investigations of the site have not revealed many details of site structure; the presence of a palisade is possible but is not demonstrated. A partial circular posthole pattern was identified in the mound vicinity, but it is uncertain whether this represents a domestic structure.

Other aspects of Burke phase material culture include ground stone and pottery disks, small triangular projectile points usually made from chert, and small ceramic elbow pipes.

Burke phase mortuary practices are not well documented, but two burials excavated at the Berry site provide some insight. Both burials were placed in shaft and chamber type pits. These are characteristic of the Pisgah phase in the North Carolina mountains (Dickens 1976:102–132) and are also common in the Dan River and Eno River area from as early as the fifteenth century to the early eighteenth century (Hogue 1988; Navey 1982; Ward and Davis 1993:407–432; Wilson 1983).

Burial 2 was a standard circular shaft and chamber pit. Two individuals were interred within the single chamber. This is not a common practice among either the Pisgah phase or the historic period Piedmont Siouans; Milner (1980:48) and Smith (1987:61) suggest that multiple bodies interred in the same burial pit may result from European disease epidemics of the sixteenth and seventeenth centuries.

Burial 1 was a fully extended adult male placed in a rectangular pit with a full-length side chamber. This type of extended interment is rare among the Piedmont Siouans and is also rare during the prehistoric Cherokee Pisgah phase. A burial bundle consisting of a possible turtle-shell container, clay pipe, projectile points, and stone abraders accompanied the individual. Similar assemblages of artifacts have been found at the King site in Georgia (Hally 1975) and at the Cherokee site of Toqua in east Tennessee (Polhemus 1987), where they are dated to the sixteenth century. An iron knife was also placed across the upper chest.

A final characteristic of Burke phase mortuary practice is the occurrence of Citico style shell gorgets. Although none were found at the Berry site, two were recovered from a disturbed burial at 31BK56 (Ward 1980b). In addition, a collector reportedly recovered one Citico style gorget at 31BK18, the Edwards Tree Nursery site, although I have been unable to confirm this. These gorgets are known from Alabama to North Carolina and are generally accepted as fifteenth- to early seventeenth-century markers (Smith 1987:108–112).

Other sites in this study with probable Burke phase components include 31BK1, 31BK12, 31BK17, 31BK18, 31BK23, 31BK24, 31BK39, 31BK44, 31BK56, 31CT115, the Nelson Mound (31CW1) and Triangle, the Davenport Mound, the Lenoir Indian Burial Pit, the Broyhill-Dillard site (31CW8), and the Jones site (31WK33). Also, subsequent to the completion of this study, Beck (1997a) identified 25 additional Burke phase sites on Upper Creek.

Happy Valley Phase

The Happy Valley phase (A.D. 1600–1700) is extremely provisional. It is distinguished from the Burke phase on the basis of the late radiocarbon date and "late" ceramics from the Broyhill-Dillard site. At this time, there is some evidence in the upper valley of ceramic attributes that suggest a seventeenth-century date for certain characteristics of Burke pottery. There are a few examples of "exploded" complicated-stamped motifs from the Berry site, 31BK17, and 31BK18, and a few examples of Lamar incised designs with more than four lines. If the Lamar pottery temporal patterns observed elsewhere are also consistent in the Catawba valley, these will be the seventeenth-century pottery attributes. In addition, the Broyhill-Dillard site ceramic assemblage also features an extremely high percentage (15.5 percent) of the large, "exploded," curvilinear complicated-stamped motifs, which are believed to be late Lamar attributes.

I suggest that this phase is represented by site components at the Nelson Mound (31CW1) and Triangle, the Davenport Jones Mound, the Lenoir Indian Burial Pit, the Broyhill-Dillard site (31CW8), the Berry site, 31BK17, and possibly the sites in the Michaux Farm vicinity. Its geographic range is restricted to this small area that spans portions of the upper Yadkin and Catawba valleys.

Upper Yadkin Valley Phases

Elkin Phase

A provisional phase, the Elkin phase, is proposed to represent upper Yadkin River valley sites that date ca. A.D. 1400–1600. These sites feature Dan River and Smyth ceramics as well as ceramics with attributes of the Burke series and/or Pisgah series. The Porter site (31WK6) is one example of an Elkin phase site. The use of this term resurrects Coe and Lewis's (1952) description of Elkin pottery thought to represent protohistoric Catawba pottery in North Carolina. The name was apparently used with reference to a large site on the Yadkin River in the Elkin, North Carolina, vicinity at which Burke ceramics were found. These may be the materials with which Coe first made the association between the soapstone-tempered pottery and the historic Catawba Indians (see Fewkes 1944:108). The use of the Elkin name and its association with Burke series pottery in the Yadkin valley assures some historical continuity of the term.

Burke Phase and Happy Valley Phase

The Burke (A.D. 1400–1600) and Happy Valley (A.D. 1600–1700) phases (described above) also are represented at upper Yadkin valley sites including the Nelson Mound (31CW1) and Triangle, the Davenport Jones Mound, the Lenoir Indian Burial Pit, the Broyhill-Dillard site (31CW8), and the Jones site (31WK33).

Middle Catawba Valley Phases

Low Phase

The Low phase (A.D. 1400–1600) is applied to sites in the middle Catawba valley that feature ceramic assemblages consisting primarily of Cowans Ford Complicated Stamped, Cowans Ford Plain/Smoothed, and Cowans Ford Burnished pottery types, with a minority of Burke types. Incised carinated and hemisphere bowls are common. These ceramics are believed to be basically coeval with the upper valley Burke series inasmuch as they differ only in temper and paste characteristics.

The ceramic assemblage from the Low site, 31ID31, is characteristic of this phase. As discussed earlier, this assemblage has been viewed as representing protohistoric Catawba Indian pottery (Wilson 1983; also see RLA site form for 31ID31). Low phase sites are located on the floodplain and terraces of the middle Catawba River valley. They include 31CT1, 31CT18, 31CT30, 31CT94, 31CT94A, 31CT96, 31ID31, 31ID46, and 31ID51. Future investigations may identify Low phase sites with sixteenth-century Spanish artifacts; these would be likely candidates for the towns of Guaquiri and Quinahaqui visited by Juan Pardo.

Iredell Phase

The Iredell phase (A.D. 1600–1725) is represented by several components in the middle Catawba valley. It is characterized by the presence of Cowans Ford Complicated Stamped with large, "exploded" motifs and wide, folded, and punctated jar rims. Further investigations of Iredell phase sites may reveal a limited presence of European artifacts that resulted from the beginnings of trade with Carolina and Virginia traders.

Iredell phase sites are located on the middle Catawba River. They include 31CT94, 31CT94A, 31ID31, 31ID42, 31ID46, 31ID51, and 31LN19.

Lower Catawba Valley Phases

I hesitate to establish even preliminary phases in the lower Catawba valley for three reasons. First, the number of sites and analyzed ceramic assemblages is extremely low. Second, I believe that the ceramics of this area will be found to be similar to upper Wateree River valley assemblages. This is within the critical region of historic Catawba coalescence and I believe that it is more appropriate to withhold phase designation until the sites and ceramics of the area are better understood. It is likely that current research at Spratt's Bottom (38YK3) and other sites in York County, South Carolina, will provide relevant data (May and Tippett 2000).

Third, the formulation of lower valley phases should proceed cautiously since these phases will be more closely linked with the historic Catawba Indians. Before these phases can be reliably established, it is necessary to have explicit research conducted on sites attributed to the Catawba Indians. However, until such work is accomplished, the Belk Farm site remains the best-documented early historic period site in the lower valley. Therefore, I propose the Belk Farm phase for the latest component at the site.

Belk Farm Phase

The Belk Farm phase (A.D. 1680–1725) is defined as the early historic period component at the Belk Farm site, 31MK85. Glass trade beads are present and the ceramic assemblage features Cowans Ford Complicated Stamped, Burnished, Plain/Smoothed, and Corncob Impressed pottery along with fine cord-marked pottery.

Chronology of the Historic Period Catawba Indians

One of the stated goals of this study was to try to identify links between the makers of protohistoric period ceramics in North Carolina and the historic period Catawba people. This study suggests that such a link exists on the basis of ethnohistoric accounts and the corresponding distributions of Burke and Cowans Ford ceramics. However, because of a lack of ceramic analysis from clearly documented eighteenth-century sites, it remains difficult to compare the protohistoric and historic period ceramic traditions. The difficulty is exacerbated by the fact that the geographic ranges of protohistoric and historic period sites do not greatly overlap. Nonetheless, it has been common in the past to refer to "Catawba" pottery without clear temporal or cultural referents.

Specifically, Burke (Dickens 1976; Keeler 1971), Elkin (Coe and Lewis 1952), and Chicora (South 1973) ceramics have been attributed to the protohistoric Catawba Indians. More recently, Wheaton et al. (1983:226–229) defined the *Catawba* type as an Indian-made version of colonoware. While Wheaton et al. (1983) may be absolutely correct in having identified an *Indian-made* colonoware, the Catawba appellation implies an association with Catawba Indians and thereby confuses the issues of both the origin of this pottery and its widespread tradition (see Ferguson 1989). The current study has clearly shown that an indigenous ceramic tradition of plain and burnished pottery existed in the Catawba valley for at least several centuries before the colonial period. Therefore, it should not be surprising if a tradition of plain wares is found to continue into the Historic period within the Catawba/Wateree drainage. However, applying the Catawba label to such wares without a demonstrated cultural link is inappropriate.

To avoid this problem, and given the ubiquity with which a "Catawba" affiliation has been used for Catawba valley ceramics (and Wateree valley ceramics as well), I suggest that future researchers carefully consider their use of the term *Catawba* when describing pottery, archaeological sites, or historically documented settlements. Furthermore, I would urge the use of new terms to separate the Catawba/Wateree region chronological phases and ceramic types from inadvertent cultural implications; terminology should be used that more clearly distinguishes sixteenth-century Catawba Indian material culture from that at the time of the founding of Charles Town (1670), at the time of John Lawson's visit (1701), and after the turmoil of the Tuscarora and Yamasee Wars (ca. 1720).

The cultural chronology presented here has, for the first time, created a temporal framework in which sites from the entire Catawba valley may be placed. It is now clear that Burke pottery is primarily distributed at sites in the upper Yadkin and Catawba River valleys and that Cowans Ford pottery is found throughout the middle and lower Catawba valley in the western Piedmont. The use of radiocarbon dates, patterns of Lamar pottery attributes, and the presence of historic Spanish artifacts at the Berry site and possibly in the Yadkin valley also help to distinguish some degree of temporal difference within the region during the late prehistoric and early historic eras. We are now able to identify sites representing Catawba Valley Mississippian peoples and to distinguish these sites from sixteenth-century sites representing their descendants, the protohistoric Catawba peoples.

Future investigations will further explore the nature and evolution of Catawba Valley Mississippian culture as well as later changes that show proto-Catawba peoples moving out of the region and coalescing into their historic-era homelands. I have no doubt that continuing research in the Upper Creek/Johns River area of the upper Catawba valley, in the upper Yadkin valley, and in the lower Catawba valley will establish a more detailed chronology in the near future.

Conclusion

Although the Catawba and Yadkin valley phases introduced in the previous chapter lack the temporal precision of other Lamar phases (Williams and Shapiro 1990), we are able for the first time to view the late Prehistoric period in this region as a coherent temporal unit. The chronology also provides a cultural context for sites and artifacts that have been viewed in isolation, such as the anomalous Caldwell County mounds explored in the nineteenth century and the ancestral Catawba pottery described from assorted seemingly independent sites. Further, it is now clearly established that groups practicing South Appalachian Mississippian lifeways occupied not only the south-central Piedmont of North Carolina (Pee Dee culture), but also an equally large portion of the western Piedmont region as well.

It remains to consider how the new chronology complements the ethnohistoric model of Catawba origins presented in chapter 1. At first glance, it may be argued that this model of Catawba ethnogenesis is to some extent tautological. That is, Hudson's (1990; DePratter et al. 1983) interpretation of Juan Pardo's route establishes an ethnohistoric basis for identifying Catawba towns in North Carolina's Catawba River valley—therefore, sixteenth-century sites located within the area traversed by Pardo must be Catawba towns. This study, however, has established an archaeological basis for characterizing fifteenth- and sixteenth-century peoples in the Catawba valley. The archaeological model can be evaluated independently of, and in relation to, the ethnohistoric model.

Much of the recent discussion on Catawba origins has focused at least in part on the relationship between the so-called Siouan hill tribes and the southern chiefdoms, especially the chiefdom of Cofitachequi (e.g., Baker 1974, 1976; Hudson 1965, 1970, 1990; Merrell 1989). Some researchers have suggested that the Catawba of the eighteenth century evolved out of the dissolution of the chiefdom of Cofitachequi in the seventeenth century (Baker 1974, 1976). Others have suggested that the Siouan-speaking Catawba Indians remained outside the orbit of Cofitachequi, but may have developed a greater degree of political sophistication as a result of their interactions with the chiefdom (Merrell 1989). Still others suggest that Catawba ancestors, while linguistically and perhaps politically distinct from Cofitachequi, were nonetheless subject to the chiefdom in the sixteenth century to a greater (DePratter et al. 1983; Hudson 1990) or lesser degree (DePratter 1994; Levy et al. 1990).

Charles Hudson has been particularly influential in his pursuit of the Catawba past. He (Hudson 1965:66–71) originally traced Catawba roots from Coe's (1952a) Siouan hill tribes to their chiefdom status in the seventeenth century and has continued related research with investigations of Hernando de Soto and Juan Pardo in the southeastern United States (Hudson 1990, 1997; Hudson et al. 1984). Most recently, Hudson (1990:185–189) has presented a compelling model of Catawba origins by directly linking sixteenth-century Siouan-speaking chiefs with the Esaw and Catawba tribes encountered by John Lawson in 1701. The current study relies heavily on this scholarship.

The perspective presented here, however, focuses on establishing an archaeological interpretation of the Protohistoric period; that is, what are the origins of the protohistoric populations in the Catawba River valley? Here, the model diverges dramatically from that of Hudson. In framing the Mississippian cultural landscape for the sixteenth-century chiefdom of Cofitachequi, Hudson (1990:70–73) describes very briefly the evolution of Mississippian chiefdom societies in South Carolina and the intrusion into the Yadkin River valley by Mississippian peoples of the Pee Dee culture around A.D. 1300. The Pee Dee, a chiefdom society, pushed native peoples of the Uwharrie culture out of the southern Piedmont. In contrast to the Pee Dees, the Uwharrie peoples were not organized into chiefdoms (Hudson 1990:72). Uwharrie ancestors continued to live on the upper Yadkin River and elsewhere throughout the northern Piedmont. Thus, while acknowledging that the archaeology of the Catawba and Broad river valleys was poorly understood, Hudson paints a picture of the North Carolina Piedmont's "Mississippian transformation" that leaves the Catawba River valley blank—though this was the very region into which Pardo traveled and met with "chiefs" in the sixteenth century.

It is now clear that Hudson's most recent model, as well as the earlier perspectives on Catawba origins, lack an archaeological foundation with which they might establish the prehistoric past of the Catawba Indians and by which the protohistoric past would become more clear. From the preceding chapters, there is solid evidence of fifteenth- and sixteenth-century native occupations throughout the Catawba and upper Yadkin valleys represented by sites of the Pleasant Garden, Burke, Low, and Elkin phases. Earlier phases are poorly understood and undefined, but it is likely that occupation by peoples making Burke and Cowans Ford pottery occurred in the fourteenth century and possibly earlier.

Additionally, Hudson relies on a model of "Mississippian transformation" that is unsupported by the archaeological evidence. The Pee Dee culture was once referred to as "one of the best archaeological records of the movement of a people in the southeast" (Coe 1952a:308). Pee Dee peoples, practicing a radically different culture, were seen as invaders who arrived in the southern Piedmont around A.D. 1550 and displaced resident villagers of the Piedmont Siouan tradition (Coe 1952a:308). In contrast, recent chronological developments emphasize that Pee Dee culture evolved over a period of more than 500 years from ca. A.D. 950–1600 (Oliver 1992). Equally important, Pee Dee culture is now seen not as an invading culture, but as a "regional center of South Appalachian Mississippian that interacted and evolved with other regional centers scattered from the Coastal Plain of Georgia and South Carolina to the western North Carolina mountains" (Ward and Davis 1999:125). Again, the current study shows that the late prehistoric peoples of the Catawba valley were also independent participants in the same interregional cultural system.

To characterize these cultures as regionally interacting centers still begs the question: what is the mechanism by which Lamar culture spread into North Carolina, represented not only by Pee Dee culture, but by the Burke and Low phases as well? Undoubtedly, multiple mechanisms were operational throughout the fourteenth and fifteenth centuries. They involved not replacement of Siouan tribes, but interaction between a variety of "chiefdom" and "tribal" communities in these and surrounding regions. Recently a model has been proposed for the development of Burke phase chiefdoms. The model views the upper Catawba and Yadkin region and the Burke phase as a Mississippian frontier, a part of the northernmost extent of Lamar from the fourteenth through the seventeenth centuries (Beck and Moore 2001).

Burke phase sites are located in foothill valleys that represent a major ecotone at the juncture of the Piedmont and the Blue Ridge Mountains. Ecotone settings for Lamar chiefdoms have been thought to offer both subsistence and economic advantages including fertile soils and resource variability (Hally 1979:10–11, 1994:163; Larson 1971:24–25; Meyers 1995:95). It is likely that the upland valley ecotone provided a favorable setting in which local leaders could pursue a variety of group-building strategies. Archaeological evidence suggests that these upper valleys had a significantly higher population density than adjoining areas of the Piedmont, a density that was more easily sustained by the productive potential of the foothills ecotone (Beck and Moore 2001).

In addition, the model suggests that Mississippian chiefdoms in the upper Catawba and Yadkin region were situated in this particular locale to take advantage of a system of trails connecting the region to polities in northeast Georgia, east Tennessee, southwest Virginia, and the South Carolina Piedmont (Beck 1997b). Beck and Moore (2001; emphasis in original) state, "Long-distance communication and exchange may have provided emergent leaders . . . with knowledge of the Mississippian ideas and strategies being successfully pursued by distant people, and may also have contributed to a local political economy based upon the production of a staple surplus *and* access to exotic goods such as shell, copper, and salt."

Finally, it is suggested that social power in frontier Mississippian groups was less secure than that seen in core Mississippian chiefdoms such as Moundville. As a result, leaders in the upper Catawba and Yadkin region emphasized group-building activities such as mound construction and the use of corporate mortuary facilities to achieve their persuasively organized regional chiefdoms (Beck and Moore 2001).

It has also been proposed that the presence of multiple elite burials at the Jones site in Wilkes County, just downstream from the Broyhill-Dillard site, reflects competition between lineages of local tribal-level polities in an effort to enhance their standing relative to nearby Burke phase chiefdoms with access to rare goods (Idol 1996). Such competition involving marriage patterns and trade among Lamar chiefdom groups and local tribal level groups may have been one of the mechanisms by which Lamar lifeways spread into the Catawba region. Such a model may be especially appropriate within the Mississippian frontier framework, in which one expects interaction to have occurred between Catawba Valley Mississippian peoples and nearby tribal-level polities.

What is the evidence that the spread of Lamar style pottery vessels into the Catawba valley was accompanied by the same level of social and political complexity with which Lamar culture is associated in other parts of the South Appalachian region (Hally 1994; Williams and Shapiro 1990)? As pointed out in the introduction, chiefdoms have been variously defined and are extremely variable in character and complexity. Therefore, it is difficult, if not impossible, to analyze the Catawba Valley Mississippian societies in terms of any specific chiefdom models because of the lack of comprehensive regional settlement data and extensive site excavation data. However, it is possible to consider some features of the region that may reflect the organization of chiefdom-level societies. In other words, we should not now assume a priori that Burke phase polities were chiefdoms, but must ask instead to what extent the Catawba valley societies conform to our expectations of a southeastern chiefdom society. For the Catawba valley we must consider both archaeological and ethnohistoric data. On the basis of ethnohistory, we must once again rely on the strength of the Spanish documents and the interpretations that place the towns of Otari, Yssa, Guatari, Guaquiri, and Joara within the study area. If these interpretations are accurate, then the Spanish documents show evidence of mid-sixteenth-century regional political integration, multicommunity organization, social ranking, and perhaps economic stratification within the study area, these being some basic characteristics of chiefdoms (Anderson 1994a; Earle 1987).

Archaeological settlement data in the Catawba valley are extremely limited, but late prehistoric and protohistoric towns are based in productive floodplain settings, and limited subsistence data show that an active maize agricultural system was operative. Survey data from the Upper Creek/ Warrior Fork area strongly suggest that the local settlement system contains at least four different sizes of sites (Beck 1997a:31). It is unclear how functionally discrete these sites are, but Beck (1997a:33) argues that sites representing all four size classes were probably occupied simultaneously. He (Beck 1997a:40–42) suggests that the contemporaneous occupation of one mound site (Berry) and three smaller classes of sites is evidence of multi-community integration and supports the characterization of a chiefdom-level society for this locale. It is also interesting to hypothesize whether the site size range may reflect changes in the degree of population dispersal resulting from the effects of regional competition or peaceful interactions among rival towns or polities.

We also see, in the upper Catawba and upper Yadkin valleys, that these groups constructed substructure mounds and corporate mortuary facilities. Substructure mounds are present at the McDowell and Berry sites. Earlier descriptions of the mounds suggest that the Berry mound may have been considerably larger than the McDowell mound. It is uncertain whether mound size reflects its length of service or other factors. Of course, evidence for elite structures on mound summits would provide more compelling evidence for the existence of chiefdoms and some level of hierarchy. Unfortunately, earlier excavations and plowing have effectively destroyed that potential evidence. Nonetheless, though much more work is necessary to analyze the distribution of these mound sites, archaeological evidence supports some potential for a hierarchical settlement system in the region.

In addition, the known mound sites feature several common elements with respect to their location. First, the mounds that have been identified, as well as the Yadkin valley mounds reported by Cyrus Thomas in the nineteenth century, are confined to a relatively restricted area: the large headwater valleys at the foot of the Blue Ridge. With only three exceptions, mounds are not reported downstream. Thomas (1891:153) reported one unconfirmed mound in the Lake Norman area and Ferguson (1971:148) reports one mound on the Yadkin River in Davie County. The third is the well-known Town Creek site in the Pee Dee valley (Oliver 1992; Reid 1967). Second, it is perhaps noteworthy that both the Nelson mound and the Berry mound are located as far upstream as practical to allow access to both large fields of easily tillable soil and natural routes into and through the mountains. These locations not only confer economic and subsistence advantages, but also possibly play a role in defining or defending polity boundaries as well.

Large corporate burial facilities were located at the Nelson, Davenport Jones, and Lenoir Burial Pit sites. These facilities are seemingly unique to this region and the large quantity of "exotic" artifacts such as spatulate axes, shell gorgets and masks, copper plates, and European metal tools that accompanied the burials suggests that they were burials of high-status individuals. The facilities appear to be similarly constructed and are unlikely to represent substructure mounds. While high-status burial mounds are often associated with platform mounds on other Mississippian sites (Etowah being the best example), the burial facilities in the upper Yadkin valley do not conform to this general pattern. In any event, this is a striking distribution of a wide range of mound and burial facilities found in this rather restricted geographic area.

Aside from the notable grave associations from the upper Yadkin valley sites, there are few mortuary data available elsewhere in the study area; certainly none that suggest significant status differentiation. The presence of the European knife and other grave associations in Burial 1 at the Berry site are suggestive of marked status differentiation, but little more understanding can be gained without further examples of Berry site mortuary practices. Finally, it should be noted that there are several examples of the spatulate axes, which are usually viewed as high-status artifacts associated with chiefly elites (Hatch 1975; Smith 1987:98). Spatulate axes have been found in burial contexts at the Nelson and Davenport Jones mounds in the upper Yadkin valley (Thomas 1887), at the Porter site, 31WK6 (Rogers 1993:205), located on the Yadkin River about 35 miles downstream from the Nelson site, and at the Hardins site, 31GS29 (Keel 1990), in the lower Catawba valley. Such a sample is interesting but, of course, hardly evidence of ascribed ranking in the region.

In sum, settlement data, mound construction, and mortuary evidence suggest that Catawba Valley Mississippian peoples exhibited some level of hierarchical and/or multicommunity integration during the Burke and Low phases (ca. A.D. 1400–1600). On the basis of archaeological evidence alone, the social organization of these peoples appears to have been consistent with that of other Lamar peoples organized in chiefdom societies. Ethnohistoric evidence drawn from the accounts of Juan Pardo's expeditions into the interior is also consistent with the archaeological evidence. Pardo appears to have met with individuals and groups of native chiefs on multiple occasions and at different town locations in such a manner as to suggest that various levels of political authority existed between these chiefs and between different towns. It is suggested that the towns of Joara and Guatari held a greater degree of authority than did any of the other multitude of towns in the study area represented at these gatherings among the native chiefs and the Spaniards (Hudson 1990).

There now seems little doubt that some level of contact between native Catawba valley peoples and Spanish explorers occurred during the sixteenth century. While we must remain cautious about the veracity of the Spanish accounts and the strength of interpretations based on these accounts, we should not hesitate to explore this source of information. Regardless of the specific location of the towns of Joara, Guatari, Yssa, or Suhere, Hudson's (1990) Pardo route reconstructions suggest that North Carolina's Catawba valley was occupied by a number of different polities among whom Catawban languages were spoken.

Some have questioned the basic premise of reconstructing individual historical events such as the De Soto or Pardo expeditions (Boyd and Schroedl 1987:843; Ward and Davis 1999:264). I prefer, rather, to suggest that the Spanish documents offer modern scholars an opportunity to understand the dynamic interaction of polities and populations in the sixteenth-century Southeast. These documents, and the reconstructed routes, enable us to explore and recognize the archaeological manifestations of the towns, villages, and polities encountered by these expeditions. Regardless of whether the routes are ever proved beyond doubt (an unlikely event), archaeological investigations of the proposed town and polity locations will eventually enable us to interpret the type of cultural geography Hudson envisions. This is not to say that testing entails proving the veracity of individual site designations; rather, such testing entails demonstrating that the settlement types, social relationships, populations, and other cultural features correspond to those described in the documents. It may indeed prove impossible to identify individual town locations, but regional investigations may, at a minimum, reveal the cultural landscapes in which recorded events are likely to have occurred. In fact, I submit that this is the case for the current study.

Let us assume, for the moment, that the Hudson route is incorrect and that the towns of Catawban-speaking peoples encountered by Pardo were located somewhere in the upper Savannah or Broad river drainages of South Carolina instead of the upper Catawba valley—regardless, the archaeological evidence for the Burke and Low phases (ca. A.D. 1400–1600) remains unaltered. A relatively dense population of Lamar chiefdom societies occupied the Catawba valley from at least as early as the fourteenth to at least the sixteenth century A.D. This population consistently produced Lamar style pottery with an overwhelming emphasis on complicated-stamped, plain, and burnished vessel surfaces. The presence, quantity, and type of European artifacts at the Berry site and at mortuary sites in the upper Yadkin valley make clear that Burke phase sites were occupied in the sixteenth century and possibly into the early seventeenth century.

However, pottery attributes (wide appliqued or folded rims, very large complicated-stamped designs, carinated vessels with multiple fine incised decoration) that are thought to reflect seventeenth-century Lamar ceramic assemblages are present in very low numbers and are most common in the middle Catawba valley where the Iredell phase (ca. A.D. 1600–1725) is proposed. A drastically lower population density is suggested at this time, especially in the upper valley. Outside of the upper valley, the only site from which European artifacts have been recovered is the Belk Farm site, which is dated ca. A.D. 1680 to 1725 in the lower valley. Though there are no other obvious candidates for late seventeenth-century sites anywhere in the study area, it is possible that our lack of fine-grained temporal markers may render invisible sites of this time period. However, it should be emphasized here again that there is scant ethnohistoric evidence for any substantial occupation of the study region in the seventeenth and early eighteenth century. Thus, assuming that no ethnohistoric evidence exists to place Catawban-speaking peoples in North Carolina's Catawba valley in the sixteenth century, the archaeological evidence still clearly suggests that local Lamar chiefdoms underwent major transformations resulting in a regional depopulation during the Protohistoric period. Future archaeological research in the study region must be guided by working hypotheses regarding the causes, the scope, and the timing of this depopulation.

Thus, the current study is strengthened, not weakened, by the sixteenth-century Spanish accounts. The archaeological chronology and settlement pattern analysis outlined in chapter 5 is congruent with the ethnohistoric model of Catawba origins presented in chapter 1. Both archaeological and ethnohistoric data suggest that the sixteenth and seventeenth centuries comprise perhaps the most critical period in the history of the Catawba valley peoples. It is during this time that protohistoric aboriginal populations of the southeastern United States were irreversibly disrupted by the arrival of Europeans, and native depopulation must be considered among the most serious consequences of the invasion.

Galloway's (1995) comprehensive treatment of the genesis of the historic Choctaw confederacy may serve as a model for future investigation of Catawba origins. Galloway (1995:5–6) describes the complexity of factors involved in understanding Choctaw prehistory, including depopulation, changes in town locations, changes in sociopolitical organization, and changes in regional geopolitical relationships. All of these factors are likely to have been integral to Catawba ethnogenesis and the formation of the Catawba confederacy. Galloway (1995:5) suggests that while the causes of depopulation are complex and may include the effects of Mississippian political "cycling," tribal aggression, and slave trading, European disease was the most important factor in depopulation experienced by the proto-Choctaw. As summarized above, the archaeological and ethnohistoric evidence suggest that depopulation also occurred in the Catawba valley following the contact between Spaniards and local native peoples. The effects of that depopulation may have influenced the course of Catawba ethnogenesis and deserve special attention here.

I am not the first to make such a proposal. Baker (1976) argues that the Catawba tribe emerges in the Protohistoric period from the dissolution of the chiefdom of Cofitachequi. Baker (1974), Hudson et al. (1984), DePratter et al. (1983), and Anderson (1994a) also argue that the scope of the chiefdom of Cofitachequi's influence and power waned between 1541 and 1565 as the result of disease brought by the De Soto entrada. Under this interpretation, one could argue that similar devastating effects had been felt throughout the Catawba valley. DePratter (1994), on the other hand, questions whether such a catastrophic impact was ever felt in the region. Clearly, the relative impact of sixteenth- and seventeenth-century epidemics would significantly affect the Catawba valley population size and distribution.

Despite considerable debate regarding the timing, the mechanisms of transmission, and ultimate effects, there is little doubt that the introduction of European diseases is one of the major factors in population dynamics among protohistoric and early historic period southeastern Native Americans (see Blakely and Detweiler-Blakely 1989; Dobyns 1983; Galloway 1995; Milner 1980; Ramenofsky 1987; Smith 1987; Snow and Lanphear 1988; Storey 1985; Ward and Davis 1993, 1999). However, the Catawba valley woefully lacks the data needed to consider the effect of disease and population changes. Catawba valley researchers are unable to control the variables of chronology, settlement patterns, and village populations that are necessary to document population losses caused by disease (Ramenofsky 1987). Ward and Davis (1989, 1993:430–432, 1999:257–260) emphasize this point with convincing mortuary data from numerous sites that suggest that the Siouan populations of the central and northern North Carolina Piedmont suffered minimal effects of European diseases until the late seventeenth or early eighteenth century. They (Ward and Davis 1999:266) further suggest that the lack of burials from excavated sites in the Catawba valley argues against a massive sixteenth-century depopulation in the study area. It must be pointed out that the scale of site excavation in the Catawba region is dwarfed by that carried out in the Piedmont Siouan region, and I would prefer to have somewhat comparable data before assuming that no sixteenth-century depopulation occurred within the study area.

It is interesting, however, to recall the Burke phase burial mounds in the upper Yadkin valley. The skeletons of at least 125 individuals were reported from the Nelson Mound and Triangle, the Davenport Jones Mound, and the Lenoir Burial Pit (Thomas 1887, 1894). It is not clear whether these interments occurred throughout the Burke phase or rather occurred during a much shorter interval of time. It is even possible that such a marked display of corporate burial practice is a direct response to one or more episodes of European disease–related deaths. Clearly, much additional information is necessary to evaluate such a hypothesis.

In any event, it would be dangerous to assume that the effects of European disease on Catawba valley populations should necessarily be similar to those demonstrated for the Piedmont Siouan region. Disease effects may have varied within the more heavily populated Catawba valley, and it is possible that the Catawba populations were potentially exposed to more disease effects because of their proximity to Cofitachequi and the probability of direct contact with the Spanish. At this point it is best to recognize that there are a range of opinions and data regarding the transmission, timing, and effect of sixteenth- and seventeenth-century European diseases on native populations that cannot yet be evaluated in the Catawba valley. Further enlightenment will require extensive investigations of individual sites and regional settlement studies.

Finally, even if depopulation of the Catawba valley did not occur until the late seventeenth century, the overall model presented here remains the same. What is important is that a significant shift of Catawba valley population occurred sometime between the late sixteenth century and the early eighteenth century. That shift may have resulted from loss of lives due to European disease, dislocation of the population resulting from the breakup of the chiefdom of Cofitachequi, the introduction of the Virginia trade, or the later establishment of trade with South Carolinians. Very likely, a combination of these and other factors was responsible.

Depopulation of the Catawba valley was accompanied by a coalescence of peoples farther to the south near the North Carolina–South Carolina border, probably after the mid-sixteenth century. By the late seventeenth century the activities of Charles Town traders may have served to focus the coalescing group on their historically recognized homeland. At this time we are in no position to understand the complete range of peoples who may have been a part of that coalescence. The sixteenth-century Spanish accounts suggest that numerous sixteenth-century polities were distributed across the western Piedmont from the central Yadkin valley to the foothills of the Blue Ridge. Some of these peoples spoke Catawban languages, but other languages were also spoken within the region. Ethnic diversity may have been the rule rather than the exception within this region. It is also possible that such diversity characterized the late Prehistoric period within the region, resulting perhaps from the very processes that helped to spread the Lamar culture. Indeed, though the Lamar ceramic tradition is quite consistent across the region, intraregional diversity was such that we recognize distinct phases, the Burke and Low phases.

The prehistoric diversity is still reflected after the coalescence in the association of the Esaws, Kadapaus, Sugarees, and others in 1701. Initially, the coalescence appears to have been a successful response. I suspect it succeeded in part because it represented the continuation of some aspects of a cultural system in place since at least the fourteenth century and, very possibly, earlier. That system incorporated a reliance on mound building and long-distance trade to help integrate and regulate regional chiefly elites. Though it is likely that much of the earlier chiefdom-level social and political structure had broken down in the course of coalescence, these groups, though smaller in numbers, retained some of their independent identities.

The study described here is broadly limited by the nature of the archaeological data on which it is based. The region has seen little systematic, long-term directed research and many gaps exist in regional site surveys and excavations. Yet, this synthesis of widely disparate sources of archaeological and ethnohistoric data enables us to regard the late Mississippian and protohistoric cultural landscape of the North Carolina Piedmont through a clearer lens. It also reveals many gaps in our understanding of the sixteenth- and seventeenth-century forces that buffeted the Piedmont region and to which Catawba ancestors reacted and adapted. Future research directed toward the questions raised above will do much to further our understanding of that period. Most obviously, it will be essential to conduct extensive investigations within the historic period Catawba region, to try to identify specific sites and phases related to the coalescence of peoples called the Catawba confederacy. The effort to identify cultural and ethnic diversity among the early eighteenth-century Esaws, Kadapaus, Sugarees, and others should provide additional models by which the diversity of their sixteenth- and seventeenth-century ancestors may also be explored.

This work also suggests that we revise the Siouan hill tribe and southern chiefdom dichotomy that has driven past perspectives on Catawba origins. Peoples of the Piedmont Siouan tradition undoubtedly interacted in various ways with Mississippian chiefdoms. Significant differences existed in the social fabric of these two diverse groups and interactions between and among all of these Piedmont peoples generated the cultural landscape of the late Mississippian frontier. It now seems clear, however, that the "southern chiefdoms" were present not only on the Pee Dee and Wateree, but throughout the entire Catawba River valley as well. The ancestors of the nucleus of the Catawba confederacy were, in fact, Mississippian societies in their own right for at least three centuries before the Kadapau King entertained John Lawson in 1701.

Appendix A

The McDowell Site

This appendix briefly describes the results of fieldwork conducted at the McDowell site in 1977 (Ward 1977) and by the author in 1986 during the Upper Catawba Archaeological Project. The McDowell site (31MC41) is located on the floodplain of the Catawba River west of Marion in McDowell County (Figures 5 and 13). The alluvial bottoms surrounding the site encompass more than 200 acres, while the site itself is limited to an area of about 3 to 4 acres, 250 ft south of the river. Today, a narrow, flood-prone, abandoned channel separates the site from the river. The site is known locally as the location of a large 'mound,' which is actually a conical monadnock more than 60 ft high. The archaeological site is approximately 1,000 ft east of the monadnock. However, the site includes what has generally been interpreted as the remnant of an earthen substructure mound (Ward 1977:5). Years of cultivation have reduced the mound to a low rise about 100 ft in diameter and less than 4 ft high.

Excavation Results: 1977 and 1986

The 1977 report (Ward 1977) on field investigations describes artifacts scattered over nearly a 2-acre area (about 250 × 300 ft). Within these boundaries higher concentrations of surface material were noted in the east-central and southeastern sections of the site, while very little material was found on or south of the mound (Ward 1977:4–5). The 1986 investigations recorded a surface scatter of artifacts that covered 3 to 4 acres. However, consistent with earlier observations, surface artifact density dropped rapidly south of the mound. In 1977, a permanent grid was established by placing iron pipes at the corners of a 200-x-200-ft block. Test excavations revealed a plow zone of brown silty loam .5 to .9 ft in depth overlying a tan silty-clay B horizon (Ward 1977:5). Plow zone was removed from about 750 ft^2 of the site in 1977. This included four 5-x-5-ft units and a 10-x-50-ft trench designated Block A (Figure 14). Twenty-eight postholes and 4 features were identified in Block A. The postholes included portions of a possible house structure (Structure 1) and a palisade running west to east across the trench (Ward 1977:6–8).

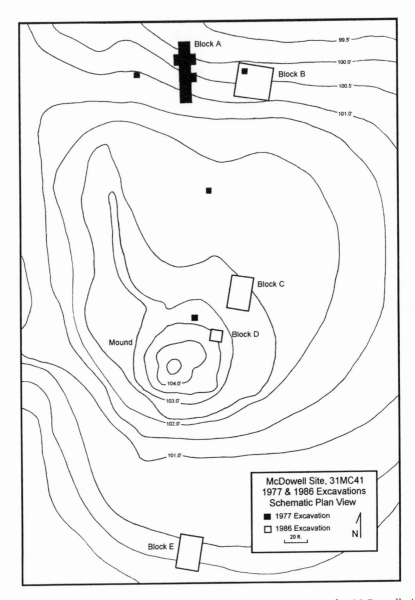

Figure 13. Plan view of the 1977 and 1986 excavation area at the McDowell site (31MC41).

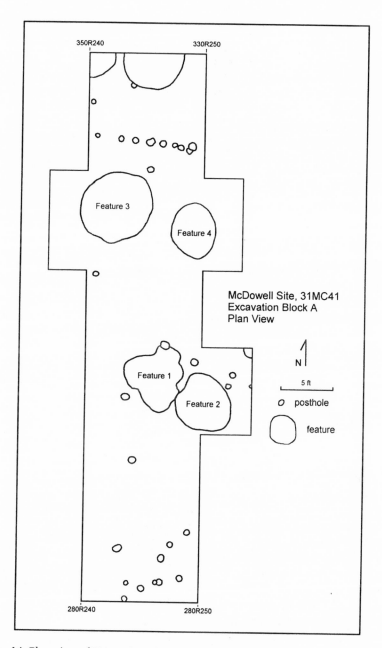

Figure 14. Plan view of Excavation Block A at the McDowell site.

Further investigations at the McDowell site were carried out as part of the Upper Catawba Archaeology Project from September 12 to October 12, 1986. Complete access to the site was not possible; our investigations were limited by crop cover to a narrow 80-ft transect that bisected the site and ran north-to-south through the site, crossing the mound. An attempt was made to locate the permanent datum rods placed along the woods just north of the site in 1977, so that recording could continue within the original grid system. Unfortunately, the edge of the wooded area had been graded to realign a dirt road and we were able to locate only one of the three original datum rods; though hit by the bulldozer blade and badly bent, it appeared to be in its original location. We were also unable to re-locate the 1977 excavation units since they were located outside of our access area. Therefore, the relationship of the 1986 excavation grid to the 1977 grid is based on only this single point. It is likely that some error occurred in attempting to replicate the grid's north-south orientation from the single point. The site map (Figure 13) is based on Ward's 1977 topographic map. Without the accurate datum points or a new topographic map, I have placed the 1986 grid as accurately as possible relative to the 1977 grid. While this placement was made as carefully as possible with respect to the existing datum, the mound, and the farm road, the relationship of the 1977 units to the 1986 units is still subjective.

Four areas (Blocks B–E) totaling 2,200 ft² were excavated in 1986. Each block was shoveled to remove the plow zone, but because of time limitations the entire plow zone was screened for artifacts in Blocks C and D only. In Blocks B and E, those units in which the plow zone was not completely screened, a 100-liter soil sample of plow zone was water screened to obtain a sample of artifacts from these units. Although the plow zone character and depth appeared to be consistent with that reported in 1977, there since had been a significant change in the plowing practice. On two occasions a chisel plow had been utilized to break the subsoil to a greater depth. The resulting plow scars occurred at 5-ft intervals in the north-south and east-west directions. Though narrow (.2–.3 ft wide), these scars penetrated the subsoil at least .6 ft below the normal plowing level.

Table 25 provides a comparison of the artifact densities from several excavation squares in Blocks A, B, C, and D. It is perhaps not surprising that ceramics are heavily represented, but the paucity of lithic remains is striking. The use of ½-in screen is certainly a factor that eliminated smaller flakes from representation, but aside from hammerstone fragments there are almost no lithic tools either. It is difficult to draw any conclusions from these distributions except that there is a clear increase in the quantity of ceramics on the mound and to the northeast in Block C. Similarly, Block C shows a striking concentration of daub representing the remains of Structure 3 (described below).

Table 25. Distribution of artifacts from Excavation Blocks A, B, C, and D at the McDowell site

Excavation Unit	280R250	290R250	300R250	310R250	320R250	90R350	90R350	120R360	130R360	140R360	140R360
	Block A	Block A	Block B	Block B	Block B	Block D	Block D	Block C	Block C	Block C	Block C
Level	Plow zone	Plow zone	Plow zone	Plow zone	Plow zone	Plow zone	Mound fill	Plow zone	Plow zone	Plow zone	Fea. 12
Approx. volume (cubic feet)	85	85	85	85	85	85	45	95	95	80	15
Contents											
Lithics											
Chipped stone projectile point	·	·	·	·	·	·	·	·	·	·	·
Biface/misc. tool	3	1	2	1	1	2	2	1	2	4	·
Hammerstone	2	2	4	8	2	2	2	1	·	·	·
Disk	·	·	2	1	2	·	·	1	·	1	2
Pipe	·	·	·	·	·	1	·	·	·	·	·
Polished object	4	·	·	·	·	·	·	1	·	·	·
Flakes	5	5	5	·	2	5	·	4	·	·	·
Ceramics											
Potsherds	763	616	670	688	436	1129	279	945	1124	1086	109
Disk	·	1	·	1	·	·	·	2	2	1	4
Pipe	·	1	2	·	·	·	·	1	1	·	1
Daub											
Daub pieces (#)	·	·	·	·	·	3	·	3	82	113	40
wt. (g)	·	·	·	·	·	5	·	3	184	240	242

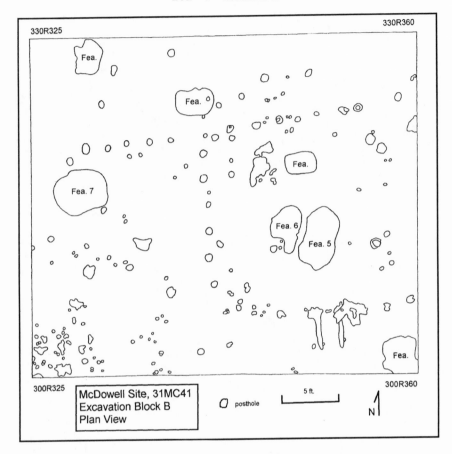

Figure 15. Plan view of Excavation Block B at the McDowell site.

Although 21 features were identified, limited time allowed the excavation of only three. Numerous postholes were recorded; several from alignments that represent a palisade and a domestic structure (Structure 2). Another, possibly public, structure (Structure 3) was represented by Feature 12. Finally, the low mound was determined to consist partially of basket-loaded fill, confirming its cultural origin.

Block B (900 ft²; Figure 15) was located at the north edge of the site adjacent to the dirt road. This area was about 100 ft east of Block A and was selected for investigation in the hope of extending the palisade identified in 1977. Block B revealed a density of features and postholes similar to that of Block A. Seven features were observed; the three excavated features (5–7) are described below. Two posthole patterns were also observed (see Figure 15). The first was a row of 16 posts running 25 ft west to east across the unit. This is undoubtedly a palisade and may represent the same palisade observed in Block A in 1977. The second pattern is clearly a domestic structure (Structure 2). It is represented by at least 19 postholes forming approximately 60 percent of the structure. This pattern appears to be similar to the house patterns described by Dickens (1976:32) at the Warren Wilson site, a Pisgah phase site located 30 miles west of the McDowell site: "Houses at the Warren Wilson site were constructed of vertical posts that were set individually in the ground, except for the vestibule entrances where they were set close together in short trenches. The buildings were square or slightly rectangular in plan [usually with slightly rounded corners], with an average measurement along the outer walls of about 20 feet." Structure 2 fits this pattern very closely; the west-side outer wall is approximately 20 ft in length and both the southwest and northwest corners are slightly rounded. The palisade line intrudes Structure 2, but it is not possible to determine which precedes the other temporally.

Although the Block B plow-zone soils were not sifted, it was clear that a large quantity of material, primarily ceramics, was present. Interestingly, the water-screened plow-zone samples from three of the excavation squares yielded small fragments of ferrous metal. Three metal fragments were recovered from the water-screened materials by the use of a magnet. Each piece resembles a thin wire and two of them are slightly twisted and curved. These pieces resemble fragments of sixteenth-century Spanish chain mail recovered from the Governor Martin site in Tallahassee, Florida, the presumed location of the town of Anhaica at which De Soto's army spent the winter of 1539–1540 (Ewen 1988, 1989). According to Charles Ewen, these pieces are the same size and exhibit the same curve and twist as examples of chain mail from the Governor Martin site, but they lack a rivet. Had these pieces been found at the Governor Martin site, they would have been included among the chain-mail sample, but, lacking the diagnostic rivet, they cannot be identified as chain-mail pieces on their own (Charles Ewen, personal communication 1987).

The presence of chain mail, if confirmed, could indicate a connection to the sixteenth-century Spanish explorers Hernando de Soto and Juan Pardo. It is known that De Soto's men wore chain mail, but it is also suspected by many that the Spaniards had abandoned its use by the time they left Florida because of its weight and negligible protective powers against cane arrow shafts. Nonetheless, even if the McDowell site pieces represent chain mail, their presence does not confirm a Spanish presence. They could as easily represent a piece of chain mail that was gathered elsewhere by McDowell site inhabitants or obtained by them in trade.

Block C (600 ft²; Figure 16) was located adjacent to and just northeast of the mound. This area was selected for investigation because of a heavy surface concentration of pottery and large chunks of charcoal in mixed dark loam soils. In addition, reconnaissance coring conducted in this area in April 1986 identified what were believed to be undisturbed midden or

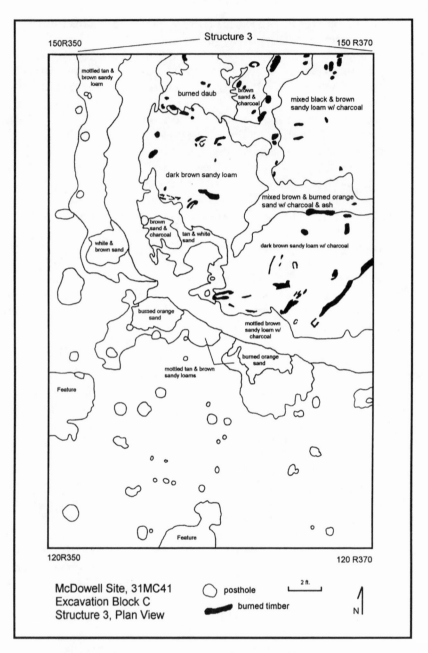

Figure 16. Plan view of Excavation Block C at the McDowell site.

Plate 34. Portion of Excavation Block C (McDowell site) showing Feature 12, Structure 3 (view to east).

mound-fill soils. Removal of the plow zone revealed a large feature that covered more than one-half of the excavation block. The feature soils consisted of a variety of light and dark compact soils, sands, burned soils, burned daub, and charred wood. However, the recent deep chisel plowing had severely disturbed this area, and it was necessary to skim off about .1 to .2 ft of feature soil to obtain a clear view of the feature (Figure 16, Plate 34). The archaeological feature (Feature 12) that emerged from the skimming covered approximately 340 ft^2.

Only a portion of the feature was exposed, but it appears to have a core of dark-brown and black loamy soil at least 20 ft in diameter. Within this core area were concentrations of ash, burned soils, orange and brown sand, charcoal, and chunks of burned timbers. Two bands of mottled brown soil, each about 2 ft wide, surround the core. This feature is believed to represent the remains of a burned structure (Structure 3). Because of time constraints, excavation of the feature was not attempted. By projecting the curve of the core and the concentric bands, the final diameter is expected to be at least 25 ft to perhaps as much as 50 ft. It is also impossible to determine whether the structure is square or round.

The position of Structure 3 next to the mound (recognizing that contemporaneity of the two is not established) and its potentially large size suggest that the structure may have had a public or ceremonial function, as opposed to Structure 1, which probably served as a domicile. Such a public structure would not be unusual (see Rodning 1996:20 for an example of such a structure at the Coweeta Creek site, 31MA34, in Macon County).

The overall characteristics of this feature/structure are unusual, but it is possible that the outlying concentric bands of soil represent the plowed remnants of earthen embankments, perhaps representing an earthlodge. Rudolph (1984:33) states that at least 19 earthlodges are reported in the southeastern United States including three in North Carolina: one at the Town Creek site (Coe 1952a, 1995), one at the Garden Creek site (Dickens 1976), and one at the Peachtree site (Setzler and Jennings 1941). Rudolph (1984:33) defines an earthlodge as "an above-ground building that had either an earth covered roof or an earth embankment buttressing the walls." A comparison of Structure 3 with Rudolph's (1984:37–39) Figures 3 and 4 shows that a heavily plowed earth-embanked structure could look much like Structure 3 at the McDowell site with its concentric bands surrounding the dark core. It should be noted that this description differs from Dickens's (1976:87) description of semisubterranean earthlodges at the Garden Creek site.

Although we were unable to excavate this feature, several samples of charcoal were selected from the burned structure timbers. One of the burned timbers yielded a radiocarbon age of 890 ± 50 B.P. (Beta-21818) and a calibrated date of A.D. 1168. At 1 sigma, the age range is A.D. 1041–1226. At 2 sigma, the range is A.D. 1019–1279.

Excavation Block D consisted of a single 100-ft^2 unit (90R350) placed on the mound to determine whether the mound was a natural or cultural feature. The crest of this low rise is 3 to 5 ft above the surrounding field. However, at least 1.5 ft of this elevation seems to be accounted for by the presence of an eroded terrace or knoll that incorporates much of the site area. Soils from this unit were also screened through ½-in hardware cloth.

A zone of mixed dark, loamy soils, representing probable basket-loaded mound fill, was found beneath the plow zone. However, this zone was only about .5 ft thick above the subsoil. An examination of the profiles of the respective excavation areas thus suggests that the mound was placed on a natural rise such as a terrace remnant as described above. It is impossible to determine the original height of the mound, although elderly residents in the area claim that it was once 6 to 8 ft tall.

Despite previous observations that few artifacts were found on the mound, Table 25 shows that the plow zone in this unit contained a relatively large quantity of artifacts. Of particular interest was a soapstone pipe (Plate 35, Figure 17) found in the plow-zone soil. Carved around the pipe bowl is an image of a creature, first thought to be the Uktena, a mythical Cherokee creature: "Those who know say that the Uktena is a great snake, as large around as a tree trunk, with horns on its head, and a bright, blazing crest like a diamond upon its forehead, and scales glittering like sparks of fire. It has rings or spots of color along its whole length" (Mooney 1982 [1900]:297).

Plate 35. Carved soapstone pipe from square 90R350 at the McDowell site.

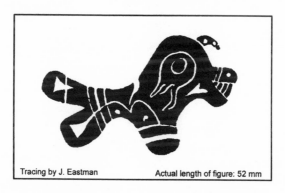

Tracing by J. Eastman   Actual length of figure: 52 mm

Figure 17. Zoomorphic design traced from carved stone pipe at the McDowell site.

Hudson (1976:131–132) also describes the Uktena as "a creature combining features of all three categories of normal animals. It had the scaly body of a large serpent, as big around as a tree trunk, with rings or spots of color along its entire body, but it had deer horns on its head, and it had wings like a bird. On its forehead it had a bright diamond-shaped crest that gave off blinding flashes of light."

However, the creature engraved on this pipe has a body that is somewhat serpentine but more mammal-like, and it has a single horn, a large mouth with teeth, and a weeping eye. Stylized wings or scales surround the body. Hudson (1986:145) also states that the Uktena was sometimes portrayed with the head of a cougar, representing the Water Cougar, an-

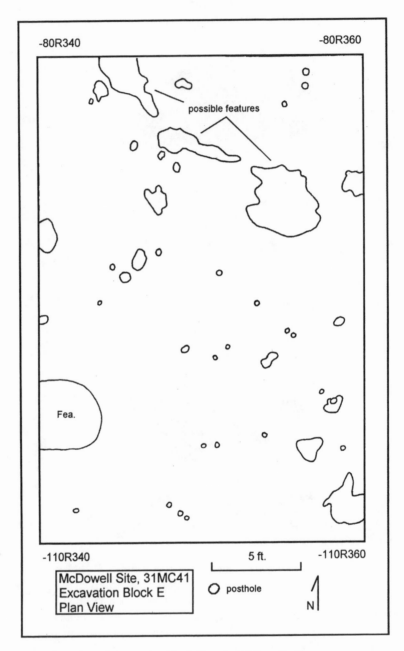

Figure 18. Plan view of Excavation Block E at the McDowell site.

other anomalous creature of the Under World. Though the creature depicted is unlike the usual Uktena symbol, it is possible that it is some sort of anomalous Under World creature.

Excavation Block E (600 ft²; Figure 18) was placed 200 ft south of the mound, where a falloff in surface material indicated the southern limits of the site. Ward (1977:4) reported a surface scatter of artifacts that covered an area approximately 250 ft north to south and 300 ft east to west. Though we were unable to conduct a surface collection over the entire site in 1986, the surface scatter covered nearly 400 ft north to south. It is possible that an additional 10 years of plowing (as well as deeper plowing) is responsible for this discrepancy. However, this unit yielded several vague features (some of which may be natural as opposed to cultural features) and a limited number of postholes. It is uncertain what the relative paucity of postholes and cultural material means with respect to the overall village structure.

Features

Seven archaeological features were excavated at the McDowell site (Features 1 through 4 in 1977 and Features 5 through 7 in 1986). The feature contents are summarized in Table 26. A brief description of the features follows below.

Feature 1 (Ward 1977:7): Feature 1 (Figure 19) was a shallow oval basin, 6.7 × 5.5 ft in diameter and less than .3 ft deep. The mottled brown silty fill included a small amount of pottery and a few lithic artifacts and small bits of animal bone and charcoal. No function was assigned to this feature.

Feature 2 (Ward 1977:7): Feature 2 (Figure 19) was a shallow basin similar to Feature 1, but nearly circular with a diameter of about 5.2 ft and a depth of .4 ft. The mottled brown sandy clay fill contained potsherds, chert flakes, and small bits of animal bone and charcoal. The feature function is uncertain.

Feature 3 (Ward 1977:7–8): Feature 3 (Figure 19) was the largest feature identified. It was nearly circular with a diameter of almost 6.7 ft and a depth of .5 ft. The fill consisted of three levels. The first was a dark-brown zone with large potsherds and charcoal; the second was a black fill containing an abundance of charred corn kernels and cobs, beans, squash seeds, and nutshell. Zone 3 was a thin lens of red burned clay that covered a small portion of Zone 2. The base of the feature was covered with large chunks of wood charcoal and cane among pockets of burned silty clay and ash. Feature 3 was the only feature to contain a substantial number of potsherds. It also included three clay disks and the largest number of lithic artifacts. The feature is believed to have served some function in food preparation.

Wood charcoal from Feature 3 yielded a radiocarbon age of 460 ± 75 B.P. (GX 11057; Boyd 1986a:67). Boyd provides two corrections to obtain radio-

Table 26. Distribution of artifacts from features at the McDowell site

	Feature No.						
	1	2	3	4	5	6	7
Contents							
Lithics							
Chipped stone projectile point	·	·	1	·	·	·	·
Hammerstone	2	1	1	·	·	·	·
Disk	·	1	·	·	·	·	·
Ground stone	·	·	5	2	·	·	·
Flakes	2	2	2	·	·	1	1
Ceramics							
Potsherds	25	34	206	35	15	10	18
Disk	·	·	3	·	·	·	·
Animal bone(*=present)	*	*	*	·	·	·	·
Fire-cracked rock	·	1	6	·	1	·	·
Daub	·	·	·	·	·	·	1

carbon dates of A.D. 1458 and A.D. 1434 ± 75. Additional calibrations yield a date of A.D. 1435. At 1 sigma there is a 91-percent probability of an age range from A.D. 1394–1509. At 2 sigma there is a 71-percent probability of an age range from A.D. 1386–1531 and a 17-percent probability of an age range from A.D. 1543–1636.

Feature 4 (Ward 1977:8): Ward interpreted Feature 4 as a modern agricultural remnant. The shallow, oval pit (5.1 × 3.8 ft in diameter and .4 ft deep) contained "a very black, 'greasy,' somewhat fibrous fill that produced little in the way of artifacts or food remains" (Ward 1977:8). However, in terms of artifactual contents it is similar to each of the other features except Feature 3.

Feature 5: Feature 5 was oval, 5.5 ft long × 3.5 ft wide. It consisted of a dark-brown loam that extended to a depth of about .3 ft. Beneath this was a zone of light-tan silty clay. The configuration of the feature form and soil zones and its association with Feature 6 suggested the possibility of a shaft-and-chamber burial. However, Feature 5 evidenced relatively straight-sided walls to a depth of nearly 3 ft, where subsoil was reached without any indication of the presence of a burial or a definite association with Feature 6. A small amount of pottery was found scattered throughout the fill.

Feature 6: Feature 6 was located adjacent to Feature 5 and was thought

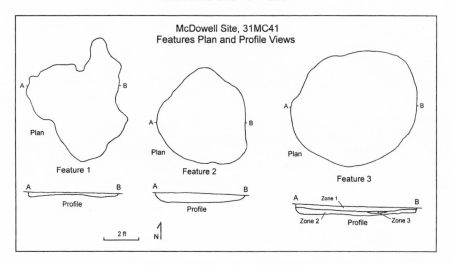

Figure 19. Excavation plan and soil profiles for Features 1, 2, and 3 at the McDowell site.

initially to represent the burial chamber of a shaft-and-chamber burial. Its surface fill was mottled but was less than .5 ft deep. This feature was excavated to a depth of 3 ft below subsoil level, without any evidence of the presence of a burial. Very little artifactual material was present. The feature walls and bottom were extremely difficult to trace, leading to an ultimate uncertainty about the integrity of the pit as it was excavated.

Feature 7: Feature 7 was a slightly oblong pit 5 × 4 ft across with a mottled dark, silty loam fill. Unfortunately, lack of time prevented more than a cursory examination of the feature. The feature was bisected and the eastern half excavated only to a depth of about .5 ft. Few artifacts were recovered.

Summary

The McDowell site excavations of 1977 and 1986 determined that this site is a relatively large village whose major component probably dates to the Pleasant Garden phase, A.D. 1400–1600. At least two domestic structures and one possible public structure were discovered, as well as the small remnant of a possible substructure mound. On the basis of the ceramic attributes found on Pisgah, McDowell, and Burke pottery from the site, it is likely that the people occupying this site during the Pleasant Garden phase (A.D. 1400–1600) participated in regional activities with Pisgah phase peoples to the west and Burke phase peoples to the east.

Appendix B

The Berry Site

The excavations described here were conducted by the author as a part of the 1986 Upper Catawba Archaeological Project. The Berry site (31BK22) is located on Upper Creek, a tributary of the Catawba River, about eight miles north of Morganton in Burke County (Figure 5). The site is situated on the extreme northeast margin of a 200-acre alluvial bottomland formed by the confluence of Upper Creek and Irish Creek. Warrior Fork flows south to the Catawba River from this confluence. The site is named for the Berry family, property owners of the site and its surroundings for four generations.

The Berry site was first identified in Cyrus Thomas's 1891 report, where it is described as "Mound on the west Bank of Upper Creek 8 miles north of Morganton (about 15 feet high and unexplored)" (Thomas 1891:151). The mound and surrounding site were regularly plowed and in 1964 the mound was bulldozed by the landowner to provide fill for low-lying areas of the field west of the mound. This area was often subject to flooding. A human skeleton was reportedly unearthed at this time, but no further details are known. A cracked but complete clay pot was also recovered at this time. After bulldozing, the surface of the mound remained about 2 ft above the level of the surrounding field.

Charles Carey and Robert Keeler recorded the site in the state site files in 1970, noting an earlier designation as 31BK2 on the basis of the mound report in Thomas (1891). However, the village site was renumbered as 31BK22 because of the uncertainty of the identification. At a later date the mound is identified on the site form as a "refuse mound" because of the high concentration of artifacts, charcoal, and faunal remains found on the mound surface. The entire site covers at least 12 acres, on the basis of the extent of surface artifacts (Beck 1997a).

The Berry site was selected for excavation in 1986 because of its large size, the presence of the mound, and surface indications of abundant artifactual, floral, and faunal remains. The site was especially important because of the overwhelming presence of Burke ceramics, and I hoped that these excavations would yield productive chronological information regarding the age of the Burke ceramic series. Most of the site was covered with a corn crop and a permanent alfalfa crop that restricted our investigations to a block 120 ft wide and nearly 400 ft long. Fieldwork began on June 9 and was completed September 11, 1986. The goal of the investigation was to remove the plow zone from several large block excavation areas and to record and excavate as many features as possible. However, the unexpected depth of the archaeological deposits encountered around the mound considerably reduced the area excavated and, consequently, the quantity of features found.

Excavation Results

The mound dominated the study block; therefore, two areas were selected initially for excavation trenches (Figure 20). The first trench (A) totaled 700 ft^2 and was placed across the mound from west to east. We hoped to determine the western edge of the mound and to investigate the area at the center of the mound, where large amounts of pottery, charcoal, and faunal remains were usually visible from the surface. The second trench (B) totaled 1,300 ft^2 and was located about 50 ft south of the mound. This area was selected to discover whether intact features existed in the area adjacent to the mound. This trench was also extended north across the southern edge of the mound to determine how much of the mound remained intact. Investigations of other site areas had been planned, but were precluded by the unexpected deep stratigraphy of the deposits found in Area B.

All excavation levels were removed by shovel in 10-×-10-ft units and the soil dry-screened through one-half-inch hardware cloth. Ten-liter soil samples and ten-liter water-screened samples were also obtained from each level. The base of each level was flat-shoveled and then troweled to reveal posthole and feature stains. Each level was photographed and drawn to scale.

Area A consisted of seven units placed in a 10-×-70-ft trench. Excavation here was generally limited to the removal of the plow zone, which varied in depth from about .8 to 1.1 ft. Beneath the plowed soil, mixed soils represented an undisturbed, basket-loaded, mound fill (Plate 36). Each basket load was clearly visible and there appeared to be at least two depositional episodes, on the basis of changes in soil deposition. Soils included light-grey to brown sands, light-brown to dark-brown sandy loams, and light-yellow to orange sandy clays. A deeper 5-×-5-ft unit excavated at the west end of this trench demonstrated that more than 1 ft of basket-loaded mound fill remained despite the bulldozing of the mound. In this small unit, the basket-loaded fill was underlain by three soil horizons (A–C) that together were nearly 1 ft deep (Figure 21). All three horizons consisted of sandy loams with the upper being a mixed brown to grey color, the middle

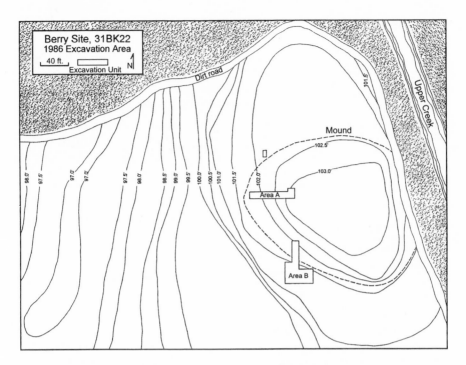

Figure 20. Plan view of the 1986 excavation area at the Berry site (31BK22).

Plate 36. Plan view of basket-loaded mound fill in excavation unit 380R290 at the Berry site.

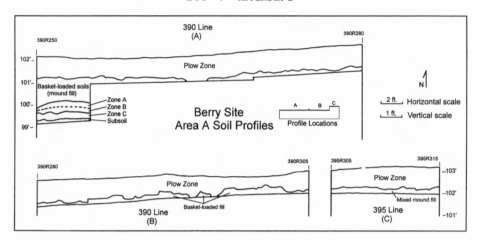

Figure 21. Soil profiles for Area A at the Berry site.

being reddish brown, and the lower being a mottled tan brown. On the basis of the small area excavated, it is unclear whether these soil zones also reflect episodes of mound construction.

There are at least two likely sources for the mound fill. The Berry family reported that originally there existed a large "sink-hole" in the woods about 500 ft northwest of the mound. It is possible that this pit was actually a borrow pit. Second, it is possible that soil was borrowed from an area 200 to 300 ft west of the mound. This was a low-lying area prone to flooding and was, in fact, partly filled in 1964 by leveling the mound. If this were the original borrow area, it is sadly ironic that the mound was leveled to fill it to reduce the problem of standing water in the field. Unfortunately, excavation was impossible in this area, but future excavation could determine whether and to what extent borrowing had occurred here.

The plowed soils of Area A contained large quantities of pottery, charcoal, and animal bone. Table 27 shows the distribution of plow-zone–level materials in four excavation units of Area A. Squares 380R270, 380R290, and 380R310 are each 100 ft^2 in area and are located at the west margin, the mid-slope, and the crest of the mound, respectively. Square 380R315 is also located at the crest of the mound, but is only 25 ft^2 in area.

Although most materials were represented in each unit, there was a heavier distribution of pottery, flakes, and animal bone at the crest of the mound, where an abrupt transition from basket fill to a mottled fill occurred. Whereas the plow zone over the basket-loaded soils contained a moderate amount of pottery and lithic artifacts, the mottled-soil plow zone contained larger amounts of pottery as well as charcoal and animal bone. In fact, this area contained the only significant quantities of faunal remains recovered from the site.

Table 27. Distribution of artifacts from Area A excavation levels at the Berry site

Excavation Unit → Contents	380R270			380R290				380R310				380R315 (5X10')		
Level	PZ	PZ & Mound fill	Total	PZ	PZ & Mound fill	Mound-fill	Total	PZ	PZ & Mound fill	Mound-fill	Total	PZ	PZ & Mound fill	Total
Lithics														
Chipped stone projectile point	.	.	0	.	.	.	0	1	1	.	2	.	.	0
Biface/misc. tool	1	.	1	1	.	.	1	3	2	.	5	1	.	1
Hammerstone	.	.	0	.	.	.	0	.	.	.	0	.	1	1
Anvil	.	.	0	.	.	.	0	.	.	.	0	.	.	0
Pipe	.	.	0	.	.	.	0	.	.	.	0	.	1	1
Disk	1	.	1	.	.	.	0	.	.	.	0	.	1	1
Polished object	.	.	0	.	.	.	0	1	.	.	1	.	.	0
Flakes (#)	4	2	6	8	3	.	11	14	3	.	17	4	7	11
Flakes (g)	11	5	16	42	5	.	47	136	18	.	154	16	51	67
Soapstone (#)	17	5	22	17	4	1	22	10	3	.	13	2	3	5
Soapstone (g)	110	29	139	121	28	3	152	64	11	.	75	8	7	15
Ceramics														
Potsherds	290	41	331	441	164	23	628	754	.	22	776	243	330	573
Disk	.	1	1	1	3	.	4	1	.	.	1	.	3	3
Pipe	.	1	1	1	.	.	1	3	.	.	3	.	.	0
Bead or effigy	.	.	0	.	1	.	1	.	1	.	1	.	1	1
Fired clay (#)	.	.	0	.	.	.	0	.	2	.	2	.	1	1
Unfired clay (g)	.	.	0	.	.	.	0	.	.	.	0	.	2	2
Faunal														
Animal bone (#)	1	.	1	56	3	.	59	90	22	.	112	153	195*	348*
Animal bone (g)	1	.	1	106	2	.	108	202	33	.	235	342	417	759
Shell bead	.	.	0	.	.	.	0	.	.	.	0	.	1	1
Shell (#)	.	.	0	.	.	.	0	1	.	.	1	.	7	7
Shell (g)	.	.	0	.	.	.	0	1	.	.	1	.	4	4
Fire-cracked rock														
Fire-cracked rock (#)	2	.	2	5	5	.	10	3	.	.	3	.	.	0
Fire-cracked rock (g)	117	.	117	350	351	.	701	64	.	.	64	.	.	0
Daub														
Daub (#)	2	.	2	.	.	.	0	.	.	.	0	.	2	2
Daub (g)	3	.	3	.	.	.	0	.	.	.	0	.	220	220

*Small uncounted fragments present.

The area of mottled fill is believed to represent an additional feature of mound construction distinct from the basket loading. The high concentration of animal bones and charcoal in this fill apparently contributed to the earlier interpretation of the mound as a "refuse" mound. The presence of the basket-loaded soils argues instead for an intentionally constructed mound and because early reports describe the mound as 12 to 15 ft tall, it is likely that the mound was built as a substructure platform mound.

Excavation Area B (Figure 22; Plate 37) included 13 100-ft^2 excavation units and yielded an unexpected but not surprising stratigraphy. Four separate levels (Figure 23), referred to as Plow zones 1–4 in the field, were encountered. Table 28 illustrates the contents of two excavation units in Area B. Zone 1, a dark-brown sandy loam, averaged 1.2 ft in depth. Zone 1 represented the modern plow zone and the soil included large amounts of pottery and minor amounts of lithics. This most recent plow zone was underlain by Zone 2, a light-grey to light-tan sandy soil. Zone 2 appeared to be a relatively recent alluvial deposit ranging from .1 to .6 ft in depth. Zone 2 occurred in every excavation unit in Area B; however, it appeared to be nearly plowed away in square 310R320. The age of this deposit is unknown, but it probably resulted from flooding in either 1914 or 1940 during which thick sediments were deposited in other areas of the Catawba drainage (Mike Ortosky and Roy Mathis, Soil Conservation Service, personal communication 1986).

Zone 3, a dark-brown sandy loam, underlay Zone 2 and varied from .5 to 1.4 ft in depth. The artifact density generally was higher in Zone 3 than in any other level. This zone probably resulted from a soil accumulation caused by plowing and erosion of the mound—erosion that had been accelerated by plowing on and around the mound. Zone 3 had nearly the appearance of a midden, but was completely plowed throughout.

Zone 4, on the other hand, was only partially plowed. This dark-brown to black sandy loam varied from .2 to 1.0 ft in depth, but was usually about .3 to .4 ft thick. In some cases it was difficult to separate Zone 3 from Zone 4; however, the texture of the latter was more compact and the looser plow scars of Zone 3 could be scraped away with care. Zone 4 represented a disconformity above the mottled subsoil, which appeared to be a buried A horizon with normal soil development over a B horizon (Ortosky and Mathis, SCS, personal communication 1986). Therefore, Zone 4 is interpreted as a cultural deposit that accumulated around the margin of the mound. It may also represent soils on an early mound summit. However, this level was labeled in the field as a plow zone since distinct plow scars were found in the subsoil below it. Interestingly, these scars were narrow (.1–.2 ft) and shallow (.1–.3 ft), suggesting a horse- or mule-drawn plow as opposed to the broader and deeper plow scars seen on the surfaces of Plow zones 2, 3, and 4. Though it was labeled a plow zone it was not entirely disturbed by the plowing. Many features (e.g., Feature 2 and

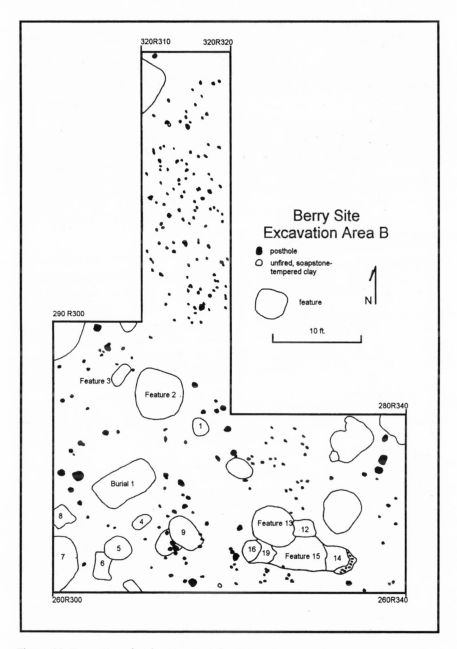

Figure 22. Excavation plan for Area B at the Berry site.

Plate 37. Berry site excavation area B (view to the east). (Note: Features 1, 2, and 3 and Burial 1 are shown after excavation and back-filling. Excavation of Features 17 and 18 is under way.)

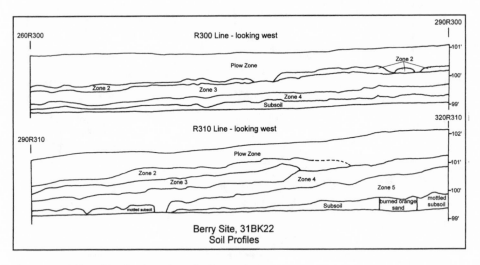

Figure 23. Soil profiles for Area B at the Berry site.

Burial 1) were visible at the top of this level. While the plow had occasionally passed through these soils, the basic integrity of the level was not destroyed. Unfortunately, within the zone, it was impossible to distinguish plow scars from the undisturbed soils, hence the entire level was labeled and treated as plow zone.

Table 28. Distribution of artifacts from selected Area B excavation units and levels at the Berry site

Excavation Unit	260R320						310R320								
Level	1	2	3	4	Subsoil	Total	1	2	4	5	6	7	8	Subsoil	Total
Contents	n	n	n	n	n	Total	n	n	n	n	n	n	n	n	Total
Lithics															
Chipped stone projectile point	·	·	5	1	·	6	3	1	1	·	·	·	1	·	6
Biface/misc. tool	1	2	·	1	2	6	9	·	5	1	1	2	2	2	22
Hammerstone	·	1	3	·	·	4	3	1	·	·	1	·	·	·	5
Pipe	·	·	·	·	·	0	2	·	·	·	·	·	·	·	2
Disk	·	·	1	·	·	1	·	·	1	·	·	1	·	·	2
Polished object	·	·	·	·	·	0	·	·	·	2	·	·	·	·	2
Flakes (#)	6	2	3	4	3	18	21	15	15	4	3	5	8	1	72
Flakes (g)	250	4	20	43	3	320	216	105	121	3	47	32	224	3	751
Soapstone (#)	3	·	8	1	·	12	13	6	8	2	·	2	6	1	38
Soapstone (g)	100	·	111	29	·	240	76	52	137	33	·	10	58	7	373
Ceramics															
Potsherds	341	100	362	117	48	968	709	199	490	144	137	153	176	46	2054
Disk	·	·	1	·	·	1	·	·	·	·	·	·	1	·	1
Pipe	1	·	2	1	·	4	1	2	2	1	2	·	·	·	8
Fired clay (#)	·	·	·	·	·	0	1	·	·	·	1	·	·	·	1
Unfired clay (g)	·	·	·	·	2014	2014	·	·	·	·	·	60	1054	675	1789
Faunal															
Animal bone (#)	·	·	·	3	·	3	1	*	·	·	·	7	·	·	8
Animal bone (g)	·	·	·	1	·	1	4	10	·	·	·	10	·	·	24
Fire-cracked rock															
Fire-cracked rock (#)	4	·	16	3	·	23	9	5	20	10	7	4	29	·	84
Fire-cracked rock (g)	2699	·	1020	49	·	3768	569	399	734	812	322	298	4214	·	7348
Daub															
Daub (#)	·	1	·	·	1	2	2	1	4	1	4	·	·	·	12
Daub (g)	·	8	·	·	2	10	5	2	6	6	13	·	·	·	32

* Small uncounted fragments present.

Zone 5 was located beneath Zone 4 in 300R320 and 310R320. Figure 23 shows that this level is deeper to the north and that Zone 4 overlays it to the north. The level consists of dark-brown to black sandy gravel. These quartz sediments with sand and gravel were inconsistent with the fine sands of the subsoil and as a result, Zone 5 is believed to be a cultural deposit associated with the construction of the mound. The possibility that these soils represented a natural terrace or sand bar was discounted because of the irregularity of the deposition. The sands and gravels did indicate alluvial deposits and must have been gathered from the floodplain (Ortosky and Mathis, SCS, personal communication 1986). Zone 5 was excavated in arbitrary .2-ft levels. These are reflected in Table 28 as Levels 5–8. However, no natural stratigraphy was observed within the level either during excavation or by an examination of the profiles after excavation.

Although it is not possible to correlate Zone 5 with the mound-fill soils from Area A, it seems reasonable to assume that this level equates to the three submound fill soil zones identified at the west edge of the mound in excavation trench A. Each occurs at a similar elevation and each is approximately 1 ft in depth.

In sum, the stratigraphy in Areas A and B is quite complex. Levels 5 through 8 represent undisturbed mound deposits whereas Zone 4 represents a cultural deposit that is associated with mound construction or use. It was plowed during the earliest plowing of the site. The depth and intensity of the early plowing was probably much lower than that of modern plowing, since although plow scars are present in the subsoil, features can still be seen extending from this zone into the subsoil.

Zone 3 is a thicker plow zone that represents a longer period of plowing. This zone probably developed as plowed soils were pushed or eroded off the mound surface. At some point, Zone 2 alluvial deposits covered Zone 3. Since Zone 2 is of variable depth, I suggest that these flood deposits were later covered with soil that was eroded and ultimately bulldozed off the mound and plowed, thus reducing its depth. Thus, Zone 1, today's plow zone, is a heavily plowed zone of soil that was formerly mound fill.

The interpretation of stratigraphy presented above is preliminary. Obviously, the stratigraphy of trench A is complicated by the history of mound construction and demolition. Additional testing around the mound and, more important, away from the mound will provide better data to determine whether this interpretation is accurate.

Site Structure

Unfortunately, very little can be said about site structure on the basis of the 1986 excavations. One probable circular structure (see Figure 22) is represented by a set of postholes immediately north and east of Burial 1. The density of postholes in excavation Area B suggests that additional structures were present adjacent to the mound. Also, the large quantity of postholes beneath Zone 5 in 310R320 suggests the possibility of structures that predate the period of mound construction.

Other elements of the overall village structure including the number or arrangement of domestic or public structures and the presence of palisades, a plaza, and additional features cannot be determined at this time. However, Beck (1997a) suggests that the overall size of the Berry site may be as large as 12 acres. He bases his estimate on the results of a systematic surface collection in which artifacts were found distributed over nearly 12 acres. The density of artifacts (gathered from 25-m² units), primarily potsherds, was relatively consistent across the site, although lower densities were found southwest of the mound. However, the density of the three collection units that included the mound was 10 times higher than the average density. This is probably a function of the fact that midden soils were used to build the mound and these same soils have been spread around it as described above.

Features

Twelve of 19 recorded archaeological features were excavated. These features consisted of pits representing a variety of functions including roasting pits, gaming-post holes, and burials. Table 29 presents an inventory of the contents of the excavated features. A number of soil stains representing other possible features were observed during the excavations, but feature numbers were only assigned to well-defined features.

Features were selected for excavation to provide as large a sample as possible of the various feature forms. Therefore features were selected on the basis of an evaluation of their form, fill, presence of artifacts, and presence of animal bone to provide subsistence data (plant foods and faunal remains) or charcoal for radiocarbon dating. Unfortunately, time limitations prevented excavation of all the identified features.

Feature 1 (Figure 24): Feature 1 was a roughly circular soil stain located at 278R317. The fill was dark-brown sandy soil with charcoal inclusions. Surrounding the dark circle was a less-well-defined, mottled, brownish-yellow soil. Artifact density was low, but a relatively large amount of fire-cracked rock was present, possibly suggesting a hearth area. At the subsoil level, the circular area did appear to be distinct from the surrounding soil. However, the feature edges and bottom were indistinct.

Feature 2 (Figure 25): This large circular feature was located at 282R311.75. It was easily observed in the subsoil level with a dark-brown sandy fill. Potsherds, charcoal, and fire-cracked rock were observed at the surface. Two major depositional levels were revealed, the uppermost of which included a cluster of more than 20 fragments of fire-cracked rock and nearly two dozen potsherds. This feature contained the most ceramics and fire-

Table 29. Distribution of artifacts from features at the Berry site

| Contents | \nFeature No. | | | | | | | | | | | | Burials | |
	1	2	3	5	9	11	12	13	14	16	17	18	1	2
Lithics														
Chipped stone projectile point	1	3	·	·	1	·	·	·	·	·	·	·	2	·
Biface	·	2	·	·	2	1	·	·	·	·	·	·	·	1
Hammerstone	1	·	·	·	3	·	·	2	·	·	·	·	·	·
Anvil	·	·	·	·	1	·	·	2	·	·	·	·	·	·
Disk	·	·	·	·	·	·	·	1	·	·	·	·	1	·
Soapstone (#)	3	12	1	18	8	4	·	·	1	·	2	8	6	·
Soapstone (g)	4	133	4	97	85	18	·	·	8	·	4	122	11	·
Flakes (#)	·	10	·	4	6	8	·	4	·	·	2	2	73	1
Flakes (g)	·	6	·	5	4	13	·	5	·	·	3	3	54	1
Ceramics														
Potsherds	30	358	5	101	149	183	2	274	6	32	69	124	63	11
Disk	·	4	·	1	1	·	·	·	·	·	·	·	·	·
Pipe	·	·	·	·	·	·	·	1	·	·	1	·	·	·
Bead	·	·	·	1	1	·	·	1	·	·	·	·	·	·
Unfired clay (g)	·	·	·	·	68	13	·	·	·	·	·	549	·	·
Faunal														
Animal bone (#)	·	7*	·	·	1*	80	·	2	·	·	1	·	·	·
Animal bone (g)	·	23	·	·	4	57	·	15	·	·	11	·	·	·
Fire-cracked rock														
Fire-cracked rock (#)	14	209	1	·	35	·	·	·	·	·	·	2	·	·
Fire-cracked rock (g)	1110	13,374	10	·	910	·	·	·	·	·	·	1050	·	·
Daub														
Daub (#)	·	·	·	·	·	14	·	7	·	·	·	·	6	·
Daub (g)	·	·	·	·	·	9	·	7	·	·	·	·	5	·
Wood post frag.														
(uncarbonized) (#)	·	·	·	·	·	·	·	·	·	·	2	10	·	·
(g)	·	·	·	·	·	·	·	·	·	·	165	43	·	·

*Numerous uncounted small fragments present.

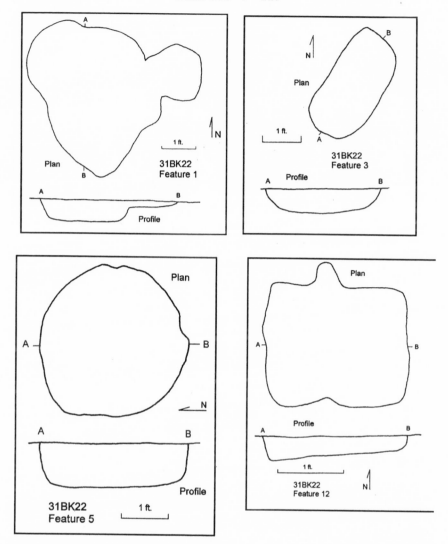

Figure 24. Plan view and profile drawings for Features 1, 3, 5, and 12 at the Berry site.

cracked rock of all the excavated features. An irregular soil stain at the north end of the pit also included fire-cracked rock and may represent an earlier pit hearth intruded by Feature 2.

Level 1 (.2 to 1.0 ft deep) consisted of a dark-brown sand mixed with occasional thin lenses of light-tan sand. The majority of artifacts, fire-cracked rock, and charcoal were found within the first .5 ft of the feature surface in a cluster located just west of the center of the pit. The second

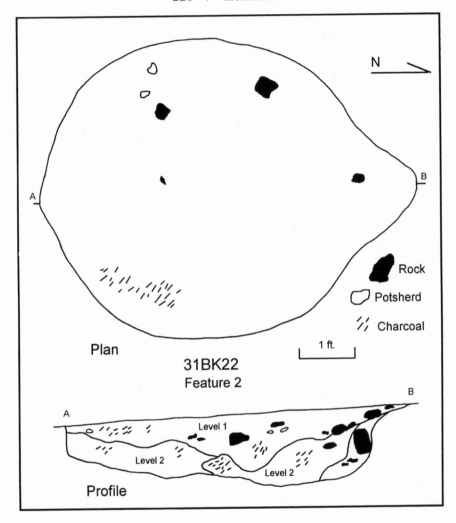

Figure 25. Plan view and profile drawings for Feature 2 at the Berry site.

level was less homogeneous. The south side of the pit was filled with a light-brown mottled soil and occasional artifacts, whereas the northeast portion of the pit was filled with a reddish-brown sand, more fire-cracked rock, and a greater abundance of charcoal. The pit edges were relatively distinct but the bottom was less so. There was no apparent hardening or color change from fires in the pit. As a result this pit is interpreted as a shallow basin utilized in short-term roasting episodes.

Feature 3 (Figure 24): This small (2.9 × 1.4 ft) feature was located at 284R308.25 and was quite distinct at the subsoil level. However, the mixed dark and light sandy soil matrix appeared more as a stain than as a pit. The feature was excavated to a depth of .6 ft and the fill graded into the subsoil without any discernible pit walls or bottom. No artifacts or charcoal was recovered. This feature may be of a natural rather than cultural origin.

Feature 4: This feature occurred as a lens of bright orange-red (burned) sand in Plow zone 4. It remained intact within the plow zone level, but appeared to be merely a thin lens of mixed red and brown sands at the subsoil level. One ceramic elbow pipe was recovered from the feature in Plow zone 4. The feature was not excavated into the subsoil level and its function is uncertain.

Feature 5 (Figure 24): Feature 5 was a circular pit 3 ft in diameter located at 267.5R305.75. Two soil levels were present. The first (.3 ft deep) was filled with a mottled dark-brown to dark yellowish-brown sandy (10YR4/3–4/4–3/3) soil with potsherds, charcoal, and ocher. Below this level the soil was mottled with a light-colored sand that also contained potsherds, charcoal, and ocher. The base of the pit was well-defined at a depth of about .8 ft. Despite the relative abundance of charcoal, fire-cracked rock was scarce and there was no evidence of firing on the walls or pit bottom. Therefore, this pit is interpreted as a trash-filled storage pit.

Feature 6: This feature was located at the south end of, and was intruded by, Feature 5 (Figure 22). The feature was shaped in an irregular oblong 3 ft long and 1.5 ft wide. It is possible that the irregular outline included postholes that could not be discriminated. The feature fill was similar to that of Feature 5 though it did not exhibit artifacts at the surface. This feature was not excavated and its function is uncertain.

Feature 7: This feature was observed at the top of Plow zone 4. It was located in the southwest corner of square 260R310 and continued into the south and west profiles of the square (Figure 22). Though it was not entirely exposed, it appeared to be a large pit at least 7 ft long by 5 ft wide. The dark-brown sandy soil contained fire-cracked rock and charcoal. Its size suggests that this pit served as a storage pit or as a roasting pit. It was not excavated.

Feature 8: Feature 8 was also observed within Plow zone 4. This was a small feature about 3 ft in diameter that was located on the west side of 260R310 and continued into the west profile (Figure 22). Its fill was light-tan sand with fine gravel. Feature 8 was not excavated and its function is uncertain.

However, the east side of the feature was intruded by a large cluster of charred hickory nuts in a dark-brown soil. Though Feature 8 was not excavated, the hickory nuts were removed for further analysis. The charred nuts were radiocarbon dated and yielded a radiocarbon age of 520 ± 50 B.P. (Beta-21817). The calibrated intercept is A.D. 1421. The 1-sigma range is A.D. 1400–1441 and the 2-sigma range is A.D. 1307–1473.

Feature 9: This feature is described under Burial 2 below.

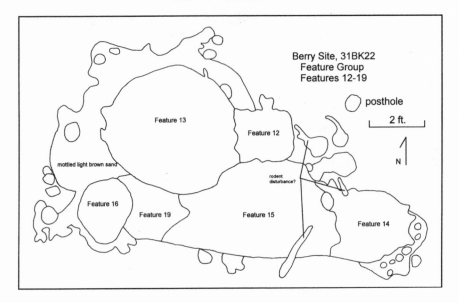

Figure 26. Plan view of the feature group (Features 12–19) at the Berry site.

Feature 11: This feature was located within the midden-like deposit at the east end of Trench A. The feature appeared to be well defined beneath the plow zone. It had an oval shape and was 4.5 × 3.5 ft in diameter. The fill was distinct from the midden matrix, being mottled dark- and light-tan/brown soil that contained an abundance of pottery and other materials. However, excavation of the feature proved to be problematical. It was extremely difficult to determine either walls or a floor for this feature. The excavation units in which the feature was located were expanded to try to find the feature edges, but we were not successful in doing so. We eventually abandoned work in this feature after deciding that the feature represented a disturbance (pothole) of the mound and that we were excavating disturbed mound fill. Interestingly, this is the only feature that contained more than a few fragments of faunal material, corroborating the overwhelming presence of faunal material scattered across the surface of the mound.

Features 12–19—Feature Group (Figure 26): Features 12 through 19 occurred as contiguous features and are termed a feature group as a result. The group was located in excavation units 260R330 and 260R340 and was first observed and drawn as Features 12–17. During excavation, Feature 18 was defined beneath Feature 13 and Feature 17 was defined beneath Feature 16. The entire cluster was approximately 14 ft long and 7 ft wide and was especially noteworthy for the variety of soil fills observed. Portions of the features were quite distinct, but mottled soils surrounded and obscured certain areas. This was particularly true at the east and west ends of the group. Another unusual aspect of the feature group was the common southern edge shared by Features 14, 15, and 19.

The feature group was initially observed at the base of Plow zone 4. However, it was extremely difficult to define the pit edges at the initial subsoil level; therefore, the subsoil was flat-shoveled in several thin layers until the individual feature outlines were more distinct. At this point the two excavation units were cleaned by trowels and drawn. The complexity of the feature group was such that several trowelings were completed before we drew a final plan view of the entire group. At this point additional mottling had been removed and we were left with a more simplified picture of the individual features.

It was not possible to excavate the entire feature group because of its size and the time available. However, we felt it necessary to try to determine the nature of the group or of individual pits as best as possible. We therefore determined to excavate those features whose edges were most distinct and/or least complicated by intrusions. Features 12, 13, and 16 were selected. However, because of the subsequent developments, Features 17 and 18 were excavated as well. The excavated features are described below, not in numerical order, but by their excavated order as a result of their associations.

Feature 12 (Figure 24): Feature 12 was nearly square with a diameter of about 2 ft. It intruded the east edge of Feature 13. The shallow feature (less than .2 ft deep) consisted only of a dark greyish-brown clayey sand fill, a fill unique for color and clay content among all those observed at the site. No artifacts were present. The function of Feature 12 is uncertain.

Feature 13 (Figure 27): Feature 13 was the focal point of the group because of its size and color; it seemed to anchor the entire feature group. Its large size (circular; nearly 5 ft in diameter) and distinct dark fill dominated the other features. The east side of the feature was excavated first. The pit edges were distinct and several depositional levels were observed. The uppermost was a dark-brown and grey sand with lighter-colored sand inclusions. The quantity of sand in the fill was such that it blocked the $\frac{1}{16}$-in screens at the water-screening table. Charcoal was abundant and moderate amounts of pottery and fire-cracked rock were present. A charcoal sample from this level yielded a radiocarbon age of 520 ± 50 B.P. (Beta-21817). The calibrated age is A.D. 1415. A second correction yields a 75-percent probability for the age range A.D. 1392–1435 (Stuiver and Becker 1986). This soil level covered the entire pit; below this a series of shifting levels included dark-black/purple sand with charcoal, grey sand and ash, a mottled grey-brown sandy soil, and a mottled light-brown soil. The depth of the pit sloped from about 1.0 ft at the south end to more than 1.5 ft at the north. Similar levels and artifact content occurred on the west side of the feature.

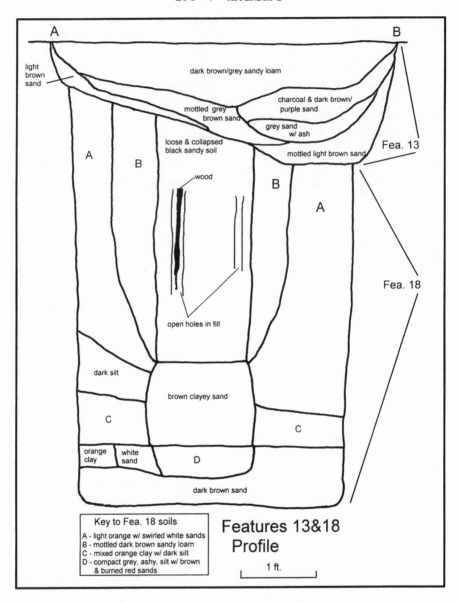

Figure 27. Soil profiles for Features 13 and 18 at the Berry site.

Feature 13 is believed to be a trash or roasting pit. However, this feature also coincides with the uppermost portion of Feature 18 (see below), a posthole for a large gaming post. Feature 13 appears to postdate Feature 18 on the basis of the stratigraphy seen in Figures 26 and 27. However, its placement over Feature 18 suggests that it may be related to the removal

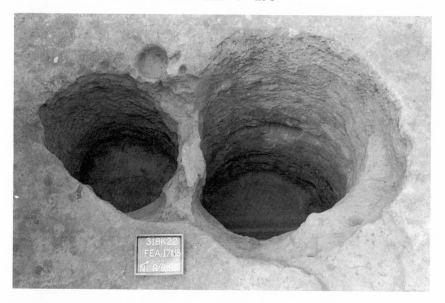

Plate 38. Features 17 and 18 (Berry site) after excavation was completed.

of the game post or to the point in time that the game post was no longer used.

Feature 18 (Figure 27; Plate 38): When the excavation of Feature 13 was completed, we observed that the soil beneath the feature was not consistent with the surrounding subsoil matrix. A variety of mixed soils covered most of the area of the base of Feature 13. Mottled light orange and brown soils surrounded a darker black core that consisted of loose black soil, some of which had collapsed into small holes. The combination of fills and the collapsed holes were interpreted as the top of a collapsed burial chamber. Since a similar configuration of fills and collapsed soil had been observed in the adjoining Feature 16, it was thought that both features represented burials or that one large burial chamber was located beneath both of them.

Feature 18 was excavated in arbitrary levels of about .1 ft and discrete fills were kept separated. At a depth of about 1.8 ft, the mottled soils on the northern edge of the pit appeared more clearly as a series of small post-holes. Also at this depth a small fragment of uncarbonized, decayed wood was observed on the edge of one of the collapsed holes within the loose black fill area. After the next .1 ft of fill was removed, a second small hole collapsed, revealing a small piece of wood standing vertically within the hole. The hole seemed to be a cast of what might have been a stick nearly .1 ft thick. The wood was removed and found to be a decayed stick more than 1 ft long. An additional .1 ft of the dark fill was removed and three more open holes appeared, each with a piece of wood standing vertically within it. The sticks were left in place while an additional .3 ft of fill was removed around them. Feature 18 was cleaned, photographed, and drawn at this point.

Leaving the sticks in place, we continued excavation by .1-ft levels, keeping all fills separate. By this time a ring of 16 postholes was clearly visible around the northern edge of the pit. These represented posts, .2 to .4 ft in diameter, that slanted slightly to the east. The postholes turned out to be more than 1.5 ft deep and the wooden sticks also turned out to be 1.0 to 1.5 ft in length. The bottom of the sticks was at a depth of about 3.4 ft. The loose black fill continued to a depth of 4.15 ft, at which point an irregularly shaped cavity appeared filled with a red/brown clayey fill. The surrounding brown fill remained intact to a depth of 5.0 to 5.4 ft. Beneath this depth no central column was discernible. A variety of fill was encountered to a depth of 6 ft, where fine and medium sands and river gravel marked the base of the feature.

Feature 18 is interpreted as a posthole for a large gaming post. The central column of brown fill surrounded the post itself which, on the basis of the width of the loose black fill, is believed to have been about 1.0 to 1.5 ft in diameter. Coe (1995:93–96), using the examples from the Town Creek site, provides a vivid description of the techniques used to raise such a large pole. A stepped ditch is dug beside the hole prepared for the post. The post is then placed into the base of the trench at an easily managed low angle and gradually pulled to a vertical alignment with the help of a supporting wooden frame. It is possible that the common border of Features 14, 15, and 19 represents the edge of such a stepped trench. The ultimate function of the entire feature group can only be determined with complete excavation.

Feature 14 (Figure 26): Feature 14 represented the easternmost portion of the feature group. It was not excavated, but the light-tan fill suggests burial fill if it is not otherwise associated with Features 17 and 18.

Feature 15 (Figure 26): Feature 15 was not excavated, but it resembled Feature 14 and may represent a burial if it is not associated with Features 17 and 18.

Feature 16 (Figures 26 and 28): Feature 16 was located at 264.5R332.5 on the southwestern edge of the feature group. It appeared as a dark circle (2 ft in diameter) surrounded by indistinct mottled soils. The surface of the feature was notable for the large quantity of heavy sands and gravel mixed in the dark-brown (10YR3/2–3/3) sandy soil. On excavation, we found the feature fill consisted of nearly 20 percent gravel and sand. Several potsherds were recovered from the feature. The bottom of the gravely matrix was reached at a depth of .9 ft. As the last of the gravel was removed, the bottom of the small pit collapsed, revealing several inches of loose fill below. Because there had been no indication of any recent disturbances at the surface, this was interpreted to be a collapsing burial chamber. The new

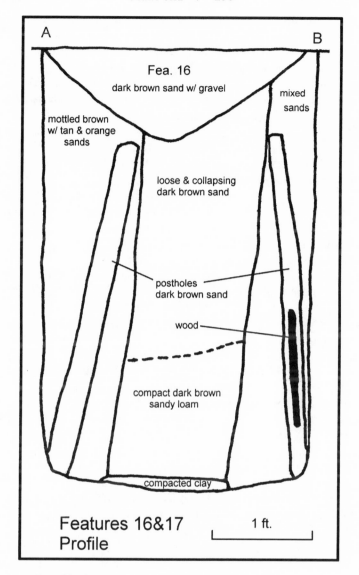

Figure 28. Soil profiles for Features 16 and 17 at the Berry site.

feature was designated Feature 17 and was thought to represent the remainder of the burial pit. This turned out not to be the case, as will be seen
below.

Feature 17 (Figure 28; Plate 38): Rather than a burial, Feature 17 turned
out to be nearly identical to Feature 18. The feature consisted of a small
circular column of loose black fill (1 ft in diameter) surrounded by a ring

of mottled soils all of which filled a pit 2.5 ft in diameter. At a depth of 1.9 ft a series of 15 postholes .2 to .4 ft in diameter became apparent in the surrounding mottled soils. A small piece of uncarbonized wood was encountered in posthole 3 at a depth of 2.5 ft. This turned out to be 1.1 ft in length and nearly .2 ft in diameter despite obvious decay. The fill and the postholes continued to a depth of 4 ft. At this level the postholes were located close together against the edge of the pit, indicating that they had all leaned inward toward the central column. Beneath this level a compact clayey base was found over original subsoil sand.

Feature 17 is believed to represent a smaller version of Feature 18. Each of these features included a column of dark loose fill surrounded by a mottled fill in which were found a series of posts flanking the outside wall of the pit. It is suggested that the interior column represents the pole and the remainder of the pit represents the hole dug to receive the pole. The wooden posts may have been placed on the edges of the pits to help provide a grip for the base of the pole as it was lowered into the pit and bumped against the pit wall (Joffre Coe, personal communication 1986). In the case of Feature 18, the posts found in the interior collapsed fill are believed to have been placed at the side of the main pole to stabilize it as the fill was placed into the pit. According to Richard Yarnell and Kristen Gremillion (personal communication 1986), the wood sticks are most likely to be heart pine.

Burial 1 (Figure 29): Burial 1 was first observed at the subsoil level in 270R320. The light-tan sandy fill immediately suggested burial fill, but the pit was unusual in its large size (6.5 × 3.5 ft) and rectangular shape. On the basis of the size and shape, we initially considered it possibly a historic period grave. However, excavation revealed a shaft and chamber burial. The interior dimensions were equally large: 3.2 ft from the top of the pit to the bottom of the shaft and .9 ft to the bottom of the chamber for a total depth of 4.1 ft. Few artifacts were found in the fill. One individual was interred in the chamber. The extended skeleton was complete but the bones were extremely fragile; none were removed from the ground intact and many were reduced to mere fragments upon being exposed. The interred individual was an older adult male, but the poor condition of the bone prohibited any further analysis (Weaver 1988). It was also impossible to determine the effect on the individual of a stone projectile point recovered next to the left innominate. Field observations suggested that the point was embedded in the body though perhaps not in the bone. It is uncertain whether the wound contributed to the death of the individual.

Despite the paucity of biophysical information, Burial 1 contained examples of personal adornment and striking examples of burial furniture. Copper disks were located above each parietal bone. Also, a bundle of artifacts was located on the floor of the chamber just above the skull. A dark organic stain, probably representing the remains of a container of

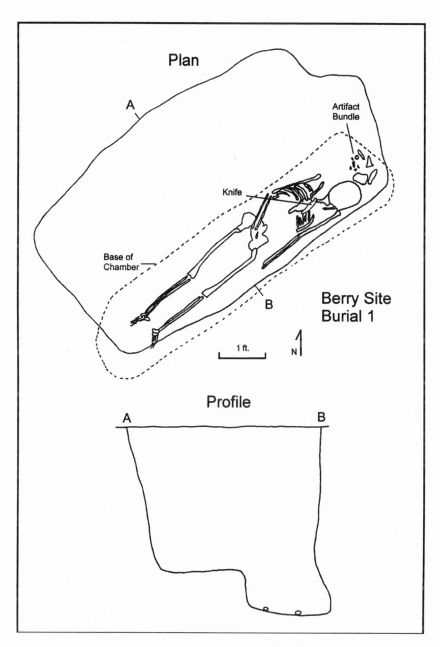

Figure 29. Plan view and profile of Burial 1 at the Berry site.

Plate 39. Iron knife from Burial 1 at the Berry site.

some sort, surrounded the artifacts. The artifacts were clustered around an intact turtle carapace that held a ceramic elbow pipe made from soapstone-tempered clay. A large, early Archaic, corner-notched point lay on one side of the carapace and a stone-working toolkit lay on the other. Included in the toolkit were two stone abraders, one small quartz cobble, one chert chunk, four small triangular projectile points, one thumbnail scraper, and eight flakes. All of the lithic artifacts were made from Knox chert except for the quartz cobble.

In addition to the artifact bundle, an iron knife was located across the upper chest of the individual. It is uncertain whether the knife was placed on the individual or was perhaps hung from the neck. The knife is approximately 14.5 cm long with a short (2.1 cm), apparently intact, tang (Plate 39). The blade is straight-backed with a slightly tapered tip and a beveled edge.

Dating this knife style is difficult. Its style most closely resembles the Type C knife dated by Hagerty (1963:98–101) to the late sixteenth to early seventeenth century. However, according to Jonathan Leader (personal communication 1988), the knife resembles "a popular style of utility knife manufactured in Europe prior to the contact period and [that] continues to be used to the present." Leader feels that the short tang argues for its manufacture as a trade item rather than a standard utility blade. Gregory Waselkov (personal communication 1986) points out that though the knife form is identical to eighteenth-century knives, that form is not temporally diagnostic and it may be earlier. Marvin Smith (personal communication 1986) accepts a sixteenth-century age for the knife.

Despite the occurrence of other sixteenth-century Spanish artifacts at the Berry site (see below), it is difficult to associate the knife with those other artifacts. The presence of the knife blade can be explained by at least two alternative hypotheses concerning the age of the burial. In the first, the age of the knife is accepted as late seventeenth to early eighteenth century, and it was probably obtained in trade from the Carolina traders. However, the major component of the site appears to date 100 to 300 years earlier. Also, on the basis of the otherwise total absence of European artifacts from that period, there is little evidence for a late seventeenth- to eighteenth-century occupation at the Berry site. It may be necessary by this hypothesis to view the burial of this individual as a later, intrusive burial; perhaps that of an important high-status individual at an unoccupied but revered location of ancient ceremony.

The second hypothesis accepts a sixteenth-century date for the knife as consistent with the other articles buried with the individual. The only source of such a knife in the sixteenth century is directly or indirectly from the Spanish explorers, and it is possible that this knife was one of the many knives distributed by Juan Pardo while at the town of Joara (DePratter and Smith 1980). According to Worth (1994a) and Beck (1997b), this is a possible scenario. Given the presence of other sixteenth-century artifacts and the lack of any later European artifacts, I also suggest that the knife and the burial date to the sixteenth century.

Burial 2/Feature 9 (Figure 30): This feature was originally observed and drawn as a dark circular pit about 3 ft in diameter with associated mottling on the southwest side. The dark-brown/black sandy fill included rock, pottery, and charcoal. However, after several re-trowelings we defined a series of small postholes on the east side of the pit and a cluster of larger postholes in the mottled area on the southwest side of the pit. The postholes on the east side turned out to be very shallow (.1–.3 ft), but those on the west side were deeper (to 1.1 ft) with well-defined sides and bottoms.

We suspected that the southeastern area of mottling might include additional postholes, but we also suspected the area might represent a collapsed burial chamber. We therefore began excavation of the larger, dark fill portion of the feature. This pit contained numerous pieces of rock, pottery, and mica, and abundant charcoal. The sides of the pit were all clear except on the west, where a stain on the floor of the pit extended into the mottled wall of the pit, indicating that the mottled area was either intrusive or represented the chamber portion of a shaft-and-chamber burial. We believed it to be the latter since there was no evidence of an intrusive feature at the surface.

A human skull was encountered very near the surface of the mottled area. Continued cleaning exposed two flexed individuals within the small (2 × 3 ft) chamber. Bone preservation was extremely poor. Each individual was tightly flexed and the condition of the bone made it impossible to determine their exact relationship to one another. However, it appeared that the first individual had been pushed as far into the chamber as possible so that the head was pushed up against the south wall. The second individual was forced into the remaining portion of the pit. An abundance of decayed

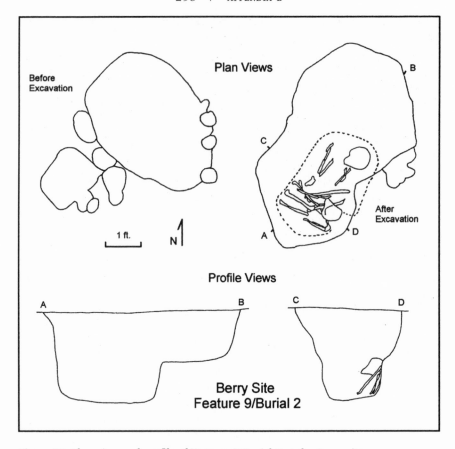

Figure 30. Plan view and profile of Feature 9/Burial 2 at the Berry site.

organic material on the east edge of the chamber suggests that wood or bark was probably placed over the chamber before the shaft was refilled with soil.

The condition of the bones was poor as a result of postmortem ground damage. No measurements were obtainable on axial or appendicular skeletons. The crania were relatively intact; both individuals appear to be adult males. No age estimate was made for Individual 1 but Individual 2 appears to be less than 25 years of age on the basis of the lack of occlusal wear on dentition. No other details of stature, robusticity, pathologies, or indications of probable cause of death were determinable (Weaver 1988).

No artifacts were found within the burial chamber and though this burial was located in the vicinity of Burial 1 there is no direct evidence of contemporaneity with Burial 1. Shaft-and-chamber burials are common to the west of the project area, where they appear as the predominate burial type for the Pisgah phase (Dickens 1976).

Subsistence Remains

Faunal remains were found in relative abundance only on the mound, including surface, plow zone, and Feature 11 contexts. They were nearly absent from other site contexts. They included primarily deer and bear, but also included turkey and other bird bones (Mary Ann Holm; personal communication 1987). A complete description of the ethnobotanical analysis from feature contexts at the Berry and McDowell sites is presented in appendix E (Gremillion 1993). The following is a brief excerpt.

Plant food remains were abundant in the Berry site samples and averaged 1.15 g per liter of fill. Hickory shell, maize cupules, and acorn shell were particularly abundant. Other domesticates present included the common bean and rind fragments of pepo squash. Seeds representing a wide range of grains and/or weeds and fruits were also present. These included chenopod, little barley, giant ragweed, jimsonweed, amaranth, ragweed, plantain, lespedeza, morning glory, poke, bearsfoot, spurge, and grass. Seeds of plants yielding edible fleshy fruits included maypop, sumac, brambles, grape, persimmon, and plum or cherry.

Gremillion feels that the plant food component of the diet at the Berry site was primarily maize, acorns, and hickory nuts, supplemented by cucurbits, the common bean, several fruits, and perhaps some weedy plants used for grain or greens.

Finally, Gremillion suggests that most of the features analyzed support estimates of summer and fall deposition on the basis of the fruiting dates and availability of the seeds represented within the fill. She also suggests that the seed contents of several of the features represent simultaneous deposition and that the wide diversity of burned weed/grain seeds may represent a burning episode within or around the village.

Artifacts

Projectile Points

There are no projectile point types specifically defined for the Catawba valley. Previous researchers (see Keeler 1971; Levy and May 1987) have relied upon typologies formulated by Coe (1964) for the Piedmont region, but primarily defined in areas east of the Catawba valley. A non-typological approach to projectile points has also been applied in the Piedmont region (Tippett and Daniel 1987). However, because of the proximity of the upper Catawba region to the Appalachian Summit region, the following typological descriptions are made with reference to both Piedmont and Mountain typologies.

Forty-three whole and partial projectile points were recovered; whole points and identifiable types are described below.

Side notched (n = 3): None of these points is assigned to a specific type, though they show some similarity to the Coosa Notched point (Cambron and Hulse 1969; Keel 1976). One point is made from Knox Black chert, one is manufactured from a variegated light-tan and brown chert, possibly from central Tennessee, and the third is from a light-tan chert of unknown source. These specimens may represent Middle Woodland points.

Small Savannah River Stemmed (n = 1): This type is defined as a "small, triangular bladed point with a relatively small rectangular straight stem and a straight base" (Oliver 1981:125; also South 1959). This specimen is made from quartzite. Oliver (1981:160) suggests that this type dates to the late Savannah River phase (ca. 1800 B.C.) at the Warren Wilson site.

Small lanceolate stemmed (n = 1): This point is a narrow, lanceolate point with a small, straight stem. It is made from rhyolite and does not appear to fit any described point type for the area.

Yadkin Triangular (n = 1): This type is represented by one specimen made from rhyolite. This is a medium-sized triangular point associated with the Woodland Yadkin phase in the Piedmont (Coe 1964).

Dallas Triangular (Lewis and Kneberg 1946:113) (n = 4): Four examples of this small to medium point were recovered. These are thin (2–3 mm) bifaces with straight bases and excurvate, pressure-flaked lateral edges. They are associated with the Late Mississippian Dallas phase (A.D. 1300–1600) at Toqua (Polhemus 1987). All specimens are made from Knox chert.

Pisgah Triangular (Dickens 1976:135) (n = 9): These are small isosceles or equilateral points. Five of these points are made on flakes and lack extensive retouching; the other four are bifacially worked with finely pressure-flaked lateral edges. Two specimens are manufactured from Knox chert, one from rhyolite, and the remainder from quartz. This type dates to the Mississippian period Pisgah phase (A.D. 1000–1450).

Corner-Notched Triangular (Davis 1990a:66; Kimball 1985) (n = 1): One example of this small corner-notched triangular type was present. It is manufactured from Knox chert. It is accorded a Mississippian period association in east Tennessee.

Pentagonal (n = 2): Two pentagonal points were recovered. They do not closely match the type descriptions for either South Appalachian Pentagonal (Keel 1976:133) or Pee Dee Pentagonal (Coe 1964:49). Each of these examples is small, measuring about 20 mm in length and width, but relatively thick (5–6 mm). One is made from Knox chert; the other from jasper. The latter specimen shows resharpened lateral edges. Dating these specimens is difficult. Pee Dee Pentagonal is associated with the Pee Dee phase, whereas South Appalachian Pentagonal has been associated with the Connestee phase (Keel 1976:133) in western North Carolina and has been assigned a general Mississippian context in the Little Tennessee River valley (Davis 1990a:66).

Incurvate base, straight blade triangular (Davis 1990a:66; Kimball 1985) (n = 1): One example of this type was present. It is a small triangular point with a general Mississippian context.

Straight base, straight blade triangular (n = 5): These small triangular forms do not easily fit established types. Five examples are present; four manufactured from Knox chert and one from quartz.

Carved and Ground Stone

Stone pipe: One piece of incised soapstone was recovered from the Plow zone 2 context in unit 290R320. It is thin (3 mm) and curved as if part of a large straight-sided pipe bowl. The incising includes line-filled triangles separated by parallel lines. Three other fragments of drilled soapstone are interpreted as pipe fragments, though they are too fragmentary to suggest size or shape. All pieces are from plow zone contexts in 310R320 and 260R340.

Stone disks: Nine complete or fragmented stone disks were recovered. These are comparable to the clay disks described below and possibly also served as gaming pieces or counters. They range from 19 to 55 mm in diameter. Four of the disks are soapstone and are finely finished. Another four have been roughly chipped to shape and are in various states of finishing. The final disk is drilled soapstone. It is roughly symmetrical, 30 mm in diameter, and about 14 mm thick, with concave sides and grooved to a depth of 2 to 3 mm on the outer edge. It is possible that this disk functioned as an ear spool.

Chunkey stone: One fragment was found in unit 300R320 at the base of Plow zone 4 that is part of a quartzite chunkey stone approximately 70 mm in diameter and 33 mm thick. It is well polished with at least one concave side.

Non-vessel ceramic artifacts

Non-vessel ceramic artifacts from the Berry site include clay disks, pipes, effigies, and beads. Two deposits of unfired, tempered clay also were found. Each artifact category is discussed below.

Clay disks: Numerous (n = 45 complete/2 fragments) clay disks were recovered. They are made from potsherds whose edges were broken to make a roughly circular disk, then ground smooth to form nearly symmetrical disks. The degree of grinding varies; 36 percent (n = 17) of the disks exhibit little to no grinding, whereas the remainder exhibit complete or nearly complete smoothing. Diameters range from 18 to 44 mm with an average of 27.1 mm, although most (55.8 percent) are 20 to 24 mm in diameter. The disks have complicated-stamped, plain, and burnished surface treatments and all are soapstone tempered. These disks are believed to be gaming pieces or counters and are commonly found on Pisgah (Dickens 1976:144) and Dallas (Lewis and Kneberg 1946:106) phase sites in the southern Appalachians.

Pipes: Three complete pipes and 37 pipe fragments were recovered. On the basis of this small sample, it appears that the standard clay pipe was a relatively small elbow pipe with bowl and stem meeting at a nearly 90-degree angle, though some examples are slightly oblique. Bowls include straight-walled, slightly everted, and keeled forms. Lips are plain, flared, or L shaped. Pipe surfaces are finely burnished (72 percent) or smoothed. Several bowls and stems exhibit ridges or incised lines around their circumference and one is decorated with circular nodes placed evenly on either side of a keeled bowl. Ninety-five percent (n = 38) of the pipes are sand tempered, whereas the remaining two pipes are soapstone tempered.

Clay beads: Four clay beads were recovered. Interestingly, each is of a different type, including tubular, spherical, large barrel, and flattened barrel with expanded center. Dickens (1976:146–147) also notes a wide range of similar clay bead types for the Pisgah phase in western North Carolina.

Clay effigies: Five fired-clay pieces are identified as possible effigy fragments. None, however, exhibits any identifying characteristics and it is possible that some of these may represent fired clay coils.

Unfired, tempered clay: Unusual caches of unfired, soapstone-tempered clay were found in two locations. The first (2,014 g), located at 261R316, was a clay-filled posthole. A second clump (1,114 g) was found in unit 310R320, apparently at the top of Level 8. It is uncertain whether these represent intentional or accidental caches or some other function, but clearly the clay was tempered as if for vessel manufacture.

Ceramic Vessels

Aside from the Burke vessel found by the landowners, ceramic vessels from the Berry site are represented entirely by vessel fragments (sherds). Berry site pottery was reviewed in chapter 2 with respect to other site assemblages in the upper Catawba valley. This section reviews the results of the attribute analysis for the Berry site assemblage and presents a more in-depth description of the assemblage. Sherds were analyzed from all excavated features (n = 13) and 10 excavation levels. The excavation levels include two plow zones (3 and 4), subsoil, and six mound fill levels. A total of 4,730 sherds were present in these contexts; after size sorting, 3,692 sherds greater than .5 in were analyzed. It should also be noted that an additional 1,216 sherds were analyzed for exterior surface treatment, rim form, and decoration only (the figure of 4,908 in Table 30 reflects the addition of the surface materials, which are not included in Tables 5 and 6 where the analyzed Berry site assemblage is presented). These extra sherds represent the entire Charles Carey and Tommy Stine surface collections

Table 30. Percentages of exterior surface treatments on pottery from Burke County sites

Site No.	Curv Comp St	Rect Comp St	Comp St Indet	Large Curv Comp St	Indet St Linear	Simple St	Pisgah	Smoothed-Over Comp St	Burnished	Corncob Impressed	Plain/Smooth	Check St	Cord Marked	Fabric Impressed	Net Impressed	Brushed	Misc/Indet	No.
31BK1	52.1	0.0	5.3	0.0	0.6	0.0	0.0	0.0	33.5	0.0	3.3	0.0	0.8	0.0	0.0	0.3	4.2	361
31BK5	0.0	0.0	0.0	0.0	0.0	0.0	0.0	0.0	0.0	0.0	0.0	0.0	0.0	0.0	0.0	0.0	100.0	2
31BK6	0.0	0.0	0.0	0.0	0.0	0.0	0.0	0.0	0.0	0.0	0.0	0.0	0.0	100.0	0.0	0.0	0.0	4
31BK9	6.5	3.2	12.9	0.0	6.5	0.0	0.0	0.0	0.0	0.0	32.3	3.2	16.1	9.7	0.0	0.0	9.7	31
31BK11	4.1	0.0	12.2	0.0	0.0	0.0	1.4	0.7	0.0	0.0	12.2	0.0	12.2	6.1	18.4	2.0	32.7	49
31BK12	29.3	0.0	10.7	0.0	0.7	0.0	3.3	0.0	14.3	6.6	28.6	0.7	1.4	0.7	0.7	2.1	8.6	140
31BK16	4.4	0.0	12.1	0.2	0.0	1.1	0.2	2.8	4.4	0.6	8.8	0.1	1.1	1.1	45.1	0.4	15.4	91
31BK17	35.8	1.2	5.0	0.0	1.8	0.1	0.4	1.7	17.0	0.2	24.1	0.1	0.7	0.2	0.5	0.3	9.2	3293
31BK18	31.9	1.1	11.1	0.1	4.8	0.0	0.0	0.0	12.6	0.0	20.9	0.5	0.3	0.4	0.5	0.0	9.2	1860
31BK19	0.0	0.0	0.0	0.0	0.0	50.0	0.0	0.0	0.0	0.0	0.0	0.0	0.0	0.0	0.0	50.0	0.0	2
31BK20	0.0	0.0	0.0	0.0	0.0	0.0	0.0	11.1	0.0	0.0	44.4	0.0	11.1	11.1	0.0	0.0	22.2	9
31BK21	5.6	0.0	10.0	0.1	1.1	0.0	0.6	1.1	4.4	1.1	50.0	4.4	1.1	3.3	1.1	3.3	13.3	90
31BK22	29.7	1.3	7.0	0.0	1.8	0.1	0.0	3.4	20.0	0.4	17.0	0.1	2.2	1.2	0.4	0.8	13.1	4908
31BK23	18.5	0.0	18.5	0.0	3.7	0.0	0.0	0.0	3.7	0.0	18.5	3.7	7.4	14.8	0.0	0.0	11.1	27
31BK24	40.0	0.0	0.0	0.0	0.0	0.0	0.0	0.0	0.0	0.0	33.3	13.3	0.0	6.7	0.0	0.0	6.7	15
31BK25	0.0	0.0	0.0	0.0	16.7	0.0	0.0	0.0	0.0	0.0	16.7	0.0	50.0	0.0	0.0	0.0	16.7	6
31BK26	0.0	0.0	0.0	0.0	0.0	0.0	0.0	0.0	10.8	2.7	5.4	0.0	10.8	35.1	0.0	8.1	27.0	37
31BK27	0.0	0.0	0.0	0.0	0.0	0.0	0.0	0.0	0.0	0.0	6.3	6.3	0.0	0.0	68.8	0.0	18.8	16
31BK38	2.1	2.1	8.5	0.0	2.1	0.0	0.0	7.4	6.4	0.0	44.7	2.5	12.8	2.1	0.0	6.4	12.8	47
31BK39	14.8	3.7	8.6	0.0	2.5	0.0	3.2	6.5	9.9	0.0	35.8	3.2	2.5	0.0	0.0	0.0	12.3	81
31BK44	0.0	3.2	22.6	0.0	0.0	0.0	0.0	0.0	9.7	0.0	45.2	0.0	0.0	0.0	0.0	0.0	6.5	31
31BK56	11.5	0.0	5.8	0.0	0.0	0.0	0.0	0.0	23.1	1.9	15.4	1.0	3.8	25.0	0.0	0.0	13.5	52
31BK209	7.8	2.6	14.7	0.0	0.5	0.0	2.1	6.9	7.5	0.0	35.7	0.3	2.3	0.3	1.2	0.7	16.6	577
Total	30.3	1.2	7.6	0.1	2.1	0.1	0.5	2.9	17.0	0.5	20.7	0.3	1.6	1.0	1.0	0.6	11.4	11729

from 31BK22 and were analyzed to compare the excavated and surface assemblages.

Tables 5 and 6 (chapter 2) present assemblage summaries organized according to temper and exterior surface treatment, respectively. It is clear from these tables that a wide variety of surface treatment attribute states are represented, as well as a variety of tempers. In terms of relative frequency, the most common exterior surface treatments are complicated stamped, plain smoothed, and burnished, which together are found on over 89 percent of the sherds with identifiable surface treatments. The remaining surface treatments include simple stamped, check stamped, cob impressed, cord marked, fabric impressed, net impressed, brushed, and indeterminate. The "indeterminate" code was used (perhaps excessively) if the surface treatment could not be determined with absolute certainty.

There was also a relatively large range of aplastics added to the ceramics in the Berry site assemblage. Soapstone (79.7 percent) was most frequently used, along with sand (9.3 percent), grit (5.9 percent), and crushed quartz (3.9 percent). Hornblende (.6 percent) and shell (.1 percent) occurred rarely. Given the importance of temper in helping to define most ceramic types (and particularly, in this case, the soapstone-tempered Burke series), the following discussion considers the overall ceramic assemblage in terms of the temper groups: soapstone, sand, quartz, and grit. Following this is a more in-depth description of the soapstone-tempered Burke ceramics.

Grit-tempered sherds (n = 217; the small number of hornblende-tempered sherds have been added to grit-tempered sherds for the purposes of this discussion) consist primarily of plain (47.8 percent; percentages in the following discussion include only sherds with identified exterior surface treatments unless otherwise specified), cord-marked (17.2 percent), fabric-impressed (10.7 percent), and burnished (10.2 percent) surface treatments. Complicated stamping occurs on 4.3 percent and linear stamping on 5.4 percent of the grit-tempered sherds. Brushed (2.7 percent), net-impressed (1.1 percent), smoothed-over complicated-stamped (1.1 percent), and corncob-impressed (.5 percent) treatments occur rarely.

Interior surfaces are usually plain or smooth (73.0 percent), though burnishing (15.3 percent) and scraping (10.2 percent) also occur. Sherd thickness was most often 6 to 8 mm (73.3 percent), followed by less than 6 mm (17.1 percent) and more than 8 cm (9.5 percent). Little information regarding vessel form is available and although more than 10 percent of the grit-tempered sherds were rim sherds, all but one of them was unmodified (the one exception being an appliqued rim). As described in chapter 3, these sherds are now typed as McDowell series pottery.

The quartz-tempered sherd group (n = 147) corresponds very closely with the grit-tempered group. Individual percentages vary slightly, but all of the overall patterns hold. Sherds are primarily plain or smoothed (51.1 percent), cord marked (13.5 percent), fabric impressed (13.5 percent), or burnished (8.3 percent). Interiors are overwhelmingly (73.0 percent) plain and sherds tend to be 6 to 8 mm in thickness (73.3 percent). All rim sherds were unmodified.

Crushed quartz is a very common temper among Piedmont ceramic types; however, like the grit-tempered group, the quartz-tempered sherd group bears little resemblance to previously established types. Individually, some of these sherds might appear similar to Yadkin (Coe 1964) or Uwharrie (Coe 1952b:307–308) ceramics.

The characteristics of the sand-tempered sherds (n = 345) are slightly different from those of the previous groups. While plain and smoothed surface treatments predominate (46.9 percent), burnishing (27.0 percent) occurs in large numbers, followed in frequency by curvilinear and linear stamped (8.6 percent), cord marked (6.8 percent), fabric impressed (5.5 percent), corncob impressed (1.0 percent), net impressed (.7 percent), and smoothed-over complicated stamped (.3 percent).

Burnished interiors also occur more frequently (29.8 percent) among sand-tempered sherds than among the grit- and quartz-tempered sherds. However, most interiors remain smooth or plain (59.9 percent) or occasionally scraped (6.4 percent). Sand-tempered sherds tend to be thinner also, with 40 percent less than 6 mm. Identifiable vessel forms include straight-sided and everted-rim jars as well as carinated bowls. Rims are nearly exclusively (97.7 percent) unmodified, with the exception being one folded rim.

Sand-tempered ceramic types are also well represented in the Piedmont region. However, as a group, these sherds are not related to the Badin (Coe 1964:28–29), Haw River (Ward and Davis 1993:65–67), Dan River (Coe and Lewis 1952), or Pee Dee (Reid 1967) types. These sherds represent Cowans Ford pottery (appendix C) and consist of plain, burnished, and complicated-stamped exterior surface treatments (also small numbers of the minority surface treatments).

The three temper groups described above represent a minority (19.2 percent) of the Berry site ceramic assemblage. The soapstone-tempered ceramics are by far the largest group among Berry site sherds (n = 2,942) and they represent examples of the Burke series as defined by Keeler (1971:31–37). Keeler (1971:32) describes well the distinctive nature of the soapstone temper added to Burke ceramics as well as the wide range of temper characteristics. However, the assemblage of Burke ceramics at the Berry site (and throughout the region) exhibits an even larger range of variation than Keeler described.

Soapstone temper ranges in size from miniscule flecks to individual pieces in excess of 6.0 mm. The largest piece observed was at least 12.0 mm. Although the temper particles tend to be similarly sized there is often a range from very small to very large within a single sherd. Keeler also noted the presence of sand or crushed quartz along with the soapstone and was uncertain as to whether it was intentionally added as tempering material. I suspect that sometimes it was and sometimes it was not. It is possible that fragments of quartz (or other material) hammerstones became mixed with soapstone as it was crushed and crumbled. In any event, I also observed the addition of grit, schist, and possibly grog to the usual soapstone temper. Sherds with these additional materials are coded as "plus" on Table 2 and subsequent tables. They represent a sizable (12.3 percent) portion of the Burke sherds. Most sherds are tempered with medium (2–5 mm; 46.4 percent) or fine (<2 mm; 40.4 percent), and rarely coarse (>5 mm; .9 percent), pieces of soapstone.

Keeler (1971:31–32) reports that paste and temper characteristics reflect spatial relations, as paste "exhibits a trend toward fineness from west to east or downriver. . . . [and hardness] tends to increase from west to east or downriver. . . . The trend toward less steatite in the temper is roughly west to east or downriver." Although the current analysis did not specifically examine hardness or paste characteristics, temper density was examined and I find it difficult to support any of these observations.

Keeler's Burke series includes the following types (based on surface treatment) in descending order of frequency: Burke Complicated Stamped (61.6 percent), Burke Plain (19.4 percent), Burke Plain/Burnished (16.4 percent), Burke Roughened (.3 percent), Burke Check Stamped (.2 percent), Burke Simple Stamped (.2 percent), Burke Plain/Brushed (.2 percent), and unidentified (1.7 percent). The relative frequencies reported in Table 6 (chapter 2) for the Berry site Burke ceramics are similar, but with a few significant differences. Most significant is the large number of unidentified surface treatments.

My analysis is slightly different from Keeler's. Keeler's use of "plain" in three different types is somewhat confusing, and I tried to simplify this by using it only in a single category. Plain sherds here include smoothed and unsmoothed sherds, but not burnished sherds. The burnished type includes only those sherds that have been smoothed to the point where compaction occurs on the surface and in many cases polishing facets are observed. It should be noted that the amount of smoothing and burnishing is quite variable. Also, I was unable to recognize "roughened" sherds. I may have included some of these in the "plain" group and some may have been cob impressed. As for the remainder of Keeler's descriptions, the current analysis provides some additional information.

Sherds with complicated stamping are consistent with Keeler's descriptions in terms of quantity and in the very low frequency of rectilinear stamping. However, Keeler included no examples of Pisgah ceramics in his tables and I suspect he considered Pisgah style rectilinear-stamped sherds to be Burke sherds if they were soapstone tempered. I suggest that these sherds are probably earlier than the majority of the assemblage and should rightly be classified as Pisgah sherds regardless of their temper.

Curvilinear complicated-stamped designs most often include combinations of whole or partial spirals or concentric circles joined by fields of arcs, straight lines, or diamond or square motifs. Formal figure eights or filfot crosses are rare (cf. Keeler 1971:34). Table 6 illustrates the wide variety of surface treatments on Burke ceramics at the Berry site. The vast majority (89.3 percent) are represented by the group that includes complicated stamped (49.8 percent of identified sherds), burnished (24.3 percent), and plain (15.2 percent). (Percentages in the following discussion include only sherds with identified exterior surface treatments unless otherwise specified.) Other surface treatments include smoothed-over complicated stamped (4.3 percent), simple or linear stamped (2.6 percent), cob impressed (.6 percent), check stamped (.2 percent), cord marked (1.0 percent), fabric impressed (.1 percent), net impressed (.6 percent), and brushed (.4 percent). Finally, a small number (n = 22; .9 percent) of soapstone-tempered sherds feature clear Pisgah (Dickens 1976) type rectilinear complicated-stamped motifs.

The above distribution becomes even more striking if the linear/simple-stamped sherds are combined with complicated-stamped sherds (since it is likely that many of them are portions of complicated-stamped sherds) and smoothed-over complicated-stamped sherds are combined with plain sherds. The trio of complicated-stamped, burnished, and plain surface treatments then makes up 96.2 percent of the Burke ceramics at the Berry site.

Burke sherd interiors are smoothed (44.5 percent) or burnished (50.6 percent) and rarely scraped (3.6 percent). However, among fine soapstone–tempered sherds burnishing predominates (58.4 percent) whereas plain/smoothed is most common (48.8 percent) among medium, coarse, and "plus" categories (48.8 percent, 65.4 percent, and 49.2 percent, respectively).

Vessel forms (where identifiable) include straight-sided jars (19.2 percent), everted-rim jars (66.7 percent), hemisphere bowls (.8 percent), and carinated bowls (13.3 percent). A much wider variety of rim forms occurs than among the non-soapstone-tempered sherds. Most rims are unmodified (73.4 percent), but 22.1 percent are folded or thickened, and 2.4 percent feature an appliqued strip beneath the rim.

The relationship between decoration, vessel form, and exterior surface treatment appears to be significant in the Berry site ceramic assemblage. This relationship would be more clear with the addition of a sample of complete vessels, but a number of the above relationships can be well described on the basis of the available sherd data. Vessel form is indicated by examining three attribute states: vessel portion, rim form, and rim/vessel profile. Decoration is indicated by the attribute states exterior decoration and decoration location.

More than 40 discrete modes of decoration were recorded for the Berry

Table 31. Frequency of decoration attribute states at the Berry site and 31BK17

| | | Berry | 31BK17 | |
Decoration	No.	%	No.	%
Incised lines				
Horizontal lines w/ loops	6	2.4	13	3.5
Loops below horizontal lines	2	0.8	6	1.6
H. lines w/ arches/brackets	5	2.0	55	14.7
Single line parallel to rim	2	0.8	0	0.0
Mult. lines parallel to rim	21	8.4	55	14.7
Short lines perpend. to rim	1	0.4	1	0.3
Inverted V	2	0.8	2	0.5
Rectilinear pattern	0	0.0	1	0.3
Complicated curvilinear lines	19	7.6	12	3.2
Complicated rectilinear lines	1	0.4	1	0.3
Parallel lines oblique to lip	2	0.8	4	1.1
Miscellaneous lines	7	2.8	14	3.8
Multiple V	0	0.0	2	0.5
Line-filled triangles	0	0.0	2	0.5
Multiple X	0	0.0	1	0.3
Notching				
V-shaped	6	2.4	9	2.4
U-shaped	20	8.0	12	3.2
Square	0	0.0	3	0.8
Vertical	1	0.4	2	0.5
Finger-applied				
Fingertip impressed parallel to rim	0	0.0	1	0.3
Fingertip impressed perpend. to rim	0	0.0	7	1.9
Fingertip impressed oblique to rim	0	0.0	2	0.5
Vertical pinch parallel to rim	4	1.6	9	2.4
Pinched	0	0.0	1	0.3
Punctation				
Circular reed	6	2.4	4	1.1
Rows of circular reed	1	0.4	0	0.0
Circular reed applied obliquely	1	0.4	16	4.3
Circular	0	0.0	2	0.5
Oblong	36	14.4	24	6.4
V-shaped	15	6.0	15	4.0
U-shaped	13	5.2	24	6.4
Multiple rows	17	6.8	1	0.3
Triangular, parallel to rim	0	0.0	3	0.8
Tiny circular	0	0.0	7	1.9
Linear oblique	2	0.8	7	1.9
Linear vertical	9	3.6	20	5.4
Roughly circular	2	0.8	4	1.1
Square	8	3.2	9	2.4
Tiny pointed	1	0.4	2	0.5
Long vertical	1	0.4	2	0.5
Elongated linear triangular	1	0.4	1	0.3
Misc. pattern of small circles	1	0.4	0	0.0
Multiple X's	1	0.4	0	0.0
Alternating oblique lines	1	0.4	0	0.0
Adornos	7	2.8	5	1.3
Miscellaneous	27	10.8	12	3.2
Total	249	99.9	373	100

ceramic assemblage (see Table 31). The discrete modes may be joined in groups according to the technique of application; i.e., incised (incised Lamar style, incised miscellaneous styles), punctated, finger impressed or pinched, notched, smoothed or brushed, scraped or brushed, stamped, added fillet, and added rosette or node (Tables 32 and 33). Despite a wide range of decoration, the frequency of decorated sherds is relatively low (n = 233; 6.3 percent of total sherds). However, this figure slightly overstates the actual number of decorated sherds since there are a small number of sherds that exhibit two or more different elements of decoration (i.e., there are examples of circular punctations on the shoulder associated with an incised scroll on the neck).

Punctation (46.3 percent of decorated sherds), notching (11.6 percent), and incising (28.3 percent) represent the overwhelming majority of decoration examples. Punctation occurs most often as single rows of circular or oblique (oblong) impressions placed on the unmodified, folded, or appliqued rim or the vessel lip. Nearly 20 percent of the punctated sherds exhibit multiple rows of circular or angled linear punctations; this form is associated with sherds of the Pisgah series (Dickens 1970, 1976).

Notching (11.6 percent of decorated sherds) occurs as U- or V-shaped impressions on lips and shoulders. Incised decorations (28.3 percent of decorated sherds) primarily consist of concentric scrolls, loops, semicircles, or brackets separated by extension of the parallel lines horizontally around the neck, shoulder, or upper body of the vessel. The great majority of these are decorative forms that are usually associated with the Lamar Incised ceramics reported in Georgia and South Carolina.

Tables 32 and 33 explore the relationships between decoration, vessel form, and exterior surface treatment. Table 32 provides associations between decoration type, location, and selected exterior surface treatments. Table 33 provides the associations between decoration and location according to rim forms.

To summarize, Tables 32 and 33 provide a good overview of the entire Berry sherd assemblage and as such may be used to characterize the ceramic vessels in use at the Berry site. In general, modified (folded, appliqued, etc.) rims occur on straight-sided or constricted-neck jars with everted to flaring rims. Vessels generally have small flat bottoms. A minority of these vessels feature unmodified rims. The modified rims are often decorated by notching, pinching, or punctation. These vessels may exhibit any exterior surface treatment, but are overwhelmingly complicated stamped, plain, or burnished. They are sometimes decorated by punctation at the shoulder or by incising at the shoulder or neck. Bowls are usually plain or burnished with unmodified rims. Carinated bowls are usually decorated with a field of incised lines placed between the shoulder and the lip. These are sometimes accompanied by punctations as well.

Table 32. Frequency of decoration and decoration location attributes for selected exterior surface treatments for Berry site potsherds

Decoration	P	F	N	IL	IM	S/B	CS	B	FL	R/N	Total
Curvilinear Comp. St.											
Decoration location											
Rim fold	3	–	–	–	–	1	–	–	–	–	4
Collar	–	–	–	–	–	–	1	–	–	–	1
Lower edge/scallop	5	–	–	–	–	–	–	–	–	–	5
Lip	–	–	–	–	–	1	–	–	–	–	1
Exterior edge lip	2	–	–	–	–	–	–	–	–	–	2
Just below lip	–	–	–	–	–	1	–	–	–	–	1
Shoulder	–	–	–	–	–	2	–	–	–	–	2
Total	10	0	0	0	0	5	1	0	0	0	16
Burnished											
Decoration location											
Rim	3	–	–	6	–	–	–	–	–	–	9
Rim fold	3	–	–	–	–	–	–	–	–	–	3
Applique/thickened	1	–	–	–	–	1	–	–	–	–	2
Lower edge/scallop	–	1	–	–	–	–	–	–	–	–	1
Lip	–	–	1	–	–	1	–	–	–	–	2
Exterior edge lip	6	–	8	–	–	–	–	–	–	–	14
Just below lip	2	–	–	–	–	–	–	–	–	–	2
Neck	–	–	–	4	–	–	–	–	–	–	4
Neck/shoulder	–	–	–	5	–	–	–	–	–	–	5
Shoulder	1	–	–	17	–	–	–	–	–	–	18
Shoulder tangency	1	–	–	–	–	–	–	–	2	–	3
Total	17	1	9	32	0	2	0	0	2	0	63
Plain/Smoothed											
Decoration location											
Rim	–	–	–	3	–	–	–	–	–	–	3
Rim fold	2	–	–	–	–	–	–	–	–	–	2
Lip	–	–	1	–	1	–	–	–	–	–	2
Exterior edge lip	1	1	2	–	–	–	–	–	–	1	5
Just below lip	3	–	–	–	–	–	–	–	–	–	3
Neck	1	–	–	2	1	–	–	–	–	–	4
Shoulder	–	–	–	4	–	–	–	–	–	–	4
Shoulder tangency	2	–	–	–	–	–	–	–	–	–	2
Total	9	1	3	9	2	0	0	0	0	1	25
Indeterminate											
Decoration location											
Rim	25	–	–	4	–	–	1	–	–	–	30
Rim fold	9	–	–	–	–	–	–	–	–	–	9
Collar	2	–	–	–	–	–	–	–	–	–	2
Applique/thickening	4	1	–	–	–	–	–	–	–	–	5
Lower edge/scallop	11	1	–	–	–	–	–	–	–	–	12
Lip	1	–	2	–	–	1	–	–	–	–	4
Exterior edge lip	2	–	7	–	–	–	–	–	–	–	9
Just below lip	8	–	–	1	–	–	–	–	–	1	10
Neck	–	–	–	2	–	–	–	–	–	–	2
Shoulder	–	–	–	1	–	–	–	–	–	–	1
Total	62	2	9	8	0	1	1	0	0	1	84

P, Punctated; F, finger impressed or pinched; N, notched; IL, incised Lamar style; IM, incised miscellaneous styles; S/B, smoothed or brushed; CS, stamped; B, scraped or brushed; FL, added fillet; R/N, added rosette or node.

Table 33. Frequency of decoration by rim form and decoration location at the Berry site

Decoration	P	F	N	IL	IM	S/B	B	FL	R/N	Total
Appliqued Rims										
Decoration location										
Appl. thick	4	1	0	0	0	0	0	0	0	5
Lower edge	0	1	0	0	0	0	0	0	0	1
Total	4	2	0	0	0	0	0	0	0	6
Folded Rims										
Decoration location										
Rim	1	0	0	0	0	0	0	0	0	1
Ext. edge lip	0	0	2	0	0	0	0	0	0	2
Just below lip	1	0	0	0	0	0	0	0	0	1
Appl. thick	18	0	0	0	0	0	1	0	0	19
Lower edge fold	15	1	0	0	0	0	0	0	0	16
Shoulder tangency	1	0	0	0	0	0	0	0	0	1
Total	36	1	2	0	0	0	1	0	0	40
Thickened Rims										
Decoration location										
Rim	1	0	0	0	0	0	0	0	0	1
Ext. edge lip	1	1	1	0	0	0	0	0	0	3
Just below lip	1	0	0	0	0	0	0	0	0	1
Appl. thick	1	0	0	0	0	0	1	0	0	2
Lower edge fold	1	0	0	0	0	0	0	0	0	1
Total	5	1	1	0	0	0	1	0	0	8
Unmodified Rims										
Decoration location										
Rim	17	0	0	12	0	0	0	0	0	29
Lip	2	0	4	0	1	0	5	0	0	12
Ext. edge lip	11	0	20	0	0	0	0	0	0	31
Just below lip	12	0	0	1	0	1	0	0	3	17
Neck	1	0	0	7	1	0	0	0	0	9
Neck/shoulder	0	0	0	3	0	0	0	0	0	3
Shoulder	1	0	0	13	0	0	1	1	0	16
Shoulder tangency	1	0	0	0	0	0	0	0	0	1
Total	45	0	24	36	2	1	6	1	3	118
Indeterminate Rims										
Decoration location										
Rim	9	0	0	1	0	0	0	0	1	11
Just below lip	2	0	0	0	0	0	0	0	0	2
Neck	0	0	0	1	0	0	0	0	0	1
Neck/shoulder	0	0	0	2	0	0	0	0	0	2
Shoulder	0	0	0	8	0	0	0	0	0	8
Shoulder tangency	1	0	0	0	0	0	0	1	0	2
Indeterminate	1	0	0	0	0	0	0	0	0	1
Total	13	0	0	12	0	0	0	1	1	27

P, punctated; F, finger impressed or pinched; N, notched; IL, incised Lamar style; IM, miscellaneous style; S/B, smoothed or brushed; B, scraped or brushed; FL, added fillet; R/N, added rosette or node.

Historic Artifacts

The historic period artifacts from the Berry site were first reported in 1994 (Moore and Beck 1994) following Robin Beck's recognition of Spanish Olive Jar sherds from a surface collection he made at the site in the fall of 1993. Beck subsequently reexamined the entire assemblage of ceramics from the Berry site (including plow-zone samples that were not analyzed in this study) and found two additional Olive Jar sherds, one of which had been erroneously identified as eighteenth- to nineteenth-century Moravian pottery. Since 1994 additional Spanish sherds have been found during surface collections at the Berry site. The following descriptions are from Moore and Beck (1994) with revisions to include those artifacts found since 1994.

The entire assemblage of historic artifacts from the Berry site consists of only 30 items out of a total of more than 80,000 artifacts (Plate 40). The assemblage includes 13 potsherds, 1 iron knife, 3 nails, 1 cut spike, 3 gunflints, 1 glass bead, 1 piece of melted lead, 2 buttons, 1 rolled brass bead, 1 piece of curved strap iron, 1 wrought-iron buckle, 1 wrought staple, and a piece of unidentified metal, perhaps pewter. Although a few of these items are clearly eighteenth century or later, at least 23 are sixteenth-century Spanish artifacts.

CERAMICS

A total of 13 sherds are believed to represent at least six distinct vessels. Vessels 1, 2, 3, and 4 have been identified as olive jars; Vessel 5 has been identified as Caparra Blue Majolica, and Vessel 6 has been identified as Grayware.

Olive jars are the most common earthenwares recovered from Spanish colonial sites in the New World, their use having spanned a period from the 1490s to the nineteenth century (Deagan 1987:28). These amphora-like vessels were used primarily to store and transport olive oil and wine, but were also used for olives, lard, condiments, and vegetables such as beans and chickpeas (Goggin 1960:256).

Goggin (1960) defined three forms of olive jar on the basis of variations in form and paste: early, middle, and late styles. New World dates for the early style range from A.D. 1500 to 1570. Middle-style olive jars seem to have been in use by about 1560 and were replaced with the late-style jar by 1800; late-style olive jars were used throughout the nineteenth century. Olive jars were used widely throughout the Caribbean area, into Mexico and Central America, and are occasionally found in the American Southwest (Deagan 1987:32). Though common throughout Florida and coastal areas along the Atlantic seaboard, olive jars are rarely recovered from the interior of the Southeast.

At the Berry site, four Olive Jar sherds are associated with Vessel 1, a

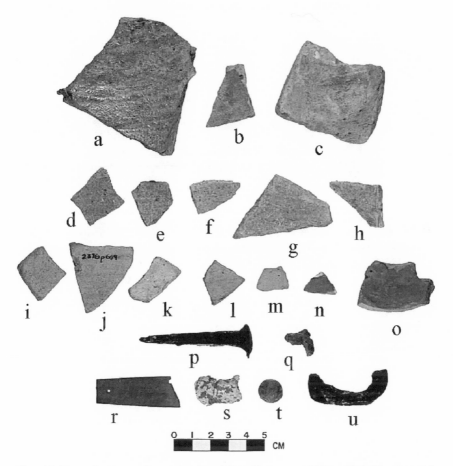

Plate 40. Berry site sixteenth-century Spanish artifacts. *a, c,* Thick-walled Olive Jar with interior lead glazing; *b, d–h,* thin-walled Olive Jar with interior lead glazing; *i–m,* thin-walled Olive Jar with plain interior; *n,* Caparra Blue Majolica; *o,* Grayware; *p, q,* wrought nails; *r,* brass clasp-knife plate (possibly sixteenth–seventeenth century), *s,* piece of melted lead; *t,* lead shot; *u,* wrought staple.

thin-walled jar with interior lead glazing (Plate 40, *a*). One sherd was recovered from undisturbed mound fill during 1986 fieldwork and three were found on the surface in 1994. Vessel 2, an unglazed olive jar with thin vessel walls, consists of three sherds that were recovered in 1986 (Plate 40, *j*). Two sherds are associated with Vessel 3, a thick-walled jar with interior lead glazing. One of these was recovered during the 1986 investigations (Plate 40, *c*); the other was recovered from the surface in 1994. According to Kathy Deagan (personal communication to Robin Beck 1996), the sherds in this assemblage are characteristic of mid–sixteenth century Spanish olive jars.

Another sherd, identified as Caparra Blue Majolica, is also temporally diagnostic (Plate 40, *n*). Caparra Blue is a common-grade tin-enameled earthenware. In the New World, Caparra Blue seems to have a chronological range of 1492 to about 1600 (Deagan 1987:63), and it is known to occur in but a single form: the albarelo, or drug jar (Lister and Lister 1982:61). This small carinated vessel is characterized by a slightly indrawn body, a short neck, a wide mouth, and a foot ring around the base.

Though never common, Caparra Blue has been recovered from many Caribbean sites, from sites in Mexico and Central America (as well as from Nueva Cadiz, Venezuela), and from the American Southeast at Santa Elena and sixteenth-century St. Augustine (Deagan 1987:63; Goggin 1968:135). Also, Charles Ewen (1990:83–91) notes that Caparra Blue has been recovered from the Governor Martin site, De Soto's first winter encampment, in present-day Tallahassee, Florida. There, Caparra Blue was discovered alongside fragments of early-style olive jars, Columbia Plain Majolica, and other examples of early sixteenth-century common-grade vessels. These forms are typical of those likely used on military-style expeditions. At the Berry site, a single sherd of Caparra Blue Majolica, Vessel 4, was recovered from the surface in 1994.

The final Spanish sherd (Plate 40, *o*), found on the surface in 1994, has been identified as Grayware by Stan South and Chester DePratter (personal communication 1995). This type, awaiting formal description, differs from the Grayware previously described by Kathleen Deagan (1987), which dates to the eighteenth century. The example recovered from the Berry site, possibly from the base of a plate-like form, is very similar to examples recovered from sixteenth-century contexts at Santa Elena.

The assemblage of sixteenth-century Spanish ceramics recovered from the Berry site is distinct from other collections of Spanish material recorded from sites in the interior Southeast. Similar Spanish wares have been found rarely in the interior Southeast. They consist entirely of one sherd of Green Bacin from the Tatham Mound in Florida (Mitchem 1989:321), a single sherd of Columbia Plain Majolica from the Pine Log Creek site in south-central Alabama (Little and Curren 1990:184), and one sherd of unidentified majolica from the sixteenth-century McMahan site in eastern Tennessee (Smith 1987:50). However, in each case, these sherds had been altered into nonutilitarian forms such as ear spools or gaming disks. That none of the Spanish ceramics recovered from the Berry site shows sign of such alteration may indicate the disposal of utilitarian waste. The only sixteenth-century site in the interior from which this type of utilitarian material has been recovered is the Governor Martin site in Florida. Also, the form of Grayware found on the Berry site, as yet, has only been reported from Santa Elena.

NON-CERAMIC HISTORIC ARTIFACTS

Though ceramics constitute the bulk of sixteenth-century material, several other artifacts, including two wrought nails (Plate 40, *p, q*), one wrought iron buckle, one wrought staple (Plate 40, *u*), one unidentified wrought object, one lead shot (Plate 40, *t*), a piece of melted lead (Plate 40, *s*), one glass bead, one brass clasp-knife plate (Plate 40, *r*), and one rolled brass bead, have also been recovered.

The single intact wrought-iron nail or spike (Plate 40, *p*) was recovered from the surface in March 1994. Stan South (personal communication 1995) has identified this nail as distinctive of sixteenth-century Spanish forms and notes that Spanish nails are characterized by a "flat to domed head, with some of the rose heads appearing like toadstools. They are usually more massive in appearance than wrought nails from eighteenth century British contexts" (South et al. 1988:43). The smaller nail fragment is similar. It was found in the plow zone during a proton-magnetometer and metal detector survey in 1997 (Hargrove 1997). On the basis of measurements of length and weight, this nail would likely be classified as the Barrote type. Documentary evidence suggests that Barrote nails were used in finishing work such as flooring, matting, and other projects requiring little strength (South et al. 1988:39–40).

A piece of melted shot of possible Spanish origin was recovered during the 1986 investigations. The heavily patinated shot seems to have been altered in the same manner as an example recovered from Santa Elena, the latter, according to Stan South, having been "subjected to heating on a flat surface, probably to melt lead for recasting" (South et al. 1988:86).

An opaque blue bead, identified as Kidd's type IIa40, was found on the surface in June 1994. This bead is round and measures 4.2 mm in diameter. Similar examples have been recovered throughout the Southeast from contexts dating to the latter half of the sixteenth century (Smith 1987:33). By the mid–seventeenth century, the round or subspherical beads of this type seem to have been replaced with longer, barrel-shaped beads, which persisted into the eighteenth century (Polhemus 1988:427).

A fragment of a brass clasp-knife plate was also recovered by surface collection. The plate appears to have been snapped and the remaining portion shows the evidence of two small drilled holes. The plate is about .6 mm thick, 47 mm at its greatest length, and expands in width from 13 mm at the original end to 18 mm at the altered end. This piece may date to the sixteenth to seventeenth century (Linda Carnes-McNaughton, personal communication 1997).

Finally, a rolled brass bead was recovered during uncontrolled excavations of the mound in the 1960s. This bead is slightly tapered and measures just over 1 cm in length. Marvin Smith (Smith 1987:37) notes that beads of this type are the earliest form of brass ornament recovered from the interior Southeast. Though usually associated with the seventeenth century, they are occasionally found on sites with early to middle sixteenth-century components.

As mentioned earlier, few diagnostic eighteenth-century items have been recovered. In fact, more items can be attributed with some certainty to the sixteenth and early seventeenth centuries than can possibly be attributed to the eighteenth century. Late historic items include three spall gunflints, a large cut spike, one porcelain fragment, two buttons, one nail, one piece of curved strap iron, and several brick fragments. Only the gunflints, buttons, and possibly the spike can be securely dated to the eighteenth century and early nineteenth centuries; it is unlikely these items predate European settlement of the area in the 1760s.

Most historic artifacts recovered from the 1986 excavations were found in disturbed contexts. However, two Olive Jar fragments and the melted lead shot were found in a partially intact humus zone (Zone 4). The only historic artifact recovered from a definite undisturbed context is the iron knife recovered from Burial 1 (discussed above).

Summary

Excavations at the Berry site in 1986 revealed the remnant of a probable substructure mound associated with a large village site. The site's major component is recognized as Burke phase and appears to date to the fifteenth to sixteenth century based on the radiocarbon dates and ceramic attributes. A wide variety of artifactual materials was recovered. Overall, site structure is difficult to determine on the basis of the small total area excavated. However, features are common, at least in the area around the mound that was explored.

Archaeologists from Warren Wilson College continue research at the Berry site. Future investigations will further define the nature of this large site and will examine the possibility that it is the location of Juan Pardo's Fort San Juan (Hargrove and Beck 2001; Moore and Rodning 2001).

Appendix C

Catawba Valley Pottery

The following sections present formal type descriptions for the Burke and Cowans Ford pottery series. Also included are tables of selected ceramic assemblages from sites in the upper and middle Catawba valley, a discussion of the use of soapstone as a tempering agent, and a brief discussion of Woodland pottery from the upper Catawba River valley.

Burke Pottery Series

Burke ceramics are first described (though not by the term *Burke*) by Holmes (1903:143–144) in *Aboriginal Pottery of the Eastern United States*. Holmes (1903) cites vessels from mounds in the upper Yadkin valley of North Carolina and remarks on how different vessels that appear to be related to the same occupation also reflect ceramic traits from the north, west, and south. He provides two examples of "southern" vessels in his Plate 129 (1903:145); these vessels are described in chapter 3 as Burke ceramic vessels. Holmes (1903:144) also reports that "from the Jones mound, in the same section, we have a series of vessels of still more modern look. So far as shape and finish go they are decidedly like the modern Catawba ware."

Keeler (1971), in his defining study of the Burke series, also recognized the southern Lamar ceramic influence along with the Catawba resemblance. These two factors have proved to be the focus of attention whenever these ceramics are discussed (Boyd 1986; Coe 1981; Moore 1987).

This study analyzed every available collection of Burke ceramics in North Carolina and, as a result, it is now possible to provide a more complete description of Burke ceramics. The following series description modifies that of Keeler (1971:31–37) on the basis of the results of this study. Modifications primarily consist of additional type designations and more discussion of attribute variability within the types.

Burke Complicated Stamped

Paste

Temper: Soapstone temper is the most distinctive attribute of the series. Soapstone is added as flakes as small as .3 mm or as particles/chunks as large as 6 mm. Occasionally, very large pieces appear; the largest chunk I observed was at least 12 mm in length. Individual sherds usually show similar sized pieces, but often a wide range of sizes is represented in the same sherd. Soapstone is extremely variable in color and texture, ranging from a soft, schisty or platy material, usually reddish orange to orange, to a finer silver-grey stone.

Additional aplastics often occur along with soapstone. These include sand, grit, schist, crushed quartz, and possibly grog. It is possible that fragments of quartz hammerstones became mixed with the soapstone as it was crushed and crumbled. It is also possible that clay sources include some amounts of sand.

Texture: Paste is generally fine, evenly mixed and compact. Temper quantity is variable from less than 5 percent to more than 50 percent, but is usually 20 to 30 percent. Temper particles are usually visible on both exterior and interior surfaces, but rarely protrude from the vessel surface. Sherds are well fired and hard: Keeler (1971:31) reports hardness from 2.0 to 3.0, and sherds have a distinctive ring when struck.

Color: Color is extremely variable, ranging from a nearly white buff to nearly black, with browns, oranges, and greys also represented. Color varies on the same vessel, firing clouds are common, and interior color often varies from exterior color, indicating that reducing atmospheres were usually present during firing.

Method of manufacture: Coils were added to a flat base. Coils were extremely well smoothed and annealed; coil breaks occur, but not frequently.

Surface Treatment

Exterior: Curvilinear complicated stamping usually comprises from 30 to 60 percent of a Burke ceramic assemblage. Stamp designs are often difficult to identify because of the large size of many of the motifs and the fact that many are overstamped, lightly applied, smoothed over, or eroded. Most designs include combinations of whole or partial bull's-eyes, spirals, or concentric circles joined by fields of arcs or straight lines. Sometimes the curvilinear elements surround diamond or square motifs. Formal figure eights, figure nines, or filfot crosses are rare.

The design motifs are quite large, but, again, it is difficult to provide accurate measurements without samples from intact vessels. However, examples from some of the larger sherds indicate that some motifs are in excess of 100 cm^2 and individual elements may be greater than 25 cm^2. Stamps generally feature lands of approximately 1 to 2 mm and grooves of

3 to 8 mm. It is possible that designs with larger lands and grooves and larger sized motifs have a later temporal distribution.

Keeler (1971) characterizes the stamps as "generally poorly made and sloppily applied." I am not sure that I would make the same characterization, but there is a wide range of expression and symmetry of the individual lands and grooves. The carved wooden paddles often leave a distinct grain impression on the sherd, especially if the clay was relatively wet when the stamp was applied. Partial smoothing over of the design often occurs and in many cases vessels have been completely smoothed or burnished over a complicated-stamped surface.

There also appears to be three groups of curvilinear stamps. The first tends to include designs such as keyholes, figure eights, and filfot scrolls or crosses. The design motif is relatively small (less than 40 cm²) and consists of even lands and grooves of 1 to 1.5 mm each.

The second group includes concentric circles, bull's-eyes, and barred ovals. The design elements generally have four lines and a design field of around 3 cm in diameter. Lands and grooves are even and around 2 cm each.

The third group consists of large elements, firmly applied, sometimes cleanly but often with considerable overstamping. They are also sometimes smoothed or brushed over. Designs tend to be concentric circles, spirals, bull's-eyes, and eccentric curves, joined by parallel arcs or sometimes nested squares or diamonds between circular elements. The circular elements have at least three to four lines and are 4 to 6 cm in diameter. Lands and grooves tend to be irregular and may range from 2.5 to 4 mm; most seem to be 3 to 3.5 mm. The entire design motif may cover over 80 cm². Again, it is possible that there is a temporal trend from early use of the first and second categories of stamps and later use of the third category of designs.

Interior: Interiors are usually smoothed or burnished, in varying frequencies. It is often difficult to distinguish between smoothed and burnished surfaces. A variety of materials may have been used to smooth, including fingers and pieces of hide. Burnishing was done with a small stone or piece of bone or cane. Scraping occurs rarely (<4 percent).

Vessel Form

Body: Curvilinear complicated stamping appears to occur exclusively on jar forms that range from open-mouth to constricted-neck varieties. The only vessels observed are those from the Yadkin valley and all are constricted-neck jars with slightly flaring rims. Below the neck, forms are usually globular to slightly conoidal.

Base: Jar bases usually feature a small flattened surface and tend to be slightly thicker than the vessel body.

Thickness: Vessel walls range from 4 to 12 mm thick. Most are 6 to 8 mm

(63.4 percent), followed by 20.9 percent that are less than 6 mm and 15.6 percent that are greater than 8 mm.

Rim: Vessel rims are usually everted or flaring and occasionally straight. Modifications to the rim include folding or otherwise thickening the rim by placement of an added coil at the lip around the exterior of the vessel. In some instances the added coil is placed beneath the lip and is referred to as an appliqued strip. Folded and thickened rim strips range from 10 to 23 mm. It is likely that rim modifications are temporally diagnostic. According to studies on the lower Wateree River (DePratter and Judge 1990), wider rim strips are later in time. I suggest that the use of the appliqued strip would be considered later as well.

Frequencies of modification vary between sites, possibly representing temporal differences. At the Berry site rims are usually unmodified (58.6 percent), whereas at 31BK17 they are usually folded or thickened (54.7 percent). The appliqued strip form occurs on less than 5 percent of the rims.

Lip: Lips are usually flattened (80 percent) and sometimes rounded (20 percent).

Decoration

Punctation and notching represent the overwhelming majority of decoration modes on Burke Complicated Stamped rim sherds. Punctation occurs most often as single rows of circular or oblique (oblong) impressions placed on the unmodified, folded, or appliqued rim or the vessel lip. Notching (11.6 percent of decorated sherds) occurs as U- or V-shaped impressions on lips and shoulders.

Very occasionally a Burke incised design occurs on the shoulder or neck of a jar with a slightly constricted neck. The design does not extend below the shoulder nor above mid-neck.

Burke Plain/Smoothed

Paste

Temper: Temper is generally the same as Burke Complicated Stamped. However, temper size is more often fine than medium and almost never coarse (43.1 percent to 37.3 percent to 0.5 percent, respectively, at the Berry site).

Texture: The same as Burke Complicated Stamped.

Color: The same as Burke Complicated Stamped.

Method of manufacture: The same as Burke Complicated Stamped.

Surface Treatment

Exterior: Keeler (1971:35) defined a Burke Plain and a Burke Plain/ Burnished type separated on the basis of the use of the burnishing technique. He also observed that it was sometimes difficult to distinguish between them. I have changed the terminology slightly while maintaining the technological distinction. Plain/smoothed sherds show more or less smoothing, but show no evidence of surface compaction or burnishing facets. Smoothing was accomplished by rubbing the vessel surface with fingers or possibly a soft hide before drying the vessel.

The frequency of plain/smoothed varies by site assemblage. In the attribute analysis, a variable percentage of sherds from most sites were coded as having smoothed-over complicated-stamped surface treatments. These were sherds that clearly had been stamped originally and then smoothed over to almost completely obliterate the stamping. They were identifiable only when the lands on the stamps had not been totally reduced. I do not believe these sherds warrant a separate type, but they should be classed as Burke Plain/Smoothed. When these sherds are added to the above figures the frequency of Plain/Smoothed becomes 19.5 percent at the Berry site and 22.6 percent at 31BK17.

Interior: Interiors are usually smoothed and occasionally burnished.

Vessel Form

Body: Few data are available; however, it appears that vessels are primarily open bowl and carinated bowl forms and occasionally (probably <10 percent) constricted-neck jars.

Base: The same as Burke Complicated Stamped.

Thickness: Similar range as for Burke Complicated Stamped; however, there is a greater frequency of thickness less than 6 mm in this type than for the curvilinear stamped.

Rim: Rims are nearly exclusively carinated or in-slanting, and occasionally straight or slightly flaring.

Lip: The same as Burke Complicated Stamped.

Decoration

Decoration most often consists of punctation or notching on the exterior edge of the lip, just below the lip, or at the shoulder tangency. If the rim is thickened or folded, the same techniques occur on the rim.

Burke Burnished

Paste

Temper: Temper is generally the same as Burke Plain/Smoothed, with an even larger percentage of fine soapstone.

Texture: The same as Burke Complicated Stamped.

Color: Generally the same as Burke Complicated Stamped, with perhaps a higher frequency of dark grey to black.

Method of manufacture: The same as Burke Complicated Stamped.

Surface Treatment

Exterior: Burnished surfaces have been rubbed to a "leather-hard" state with a polishing stone or a piece of bone or reed after initial drying. Rubbing is done with pressure so that the surface becomes smooth and compacted, and burnishing facets are often left on the surface. The degree of burnishing is variable: some vessels are lightly and irregularly burnished whereas others are finely polished such that a sheen appears on the surface.

Interior: Most often burnished but also smoothed or, very rarely, scraped.

Vessel Form

Body: Vessels are primarily carinated bowl forms, occasionally hemisphere or wide-mouth bowls, and rarely (probably <5 percent) constricted-neck jars.

Base: The same as Burke Complicated Stamped.

Thickness: This type is consistently the thinnest among the Burke sherds. The range is from 3 to 10 mm, but more than 50 percent are less than 6 mm.

Rim: Rims are nearly exclusively carinated or in-slanting.

Lip: The same as Burke Complicated Stamped.

Decoration

Decoration most often consists of punctation or notching on the exterior edge of the lip, just below the lip, or at the shoulder tangency. If the rim is thickened or folded, the same techniques occur on the rim.

Burke Incised

I have established this new type not on the basis of surface treatment, but on the use of incised decorations. I make the new designation because of its similarity to the Lamar Incised type of Georgia and South Carolina. I believe that this type designation will allow more fruitful comparisons of the Burke series with other Lamar style ceramics.

Paste

All characteristics are the same as for Burke Burnished.

Surface Treatment

Exterior: Burnished or plain/smoothed.
Interior: The same as Burke Burnished.

Vessel Form

Body: Vessels are carinated bowls or wide-mouth bowls with in-slanting rims.

Base: The same as Burke Burnished.
Thickness: The same as Burke Burnished.
Rim: Carinated or in-slanting.
Lip: Usually flattened.

Decoration

Incising is carried out with the use of a sharp instrument, probably a sharpened piece of cane. The implement is used as a graver to carve lines in the vessel surface. Incising always occurs after the vessel has been burnished or after initial drying if the surface is plain/smoothed. The incised edges are usually smooth and clean and show little evidence of curling (occurs when clay is still damp) or crazing (occurs when clay is nearly completely dry).

Burke Incised designs include brackets, scrolls, and concentric loops joined by multiple (3–10) horizontal lines. The loops and scrolls may be widely or narrowly spaced and may begin at the top line or among the middle or bottom horizontal lines.

The initial appearance, frequency, and style of Lamar Incised pottery is temporally diagnostic (Hally 1986, 1994) within many areas, including the Wateree River valley (DePratter and Judge 1990), the Savannah River valley (Anderson et al. 1986; Hally 1990), the Upper Coosa River (Hally 1990), and the Oconee River (Smith and Williams 1990). It is likely that the appearance and frequency of Burke Incised is similarly diagnostic, but examples from more dated contexts will be needed to confirm this.

Burke Minority Types

Keeler (1971:36–37) described four minority types: Check Stamped, Simple Stamped, Roughened, and Plain/Brushed, none of which accounted for more than .3 percent of his total. My analysis shows a very small number of soapstone-tempered sherds with those surface treatments, along with fabric-, corncob-, and net-impressed surfaces present at many sites. Their combined frequencies are so low that nothing can be said of them as types. It is likely that some of these surface treatments reflect holdovers from earlier Woodland period ceramic types. It is also likely that others, such as corncob- and net-impressed treatments, reflect some level of influence from the coeval Dan River ceramic tradition that is so well represented in the north-central Piedmont region. In any event, little more can be said of these ceramics.

Keeler's original Burke series description includes the following types (based on surface treatment) in descending order of frequency: Burke Complicated Stamped (61.6 percent), Burke Plain (19.4 percent), Burke Plain/ Burnished (16.4 percent), Burke Roughened (.3 percent), Burke Check Stamped (.2 percent), Burke Simple Stamped (.2 percent), Burke Plain/ Brushed (.2 percent), and unidentified (1.7 percent). Although the analysis presented here is slightly different, it remains clear that the Burke ceramic series is made up primarily of curvilinear complicated stamped, plain, and burnished pottery.

Soapstone Temper

When considering the occurrence of soapstone-tempered pottery, it is important to note that the distribution of naturally occurring soapstone has little, if any, correlation to the distribution of its use as a tempering agent.

Soapstone is sometimes referred to as steatite, and although the terms have been used almost interchangeably (see Bushnell 1939; Dickens and Carnes 1977; Holmes 1890) there are subtle but important distinctions between them. These distinctions concern the amount of talc present in the rock. According to Stuckey (1965:455), "Talc is a hydrous magnesium silicate having the general formula $H_2OMg_3Si_4O_{12}$. Theoretically, talc contains 31.7 percent MgO, 63.5 percent SiO_2 and 4.8 percent H_2O. . . . Steatite is a compact massive type of very pure talc. . . . Soapstone is a soft rock containing 10 to 80 percent talc and one or more of the minerals chlorite, serpentine, magnesite, tremolite, actinolite, diopside, enstatite, and occasionally some quartz, magnetite or pyrite."

Stuckey (1965:456) also describes the formation of soapstone: "Talc and soapstone occur in altered ultrabasic intrusive igneous rocks, while the better grades of steatite talc occur in metamorphosed dolomitic limestone. . . . The formation of talc and soapstone is due to the action of magmatic solutions during which materials are both added to and removed from the older rocks."

For the purposes of this study the term *soapstone* is used exclusively. I have made no attempt to identify the constituent minerals of the temper material; therefore, I cannot discriminate between steatite and soapstone. However, it is my impression that the relevant materials present in the region vary greatly in mineral content, hardness, and texture, and thus deserve the name soapstone.

Soapstone occurs in the Piedmont and Appalachian Mountains of the eastern United States from Newfoundland to Alabama (Ferguson 1980:7). It is especially abundant in western North Carolina as a result of the occurrence of a belt of soapstone-bearing, ultramafic rock bodies along the western edge of the Blue Ridge Mountains (Misra and Keller 1978:389). More than 275 of these formations have been identified along the 500-km belt in Georgia and North Carolina (Misra and Keller 1978:391). Principal deposits in western North Carolina are found in Jackson, Buncombe, Madison, Yancey, Mitchell, Ashe, and Alleghany counties (Stuckey 1965:456). In the Piedmont, Misra and Keller (1978:389) describe an "ill-defined belt consisting of scattered [ultramafic] bodies." The largest deposits in the North Carolina Piedmont occur in Wake and Granville counties. However, the only Piedmont deposits to have been worked commercially were located in McDowell County (Stuckey 1965:456).

Aboriginal soapstone quarry locations are obviously limited by the natural distribution of soapstone. Although there has been no systematic attempt to identify all soapstone quarry sites in western North Carolina, a substantial number have been recorded. Mathis (1981), Bohanan (1975), and the North Carolina state site files provide locations for 12 quarries west of Catawba County. This undoubtedly represents only a small fraction of all possible quarry locations in the state. Also near to our study area, Ferguson (1980) details the identification of 18 soapstone quarries in the vicinity of Spartanburg, South Carolina, and he clearly demonstrates the northeast-southwest distribution of quarries, which corresponds to the northeast-southwest trending rock deposit. A similar pattern may be present in the Yancey County area. Outcroppings of soapstone occur regularly in southwestern Virginia and northern Virginia, but the largest occur in Albemarle and Nelson counties (Allen et al. 1975a, 1975b).

Clearly, there were an abundance of potential soapstone sources available for use by aboriginal craftspersons. Indeed, soapstone artifacts are reported throughout the eastern United States. However, soapstone-tempered pottery is relatively rare and has a much more restricted distribution. The major exceptions are the abundant early Woodland wares found in Virginia, Maryland, New Jersey, and Pennsylvania reported as "steatite-tempered" Marcy Creek Plain pottery and Seldon Island Cord Marked (Evans 1955: 54–56, 142). The steatite-tempered Smyth series (Holland 1970:67–69) of southwest Virginia has a more restricted distribution and its late date suggests contemporaneity with the Burke series.

Cowans Ford Pottery Series

I believe the sand- and fine quartz–tempered ceramics found throughout the Lake Norman region generally are temporally coeval with the Burke series, with similar surface treatments and vessel forms. However, because of the difference in temper materials it is useful to introduce a new series, the Cowans Ford series, to describe the middle valley equivalents of the Burke pottery. For this purpose, I propose several new types: Cowans Ford Complicated Stamped, Plain/Smoothed, Burnished, Incised, and Corncob Impressed.

Cowans Ford Complicated Stamped

Paste

Temper: Temper is usually fine, medium, or coarse sand, with grains to 1 mm; fine crushed quartz to 2 mm also occurs. It is sometimes difficult to sort coarse sand from fine quartz, but quartz is almost always prepared, that is, sharp edges are present. Temper density varies, but is usually low to medium.

Texture: Well mixed and sandy to the touch.

Hardness: Relatively hard.

Color: Exteriors most often light tan and buff to light yellow/orange. Interiors sometimes slightly darker. Occasional firing clouds occur on either surface. Generally fired in oxidizing atmosphere.

Method of manufacture: Well-annealed coiling.

Surface Finish

Exterior: Designs are similar to those found on Burke Complicated Stamped. Curvilinear complicated stamping is by far the most common and rectilinear designs occur infrequently. Curvilinear stamped designs include concentric circles and bull's-eyes joined by arcs. Few complete designs are identifiable, but one common form is identical to a Burke design of a square within four concentric circles.

Cowans Ford Complicated Stamped is most dissimilar to Burke Complicated Stamped in the more frequent occurrence of large, "exploded," curvilinear and rectilinear designs. These designs are usually represented only by fragments, being too large to appear completely on most sherds. Lands and grooves together are wider than 6 mm and either may be as wide as 8 mm. These designs are thought to date from the mid-sixteenth to late seventeenth centuries in the Wateree valley (DePratter and Judge 1990:58). These designs seem to be more common in the lower portion of the valley than in the middle valley.

Interior: Usually smoothed but occasionally burnished.

Decoration

Decoration is limited to the rim area on jars and the shoulder and neck on bowls. Tops and exterior edges of lips of unmodified bowl forms are sometimes notched or punctated. Thickened rims or appliqued strips are usually punctated or notched.

Vessel Form

Body: Few whole vessels are represented, but they include constricted-neck jars, straight-sided jars, globular bowls, flat-bottomed bowls, and carinated bowls. Sherd assemblages prevent any estimate of relative frequencies.

Base: Slightly rounded to flattened.

Thickness: Average 5 to 6 mm.

Rim: On the basis of sherd assemblages I estimate that 50 to 60 percent of rims are everted, 15 to 25 percent are straight, and 20 to 30 percent are inverted to carinated.

Everted rims are occasionally modified by the addition of an appliqued strip placed to encircle the rim just below the lip. More often modification occurs as a folded or otherwise thickened rim. Modification occurs on a small percentage of rims and these are always jars.

Lip: Usually flattened but occasionally rounded or slightly thickened by flattening.

Appendages: Rarely short horizontal fillet strips added to shoulder.

Cowans Ford Plain/Smoothed

Cowans Ford Plain/Smoothed is similar to Cowans Ford Complicated Stamped in all attribute states except exterior surface treatment and vessel form. Vessel exteriors are usually carefully smoothed and vessel forms are predominantly hemisphere or carinated bowls. Decoration includes punctation and notching at the shoulder and sometimes incising.

Cowans Ford Burnished

Cowans Ford Burnished is similar to Cowans Ford Complicated Stamped in all attribute states except surface treatment and vessel form. Exterior surfaces are burnished and vessel forms are predominately hemisphere or carinated bowls.

Both Cowans Ford Plain/Smoothed and Cowans Ford Burnished feature incised decorated shoulders and rims on straight-sided and carinated bowls.

Cowans Ford Incised

Cowans Ford Incised is similar to Burke Incised. It is equivalent to Cowans Ford Complicated Stamped in all attribute states except surface treatment and vessel form. Exterior surfaces are burnished and vessel forms are predominately hemisphere or carinated bowls.

Cowans Ford Incised features Lamar style incised decorated shoulders and rims on straight-sided and carinated bowls.

Cowans Ford Corncob Impressed

Except for the exterior surface treatment, Cowans Ford Corncob Impressed is similar in all basic characteristics to Cowans Ford Complicated Stamped. The corncob impressions range from orderly to overstamped. They are applied with variable force, leaving shallow to deep and clear impressions.

Selected Upper Catawba Valley Ceramic Assemblages

Ceramics from 48 Burke and McDowell County sites were analyzed in this study. This represents a somewhat larger sample than that included in Keeler's (1971) survey (34 ceramic-bearing sites). At the time of the ceramic analysis, I conducted a complete survey of recorded ceramic-bearing sites from all known sources and was unable to locate any other sites with significant numbers of sherds. Since 1988, several additional ceramic-bearing sites have been recorded in McDowell County (Robinson 1996) and some of these are included in discussions in chapter 2 and at the end of this appendix. In Burke County, Robin Beck's 1996 survey of Upper Creek (Beck 1997a) identified 38 new ceramic-bearing sites and although they were recorded since the completion of my analysis, these sites also provide important data. Unfortunately, the total ceramic database for this study remains relatively limited since 19 of the 44 analyzed ceramic assemblages consist of fewer than 20 potsherds. As described in chapter 2, most of the ceramic variability from these late prehistoric and protohistoric upper valley sites is attributable to the Pisgah (Dickens 1970, 1976), Burke (Keeler 1971), McDowell, and Cowans Ford (defined in this volume) ceramic series. A small percentage is attributable to earlier Woodland period ceramic types.

Tables 30 and 34 summarize the frequency of exterior surface treatments for pottery from the Burke and McDowell county sites, respectively. Although this format does not provide a distribution of type frequencies, it is useful to look at the frequencies of surface-treatment attributes to get some perspective on ceramic attributes for the upper valley region at a glance.

The frequency of surface treatments within sites from McDowell County (Table 34) is quite distinct from that of Burke County sites (Table 30). A cursory examination shows that there is a generally similar distribution of attribute states in that complicated stamped, burnished, and plain attribute states predominate while several minority states including check stamped, cord marked, fabric impressed, net impressed, and brushed are also present. However, a closer examination of the complicated-stamped and burnished attribute states reveals distinctly different distributions between the two counties.

This is most clearly seen in the distributions of curvilinear complicated-stamped sherds and Pisgah/rectilinear complicated-stamped sherds. Curvilinear complicated-stamped sherds are present on 15 of the 23 (65 percent) Burke County sites as opposed to 9 of the 25 (36 percent) McDowell County sites. Their frequency is also markedly higher in Burke County: 9 (39 percent) Burke County sites and only 1 (4 percent) McDowell County site have more than 10 percent curvilinear complicated-stamped sherds.

An inverse relationship occurs with the distribution of the Pisgah stamped surface treatment, which occurs on more sites (44 percent to 30 percent) and in a greater frequency (7 sites with >10 percent vs. no sites with >3.3 percent) in McDowell County than in Burke County. The disparity is even greater if rectilinear complicated-stamped sherds are included. When combined, these attributes account for 13.0 percent of the identified surface treatments from McDowell County sites (occurring on 60 percent of the

Table 34. Percentages of exterior surface treatments on pottery from McDowell County sites

Site No.	Curv Comp St	Rect Comp St	Comp St Indet	Large Curv Comp St	Indet St Linear	Simple St	Napier/Etowah	Pisgah	Smoothed-Over Comp St	Burnished	Cob Impressed	Plain/Smooth	Check St	Cord Marked	Fabric Impressed	Net Impressed	Brushed	Misc/Indet	N
31MC1A	0.0	3.6	5.4	0.0	0.0	0.0	0.0	17.9	1.8	5.4	0.0	23.2	12.5	7.1	0.0	0.0	0.0	23.2	56
31MC2	0.0	0.0	0.0	0.0	0.0	0.0	0.0	0.0	0.0	0.0	0.0	0.0	0.0	0.0	0.0	0.0	0.0	100.0	1
31MC5	0.0	0.0	0.0	0.0	0.0	0.0	0.0	0.0	0.0	0.0	0.0	50.0	0.0	0.0	50.0	0.0	0.0	0.0	2
31MC8	3.4	5.6	11.2	0.0	2.2	0.0	0.0	4.5	1.1	5.6	0.0	10.1	12.4	9.0	4.5	1.1	3.4	25.8	89
31MC9	8.8	1.8	14.0	0.0	1.8	0.0	0.0	26.3	0.0	0.0	0.0	5.3	12.3	7.0	1.8	1.8	0.0	28.1	57
31MC11	4.1	0.8	23.0	0.0	0.0	0.0	0.0	0.0	0.0	0.0	0.0	34.4	4.9	4.9	0.7	3.3	0.0	24.6	122
31MC12	9.1	1.4	13.4	0.0	1.8	0.0	0.0	2.5	3.3	14.5	0.0	35.1	1.4	5.1	0.0	0.0	1.8	9.8	276
31MC13	0.0	0.0	100.0	0.0	0.0	0.0	0.0	0.0	0.0	0.0	0.0	0.0	0.0	0.0	0.0	0.0	0.0	0.0	1
31MC14	0.0	0.0	0.0	0.0	0.0	0.0	0.0	0.0	0.0	0.0	0.0	0.0	0.0	0.0	0.0	0.0	100.0	0.0	1
31MC15	0.0	28.6	0.0	0.0	14.3	0.0	0.0	0.0	0.0	0.0	0.0	28.6	0.0	0.0	0.0	0.0	0.0	28.6	7
31MC16	0.0	0.0	0.0	0.0	0.0	0.0	0.0	0.0	0.0	0.0	0.0	33.3	33.3	0.0	0.0	0.0	33.3	0.0	3
31MC17	0.0	5.0	15.0	0.0	0.0	0.0	5.0	0.0	5.0	0.0	0.0	40.0	0.0	0.0	5.0	0.0	5.0	20.0	20
31MC18	6.7	13.3	0.0	0.0	0.0	0.0	0.0	13.3	0.0	0.0	0.0	6.7	33.3	0.0	0.0	0.0	0.0	26.7	15
31MC19	0.0	0.0	0.0	0.0	0.0	0.0	0.0	0.0	0.0	0.0	0.0	100.0	0.0	0.0	0.0	0.0	0.0	0.0	2
31MC20	0.0	0.0	0.0	0.0	0.0	0.0	0.0	0.0	0.0	0.0	0.0	0.0	0.0	0.0	0.0	0.0	0.0	100.0	1
31MC39	5.3	0.5	11.6	0.0	5.8	0.0	0.0	29.6	5.3	4.8	0.0	18.5	2.6	2.1	1.1	0.5	0.1	12.2	189
31MC41	14.8	5.1	13.1	0.2	4.1	0.7	0.0	7.8	5.8	10.7	0.1	20.9	0.4	1.7	0.3	0.6	0.0	13.7	1498
31MC42	0.0	0.0	3.1	0.0	0.0	0.0	0.0	12.5	6.3	3.1	0.0	37.5	3.1	6.3	3.1	0.0	9.4	15.6	32
31MC43	9.3	1.4	12.9	0.0	1.4	0.0	0.0	6.8	3.1	4.6	0.4	21.1	3.6	5.4	14.3	0.4	0.0	15.4	280
31MC45	0.0	0.0	0.0	0.0	0.0	0.0	0.0	0.0	0.0	0.0	0.0	0.0	0.0	100.0	0.0	0.0	0.0	0.0	6
31MC47	0.0	0.0	0.0	0.0	0.0	0.0	0.0	16.7	0.0	0.0	0.0	83.3	0.0	0.0	0.0	0.0	0.0	0.0	6
31MC48	0.0	0.0	0.0	0.0	0.0	0.0	0.0	0.0	0.0	0.0	0.0	21.4	0.0	71.4	0.0	7.1	0.0	0.0	14
31MC51	0.0	0.0	0.0	0.0	0.0	26.3	0.0	10.5	0.0	0.0	0.0	26.3	0.0	0.0	31.6	5.3	0.0	0.0	19
31MC53	0.0	0.0	9.4	0.0	6.3	0.0	0.0	0.0	0.0	0.0	0.0	18.8	0.0	34.4	3.1	6.3	9.4	12.5	32
31MC157	5.5	0.7	0.4	0.7	16.2	0.0	22.4	0.0	2.6	22.1	0.0	8.8	7.0	1.1	0.0	9.6	0.0	2.9	272
Total	10.4	3.4	11.6	0.2	4.4	0.5	2.1	7.9	4.2	9.7	0.1	21.4	2.7	3.7	2.1	1.6	0.6	13.6	3001

McDowell County sites) and only 1.9 percent of the identified surface treatments in Burke County (occurring on 43 percent of the Burke County sites).

The distribution of the burnished attribute state (common to the Burke series) is also weighted to Burke County. There it occurs on more sites (61 percent vs. 32 percent) and in much higher frequencies (7 vs. 3 sites with >10 percent of identified total). It should also be noted that two of the McDowell County sites (31MC12 and 31MC41) with more than 10 percent burnished sherds also have the highest percentages of curvilinear complicated-stamped surfaces in McDowell County. The apparent spatial patterning of surface treatments is best understood as a reflection of the distribution of Pisgah and Burke series ceramics.

The frequency of plain/smoothed and check-stamped surface treatments offers additional insight into the distribution of the Pisgah and Burke ceramic series. Dickens (1976:185–186) states that check-stamped surfaces were present on 8 to 10 percent of Pisgah sherds and that plain surfaces (including rough, smoothed, and burnished) were present on 1 to 3 percent of Pisgah sherds. Keeler (1971:35–36) distinguishes Burke Plain/Burnished and Plain types and reports their occurrences at 16.4 percent and 19.4 percent, respectively, whereas check stamping was reported on .2 percent of Burke sherds. These figures contrast with those of the upper Catawba valley, where plain (excluding burnished) surface treatments occur with a high frequency throughout the region (24.7 and 23.4 percent, respectively, for McDowell and Burke counties). Check stamping is relatively more frequent in McDowell County (3.2 to .4 percent), but is found primarily within site assemblages that also include Pisgah complicated-stamped surface treatments. Interestingly, the three sites with the largest quantities of Pisgah surface treatments (31MC39, 31MC41, and 31MC43) and large sample sizes have only .5 to 4.2 percent of check stamping.

The distribution of check stamping and plain surface treatments seems to add weight to the earlier observation that Burke ceramics are more widely represented within the region than is the Pisgah series. In sum, the preponderance of curvilinear complicated-stamped, burnished, and plain surface treatments (associated with soapstone temper) characterizes the Burke series, whereas the Pisgah series is represented primarily in McDowell County by the presence of Pisgah rectilinear stamped, plain, and check stamping associated with grit and sand temper.

Finally, it should be noted that while the majority of surface treatment and temper variability seems to be explained within the parameters of the Pisgah and Burke series, some attribute variation represents other ceramic series including the McDowell and Cowans Ford series and earlier Woodland traditions (see below).

The McDowell site ceramic assemblage was characterized in chapter 2

Table 35. Summary of 31MC12 potsherds by exterior surface treatment and other selected attributes

Exterior Surface Attribute Attribute State	Curv Comp St	Rect Comp St	Comp St Indet	Indet St Linear	Pisgah Rect Comp St	Smoothed-Over Comp St	Burnished	Plain/Smoothed	Check Stamped	Cord Marked	Fabric Impressed	Brushed	Indeterminate	Total
Temper														**Total**
Soapstone (F)	1	·	5	·	·	2	15	21	1	·	·	·	2	47
Soapstone (M)	20	2	17	1	2	5	19	34	1	·	·	·	13	114
Soapstone (C)	1	·	1	·	·	·	·	·	·	·	·	·	1	3
Soapstone (In)	·	·	5	·	·	·	1	6	·	·	·	2	1	15
Sand (M)	1	·	·	·	·	·	·	7	·	1	·	·	1	10
Sand (C)	·	·	1	·	·	·	1	7	·	5	2	1	2	19
Quartz (F)	·	·	1	1	·	·	·	12	·	8	·	1	4	27
Quartz (M)	·	1	·	·	·	·	·	1	·	·	·	·	2	4
Quartz (C)	·	·	·	·	·	·	·	3	·	·	·	·	·	3
Grit (F/M)	1	1	6	1	4	2	4	4	2	·	·	1	1	27
Grit (C)	1	·	1	2	1	·	·	2	·	·	·	·	·	7
Total	25	4	37	5	7	9	40	97	4	14	2	5	27	276
Interior Surface														
Burnished	6	·	9	·	1	5	33	24	1	2	·	2	4	87
Plain/Smoothed	19	4	28	5	5	4	7	73	1	12	2	3	22	185
Scraped	·	·	·	·	·	·	·	·	2	·	·	·	1	3
Thickness														
<6 mm	6	2	7	1	3	2	14	35	1	9	·	2	7	89
6-8 mm	14	1	20	2	3	6	22	50	3	5	2	3	15	146
>8 mm	5	1	10	2	1	1	4	12	·	·	·	·	4	40
Rim Form														
Applique	·	·	1	·	·	·	·	1	·	·	·	·	·	2
Folded	·	·	·	·	·	·	·	·	·	·	·	·	1	1
Unmodified	1	·	2	·	·	3	6	8	·	2	·	1	1	24
Lip Form														
Flat	1	·	3	·	·	3	2	6	·	1	·	1	2	19
Rounded	·	·	·	·	·	·	4	3	·	1	·	·	·	8

F, Fine; *M*, medium; *C*, coarse; *In*, inclusions.

as exemplifying site assemblages in the extreme upper Catawba valley that feature varying percentages of Pisgah, McDowell, and Burke series pottery. Other sites with relatively large assemblages that illustrate the same pattern include 31MC12 (Table 35), 31MC39 (Table 36), and 31MC43 (Table 37).

The core area of Burke pottery distribution is found in Burke County east of the Linville River. The largest assemblages of Burke phase sites in the upper valley (excluding the Berry site) include 31BK1 (Table 38), 31BK12 (Table 39), 31BK17 (Table 40), and 31BK18 (Table 41).

Tables 38 through 41 show that the assemblages from 31BK1, 31BK12, 31BK17, and 31BK18 are similar to that of the Berry site, but vary in the

Table 36. Summary of 31MC39 potsherds by exterior surface treatment and other selected attributes

Exterior Surface Attribute Attribute State	Curv Comp St	Rect Comp St	Comp St Indet	Pisgah Rect Comp St	Indet St Linear	Smoothed-Over Comp St	Burnished	Plain/Smoothed	Check Stamped	Cord Marked	Fabric Impressed	Net Impressed	Indeterminate	Total
Temper														
Soapstone (F)	·	·	·	1	1	·	·	·	·	·	·	·	·	2
Soapstone (M)	1	·	1	3	1	3	1	3	·	·	1	·	2	16
Soapstone (In)	·	·	·	1	·	·	·	·	·	·	·	·	·	1
Sand (F)	·	·	·	2	·	·	·	2	·	·	·	·	·	4
Sand (M)	·	·	3	10	1	1	3	6	·	2	·	·	1	27
Sand (C)	2	·	4	7	1	3	1	10	2	1	·	1	3	35
Quartz (F)	·	·	·	·	·	·	2	2	1	·	·	·	1	6
Quartz (M)	·	·	·	1	·	·	·	·	·	·	·	·	·	1
Quartz & grog	·	·	·	·	·	·	·	1	·	·	·	·	·	1
Grit (F/M)	7	1	14	30	7	3	1	11	2	1	1	·	16	94
Grit (C)	·	·	·	1	·	·	1	·	·	·	·	·	·	2
Total	10	1	22	56	11	10	9	35	5	4	2	1	23	189
Interior Surface														
Burnished	1	·	7	11	4	5	7	6	1	·	·	·	6	48
Plain/Smoothed	9	1	14	45	6	4	1	27	4	4	2	1	14	132
Scraped	·	·	1	·	1	1	1	2	·	·	·	·	3	9
Thickness														
<6 mm	1	1	6	12	3	1	5	14	3	2	·	·	5	53
6-8 mm	6	·	12	36	3	6	4	18	2	2	1	1	9	100
>8 mm	3	·	4	8	5	3	·	3	·	·	1	·	8	35
Rim Form														
Collar	·	·	1	1	·	·	·	·	·	·	·	·	3	5
Thickened	·	·	·	·	·	·	·	·	1	·	·	·	·	1
Unmodified	·	·	1	2	·	·	·	·	·	·	·	·	·	3
Lip Form														
Flat	·	·	2	2	·	·	·	·	·	·	·	·	3	7
Rounded	·	·	·	·	·	·	·	·	·	1	·	·	·	1

F, Fine; *M*, medium; *C*, coarse; *In*, inclusions.

relative frequencies of different attributes such as exterior surface treatment. The Pitts site (31BK209) is most dissimilar with a significantly lower percentage of Burke sherds overall and a higher percentage of Pisgah sherds. As discussed in chapter 2, it is possible that the Pitts site is earlier than the main component at Berry. I had anticipated that comparisons between the Berry site pottery and pottery from the other large surface collections might reveal additional patterns of variability. The relatively minor variation in frequencies of exterior surface treatments is mirrored in the distribution of decoration attributes as well. This is best illustrated by comparing the two largest assemblages, Berry and 31BK17. Both assemblages

Table 37. Summary of 31MC43 potsherds by exterior surface treatment and other selected attributes

Exterior Surface Attribute Attribute State	Curv Comp St	Rect Comp St	Comp St Indet	Indet St Linear	Pisgah Rect Comp St	Smoothed-Over Comp St	Burnished	Corncob Impressed	Plain/Smoothed	Check Stamped	Cord Marked	Fabric Impressed	Net Impressed	Indeterminate	Total
Temper															
Soapstone (F)	.	.	2	1	3	1	6	.	7	.	.	.	.	6	26
Soapstone (M)	21	3	15	1	6	5	4	1	12	.	2	.	.	15	85
Soapstone (C)	.	.	1	.	1	1	.	.	.	.	.	.	.	.	3
Soapstone (In)	1	.	.	1	.	1	.	.	1	.	.	.	.	.	4
Sand (F)	.	.	.	.	.	.	.	.	2	.	.	.	.	.	2
Sand (M)	.	.	6	.	2	.	1	.	16	3	2	15	.	7	52
Sand (C)	.	.	4	.	3	.	.	.	11	4	5	17	.	6	50
Quartz (F)	.	1	.	.	.	1	.	.	5	.	3	4	1	2	17
Quartz (M)	1	.	.	.	.	.	.	.	.	.	.	1	.	2	4
Grit (F/M)	3	.	8	1	4	.	1	.	5	3	3	3	.	5	36
Grit (C)	.	.	.	.	.	.	1	.	.	.	.	.	.	.	1
Total	26	4	36	4	19	9	13	1	59	10	15	40	1	43	280
Interior Surface															
Burnished	6	.	5	1	4	1	13	.	8	.	.	.	.	5	43
Plain/Smoothed	20	4	31	2	14	8	.	1	50	9	14	40	1	33	227
Scraped	.	.	.	1	1	.	.	.	.	1	1	.	.	4	8
Thickness															
<6 mm	.	.	9	.	2	1	3	.	13	1	.	.	.	5	34
6·8 mm	12	2	17	2	8	5	6	.	31	8	5	16	.	21	133
>8 mm	14	2	10	2	9	3	4	1	15	1	10	24	1	17	113
Rim Form															
Collar	.	.	.	.	.	.	.	.	1	.	.	.	.	3	4
Unmodified	.	.	1	.	1	.	2	.	11	.	2	6	.	4	27
Lip Form															
Flat	.	.	1	.	1	.	2	.	6	.	1	3	.	4	18
Rounded	.	.	.	.	.	.	.	.	6	.	1	3	.	2	12

F, Fine; *M*, medium; *C*, coarse; *In*, inclusions.

feature many examples of decoration. In general, appliqued, folded, and thickened rims are decorated by punctations or notches upon the added rim portion (see Plate 12 for an excellent example of this pattern). Plain rims often exhibit notched or punctated lips. Finally, incising occurs on the shoulder area of cazuela bowls and on the shoulder/neck area of small constricted-neck bowls (Plate 13). Since the collections from these sites represent mixed assemblages I am hesitant to draw many conclusions from absolute or relative frequencies of decorative techniques, styles, or the decoration location. This is particularly true since 33.9 percent of the sherds from 31BK17 include decoration as opposed to 6.3 percent from 31BK22

Table 38. Summary of 31BK1 potsherds by exterior surface treatment and other selected attributes

Exterior Surface	Curv Comp St	Comp St Indet	Indet St Linear	Burnished	Plain/Smoothed	Cord Marked	Brushed	Indeterminate	Total
Attribute									
Attribute State									
Temper									**Total**
Soapstone (F)	32	3	·	46	2	·	·	1	84
Soapstone (M)	118	16	·	57	7	·	·	11	209
Soapstone (C)	·	·	·	1	·	·	·	·	1
Soapstone (In)	32	·	·	12	·	·	·	·	44
Sand (F)	·	·	·	·	1	·	·	1	2
Sand (M)	·	·	·	3	2	1	·	1	7
Sand (C)	1	·	1	·	·	·	·	1	3
Quartz (M)	·	·	1	·	·	2	·	·	3
Grit (F/M)	5	·	·	2	·	·	1	·	8
Total	188	19	2	121	12	3	1	15	361
Interior Surface									
Burnished	158	14	·	111	1	·	·	9	293
Plain/Smoothed	30	5	2	10	11	3	·	6	67
Scraped	·	·	·	·	·	·	1	·	1
Thickness									
<6 mm	20	5	·	38	7	·	1	8	79
6-8 mm	157	10	1	83	5	1	·	6	263
>8 mm	11	4	1	·	·	2	·	·	18
Rim Form									
Applique	·	·	·	·	·	·	·	·	0
Collar	·	·	·	·	·	·	·	·	0
Folded	1	·	·	·	·	·	·	·	1
Thickened	·	·	·	·	·	·	·	·	0
Unmodified	20	4	·	25	·	2	·	·	51
Lip Form									
Flat	20	·	·	19	·	·	·	·	39
Rounded	·	4	·	5	·	·	·	·	9

F, Fine; *M*, medium; *C*, coarse; *In*, inclusions.

(this results from the overwhelming presence of rim sherds in the surface collection from 31BK17). However, I think it may be useful to make comparisons between the two sites within the same classes of rim treatments, surface treatments, and vessel forms.

The largest samples for comparison are available for surface treatments.

Table 39. Summary of 31BK12 potsherds by exterior surface treatment and other selected attributes

Exterior Surface Attribute Attribute State	Curv Comp St	Comp St Indet	Pisgah Rect Comp St	Indet St Linear	Smoothed-Over Comp St	Burnished	Plain/Smoothed	Check Stamped	Cord Marked	Fabric Marked	Net Impressed	Brushed	Indeterminate	Total
Temper														
Soapstone (F)	9	6	.	.	.	7	10	.	.	.	.	.	2	34
Soapstone (M)	29	7	.	1	1	11	15	1	.	.	.	1	2	68
Soapstone (C)	1	.	1	.	.	.	.	.	.	.	.	.	.	2
Soapstone plus*	1	.	.	.	.	.	1	.	.	.	.	.	.	2
Sand (M)	.	.	.	.	.	.	.	.	.	.	.	.	1	1
Sand (C)	1	1	.	.	.	1	2	.	.	1	.	.	1	7
Quartz (F)	.	1	1	.	.	1	10	.	1	.	.	.	5	19
Quartz (M)	.	.	.	.	.	.	2	.	1	.	1	1	.	5
Quartz (C)	.	.	.	.	.	.	.	.	.	.	.	1	.	1
Grit (F/M)	.	.	.	.	.	.	.	.	.	.	.	.	1	1
Total	41	15	2	1	1	20	40	1	2	1	1	3	12	140
Interior Surface														
Burnished	13	3	1	1	.	14	6	1	.	.	.	.	1	40
Plain/Smoothed	27	12	1	.	1	6	33	.	2	.	1	.	10	93
Scraped	1	.	.	.	.	.	1	.	.	1	.	3	1	7
Thickness														
<6 mm	12	5	1	1	1	7	11	.	.	.	.	1	3	42
6-8 mm	22	10	1	.	.	12	23	.	2	1	.	2	8	81
>8 mm	7	.	.	.	.	1	6	1	.	.	1	.	1	17
Rim Form														
Folded	.	.	.	.	.	.	.	.	.	.	.	.	1	1
Unmodified	2	.	.	.	.	.	2	.	.	.	.	2	1	7
Lip Form														
Flat	2	.	.	.	.	.	2	.	.	.	.	2	1	7

F, Fine; M, medium; C, coarse.

* Indicates mixed temper size, see Appendix C.

Table 42 provides a comparison of decoration attributes for selected surface treatments at the two sites. Punctation is the most common type of decoration associated with curvilinear complicated-stamped and complicated-stamped indeterminate surface treatments. Punctation is most often applied to modified rims and also occurs on or just below the lip of unmodified rims. Finger impressing or pinching and notching are present at 31BK17 but do not occur at 31BK22, whereas smoothing or burnishing occurs at 31BK22 but not at 31BK17. The patterns of decoration are similar for both sites and in each case usually reflect the occurrence of jars with everted, modified rims.

Burnished and plain/smoothed sherds exhibit a different pattern, but here, again, the two sites show a great similarity. Burke Incised designs are

Table 40. Summary of 31BK17 potsherds by exterior surface treatment and other selected attributes

Exterior Surface Attribute Attribute State	Curv Comp St	Rect Comp St	Comp St Indet	Large Curv Comp St	Simple Stamped	Pisgah Rect Comp St	Napier/Etowah Comp St	Smoothed-Over Comp St	Burnished	Corncob Impressed	Plain/Smoothed	Cord Marked	Fabric Impressed	Net Impressed	Brushed	Indeterminate	Total
Temper																	
Soapstone (F)	100	4	5	2	2	.	1	4	112	1	94	7	.	.	1	56	389
Soapstone (M)	225	9	19	3	2	.	.	10	40	2	86	1	.	1	2	84	484
Soapstone (C)	13	1	1	.	.	.	.	1	1	.	5	.	.	.	.	5	27
Soapstone (In)	19	2	1	.	.	.	.	3	7	.	16	.	.	.	1	14	63
Sand (F)	1	.	.	.	.	1	.	.	10	1	8	.	1	.	.	6	28
Sand (M)	10	1	.	.	.	.	.	.	12	.	11	.	.	.	.	6	40
Sand (C)	4	.	1	.	.	1	.	.	2	.	9	2	1	.	.	4	24
Quartz (F)	.	.	1	.	.	.	.	.	1	.	.	1	.	.	.	.	3
Quartz (M)	1	.	.	.	.	.	.	.	.	.	.	.	2	.	.	1	4
Quartz (In)	.	.	.	.	.	.	.	.	2	.	.	.	.	.	.	2	4
Feldspar (C)	2	.	.	.	.	.	.	.	.	.	.	.	.	.	.	.	2
Grit (F/M)	5	.	1	.	.	.	.	1	3	.	3	.	.	.	.	1	14
Grit (C)	3	.	.	.	.	1	.	.	4	.	.	.	.	.	.	1	9
Misc./Ind.	.	.	.	.	.	.	.	.	2	.	2	.	.	.	.	1	5
Total	383	17	29	5	4	3	1	19	196	4	234	11	4	1	4	181	1096
Interior Surface																	
Burnished	160	10	12	4	2	3	.	10	142	1	48	5	.	.	4	49	450
Plain/Smoothed	220	6	17	1	2	.	.	8	53	3	182	5	2	1	.	129	629
Scraped	3	1	.	.	.	.	1	1	.	.	4	.	2	.	.	9	21
Thickness																	
<6 mm	72	2	5	.	1	1	.	2	106	1	87	4	.	.	1	40	322
6-8 mm	261	12	20	5	2	2	.	14	80	2	128	5	.	1	3	71	606
>8 mm	50	3	4	.	1	.	1	3	7	1	18	1	.	.	.	18	107
Rim Form																	
Applique	2	.	2	.	.	.	.	.	.	1	.	.	.	.	.	8	13
Folded	14	.	6	1	.	.	.	2	3	1	5	.	.	.	1	39	72
Thickened	9	1	.	.	.	.	.	.	1	.	5	.	.	.	.	32	48
Unmodified	17	1	1	.	1	.	.	2	94	.	89	.	.	.	.	33	238
Lip Form																	
Flat	33	2	5	1	1	.	.	2	59	2	51	.	.	.	.	92	248
Rounded	8	.	1	.	.	.	.	2	19	.	28	.	.	.	.	38	97

F, Fine; M, medium; C, coarse; In, inclusions.

the predominant decoration at both sites. These decorations occur on the shoulder and rim of carinated bowls and on the shoulder, neck, and rim of carinated bowls with small, everted rims (effectively forming a constricted-neck bowl form). Where punctation or other decorations occur it is striking that they rarely occur on modified rims (7 examples at 31BK17 and 8 examples at 31BK22). This results from the association of plain/smoothed and burnished surface treatments with bowls instead of jars with modified rims.

Table 41. Summary of 31BK18 potsherds by exterior surface treatment and other selected attributes

Exterior Surface Attribute Attribute State	Curv Comp St	Rect Comp St	Comp St Indet	Large Curv Comp St	Indet St Linear	Smoothed-Over Comp St	Burnished	Plain/Smoothed	Check Stamped	Cord Marked	Net Impressed	Indeterminate	Total
Temper													
Soapstone (F)	16	·	6	·	1	·	6	16	1	·	·	2	48
Soapstone (M)	34	1	16	1	5	3	1	20	·	·	1	3	85
Soapstone plus*	10	·	1	·	1	·	1	10	·	·	·	2	25
Sand (M)	·	·	·	·	·	·	2	2	·	·	·	·	4
Sand (C)	6	·	2	·	·	1	·	5	·	1	·	·	15
Quartz (F)	·	·	·	·	·	·	·	1	·	·	·	·	1
Quartz (M)	·	·	·	·	1	·	·	·	·	·	·	·	1
Grit (F/M)	·	·	·	·	1	·	·	·	·	·	·	·	1
Total	66	1	25	1	9	4	10	54	1	1	1	7	180
Interior Surface													
Burnished	·	·	6	1	4	·	10	20	·	·	1	3	45
Plain/Smoothed	·	1	19	·	5	4	·	34	1	1	·	4	69
Thickness													
<6 mm	·	·	5	·	2	·	7	18	·	·	1	1	34
6-8 mm	·	·	15	1	5	4	3	30	1	1	·	3	63
>8 mm	·	1	5	·	2	·	·	6	·	·	·	3	17
Rim Form													
Folded	·	·	·	·	·	·	·	·	·	·	·	1	1
Unmodified	·	·	·	·	·	·	·	5	·	·	·	·	5
Indeterminate	·	·	·	·	·	1	·	·	·	·	·	1	2
Lip Form													
Flat	·	·	·	·	·	1	·	3	·	·	·	2	6
Rounded	·	·	·	·	·	·	·	2	·	·	·	·	2

F, Fine; *M*, medium; *C*, coarse.

* Indicates mixed temper size; see Appendix C.

Finally, sherds with indeterminate surface treatment provide the largest number of samples. Unfortunately, the preponderance of punctated decoration results from the fact that most of these are rim sherds that have broken just below the rim treatment and therefore the associated surface treatments are not present as opposed to being indeterminate.

A comparison of rim forms between the sites is presented in Table 43. Site 31BK18 is also included in the table since it is the only other Burke

Table 42. Frequency of decoration and decoration location attribute states for selected exterior surface treatments at the Berry site and 31BK17

Decoration Location	Curvilinear Complicated Stamped							Plain/Smoothed								Burnished								
	Punctation	Misc. Incised	Finger-applied	Notched	Smooth/Burnish	Complicated St.	Total	Punctation	Burke Incised	Misc. Incised	Finger-applied	Notched	Smooth/Burnish	Rosette/node	Total	Punctation	Burke Incised	Misc. Incised	Finger-applied	Notched	Smooth/Burnish	Fillet added	Rosette/node	Total
31BK17																								
Rim	·	·	·	·	·	·	0	2	24	·	·	·	1	·	27	1	17	·	·	·	·	·	·	18
Rim fold	3	1	·	·	·	·	4	1	·	·	·	·	·	·	1	·	·	·	·	·	·	·	·	0
Applique/thickened	9	·	1	·	·	·	10	1	·	·	·	·	1	·	2	·	·	·	·	·	·	·	·	0
Lower edge/scallop	7	·	1	·	·	1	9	1	·	·	·	·	·	·	1	1	·	·	·	·	·	·	·	1
Lip	·	·	·	·	·	·	0	1	·	·	2	·	·	·	3	4	·	·	·	2	·	·	·	6
Exterior edge lip	5	·	·	4	·	·	9	1	·	·	·	2	·	·	3	2	·	·	2	4	·	·	·	8
Just below lip	4	·	·	·	·	·	4	·	·	·	1	2	·	·	3	2	·	·	·	·	·	·	·	2
Neck	·	·	·	·	·	·	0	·	12	2	·	·	·	1	15	·	10	1	·	·	·	·	1	12
Neck/shoulder	·	·	·	·	·	·	0	·	·	·	·	·	·	·	0	·	4	·	·	·	·	·	·	4
Shoulder	1	·	·	·	·	·	1	·	38	1	·	·	·	·	39	·	34	·	·	·	·	1	·	35
Shoulder tangency	·	·	·	·	·	·	0	·	·	·	·	·	·	·	0	2	·	·	·	·	·	1	·	3
Indeterminate	·	·	·	·	·	·	0	·	·	·	·	·	·	·	0	·	1	·	·	·	·	·	·	1
Total	29	1	2	4	0	1	37	7	74	3	3	4	2	1	94	12	66	1	2	6	0	2	1	90
Berry site																								
Rim	·	·	·	·	·	·	0	·	3	·	·	·	·	·	3	3	6	·	·	·	·	·	·	9
Rim fold	3	·	·	·	1	·	4	2	·	·	·	·	·	·	2	3	·	·	·	·	·	·	·	3
Applique/thickened	·	·	·	·	·	·	0	·	·	·	·	·	·	·	0	1	·	·	·	·	1	·	·	2
Collar	·	·	·	·	·	1	1	·	·	·	·	·	·	·	0	·	·	·	·	·	·	·	·	0
Lower edge/scallop	5	·	·	·	·	·	5	·	·	·	·	·	·	·	0	·	·	·	1	·	·	·	·	1
Lip	·	·	·	·	1	·	1	·	·	·	·	·	·	·	0	·	·	·	·	1	1	·	·	2
Exterior edge lip	2	·	·	·	·	·	2	·	·	1	·	1	·	·	2	6	·	·	·	8	·	·	·	14
Just below lip	·	·	·	·	1	·	1	1	2	·	1	·	·	1	5	2	·	·	·	·	·	·	·	2
Neck	·	·	·	·	·	·	0	3	·	1	·	·	·	·	4	·	4	·	·	·	·	·	·	4
Neck/shoulder	·	·	·	·	·	·	0	1	·	·	·	2	·	·	3	·	5	·	·	·	·	·	·	5
Shoulder	·	·	·	·	2	·	2	·	4	·	·	·	·	·	4	1	17	·	·	·	·	·	·	18
Shoulder tangency	·	·	·	·	·	·	0	2	·	·	·	·	·	·	2	1	·	·	·	·	·	2	·	3
Total	10	0	0	0	5	1	16	9	9	2	1	3	0	1	25	17	32	0	1	9	2	2	0	63

Table 43. Rim form percentages at 31BK17, 31BK18, and the Berry site

Sites	31BK17		31BK18*		Berry	
Rim Form	n	%	n	%	n	%
Appliqued rim	13	3.5	7	4.9	7	2.5
Folded rim	72	19.4	31	21.5	44	15.4
Thickened rim	48	12.9	6	4.2	15	5.3
Collared rim	0	0	0	0	4	1.4
Unmodified rim	238	64.1	100	69.4	215	75.4
Total	371	99.9	144	100.0	285	100.0

* Figures for 31BK18 include rims from Carey
collection that were not part of original analysis.

Table 44. Percentages of decoration attributes by rim form for 31BK17 and the Berry site

Decoration	**31BK17**		**Berry**	
Applique/Folded/	n	%	n	%
Thickened Rim				
Punctated	88	0.66	45	0.68
Finger-applied	17	0.13	4	0.06
Notched	6	0.05	3	0.05
Burke Incised	3	0.02	0	0.00
Misc. incised	1	0.01	0	0.00
Smoothed	3	0.02	0	0.00
Burnished	0	0.00	1	0.02
Cob Marked	0	0.00	1	0.02
Indeterminate	4	0.03	3	0.05
None	11	0.08	9	0.14
Total	133	1.00	66	1.00
	(35.8% of total rims)		(20.6% of total rims)	
Unmodified Rim				
Punctated	29	0.12	45	0.18
Finger-applied	3	0.01	0	0.00
Notched	19	0.08	24	0.09
Burke Incised	125	0.53	36	0.14
Misc. incised	5	0.02	2	0.01
Fillet added	1	0.00	1	0.00
Burnished	0	0.00	6	0.02
Smoothed	0	0.00	1	0.00
Comp Stamp	0	0.00	1	0.00
Node/Lug	2	0.01	3	0.01
Indeterminate	1	0.00	3	0.01
None	53	0.22	132	0.52
Total	238	1.00	254	1.00
	(64.1% of total rims)		(79.4% of total rims)	

ceramic assemblage with a large number of rim sherds. It should also be noted that the totals include additional collections (surface collections from Charles Carey) analyzed for surface treatment and rim form only. Few comments can be offered without testing the significance of these frequency distributions. The three sites appear relatively similar, though 31BK17 exhibits a somewhat larger percentage of modified rims.

Further comparison of rim forms, decoration, and decoration location at the Berry site and 31BK17 is provided in Table 44 (see Plates 14 and 15). Note that the same patterns are observed in these comparisons. Both sites feature modified rims that are usually decorated with punctations, or less frequently with notching or finger impressing and pinching. Unmodified rims are less frequently decorated, but when they are decorated exhibit incised shoulder and neck areas or punctations or notches at the rim or lip. As before, these patterns reflect the occurrence and differential decoration of jar and bowl vessel forms. Thus, there is generally little variation that can be determined among the large Burke ceramic assemblages at this point.

Selected Middle Catawba Valley Ceramic Assemblages

Chapter 4 describes the pottery from the Low site (31ID31) and also discusses patterns of ceramic variability that are observed by comparisons among the larger assemblages. Tables 45 through 50 illustrate some of those assemblages from sites in the middle Catawba valley that consisted of more than 100 sherds. The sites include 31ID4 (Table 45), 31ID38 (Table 46), 31CT10 (Table 47), 31CT94 (Table 48), 31CT96 (Table 49), and 31ID42 (Table 50).

Upper Catawba Valley Woodland Period Pottery

As described in chapter 2, small quantities of Woodland period pottery are found on numerous upper Catawba valley sites. Few of these sites have more than 15 to 20 sherds, but two sites, the Tyler-Loughridge site (31MC139) and the Lewis site (31MC157), have large and interesting Woodland ceramic assemblages.

Unfortunately, the only relatively large, seemingly single-component (or large Woodland component), Woodland period sites identified at this time have ceramics that represent cultural phases from outside the western North Carolina Piedmont. The two sites are both located in McDowell County: the Tyler-Loughridge site (31MC139) features Connestee ceramics from the Appalachian Summit and the Lewis site (31MC157) features Napier/Etowah-like ceramics from north Georgia. These two ceramic assemblages are discussed below, followed by a discussion of probable Woodland pottery found in small quantities on other McDowell and Burke County sites.

Table 45. Summary of 31ID4 potsherds by exterior surface treatment and other selected attributes

Exterior Surface Attribute Attribute State	Simple Stamped	Plain/Smoothed	Check Stamped	Cord Marked	Fabric Impressed	Net Impressed	Brushed	Indeterminate	Total
Temper									**Total**
Sand (M)	·	·	6	2	7	1	·	1	17
Sand (C)	·	4	6	2	1	4	·	3	20
Quartz (F)	·	2	·	·	9	2	1	4	18
Quartz (M)	·	·	·	·	·	·	·	1	1
Quartz (C)	·	·	·	·	·	·	·	1	1
Granite	5	41	1	10	44	·	12	15	128
Grit (C)	·	·	·	·	·	·	·	1	1
Total	5	47	13	14	61	7	13	26	186
Interior Surface									
Plain/Smoothed	5	40	13	12	59	7	9	25	170
Scraped	·	7	·	2	2	·	4	·	15
Thickness									
<6 mm	·	·	·	2	1	·	·	·	3
6-8 mm	5	39	·	7	27	2	12	15	107
>8 mm	·	8	13	5	33	5	1	10	75
Rim Form									
Unmodified	·	2	1	·	4	·	·	·	7
Lip Form									
Flat	·	·	·	·	1	·	·	·	1
Rounded	·	·	1	·	2	·	·	·	3

F, Fine; M, medium; C, coarse.

At the Tyler-Loughridge site, Robinson describes the vast majority of ceramics as Connestee, Middle Woodland ceramics best known from the Appalachian Summit region of North Carolina (Keel 1976). Connestee sherds from the Tyler-Loughridge site are thin, with fine sand temper or occasionally medium to coarse sand temper. Robinson (1996:119) reports that 1,029 (97.4 percent) of the total of 1,057 sherds recovered from Connestee component features were Connestee types: primarily plain (88.4 percent; n = 910), with small quantities of cord marked (4.2 percent; n = 43), simple stamped (1.6 percent; n = 17), check stamped (1.1 percent; n = 11), and brushed (.9 percent; n = 9).

Table 46. Summary of 31ID38 potsherds by exterior surface treatment and other selected attributes

Exterior Surface	Curv Comp St	Comp St Indet	Indet St Linear	Smoothed-Over Comp St	Burnished	Corncob Impressed	Plain/Smoothed	Cord Marked	Fabric Impressed	Net Impressed	Brushed	Indeterminate	Total
Attribute													
Attribute State													
Temper													**Total**
Soapstone (F)	·	1	·	·	·	·	2	·	·	·	1	2	6
Soapstone (M)	·	·	1	·	·	·	·	·	·	·	·	·	1
Soapstone (In)	1	1	·	·	·	·	·	·	·	·	·	1	3
Sand (F)	·	·	·	·	2	3	15	2	·	·	·	3	25
Sand (M)	6	4	·	·	8	3	94	21	1	1	8	34	180
Sand (C)	6	2	·	·	3	1	56	22	2	·	12	34	138
Quartz (F)	3	5	1	1	4	2	129	23	51	·	96	65	380
Quartz (M)	·	·	·	·	·	·	94	11	38	1	6	15	165
Feldspar (F)	·	·	·	·	1	·	7	·	·	·	1	1	10
Granite	·	·	·	·	·	·	5	·	·	·	·	4	9
Hornblende	·	·	·	·	·	·	2	·	·	·	·	·	2
Total	16	13	2	1	18	9	404	79	92	2	124	159	919
Interior Surface													
Burnished	3	·	·	1	9	1	11	·	1	·	1	2	29
Plain/Smoothed	12	13	2	·	9	8	354	56	56	2	28	133	673
Scraped	1	·	·	·	·	·	39	23	35	·	95	24	217
Thickness													
<6 mm	2	1	1	·	9	3	117	14	18	·	61	45	271
6-8 mm	11	12	1	1	9	6	230	54	42	1	57	93	517
>8 mm	3	·	·	·	·	·	57	11	32	1	6	19	129
Rim Form													
Applique	·	·	·	·	·	·	·	·	·	·	·	1	1
Thickened	·	·	·	·	·	·	·	·	1	·	1	1	3
Unmodified	1	1	·	·	1	·	13	2	3	·	9	13	43
Lip Form													
Flat	1	1	·	·	1	·	6	2	1	·	10	12	34
Rounded	·	·	·	·	·	·	6	·	1	·	·	3	10

F, Fine; *M*, medium; *C*, coarse; *In*, inclusions.

Robinson (1996:99) also points out a few fabric-impressed and cord-marked coarse sand– and grit-tempered sherds were recovered, but they did not correspond to existing Woodland or later typed pottery.

Robinson (1996:41) recorded a total of 18 prehistoric sites, only four of which evidenced Woodland ceramics. No Connestee ceramics were identified outside of the Tyler-Loughridge site. Nor were Connestee sherds found in any of the site assemblages in the ceramic analysis conducted during this study nor in the recent survey by Robin Beck (personal communication 1996). However, Larry Kimball (personal communication 1996) reports that they are present in the Happy Valley area of Caldwell County, and

Table 47. Summary of 31CT10 potsherds by exterior surface treatment and other selected attributes

Exterior Surface Attribute Attribute State	Curv Comp St	Rect Comp St	Comp St Indet	Large Curv Comp St	Large Rect Comp St	Smoothed-Over Comp St	Burnished	Plain/Smoothed	Cord Marked	Fabric Impressed	Net Impressed	Brushed	Indeterminate	Total
Temper														
Soapstone (F)	·	·	1	·	·	·	1	·	·	·	·	1	·	3
Soapstone (M)	1	·	1	·	·	·	1	·	·	·	·	1	·	4
Soapstone plus*	·	·	·	·	·	·	·	·	·	·	·	·	2	2
Sand (F)	4	·	·	2	·	·	2	7	·	1	2	4	3	25
Sand (M)	1	1	2	·	·	·	4	11	3	1	2	2	1	28
Sand (C)	3	·	·	·	·	·	5	15	2	1	3	5	3	37
Quartz (F)	5	1	12	1	·	·	22	54	4	8	9	11	24	151
Quartz (M)	·	1	·	·	1	1	·	4	·	3	1	3	6	20
Quartz (C)	·	·	·	·	·	·	·	·	·	2	·	1	·	3
Misc./Ind.	·	·	·	·	·	·	·	1	·	·	·	1	·	2
Total	14	3	16	3	1	1	35	92	9	16	17	29	39	275
Interior Surface														
Burnished	2	·	2	2	1	·	20	13	·	·	1	1	4	46
Plain/Smoothed	10	1	13	1	·	1	9	74	5	7	8	8	27	164
Scraped	2	2	1	·	·	·	6	3	4	9	8	20	8	63
Thickness														
<6 mm	1	1	3	·	·	·	5	22	·	11	4	10	5	62
6-8 mm	10	1	8	2	1	1	27	50	6	4	11	15	23	159
>8 mm	3	1	5	1	·	·	3	19	3	1	2	4	8	50
Rim Form														
Folded	·	·	·	·	·	·	·	·	·	·	·	·	1	1
Thickened	·	·	·	·	·	·	1	1	·	·	·	1	1	4
Unmodified	1	·	·	·	·	·	1	4	·	5	·	3	3	17
Lip Form														
Flat	·	·	·	·	·	·	1	3	·	1	·	3	2	10
Rounded	1	·	·	·	·	·	1	2	·	4	·	1	3	12

F, Fine; M, medium; C, coarse.

*Indicates mixed temper size; see Appendix C.

Robinson (personal communication 1996) has reported them at a site in Polk County. Thus it appears that a small number of relatively large Connestee phase sites are located along the eastern flank of the Blue Ridge. It is uncertain what the distribution of these sites means with regard to regional settlement patterns.

The Lewis site ceramic assemblage is anomalous in many respects, but particularly in the distribution of temper, exterior and interior surface, and thickness. Three temper groups are present and their distribution is unlike that of any other upper valley site. Crushed quartz is the most common aplastic (59.6 percent), followed by grit (27.2 percent) and sand (12.9 per-

Table 48. Summary of 31CT94 potsherds by exterior surface treatment and other selected attributes

Exterior Surface Attribute Attribute State	Curv Comp St	Comp St Indet	Large Curv Comp St	Large Rect Comp St	Smoothed-Over Comp St	Burnished	Corncob Impressed	Plain/Smoothed	Cord Marked	Check Stamped	Indet St Linear	Brushed	Indeterminate	Total
Temper														Total
Soapstone (F)	3	.	.	.	.	1	.	2	.	.	.	.	.	6
Soapstone (M)	1	.	.	.	.	1	1	1	.	.	.	.	.	4
Soapstone plus*	.	.	.	.	.	.	.	.	.	.	.	3	.	3
Sand (F)	2	.	1	.	.	1	.	.	.	.	.	.	.	4
Sand (M)	8	2	3	.	3	2	2	12	5	.	.	1	.	38
Sand (C)	1	5	5	1	3	2	3	7	.	1	.	4	2	34
Quartz (F)	9	1	.	.	.	4	3	9	1	.	2	.	4	33
Quartz (M)	.	.	1	.	.	.	.	.	.	.	.	.	1	2
Feldspar (F)	4	3	1	.	.	2	3	.	1	.	.	.	.	14
Misc./Ind.	.	.	.	.	.	.	.	.	1	.	.	.	.	1
Total	28	11	11	1	6	13	12	31	8	1	2	8	7	139
Interior Surface														
Burnished	14	2	7	.	1	12	3	3	2	.	.	.	2	46
Plain/Smoothed	14	8	4	1	5	1	8	26	6	1	2	4	5	85
Scraped	.	1	.	.	.	.	.	2	.	.	.	4	.	7
Thickness														
<6 mm	6	3	1	.	1	2	2	7	2	1	1	2	2	30
6-8 mm	20	6	7	1	2	8	8	20	6	.	.	5	3	86
>8 mm	2	2	3	.	3	3	2	4	.	.	.	1	2	22
Rim Form														
Folded	1	.	.	.	.	.	1	1	.	.	.	.	.	3
Thickened	.	.	.	.	.	1	.	.	.	.	.	.	.	1
Unmodified	.	.	.	.	.	2	.	1	1	.	.	.	.	4
Lip Form														
Flat	1	.	.	.	.	2	1	2	.	.	.	.	.	6
Rounded	.	.	.	.	.	1	.	.	1	.	.	.	.	2

F, Fine; *M*, medium; *C*, coarse.

* Indicates mixed temper size; see Appendix C.

cent). If one considers that grit and crushed quartz are nearly the same material as opposed to sand this is a striking pattern of quartz and grit making up 86.8 percent of the assemblage. No soapstone-tempered sherds occur.

The stamped exterior surfaces occur most often on quartz- and grit-tempered sherds and only rarely on the sand-tempered sherds. However,

Table 49. Summary of 31CT96 potsherds by exterior surface treatment and other selected attributes

Exterior Surface Attribute Attribute State	Curv Comp St	Comp St Indet	Large Curv Comp St	Indet St Linear	Smoothed-Over Comp St	Burnished	Corncob Impressed	Plain/Smoothed	Check Stamped	Cord Marked	Fabric Impressed	Net Impressed	Brushed	Indeterminate	Total
Temper															
Soapstone (F)	1	.	.	.	.	1	.	2	.	.	.	1	.	1	6
Soapstone (M)	6	.	.	.	.	.	.	1	.	.	.	.	.	1	8
Soapstone plus	2	.	.	.	.	.	2	3	.	.	.	.	1	.	8
Sand (F)	3	1	.	.	.	9	.	7	.	.	.	.	.	1	21
Sand (M)	5	1	3	.	.	5	1	25	.	3	.	1	.	2	46
Sand (C)	5	2	.	.	2	3	3	15	1	1	.	.	.	3	35
Quartz F	.	.	1	1	2	59	17	23	.	.	1	.	6	3	113
Quartz (M)	.	.	.	.	.	19	.	1	.	.	.	.	.	.	20
Feldspar (F)	2	.	.	.	.	.	.	3	.	1	.	.	.	.	6
Grit (F/M)	.	1	.	.	.	.	.	2	.	.	.	.	.	.	3
Total	24	5	4	1	4	96	23	82	1	5	1	2	7	11	266
Interior Surface															
Burnished	8	1	.	.	.	91	7	17	.	2	.	1	3	2	132
Plain/Smoothed	16	4	4	1	4	5	16	64	1	2	.	1	4	9	131
Scraped	.	.	.	.	.	.	.	1	.	1	1	.	.	.	3
Thickness															
<6 mm	4	.	2	.	2	11	1	15	.	.	.	.	3	4	42
6-8 mm	16	4	2	1	1	81	17	55	1	3	1	2	3	6	193
>8 mm	4	1	.	.	1	4	5	12	.	2	.	.	1	1	31
Rim Form															
Applique	.	.	.	.	.	.	.	.	.	.	.	.	1	.	1
Folded	1	.	.	.	.	.	.	.	.	.	.	.	.	1	2
Unmodified	.	.	.	1	.	16	4	8	.	.	.	.	.	.	29
Lip Form															
Flat	1	.	.	1	.	13	4	3	.	.	.	.	1	1	24
Rounded	.	.	.	.	.	3	.	5	.	.	.	.	.	.	8

F, Fine; *M*, medium; *C*, coarse.

* Indicates mixed temper size; see Appendix C.

each of the temper groups also includes burnished and plain exterior surfaces. The burnishing is often variably finished with many striations present. I believe that the polishing was done with something like a hard leather pad as opposed to the small pebbles that probably were used to polish Burke burnished pottery.

Interior surface treatment is usually burnished (though often poorly) and sometimes plain. Most sherds (53.3 percent) are between 6 and 8 mm thick. However, nearly as many (44.5 percent) are less than 6 mm thick and only 2.2 percent are greater than 8 mm.

The predominance of the Napier/Etowah, indeterminate stamped linear,

Table 50. Summary of 31ID42 potsherds by exterior surface treatment and other selected attributes

Exterior Surface / Attribute / Attribute State	Curv Comp St	Rect Comp St	Comp St Indet	Large Curv Comp St	Large Rect Comp St	Simple Stamped	Smoothed-Over Comp St	Burnished	Corncob Impressed	Plain/Smoothed	Cord Marked	Fabric Impressed	Brushed	Indeterminate	Total
Temper															
Soapstone (F)	.	.	.	.	.	.	.	.	.	1	.	.	.	.	1
Soapstone (M)	.	.	.	.	.	.	.	2	.	.	.	.	.	.	2
Soapstone (In)	.	.	.	.	.	.	.	1	.	2	.	.	1	.	4
Sand (F)	1	.	.	.	.	.	.	2	.	7	.	.	.	1	11
Sand (M)	4	1	.	1	.	.	1	2	3	29	3	.	4	4	52
Sand (C)	5	.	.	1	.	.	.	1	3	18	2	.	4	6	40
Quartz (F)	1	.	1	1	1	1	.	9	5	12	.	1	3	4	39
Quartz (M)	.	.	.	.	.	.	.	1	.	2	1	.	.	.	4
Feldspar (F)	3	.	.	.	.	.	.	.	1	1	.	.	.	1	6
Granite	.	.	.	.	.	.	.	.	.	5	.	.	.	.	5
Total	14	1	1	3	1	1	1	18	12	77	6	1	12	16	164
Interior Surface															
Burnished	2	.	.	2	.	.	.	12	4	8	.	.	.	2	30
Plain /Smoothed	12	1	1	1	1	1	.	6	8	68	4	.	4	14	121
Scraped	.	.	.	.	.	.	1	.	.	1	2	1	8	.	13
Thickness															
<6 mm	.	.	1	1	.	.	.	3	1	14	1	.	1	2	24
6-8 mm	11	1	.	2	1	1	.	10	7	52	3	1	10	5	104
>8 mm	3	.	.	.	.	.	1	5	4	11	2	.	1	7	34
Rim Form															
Folded	.	.	.	.	.	.	.	.	.	1	.	.	.	.	1
Thickened	.	.	.	.	.	.	.	.	.	.	.	.	.	2	2
Unmodified	.	.	.	.	.	.	.	2	.	4	.	.	2	.	8
Lip Form															
Flat	.	.	.	.	.	.	.	2	.	5	.	.	.	3	10
Rounded	.	.	.	.	.	.	.	.	.	.	.	.	2	.	2

F, Fine; *M*, medium; *C*, coarse; *In*, inclusions.

and burnished exterior surface states represents an assemblage diversity that has not been described previously. The typical sherd in this assemblage is stamped with a Napier design or burnished on the exterior, is burnished on the interior, and is generally thin. Small numbers of north Georgia Napier and Etowah pottery types are reported at isolated sites in western North Carolina (Dickens 1976:12; Keel 1976:71, 116) and they are somewhat common in the Hiwassee River valley (Dorwin et al. 1975). I also recorded a small Napier site (Cullowhee Valley School site, 31JK32) in Jackson County. However, to my knowledge, such sites are rare to absent in the Piedmont of North Carolina. Therefore, I suggest that this assemblage represents a possible site intrusion by peoples of Napier/Etowah cultures in north Georgia. This may not seem unusual when one considers the later Catawba valley ceramic development of the Burke series that is a Lamar style pottery nearly identical to Lamar pottery from north Georgia.

It is difficult to place the Lewis site temporally. The only radiocarbon dates for Napier pottery in North Carolina come from the Cullowhee Valley School site in Jackson County. Radiocarbon dates were obtained from two separate features that included cross-mending Napier sherds. Unfortunately, the dates are separated by nearly three centuries. The sample from the first feature (Beta-69964) gave a radiocarbon age of 1,260 ± 80 B.P. with a calibrated date of A.D. 872 and a 1-sigma range of A.D. 719–961. The second sample (Beta-69801) resulted in a radiocarbon age of 940 ± 70 B.P. with a calibrated date of A.D. 1162 and a 1-sigma range of A.D. 1028–1222. The two dates barely overlap at the 2-sigma range, however.

These dates seem generally in line with a late Woodland time frame for Napier pottery. However, it is uncertain whether the same applies to the assemblage at the Lewis site. I think it is likely that the Lewis assemblage represents a late Woodland assemblage. Whether it is wholly an intrusive assemblage or not may be questionable. The paste and mixed tempers seem unlike those of Napier types in north Georgia, where temper is almost always fine sand or occasionally sand and grit (Wauchope 1966:57). I think it is possible that the prominence of the plain and burnished, check-stamped and net-impressed sherds may represent a local tradition present in the late Woodland upper valley by which the plain and burnished Burke wares were influenced. Alternatively, the assemblage may have been influenced by early Burke styles and may reflect a somewhat later period. Little more can be said of this assemblage without dated contexts.

There are no other sites yet identified with similarly diagnostic ceramics, but most of the upper valley sites include small numbers of what are likely Woodland sherds. Keeler (1971:36–37) describes several extremely minor (each less than 1 percent of the total) surface treatments: check stamped, simple stamped, roughened, and plain/brushed. With the exception of "roughened" (discussed earlier in this appendix), each of these was identified in the present analysis. In addition, small numbers of net- and fabric-impressed sherds were identified. However, in most cases, the minority surface treatments occur on non-Pisgah or non-Burke type ceramics and probably represent earlier Woodland period wares.

On the basis of their ceramic assemblages, the following upper Catawba valley sites are thought to represent Woodland period sites (or components): 31MC1, 31MC8, 31MC9, 31MC11, 31MC12, 31MC18, 31MC43, 31MC48, 31MC53, 31BK9, 31BK11, 31BK16, 31BK26, 31BK27, 31BK38, and 31BK56.

Appendix D

Ceramic Analysis Methodology

As described in chapter 2, the extant literature on Catawba valley ceramics is limited to a general description of the Burke series and limited descriptions of site-specific assemblages. The attribute analysis described here was conducted to provide a more complete description of Catawba valley ceramics and to attempt to identify temporally sensitive attribute patterning within the valley.

The attribute analysis is adapted from the computerized data recording system used by the Research Laboratories of Anthropology, University of North Carolina at Chapel Hill (Davis 1987, 1988). Davis identified attributes of late prehistoric and historic period Siouan pottery in the north-central Piedmont of North Carolina. The use of a similar analytic tool in this study allows for a more reliable comparison of the ceramics of the western Piedmont Catawba valley with the better-known Siouan ceramics. I selected attributes on the basis of the characteristics of the Catawba valley assemblages and also with consideration of attributes that have proved to be analytically useful elsewhere in the North Carolina Piedmont.

I attempted to analyze pottery from every recorded site in the upper and middle Catawba River valley. The major collections I examined were curated at the Research Laboratories of Archaeology, but I also looked at materials from Wake Forest University, Appalachian State University, the Office of State Archaeology, the United States Forest Service, the Schiele Museum of Natural History, and several private collections. However, some site collections were inaccessible for a variety of reasons. I do not believe that I missed any sites with pottery collections of more than 50 sherds.

The total sample of pottery from over 300 sites was in excess of 30,000 potsherds. I did not analyze sherds less than .5 inch in diameter. This removed over 10,000 sherds from the sample, including more than 2,000 from the Low site (31ID31) alone. The final analyzed sample numbered 19,034 potsherds. The discussions in the preceding chapters and appendixes focused primarily on those 33 sites with ceramic assemblages larger than 100 sherds. They constituted 78.9 percent of the total analyzed sample.

The coding procedure recorded three stylistic attributes, four technological attributes, five morphological attributes, and four contextual or provenience attributes for each sherd. Stylistic attributes include exterior surface treatment, type of decoration, and location of decoration. Technological attributes include type, size, and density of temper and method of interior surface finishing. Morphological attributes include vessel portion, rim form, rim profile, lip form, and sherd thickness. Contextual attributes included the site number and the provenience (either surface, feature number, or excavation unit and/or level).

Stylistic Attributes

Stylistic attributes include exterior surface treatment, type of decoration, and location of decoration. Exterior surface treatment is considered to be the method by which the major portion of the vessel exterior is treated prior to firing. Decoration is also applied before firing, but it is generally applied by a different method from the exterior surface finish and is limited to a smaller portion (or smaller portions) of the vessel. Stylistic attributes are crucial to the discussions of chronology and cultural relationships below; therefore, they are introduced here in some detail.

Exterior Surface Treatment

In an attempt to describe and quantify as much variation as possible, nearly 70 attribute states were recorded originally for exterior surface treatment. Many of these were variations of complicated-stamped designs; unfortunately, the small size of most of the sherds precluded an accurate identification of designs. Therefore, the 70 states were reduced to 20 to create larger classes and to facilitate analysis. Surface treatments are described below.

Complicated Stamped

Complicated stamping employs a carved wooden paddle that is impressed or stamped upon the exterior surface of the vessel to create distinctly patterned grooves and lands. Carved designs include curvilinear and rectilinear patterns or combinations of both straight and curving lines. Variation in the Catawba valley occurs in the type of design, the size of the design elements, the size of grooves and lands, and the quality of execution of the design.

The attribute states were defined to account for the wide range of variability in complicated-stamped motifs and the fact that certain stamping characteristics are believed to have temporal significance. Specifically, I separated curvilinear from rectilinear motifs and, where possible, identified those (such as Pisgah or Etowah) whose temporal placement was distinct. Since the study assemblage consisted almost entirely of small sherds it was usually impossible to distinguish complete or individual design motifs. Eventually, more than 20 designs were identified, but sherd sizes were generally not large enough to identify many complete designs. Therefore, the following attribute states were coded for analysis:

Curvilinear complicated stamped: Any pattern that included curved lands and grooves. This included any design that consisted of curved lines for all or merely a portion of the design. Most commonly these designs appeared to be combinations of arcs and rays, concentric circles and bull's-eyes, but they also included the filfot cross, keyhole, or scroll patterns.

Rectilinear complicated stamped: Any pattern that included connected or converging straight lands and grooves with no curving elements present. This included designs made up solely of straight, angled lines such as nested diamonds or squares and zig-zag patterns. A small number of rectilinear patterns were coded under specific type names if they were recognizable as such. These included Pisgah Rectilinear Complicated Stamped and Etowah/ Napier Complicated Stamped.

Complicated stamped indeterminate: Used generally for small sherds that exhibited connected or converging straight lands and grooves, but were too small to preclude their being straight elements of curvilinear patterns such as filfot crosses or scrolls, etc.

Curvilinear stamped large: Curvilinear complicated-stamped elements with combined lands and grooves wider than 8 mm. Designs of this size were relatively rare, but their style and execution seemed to demonstrate a departure from the more finely controlled and uniform smaller designs.

Rectilinear stamped large: Same as curvilinear stamped large, except with rectilinear motifs.

Indeterminate stamped, linear: Used for smaller sherds that exhibited straight lands and grooves without connections or convergences.

Simple stamped: Used for larger sherds that appeared to preclude the likelihood of complicated stamping. Also used when lands and grooves were less regular or even.

Etowah/Napier: Used for specific rectilinear patterns attributable to these types; not intended to represent the type necessarily.

Pisgah: Used for specific rectilinear patterns attributable to the Pisgah type; not intended to represent the type necessarily.

This combination of attribute states eliminates one source of recording bias by decreasing the chances of mixing curvilinear and rectilinear states. Unfortunately, it also probably reduces the total numbers of sherds recorded with definite motifs and increases the numbers that are difficult to interpret; i.e., how do you interpret the relative frequencies of complicated stamped indeterminate; indeterminate stamped, linear; and simple stamped? Ultimately, I chose to select for the absolute distinction between rectilinear and curvilinear motifs.

Burnished

Burnished is the first of five attribute states that cover sherds with a plain surface, devoid of impressed or stamped features.

Burnished sherds exhibit a finely smoothed or polished surface. The use of a burnishing tool such as a stone or bone often leaves distinct facets on the surface. Although it was sometimes difficult to distinguish between burnished and smoothed states, the distinction was based on whether a compaction of the surface paste had occurred. If so, the sherd was coded as burnished. The burnishing technique also reduces the amount of temper visible at the surface. Some burnished surfaces were not completely finished, leaving striations or even evidence of an impressed or stamped surface treatment beneath. Most, however, evidence a highly polished or glossy surface.

Plain Smoothed

These sherd surfaces exhibit a uniform and smoothed surface.

Rough Smoothed

These sherd surfaces show irregular smoothing. I felt that ultimately this category was impossible to separate objectively from plain smoothed. Therefore, I joined the two into the category plain/smoothed, which appears on the pottery tables.

Smoothed-Over Complicated Stamped

These sherd surfaces are generally smoothed only enough to blend the lands and grooves of the underlying stamping treatment; the surface is not leveled.

Plain

This attribute state reflects those surfaces that appear to have minimal smoothing beyond that which would be required for annealing coils and shaping the vessel. Temper particles are usually readily apparent at and above the surface, rather than having been smoothed into the surface.

Simple Stamped

This treatment, like complicated stamped, also employs a carved wooden paddle to impress a pattern of lands and grooves on the surface. The lands and grooves are regular and parallel although overstamping sometimes reduces their clarity. Two attribute states make up this treatment. *Simple stamped* was coded for sherds large enough to preclude the possibility that the stamping was part of a larger complicated design, and *indeterminate linear stamped* was coded for sherds too small to preclude that possibility.

Check Stamped

The final wood-carved stamp treatment is an extremely minor one, found on less than 1 percent of the identifiable sample. Parallel grooves are usually cut at right angles to form squares, though occasionally rectangular or diamond-shaped patterns occur. Patterns are well executed, but the stamp is usually lightly impressed on the surface.

Cob Impressed

This treatment employs a corncob from which the kernels have been removed. The dried cob is impressed upon or rolled across the vessel surface, resulting in a variety of patterns.

Cord Marked

This treatment results from impressing the surface with a cord-wrapped paddle. Both S and Z twists were identified, though the latter occurs only rarely. Cord widths range from under 1 mm to 3 mm; most are 1 to 2 mm. The cords were usually wrapped in nearly parallel order, though a large number show irregular wrapping. Some overstamping also occurs.

Brushed

This category was used to subsume both the terms *brushed* and *scraped*. *Brushed* describes a smoothing process that leaves a surface marked by relatively fine linear abrasions, and *scraped* describes the use of a serrated tool that produces prominent parallel striations. This treatment results from brushing or scraping across the surface with a comblike instrument or a tool such as a serrated shell. The resulting lands and grooves are generally parallel but irregular and may be fine or large depending on the implement. It is possible that some simple-stamped sherds are represented by this state when their regular lands and grooves are obscured by overstamping.

Net Impressed

In this treatment the vessel surface is impressed with a net-wrapped paddle. In most cases knotted nets are utilized, though the use of looped nets is occasionally seen. The stamping creates both regular and irregular patterns depending on whether the net was loosely bunched or tightly stretched on the paddle and whether overstamping occurred. Net impressing is relatively rare in the Catawba valley, occurring on 2.1 percent of the identifiable sherds. This pattern also stands in contrast to that in the eastern Piedmont, where it occurs in large numbers in both the Uwharrie and Dan River series (Coe and Lewis 1952; Wilson 1983).

Fabric Marked

This treatment utilizes a paddle wrapped with plaited fabric or possibly a more rigid fabric applied without a paddle foundation. Most of the fabric-marked sherds are likely to represent Early or Middle Woodland ceramics such as the Badin and Yadkin series (Coe 1964).

Unidentified

All sherds for which the surface treatment was indeterminable were coded as unidentified. Despite removal of all sherds less than .5 inch from the analysis, most of the collections consisted of many small sherds less than 1 inch in diameter. As a result, the unidentified surface treatment attribute state made up a large percentage (14.1 percent; n = 2,677) of the total assemblage.

Type of Decoration

Decoration generally refers to a treatment of a portion of the vessel in a manner different from that employed as surface treatment. Nearly one hundred distinct decoration attribute states were observed. These states are combined for most analyses into nine groups on the basis of application technique.

Punctated

Punctated decoration is accomplished by pressing the end of a linear tool into the clay when it is soft. The tool may be solid or hollow and may leave a flat, rounded, pointed, or irregular concavity. The tool may also be applied vertically or obliquely to the plane of the vessel. Most common tools appear to be reeds, sharpened bones (or reeds), and wooden sticks. Twenty-four punctated states were identified including singular or multiple rows of circular, square, rectangular, and V-, U-, and X-shaped designs.

Incised

Incised decoration consists of one or more lines scribed into the vessel surface. All incising occurs before firing and while the clay is damp but not too soft; some incising may have occurred while the clay was "leather-hard." In most cases incised lines are extremely regular and excess clay was cleaned away from the line edges. A variety of implements may have been utilized for scribing; some lines are narrow V cuts whereas others are wider and exhibit a U-shaped or squared base. Incised lines vary in width from approximately .5 mm to nearly 2 mm, but most average about 1 mm. Among identifiable surface treatments, incised decorations are most common on plain/smoothed and burnished vessels.

Twenty-four incised attribute states were identified. These included a variety of triangular and V designs. However, the majority featured combinations of bands of multiple lines parallel to the rim. The bands were usually interrupted by loops, scrolls, arches, or brackets.

Finger Impressed

Fingertips or fingernails impressed into the surface created both notched and punctation-like decorations. They were usually applied vertically to the plane of the surface though occasionally were applied obliquely or even pressed or pinched together.

Notched

Notching is distinguished from punctation by the application of the tool edge rather than the point of the tool on the clay surface. Most notches appear as relatively wide U- or V-shaped depressions, but a small number are squared.

Punctation, incising, notching, and finger-impressing constitute the large majority of decorative techniques and specific attribute states. The following make up the remaining minority states.

Smoothed/Burnished

In rare cases, the vessel surface is decorated by zoned bands of smoothing and burnishing.

Scraped

Scraped decorations are distinguished from incised decorations by the lack of intentional or coherent design elements. This group consists of single or multiple lines applied by brushing or scraping an implement across the vessel surface.

Appliqued

This group consists of modeled pieces of clay added to the vessel in the form of fillet strips, handles, rosettes, nodes, and castellations.

Segmented Strip

This specific attribute state is formed by the combination of a rim form (appliqued strip) with a decorative technique (punctation). This state was coded when the punctation element on an appliqued rim strip completely covered the width of the strip, giving the strip a segmented appearance. This type of decoration has been demonstrated to be an important indication of temporal placement among pottery of the Wateree River valley in South Carolina, but turned out to be extremely rare in the Catawba valley.

Cob Impressed, Cord Marked, and Complicated Stamped

These groups include decorative techniques that are more commonly used as surface treatments, but occur in restricted areas of a vessel marked with a different surface treatment.

Decoration Location

The final stylistic attribute is the location of the decoration on the vessel. Twenty-six attribute states were observed, reflecting the wide variety of placement as well as motif among this assemblage. These states included portions of the vessel such as lip, rim, rimfold, shoulder, and neck as well as locations on appliqued strips or fillets, nodes, handles, and so on.

Technological Attributes

Four technological attributes were coded to describe vessel manufacturing procedures. The first three include the type, size, and amount of temper added to the paste. The fourth is interior surface treatment.

Temper

Temper is a fundamentally important attribute in the Catawba valley because of the unusual use of soapstone in the Burke ceramic series. The type of temper (aplastic) added to paste has been demonstrated to be an important factor in Piedmont ceramic classifications (Coe 1964; Coe and Lewis 1952). Recently, Boyd (1986a) has observed a wide variability of temper classes in protohistoric and historic ceramic assemblages in the region north of the upper Catawba valley. Davis (1987) has also demonstrated a wide range of temper in the Siouan pottery of the Piedmont and has suggested that temper may be less temporally sensitive than previously thought.

Temper attribute states included soapstone, soapstone plus sand, soapstone plus quartz, sand, crushed quartz, grit, feldspar, shell, hornblende, granite, and grog.

Temper Size and Density

Keeler (1971) previously suggested that the size of temper particles and the quantity of sand tempering were spatially and temporally significant. As a result, temper attribute states were created to include the size of the temper particles. They were usually coded fine, medium, and coarse (a category of "inclusions" was recorded for sherds with wide size variations).

I also attempted to record the density of temper in each sherd. I used a geological sorting scale that proved to be extremely subjective and unwieldy. I do not think it was particularly useful given the difficulties. Temper density would be better analyzed using statistical samples and fresh cross sections of sherds.

Interior Surface Treatment

The final technological attribute coded was interior surface treatment. This attribute describes the manner in which the interior vessel surface is treated prior to firing. Initially, an attempt was made to distinguish five states of interior surface treatment: plain, smoothed, brushed, scraped, and burnished. Plain surfaces show little or no evidence of smoothing whereas smoothed surfaces are evenly smoothed (the precise smoothing method is not apparent). Brushing describes a smoothing process that leaves a surface marked by fine linear abrasions, and scraping describes the use of a serrated tool that produces prominent parallel striations. Unfortunately, the variety in brushed and scraped techniques produces a wide range of striations and for the sake of consistency in analysis brushing and scraping were combined, as were smoothed and plain. Burnishing describes the highly smoothed to polished surface produced by rubbing with leather, bone, or polished stone. It is often difficult to distinguish between highly smoothed and burnished surfaces. In this study any sherds with an interior surface that evidenced burnishing facets or a compaction of the interior surface were coded as burnished. Finally, rare sherds were marked by fabric or cord impressions on the interior surface.

Morphological Attributes

It is often difficult to derive vessel morphology information from potsherd collections. In this case, the study collection includes few whole vessels and relatively few large rim sherds. However, five morphological attributes were coded for each sherd (when applicable) in an attempt to gain better morphological data for the ceramic assemblage.

Vessel Portion

All sherds were coded for the portion of the vessel they represented.

Rim/Vessel Profile

Second, the rim and/or vessel profile was coded. Unfortunately, many of the rim sherds exhibit coil breaks immediately below the rim; this is particularly true where folded rims or appliqued rim strips were present. As a result, profiles were often difficult to determine and this category did not prove to be productive.

Rim Form

Attribute states for rim form, the treatment of the upper portion of the vessel, are particularly important in this analysis since rims are often associated with the stylistic attributes of decoration. Six attribute states were used in the analysis: folded rims (the original lip remains distinguishable); appliqued strip (a strip of clay is added at or just below the lip); thickened (manner of thickening in the rim area is uncertain); collared (the final coil is added to present a vertical face above the neck); unmodified; and indeterminate.

Lip Form

Attribute states for lip form included rounded, flat, pointed, beveled, and thickened.

Sherd Thickness

Sherd thickness was measured in the following increments: less than 6 mm; 6 to 8 mm; 8 to 10 mm; 10 to 12 mm; and greater than 12 mm.

Appendix E

Report on Plant Remains from the Berry and McDowell Sites

Kristen J. Gremillion

Samples of plant remains from two sites, Berry (31BK22) and McDowell (31MC41), were submitted to the Paleoethnobotany Laboratory at the University of North Carolina at Chapel Hill for analysis. Only flotation samples are reported upon here, although some material recovered from the McDowell site by water screening during 1977 excavations was also examined. The sample from Berry is considerably larger than that from McDowell, which constrains the comparisons that can be made of plant remains assemblages from the sites. Both sites date to the middle to late fifteenth century, although McDowell appears to contain an earlier, twelfth-century component as well. When additional plant remains from these two sites are examined it should be possible to draw some conclusions about how subsistence patterns in the Catawba valley on the eve of European contact differed from earlier patterns. Viewed together, plant remains data from the two sites provide a basis for preliminary discussion of the use of plant foods by late prehistoric occupants of the western North Carolina Piedmont.

Materials and Methods

All of the samples from McDowell were analyzed. These included one from mound fill and five from features, representing a total of 60 liters of fill. The flotation samples selected from Berry were collected from 11 features, including three burials. The total assemblage represents 265 liters of fill. Although not all samples submitted were analyzed, an attempt was made to represent all zones and features by at least one sample with subsamples reflecting the total amount of material submitted for each feature.

Flotation samples were processed in the field using a modified SMAP-type water separation device (Watson 1976). A .7-mm mesh brass sieve was used to collect light fractions, and heavy fractions were recovered in ¹⁄₁₆-in (approximately 1.6 mm) window screen. Some heavy fractions were further separated by the analyst in the laboratory using tap water and a plastic tub to pour off charcoal that had settled initially into the heavy fraction tub during field processing. This was done only for samples that contained large quantities of soil, pottery, and/or stone that would have rendered hand sorting of the entire sample too time consuming.

Material remaining in the 2.0-mm and larger screens was sorted completely and each component was weighed. Material passing through the 2.0-mm screen was searched only for seeds, cultigen remains, and items not found in the larger size category. Quantities of plant remains in the .7-mm and larger size category were estimated on the basis of their representation in the greater than 2.0 mm size category. This procedure assumes equal representation of various materials in all size classes. Although this assumption is sometimes not justified, the extrapolation provides a more accurate estimate of actual quantities in each sample than do the raw data.

For each site, extrapolated quantities of plant remains are presented as well as itemizations of plant food remains (Table 51 lists the scientific names of plants mentioned in the text). Seeds and fruits appear as aggregate weights for each sample in the tables, but counts are given separately. Percentages of identified seeds were calculated using only seeds identified to genus or species level. Ubiquity values were also calculated for plant food remains at each site. Here, ubiquity represents the percentage of features from which an item was recovered and reflects the regularity of occurrence rather than quantity. This procedure eliminates some of the biases inherent in calculation of percentages by weight, which tend to exaggerate the importance of plant foods that produce dense, durable remains, such as hickory shell.

Results

McDowell Site

In addition to large amounts of wood charcoal, smaller quantities of giant cane stem were recovered from Feature 7. Several fragments of an unidentified root or tuber occurred in Feature 6 (Table 52). Among plant food remains, hickory and acorn shell and maize cupules and kernels were abundant. Fragments of common bean cotyledon were found in the mound fill sample (Table 53). A small number of seeds were recovered from the site as well (Table 54). Most of the latter are of common weeds (e.g., nightshade, plantain (?), morning glory, spurge, chenopod, ragweed, maypops, and lespedeza (?) [see below for a discussion of tentative identifications of plantain and lespedeza at the Berry site]). Maypops was probably a food plant, and although the seeds of chenopod and ragweed may have been used for food, there is no compelling reason to suspect that they were. Presumably these weed seeds blew into fires and were carbonized with other weed seeds and plant food refuse.

Table 51. Scientific names of plants mentioned in the text

Taxon	Latin Binomial and Authority
Acorn (Oak)	Quercus sp.
Amaranth	Amaranthus sp.
Bearsfoot	Polymnia uvedalia L.
Bramble	Rubus sp.
Chenopod	Chenopodium sp.
Giant cane	Arundinaria gigantea L.
Giant ragweed	Ambrosia trifida L.
Common bean	Phaseolus vulgaris L.
Grape	Vitis sp.
Grass family	Poaceae
Hickory	Carya sp.
Jimsonweed	Datura stramonium L.
Knotweed	Polygonum sp.
Legume family	Fabaceae
Lespedeza	Lespedeza sp.
Little barley	Hordeum pusillum L.
Love grass	Eragrostis sp.
Maize	Zea maize L. ssp. mays
Maypops	Passiflora incarnata L.
Morning glory	Ipomoea sp.
Nightshade	Solanum sp.
Nightshade family	Solanaceae
Panic grass	Panicum sp.
Pepo	Cucurbita pepo L.
Persimmon	Diospyros virginiana L.
Plantain	Plantago sp.
Plum/cherry	Prunus sp.
Poke	Phytolacca americana L.
Ragweed	Ambrosia sp.
Spurge	Euphorbia sp.
Sumac	Rhus sp.
Walnut (Black walnut)	Juglans nigra L.
Walnut family	Juglandaceae

Table 52. McDowell site plant remains (weight in grams)

Sample	Soil Volume (liters)	Total Plant Remains	Wood Charcoal	Cane	Unknown Plant	Root or Tuber	Plant Food Remains
Mound Fill	10	5.98	4.7	x	0.21		1.06
Feature 5	10	0.69	0.61		0.7		0.01
Feature 6	30	11.26	10.64		0.48	0.06	0.09
Feature 7	10	2.52	2.27	0.09	0.12		0.05
Site Total	60	20.45	18.22	0.09	1.51	0.06	1.21

x = present.

Table 53. McDowell site plant food remains (weights in grams)

Sample	Fraction	Hickory Shell	Acorn Shell	Common Bean	Maize Kernels	Maize Cupules	Seeds	Total Plant Food Remains
90R350	LF		x		0.13	0.51	x	0.64
Mound Fill 1	HF	0.2		0.05	0.03	0.14	x	0.42
Mound Fill Total		0.2	x	0.05	0.16	0.65	x	1.06
Feature 5 Level 2	LF					0.01	x	0.01
	HF							0.00
Feature 5 Total			x			0.01	x	0.01
Feature 6 Level 2	LF					0.01	x	0.01
	HF	0.03						0.03
Feature 6 Level 5	LF						x	x	0.0
	HF	0.05						0.05
Feature 6 Total		0.08				0.01	x	0.09
Feature 7 Level 1						0.02	0.01	0.03
E 1/2		0.02					x	0.02
Feature 7 Total		0.02				0.02	0.01	0.05
Site Total		0.3	x	0.05	0.16	0.69	0.01	1.21

LF, Light fraction; HF, heavy fraction.
x = present.

Berry Site

The larger sample of plant remains recovered from the Berry site allows for a more thorough discussion of the resulting data. As at McDowell, wood charcoal dominated the plant remains assemblage, although smaller quantities of giant cane and other monocot stem fragments were also present. Root or tuber fragments were especially common in samples from Feature 13. These fragments could not be identified other than anatomically, but their relative abundance indicates that they may be the remains of food-processing activity. The "roundish unknown" of Table 55 also occurred with some regularity in samples from Feature 13 and may also be some type of underground plant part, although this assessment is tentative (Table 55).

Plant food remains were abundant in samples from the Berry site (Table 56). Densities of plant food remains in features ranged from .07 g (Feature 17) to 1.70 g (Feature 13) per liter of fill. The complete set of flotation samples produced 1.15 g per liter. Hickory shell, maize cupules, and acorn shell were especially abundant. Walnut shell and Juglandaceae (walnut family; i.e., walnut or hickory) shell were also present, as were maize kernels, pepo rind, common bean, and a large number of fruit and grain or weed seeds (Table 57).

Nutshell. Although hickory is the most abundant nutshell type by weight, acorn shell runs a close second, comprising 27.3 percent of total nutshell from the site (Table 58). Because acorn shell represents more edible portion than an equivalent quantity of hickory shell (Lopinot 1983), multiplying the quantity of acorn shell by some number for comparison with hickory

Table 54. McDowell site seeds and fruits

	90R350 Mound fill LF	HF	Total	Feature 5 Level 2 LF	Feature 6 Level 2 LF	Level 5 LF	Total	Feature 7 / Feature 1 E1/2 Level 1 LF	HF	Total	Site Total
Fraction											
Maypops		1	1						1	1	2
Nightshade					1		1				1
Chenopod	1		1		2		2				3
Ragweed					1		1				1
Lespedeza?					2		2				2
Plantain?				7							7
Morning glory	1		1		1		1				2
Spurge								1		1	1
Nightshade fam.					1		1				1
Common bean		1	1								1
Maize kernels		3	3								3
Maize cupules		18	18	1	4	2	6	4		4	29
Unknown	3	2	5		3	2	5	2	1	3	13
Total	5	25	30	8	15	4	19	7	2	9	66

LF, Light fraction; HF, heavy fraction.

Table 55. Berry site plant remains (weight in grams)

Feature	Volume (liters)	Total Plant Remains	Wood Charcoal	Cane/ Monocot	Roundish/ Unknown	Unknown Plant	Pedicel/ Peduncle	Root or Tuber	Plant Food Remains
1	20	22.68	16.45	0.02		0.83			5.38
2	60	69.19	59.02	1.07	0.11	2.15		0.09	6.77
5	20	18.69	15.62	0.16	0.13	0.51			2.26
9	10	2.29	2.01			0.03			0.25
11	60	82.71	78.1	0.98		0.99		0.02	2.61
12	10	1.16	1.06			0.05		0.01	0.04
13	45	76.61	55.82	2.77	0.64	6.21	0.03	3.38	7.76
16	10	2.2	1.37		0.06	0.2			0.56
17	10	0.67	0.62					0.02	0.04
18	10	3.81	2.79			0.41			0.83
Burial 1	10	1.02	0.72			0.21			0.09
Site Total	265	281.03	233.58	5	0.94	11.59	0.03	3.52	26.59

Table 56. Berry site plant food remains (weight in grams)

Feature	Total Plant Food Remains	Hickory Shell	Acorn Shell	Walnut Shell	Juglandaceae Sh.	Maize Kernels	Maize Cupules	Pepo Rind	Common Bean	Seeds
1	5.38	3.08	1.22	0.13	0.13	0.2	0.59			0.02
2	6.77	2.19	1.88	0.21		0.33	1.72		0.02	0.42
5	2.26	1.21	0.35		0.12	0.25	0.26		0.04	0.03
9	0.25	0.2	0.03	x		0.01	0.01			
11	2.62	1.24	0.28	0.17		0.21	0.57	0.01	x	0.14
12	0.04	0.01	x				0.03			
13	7.77	0.92	0.04	0.12		0.16	5.87			0.65
16	0.56	0.47			0.06		0.03			x
17	0.04	0.03				0.01	x			
18	0.83	0.42	0.14	0.03		0.07	0.15			0.01
Burial 1	0.09	0.08				0.01	x			
Site Total	26.61	9.85	3.94	0.66	0.31	1.25	9.23	0.01	0.06	1.27

x = present.

Table 57. Berry site seed and fruit counts

Feature #	1	2	5	9	11	12	13	16	17	18	Burial 1	Total
Weeds or Weed Crop												
Chenopod	.	176	1	.	2	.	264	.	1	.	.	444
Ragweed (small)	.	4	2	.	1	.	6	.	.	1	.	14
Giant ragweed	.	10	.	.	.	.	8	.	.	.	.	18
Little barley	.	1	.	.	.	.	3	.	.	.	.	4
Knotweed	.	34	1	.	3	.	22	.	.	.	.	60
Subtotal												**540**
Fleshy Fruits												
Maypops	2	3	2	.	3	.	3	.	.	.	.	13
Persimmon	.	.	.	.	1	.	.	.	.	.	.	1
Bramble	.	.	.	.	.	.	1	.	.	.	.	1
Grape	.	5	2	.	3	.	7	.	.	.	.	17
Plum/cherry	1	.	.	.	.	.	.	.	.	.	.	1
Sumac	1	.	.	.	.	.	1	.	.	.	.	2
Subtotal												**35**
Weeds (?)												
Lespedeza (?)	.	150	.	.	1	.	495	1	1	.	.	648
Plantain (?)	.	1113	1	.	.	.	1193	4	.	.	.	2311
Jimsonweed	.	.	1	.	.	.	.	.	.	.	.	1
Morning glory	.	2	.	.	1	.	.	.	.	.	.	3
Amaranth	.	4	.	.	.	.	1	.	.	.	.	5
Poke	2	.	.	.	.	.	3	.	.	.	.	5
Brassica	.	.	.	.	.	.	1	.	.	.	.	1
Bearsfoot	.	.	.	.	.	.	1	.	.	.	.	1
Spurge	.	2	.	.	.	.	1	.	.	.	.	3
Subtotal												**2978**
Grasses												
Panicum (?)	.	27	.	.	1	.	9	.	.	.	.	37
Eragrostis (?)	.	52	.	.	.	.	14	.	.	.	.	66
Subtotal												**103**
Cultigens												
Common bean	.	1	1	.	.	.	.	.	.	.	.	2
Maize kernels	7	21	10	3	18	.	9	.	1	3	1	73
Maize cupules	60	158	30	4	74	2	353	4	1	11	2	699
Subtotal												**774**
Miscellaneous												
Nightshade family	.	.	.	.	.	.	2	.	.	1	.	3
Legume family	1	1	.	.	.	.	1	.	.	.	.	3
Grass family	.	.	1	.	.	.	.	.	.	.	.	1
Subtotal												**7**
Unknown	4	79	11	.	12	.	59	6	1	2	.	**174**
Total	78	1843	63	7	120	2	2457	15	5	18	3	**4611**

shell provides a more realistic estimate of relative food quantities represented. Using the factor of 50 suggested by Yarnell and Black (1985) produces an acorn-to-hickory ratio (grams acorn shell × 50/grams hickory shell) of 20.0. This indicates that acorn is actually better represented at the site than is hickory. Hickory does have higher ubiquity than acorn (100

Table 58. Nutshell percentages at the Berry
and McDowell sites

		Berry	McDowell
Hickory			
	(g)	9.88	0.3
	(%)	66.8	100.0
Acorn			
	(g)	3.95	x
	(%)	26.7	trace
Juglandaceae			
	(g)	0.31	
	(%)	2.1	0.0
Walnut			
	(g)	0.66	
	(%)	4.5	0.0
Total	**(g)**	14.8	0.3

x = present.

percent of features compared with 72.7 percent for acorn), but the difference is in three features only, and acorn shell is more fragile and therefore less likely to be preserved archaeologically. Walnut is only a minor nutshell type, although it did occur in 6 of the 11 features sampled (Table 59).

Cultigens. Two Mesoamerican crops, maize and common bean, were found at the Berry site. Maize remains were found in 100 percent of features sampled (Table 59). Maize kernels comprise only about 2.0 percent of total identified seeds (Table 60), but are exceeded in number only by three taxa of weed seeds that occurred in surprisingly large numbers at the site. Common bean cotyledons were found in two features (18.2 percent) and make up .1 percent of identified seeds. Presumably beans are somewhat underrepresented relative to the extent of their use because of their preparation by boiling rather than roasting or parching, which was probably the case with maize (Yarnell 1982).

Rind fragments of pepo squash were recovered from Feature 11. Once thought to be Mesoamerican in origin, one variety of *Cucurbita pepo* L. (var. *texana Decker*) is now thought to be an indigenous eastern North American domesticate (Decker 1988). Like common bean, pepo squash was probably either thin-skinned or prepared in such a way that the likelihood of pieces of rind being preserved through carbonization and recovered archaeologically is rather low. Paleoethnobotanical data support the expectation that maize was the single most important crop and plant dietary staple at the Berry site, as it was for other aboriginal villages of that time period.

Grain, fruit, and weed seeds. The occurrence of large numbers of grain and/or weed seeds at the Berry site raised a number of questions regarding

Table 59. Ubiquity of plant foods from the Berry site

Taxon	No. of Features*	% of Features
Hickory	11	100.0
Maize	11	100.0
Acorn	8	72.7
Walnut	6	54.5
Maypops	6	54.5
Chenopod	5	45.5
Lespedeza	5	45.5
Ragweed	5	45.5
Plantain	4	36.4
Grape	4	36.4
Knotweed	4	36.4
Panic grass	3	27.3
Little barley	3	27.3
Morning glory	2	18.2
Love grass	2	18.2
Plum/cherry	2	18.2
Spurge	2	18.2
Poke	2	18.2
Amaranth	2	18.2
Giant ragweed	2	18.2
Bean	2	18.2
Jimsonweed	1	9.1
Persimmon	1	9.1
Sumac	1	9.1
Bramble	1	9.1
Bearsfoot	1	9.1
Pepo	1	9.1

* Total number of features = 11.

their identification and interpretation. Some taxa, such as chenopod, little barley, and giant ragweed, were cultivated in some parts of the East (Yarnell 1986). The large numbers of chenopod seeds in particular are relevant to the question of the importance of native grain crops relative to staples such as maize. These chenopod seeds were found in association with large numbers of presumably non-food weed seeds such as jimsonweed, amaranth, ragweed, and plantain, although maize remains also occurred in features along with chenopod. One of the chenopod seeds examined was carbonized after it had begun to germinate, as indicated by the radicle seen emerging from the seed. B. Smith (1985) used this condition, found in some of the chenopod specimens from a woven bag full of carbonized seeds

Table 60. Percentage of identified seeds from the Berry site

Taxon	No.	Percentage
Plantain	2311	61.94
Lespedeza	648	17.36
Chenopod	444	11.90
Maize	73	1.96
Love grass	66	1.77
Knotweed	60	1.61
Panic grass	37	0.99
Giant ragweed	18	0.48
Grape	17	0.46
Ragweed	14	0.38
Maypops	13	0.35
Amaranth	5	0.13
Little barley	5	0.13
Poke	5	0.13
Spurge	3	0.08
Morning glory	3	0.08
Sumac	2	0.05
Bean	2	0.05
Bramble	1	0.03
Bearsfoot	1	0.03
Jimsonweed	1	0.03
Plum/cherry	1	0.03
Persimmon	1	0.03

and fruits in Russell Cave, Alabama, as evidence that the seeds had germinated in storage. In the case of the Berry site specimen, however, it is equally likely that the germinating seed was blown or otherwise conveyed into an open fire from the ground.

The fact that many grain crops are derived from colonizing plants of open, anthropogenically disturbed habitats makes the distinction between unutilized weeds, harvested weeds, and crops unclear in many cases, particularly since the status of many species varied temporally and spatially. In addition, there is no way to distinguish between seeds deposited in features as a result of food-processing activities and those blown in by wind or other natural means. The food plant identity of chenopod at the Berry site is therefore unclear, although association with other non-food weeds weakens the argument that it was grown or harvested for food, despite its large numbers. Other weedy potential grain crops, such as little barley, giant ragweed, and knotweed, occurred in much smaller numbers and are more likely to have been weeds than food plants.

Interpretation of the crop and food plant status of these small seeds rests partly upon their association with other taxa known to be weeds but not likely to have been food plants. Two of these, lespedeza and plantain, require further discussion because their identification was the result of considerable effort and must still be considered tentative. The seeds identified as plantain were the most abundant at the site, totaling 3,211 and comprising 61.9 percent of identified seeds. A search of manuals (Martin and Barkley 1961; Montgomery 1977) revealed no other taxon that combined the size and shape characteristics and the trait of extreme variability in shape (caused by the variable number and arrangement of seeds inside the capsule). The size of the archaeological specimens is fairly close to that given for *Plantago rugellii Duchesne* (a native North American species). A problematic feature of the archaeological specimens compared with dried material of this species, however, was that the dried seeds were flattish whereas the carbonized seeds were dorsally more rounded. Carbonization experiments determined that the dried seeds did expand somewhat when charred, producing a space inside the seed. So far, this identification is the most likely one for this abundant seed. Today *P. rugellii* typically inhabits waste ground, roadsides, pastures, and lawns (Radford et al. 1968).

The other problematic seed type appears to be a small legume with a folded embryo that overlaps on itself, producing a small "beak." The size and shape of this seed type conforms most closely to the genus *Lespedeza,* although other small-seeded legumes are possible candidates. A number of species of *Lespedeza* are found in the western Piedmont. Two of the more common species, *L. virginica* (L.) Britton and *L. repens* (L.) Barton, occur in fields and roadsides (the latter also in open woods) (Radford et al. 1968).

The largest numbers of both plantain and lespedeza (as well as chenopod) occur in Features 2 and 13, although plantain was found in two additional features (ubiquity 36.4 percent) and lespedeza in three additional features (ubiquity 45.5 percent). Both also occurred in McDowell site flotation samples. The dominance of weed seeds in the site assemblage raises questions about the sorts of behavior (e.g., burning vegetation off a large area) that might result in deposition of many carbonized weed seeds in open pits. A survey of the seed types found in Features 2 and 13 (both classified as roasting pits) shows that all taxa represented in them would have produced seeds in June (except for grape, which begins to produce fruits in July), although individual taxa fruit anywhere between April and November (see below for a full account of methods used to estimate fruiting dates). It seems likely, given the similarity in seed assemblages from the two features (particularly in having large numbers of chenopod, lespedeza and plantain as well as smaller numbers of ragweed and knotweed), that these seeds at least were deposited in a single event.

Other weed seeds from the site include jimsonweed, morning glory, amaranth, poke, bearsfoot, spurge, and grass, tentatively identified as panic grass and love grass (the latter identification rests mainly upon a cursory assessment of general shape and size characteristics and is meant to suggest only one possible identification). Jimsonweed is a weed of fields, roadsides, and waste places (Radford et al. 1968) whose roots and fruits were also used to produce an intoxicant hallucinogen by some North American groups. Reportedly jimsonweed was the chief ingredient in a concoction given to young male initiates among the coastal Algonquin or Tuscarora of North Carolina (Lefler 1967). However, since it is also a weed of disturbed ground, there is no reason to assume the plant was thus used at the Berry site. Amaranth and poke also occupy disturbed ground, as do bearsfoot (which is also found in woodlands) and spurge, although the former may have been food plants as well (probably as greens, although amaranth grains are edible). Morning glory is a common weed in cornfields and also occurs in other relatively open settings.

The remaining seeds identified to genus and species level are of plants producing edible fleshy fruits (Gremillion 1993). Maypops is a persistent weed in fields and was probably tolerated or encouraged because of its edible, citrus-like fruits. Propagation of this plant probably was unnecessary because of the tenacity of already-established populations and its colonizing ability. Bramble also grows in old fields, pastures, and other open areas, as does sumac. The trees, persimmon and plum or cherry, are found in both woodlands and old fields. Grape grows in woods or along stream banks.

Discussion

A few tentative conclusions can be offered about plant food use at the Berry site. The plant food component of diet at the site included several cultigens, several fleshy fruits, and perhaps some weedy plants used for greens or grain. The archaeological assemblage is an incomplete record of the kinds of plant foods used by site inhabitants as a result of preservational and sampling biases and perhaps its limitation to seasonally circumscribed activities. However, maize was the most important crop plant; acorns also seem to have been an important dietary item, as were hickory nuts. The bulk of plant food produced by the community was probably derived from these taxa, with other crops such as common bean and cucurbits providing supplements whose importance cannot be assessed on the basis of presently available evidence. Calculation of an index of diversity (D = .942) shows the Berry site plant food remains assemblage to be highly diverse, that is, both rich in taxa and highly equitable (no one item makes up a highly disproportionate share of occurrences). However, since many or even most of the seed taxa probably do not represent dietary components, this index is not particularly useful for assessing diet breadth. Instead it indicates a high degree of diversity for the assemblage, which may reflect good preservation of seeds and adequate recovery rates. The richness of the assemblage, particularly of seed types, may also indicate an event of burning in the village that affected a number of different kinds of plants.

The assemblage of plant food remains reflects a bias toward use of human-disturbed habitats (including gardens and agricultural fields) for plant exploitation. This is generally true for communities of subsistence agriculturalists, since gardens and/or fields are key locales for harvesting cultigens. In addition, extensive disturbance (e.g., trampling and clearing) generated by sedentary groups creates ecologically and spatially open habitats suitable for colonization by weeds. Many such weeds produce edible fruits; in fact, plants in general tend to be more productive in such open habitats than under a closed canopy (Yarnell 1982). Hunting techniques such as burning vegetation over large areas also provide prime habitat for many useful plants.

For the Berry site, plant taxa were classified according to their preferred habitats as follows: woods (W); cultivated soils and waste places, edges, thickets, old fields, and roadsides (O); gardens and fields (crop plants only) (G); and either open woods or both woods and open areas (OW). For genus-level classifications, two species common in the western North Carolina Piedmont were selected to provide habitat information (as well as the ripening dates discussed below). About 57.7 percent of plant taxa listed in Table 59 can be classified as O, 11.5 percent as G, and 15.4 percent as OW. Only 15.4 percent of taxa are found exclusively in woods. A large number of these taxa probably do not represent food plants, but they may have been used in other ways (e.g., as medicines or construction materials). Some may also have been used for food, if only opportunistically.

There is also a bias in the assemblage toward plants that produce fruit in the late summer and fall, including nut-producing trees and crops. This fact can be partly ascribed to the fact that this pattern (summer growth followed by late-summer or autumn flower and fruit production) is more common than the alternative strategy of fruit production early in the year using energy reserves stored the previous fall. Ripening periods for most of the features studied (considering only small grain, fruit, and weed seeds, since nuts and cultigens were probably stored) range from April to November. If the assumption is made that all seeds in a feature were deposited over a short period of time, say within a month, it is possible to narrow somewhat the period of seed deposition. This is done by calculating the period of overlap of ripening times, that is, the months during which all the seeds present would have been available. The following temporal profiles are thus obtained: Feature 1, June to August; Feature 2, May to June; Feature 5, August to October. Features 11 and 13 are unusual in that they each contain species whose fruiting times do not overlap, although they are quite close. In both cases, June and July can be considered the closest period of overlap, determined by the terminal month for little barley (June)

Table 61. Ubiquity of plant foods from the McDowell site

Taxon	No. of Features*	% of Features
Maize	4	100.0
Hickory	3	75.0
Maypops	2	50.0
Acorn	2	50.0
Chenopod	2	50.0
Morning glory	2	50.0
Nightshade	1	25.0
Plantain	1	25.0
Lespedeza	1	25.0
Bean	1	25.0
Ragweed	1	25.0
Spurge	1	25.0

*Total no. of features = 4.

and the beginning ripening date for maypops (July). However, grape is present in both features and no grape species found in the study area produce fruit before August. Thus in the case of these two features, the assumption of more-or-less simultaneous deposition of seeds is probably not valid.

Since many of these seed taxa were probably not harvested, this phenological study is more useful in determining the probable times of feature deposition than in adding to our knowledge of subsistence practices at the Berry site. However, the phenology of different useful species indicates that harvesting of fleshy fruits began as early as May with bramble and continued through the summer months with the readily available maypops, which would have been abundant in gardens, and into the fall with persimmon (ripe in September and October) and grape. Plums or cherries, depending on the species collected, would have been available from May into August. Greens from poke are most palatable if collected early in the spring before seed production begins. If chenopod was harvested, it would have been available between June and November. Little barley, if used, was ready to collect earlier, in April, May, and June.

Thus fleshy fruits, greens, and grains were collected primarily in the late summer and fall months, although some species were available in spring and early summer. Harvesting of weedy species may have been somewhat opportunistic, but knowledge of the location of stands of fruit-producing perennials probably made organized collecting forays cost effective. Springtime activities probably focused on planting maize and other crops as well as other subsistence activities such as fishing and hunting. Harvest time for

Table 62. Percentage of identified seeds from the McDowell site

Taxon	No.	Percentage
Plantain	7	30.42
Chenopod	3	13.04
Maize	3	13.04
Morning glory	2	8.70
Maypops	2	8.70
Lespedeza	2	8.70
Spurge	1	4.35
Ragweed	1	4.35
Common bean	1	4.35
Nightshade	1	4.35

most crops was late summer, and at this time preparation for storage of crops and of fruits would have been taking place on a large scale. Harvesting and processing for storage might have been completed before the various species of hickory found locally began producing fruit in October. Acorns generally ripen between September and November. Strategies for harvesting acorns probably varied from year to year, but it would have been advantageous to collect them as soon as they were available, since competition with squirrels and other herbivores is likely to have rendered later collection less effective.

Evidence of such activities from the earlier McDowell site is limited, but many of the same weed and fruit seed types were found there. In fact, all of the seed taxa found at McDowell were also represented at Berry. Maize was relatively abundant and common bean was present. Assemblage diversity was only slightly lower than that of the Berry site at .89. At this time, then, there is no reason to suspect that plant-use patterns were widely divergent at the two sites. On the other hand, there are strong indications that major food plants (e.g., maize and hickory) were the same at both sites. Acorn is scarce in the McDowell site samples, but its low quantity may result partly from the relatively low preservability of acorn in addition to the smaller size of the McDowell site sample. Acorn shell at McDowell also occurs in three out of four contexts sampled (Table 61), despite its low representation by weight. Even the same weed seeds appear at both sites, indicating similar types of disturbance in both villages. In fact, plantain comprises the largest percentage of identified seeds from McDowell (Table 62), and chenopod is as abundant as maize at the site.

Appendix F

National Museum of Natural History Collections: Caldwell County, North Carolina

In 1994 I examined the Caldwell County collections at the National Museum of Natural History (NMNH) curatorial facility in Suitland, Maryland. The artifacts I observed are discussed in chapter 3. A definitive analysis of the Happy Valley sites and artifacts will require an extensive review of all extant collection notes, a task I was unable to take on. If this were to be done, it might then be possible to determine whether the assumptions and discussion presented in chapter 3 are correct and whether more specific proveniences for the artifacts can be determined. Those details notwithstanding, a brief overview of the artifacts demonstrates that the sites are likely late prehistoric or early historic Burke and/or Happy Valley phase sites.

During my two-day visit to the NMNH, I examined every available storage tray and unit containing Caldwell County material. However, collections were in the process of being moved from the NMNH in Washington, D.C., to the new Suitland, Maryland, facility and I was told that it was possible some units were in transit. I made brief notes and photographed all vessels, shell gorgets, shell masks, metal artifacts, and spatulate celts that I found in the collection. I also photographed samples of potsherds, pipes, celts, and stone discoidals. The photographed artifacts appear in Plates 16 through 24 (chapter 3) and Plate 41 (this appendix) and are summarized below for each catalog provenience.

The Nelson Mound

Iron Implements

A. Cat. #82892 (Plate 16, *top*), labeled "Iron Celt," heavy, 12 cm long, base 1–1.4 cm, bit 4.8 cm, thickness is even at .4–.5 cm but tapers at bit end. This does not appear in the published illustrations nor do its measurements suggest that it is the second of the two celts described for the Triangle (Thomas 1894:337, fig. 211).

B. Cat. #82874 (Plate 16, *middle*), labeled "rusty iron," catalog describes three small pieces, but only one was present in box, length 9 cm, width

3 cm, thickness varies from .2–.4 cm, heavily rusted. This piece is likely a large portion of the blade from the Triangle illustrated as Figure 212 by Thomas (1894:337).

(Note: Aside from the three specimens in Plate 16, I saw no other European trade items in the collection, though because of ongoing moving of collections it was not possible to see every box from Caldwell County. The catalog lists only one additional metal artifact from the Nelson Mound: an eyeless brass button.)

Shell Gorgets

C. Cat. #82853, 13.5 cm wide × 11.4 cm tall (Plate 17, *a*).
D. Cat. #82854, 10.5 cm diameter (Plate 17, *b*).
E. Cat. #82855, seems to be a variant of Citico style.
F. Cat. #82856 (Plate 22, *d*).

Chunkey Stones

G. Total of eight, Cat. nos. 82955, 82958, 82959, 82960, 82961, 82964, 82968, 82970. Each of these is highly polished; raw materials are quartz, quartzite, and basalt.

Spatulate Celts

H. Cat. #82979 (Plate 18, *right*), 10.7 cm wide, 13.9 cm tall, base 5.3 cm wide × 6.3 cm tall. Described in NMNH catalog as "Stone hoe."

Ceramics

I. Cat. #82978, straight-sided cup, scraped or simple stamped but has plaster reconstruction obscuring it, 15.9 cm tall, 23.5 cm wide at mouth, flat bottom 10.2 cm.
J. Miscellaneous potsherds, Cat. #82904:

   1 small jar w/constricted neck, burnished exterior surface
   1 small carinated vessel with two lines Burke Incised plus punctations
      just above shoulder

K. Miscellaneous potsherds, Cat. #82894:

   162 soapstone tempered, Burke
   3 sand tempered, late
   5 grit tempered, cord and fabric marked, probably Early Woodland
   1 soapstone tempered, Pisgah collar

L. Miscellaneous sherds, Cat. #82881:

23 soapstone-tempered Burke sherds (most plain and burnished; 4 Burke Incised)

7 grit/crushed-quartz tempered, cord and fabric marked, Early Woodland

4 sand tempered, late

1 soapstone tempered, Dan River net impressed, scraped interior

There was one lot of ceramics listed in the catalog for the Nelson Mound that I apparently did not see. I examined a total of 208 potsherds. Of this total, 187 (89.9 percent) are Burke sherds, 7 (3.4 percent) are sand-tempered plain or burnished sherds that are probably Cowans Ford sherds, 2 (.9 percent) are Pisgah and Dan River sherds, and 12 (5.8 percent) are grit- or quartz-tempered fabric- and cord-marked Woodland period sherds.

Fort Defiance, Lenoir Indian Burial Place

Ceramic Vessels

A. Cat. #83200 (Plate 23, *top*), constricted-neck jar with two strap handles; inverted U-shaped notched applique on shoulder/neck; soapstone tempered; curvilinear complicated stamped, perhaps a figure nine, lands 1–1.5 mm, grooves 2 mm; flattened lip, flared out with tiny circular punctations on bottom outside edge of lip; 30.5 cm tall, 35.6 cm diameter.

B. Cat. #83182, bowl with separate elements of Burke Incised designs, slightly in-slanting; burnished exterior and interior; soapstone temper; 34.3 cm tall, 41.9 cm wide at lip, 46.9 cm wide at shoulder.

C. Cat. #83199 (Plate 23, *bottom*), constricted-neck jar; flat bottom (missing); soapstone tempered; large concentric circles (element 7 cm, lands 2 mm, grooves 3 mm); rim is thickened applique with punctations at lower edge of applique; 33.7 cm tall, 45.7 cm wide at lip, 35.6 cm wide at neck, 41.9 cm wide at shoulder, 21.6 cm base to shoulder.

D. Cat. #83183 (Plate 24, *top*), constricted-neck jar; burnished over complicated-stamped exterior, burnished interior; cob-marked neck; soapstone tempered, flat bottom; 24.1 cm tall, diameter at mouth 26.7 cm, diameter at neck 24.1 cm, diameter at shoulder 27.9 cm, base to shoulder 16.7 cm, 10.2 cm at base.

E. Cat. #83184 (Plate 24, *bottom*), constricted-neck jar; cob impressed with fine vertical overstamping in neck but diagonally and cleanly impressed on body; flat lip; 30.5 cm tall, 28.1 cm diameter at neck, 32.1 cm diameter at mouth, 33.6 cm diameter at shoulder, base to shoulder 20.3 cm.

F. Cat. #83185, constricted-neck jar; large, sloppy, curvilinear complicated stamped, design cannot be determined, lands and grooves both 3.5 mm.

G. Cat. #83186, low bowl, probably sand tempered (plaster effects), two opposite-side appendages are missing; burnished exterior and interior; 9.5 cm tall, 20 cm wide at mouth.

Shell Masks

H. Cat. #83179 (Plate 21, *right*), both masks are somewhat deteriorated; each has two perforated eyes that may have been weeping eyes.

Shell Gorgets

I. Cat. #83172 (Plate 22, *b*), Citico style.
J. Cat. #83173 (Plate 22, *c*), Citico style.
K. Cat. #83171, probably Citico style.
L. Cat. #83174 (Plate 17, *c*), Citico style, 13.0 cm wide, 11.0 cm tall.
M. Cat. #83170, 4.2 × 3.7 cm.
N. Cat. #83169, 5.8 × 4.8 cm.

Iron Implement

O. Cat. #83191 (Plate 16, *c*), "Iron Wedge," 6.5 cm long at top, 6.0 cm long at bottom; width 2.5 cm at base, 3.5 cm at midsection, 3.4 cm at bit; thickness .5 cm at base, .9 cm at midsection, tapers to edge; heavily pocked (not from rust). This appears to be nearly identical to the celt illustrated for the Triangle, but there is no mention of it in the report.

Pipes

P. Cat. #83050, chlorite.
Q. Cat. #83040.

Lenoir Mound (probably the Broyhill-Dillard site)

Pipes

A. Cat. #82835 (Plate 41, *top*), chlorite.
B. Cat. #82836 (Plate 41, *bottom*), chlorite.
C. Cat. #82837 (Plate 41, *middle*), soapstone.

W. Davenport Jones Mound

Ceramics

A. Cat. #83208, straight-sided cup; roughly burnished; soapstone tempered; 15.7 cm tall, 22.4 cm wide at mouth, 7.7 cm wide flat base.
B. Cat. #83009 (Plate 20, *bottom*), bowl with single effigy on rim (effigy nose broken, perhaps bear?); burnished exterior and interior, flat base, slightly in-slanting with high shoulders; fine soapstone temper; 24.1 cm tall, 42.4 cm wide at mouth, base to shoulder 21.1 cm, 17.8 cm wide at base.
C. Cat. #83201 (Plate 20, *top*), sherd from carinated vessel; Burke Incised

Plate 41. Stone pipes from the Lenoir Mound site, NMNH collection. *Top*, Catalog #82835, chlorite; *middle*, Catalog #82837, soapstone; *bottom*, Catalog #82836, chlorite.

with four-line decoration (1.5 mm); burnished exterior and interior with fine to medium soapstone temper; shoulder to lip 3 cm.

D. Cat. #83216, sherd from flat-bottomed jar 24.2 cm tall, approximately 25–28 cm diameter at mouth; plain exterior and interior.

E. Cat. #83007 (Plate 19, *bottom*), constricted-neck jar, flat bottom; notched appliqued strip with collar effect, flattened lip; plaster reconstruction over portions; temper is soapstone or sand; burnished exterior and interior; 27.8 cm tall, base to shoulder 17.8 cm, diameter 29 cm at neck, 32.3 cm at mouth, 31.5 cm at shoulder.

F. Cat. #83008 (Plate 19, *top*), constricted-neck jar, flat base; curvilinear complicated stamped (lands 2 mm, grooves 2 mm); flared flattened lip with punctation along lower outside edge; 31.6 cm tall, 32.6 cm wide at mouth, 25.0 cm wide at neck, 33.1 cm wide at shoulder.

G. Cat. #83211, miscellaneous sherds:

37 soapstone-tempered mostly plain or burnished carinated fragments

3 coarse grit–tempered sherds from flat-bottomed, slightly flaring jar; "roughened" exterior surface; brushed/scraped interior

2 sand/grit-tempered plain (?) sherds

H. Cat. #83212, two sherds: one body sherd, soapstone tempered, smoothed-over complicated stamped; one rim and body sherd, cazuela form with strong shoulder break, large chunks of soapstone temper.

I. Cat. #83213, miscellaneous sherds:

121 soapstone tempered
1 soapstone tempered, knotted net impressed (fine) (10–12 mm thick)
1 sand tempered complicated stamped, maybe filfot design

J. Cat. #83214, flat vessel bottom, burnished interior, smoothed-over complicated-stamped exterior, soapstone tempered.

Jones Mound potsherds totaled 168 of which 162 (96.4 percent) are Burke sherds, 1 (.6 percent) is a Dan River–like sherd, and 5 (2.9 percent) are sand or grit tempered (not typed).

Celt

K. Cat. #83056, 24.8 cm long, 2.2 cm thick, bit edge 6.8 cm wide, base 3.3 cm wide; possible ochre stains.

Spatulate Celts

L. Cat. #83010 (Plate 18, *left*), 10.8 cm wide blade, 14.7 cm tall total, base 5.5 cm wide and 5.3 cm tall. Described in NMNH catalog as "stone ornament."

M. Cat. #83100 (Plate 18, *middle*), 12 cm wide blade, 14 cm tall total, base 7 cm wide and 5 cm tall. Described in NMNH catalog as "stone ornament, gorget."

Shell Gorgets

N. Cat. #83166 (Plate 22, *a*), possible Citico style or variant.
O. Cat. #83163, possible Citico style or variant.
P. Cat. #83164, possible Citico style or variant.
Q. Cat. #83165, Citico style.

No Provenience

The following are unprovenienced as a result of either a missing catalog number or a catalog number that does not appear in the catalog.

A. Cat. #83198, constricted-neck jar; burnished interior and exterior; soapstone tempered; flared rim with notched lip; 17.8 cm tall, base to shoulder 10.9 cm, 18.4 cm wide at mouth, 16.1 cm wide at neck, 19.1 cm wide at shoulder.

B. Constricted-neck jar; burnished with strap handles; sand tempered;

17.8 cm tall, base to shoulder 7.7 cm, 17.8 cm wide at mouth, 14.0 cm wide at neck, 20.9 cm wide at shoulder.

C. Open-mouth bowl; burnished interior and exterior; 11.4 cm tall, 30.2 cm diameter at mouth, flat base 12.7 cm wide.

D. Cat. #82873, miniature cazuela; 15.3 cm diameter, 7.7 cm tall; burnished surface completely covered with evenly spaced hollow implement punctations 4–5 mm wide, two perforations on either side of base; soapstone tempered.

E. Cat. #61150, Caldwell County, J. M. Spainhour, from Dr. H. C. Yarrow (?), constricted-neck pot with strap handle; 25 cm tall, 31.6 cm diameter; limestone temper (?).

References Cited

Abbott, Lawrence E., and Erica E. Sanborn
1996   *Archaeological Sample Survey, NC 16, North of Lucia to NC 150, Gaston, Lincoln, and Catawba Counties, North Carolina, T.I.P. Number R-2206: A Study of Soil Type and Erosion as Variables for the Prediction of Archaeological Site Eligibility Potential.* New South Associates Technical Report 406, New South Associates, Stone Mountain, Georgia.

Allen, R. O., C. G. Holland, and R. O. Luckenbach
1975a   Soapstone Artifacts: Tracing Prehistoric Trade Patterns in Virginia. *Science* 187(4171):57–58.

1975b   Movement of Prehistoric Soapstone in the James River Basin. *Quarterly Bulletin, Archaeological Society of Virginia* 29(4): 183–203.

Alvord, Clarence W., and Lee Bidgood (editors)
1912   *The First Explorations of the Trans-Allegheny Region by the Virginians, 1650–1674.* Arthur H. Clark, Cleveland.

Anderson, David G.
1986   Stability and Change in Chiefdom Level Societies: An Examination of Mississippian Political Evolution on the South Atlantic Slope. Paper presented at the 43rd Annual Southeastern Archaeological Conference, Nashville.

1989   The Mississippian in South Carolina. In *Studies in South Carolina Archaeology, Essays in Honor of Robert L. Stephenson,* edited by Albert C. Goodyear III and Glen T. Hanson, pp. 101–132. Anthropological Studies 9, Occasional Papers of the South Carolina Institute of Archaeology and Anthropology. University of South Carolina, Columbia.

1990a   The Mississippian Occupation and Abandonment of the Savannah River Valley. *Florida Anthropologist* 43(1):13–35.

1990b   Stability and Change in Chiefdom-Level Societies: An Examination of Mississippian Political Evolution on the South Atlantic Slope. In *Lamar Archaeology: Mississippian Chiefdoms in the Deep South,* edited by Mark Williams and Gary Shapiro, pp. 187–213. University of Alabama Press, Tuscaloosa.

1994a   *The Savannah River Chiefdoms: Political Change in the Late Prehistoric Southeast.* University of Alabama Press, Tuscaloosa.

1994b   Factional Competition and the Political Evolution of Mississippian Chiefdoms in the Southeastern United States. In *Factional Competition and Political Development in the New World,* edited by E. M. Brumfiel and J. W. Fox, pp. 61–76. University of Cambridge Press, Cambridge.

1996a   Chiefly Cycling Behavior and Large-Scale Abandonments as Viewed from the Savannah River Basin. In *Political Structure and Change in the Prehistoric Southeastern United States,* edited by J. F. Scarry, pp. 150–191. University of Florida Press, Gainesville.

1996b   Fluctuations Between Simple and Complex Chiefdoms: Cycling in the Late Prehistoric Southeast. In *Political Structure and Change in the Prehistoric Southeastern United States,* edited by J. F. Scarry, pp. 231–252. University of Florida Press, Gainesville.

1999   Examining Chiefdoms in the Southeast: An Application of Multiscalar Analysis. In *Great Towns and Regional Polities in the Prehistoric American Southwest and Southeast,* edited by J. E. Neitzel, pp. 215–242. University of New Mexico Press, Albuquerque.

Anderson, David G., David J. Hally, and James L. Rudolph

1986   The Mississippian Occupation of the Savannah River Valley. *Southeastern Archaeology* 5(1):32–51.

Ayers, Harvard G., L. J. Loucks, and B. L. Purrington

1980   Excavations at the Ward Site, a Pisgah Village in Western North Carolina. Paper presented at the 37th Annual Southeastern Archaeological Conference, New Orleans.

Baker, Steven G.

1972a   *The Morphology of the Aboriginal River Peoples of the Catawba River, South Carolina, 1700–1800.* Report prepared for the Department of History and the Institute of Archaeology and Anthropology, University of South Carolina.

1972b   Colono-Indian Pottery from Cambridge, South Carolina with Comments on the Historic Catawba Pottery Trade. *South Carolina Institute of Archaeology and Anthropology Notebook* 4:3–30.

1974   Cofitachique: Fair Province of Carolina. Unpublished Master's thesis, Department of History, University of South Carolina, Columbia.

1976   *The Historic Catawba Peoples: Exploratory Perspectives in Ethnohistory and Archaeology.* Report prepared for Duke Power Co. Ms. on file, Department of History, University of South Carolina, Columbia.

Barber, M. B., and E. B. Barfield

1992   The Late Woodland in the Environs of Saltville, Virginia: A Case for Petty Chiefdom Development. Paper presented at the 5th Upland Archaeology in the East Symposium, Boone, N.C.

Beck, Robin A., Jr.

1997a   The Burke Phase: Late Prehistoric Settlements in the Upper Catawba

River Valley, North Carolina. Unpublished Master's thesis, Department of Anthropology, University of Alabama, Tuscaloosa.

1997b   From Joara to Chiaha: Spanish Exploration of the Appalachian Summit Area, 1540–1568. *Southeastern Archaeology* 16(2):162–168.

Beck, Robin A., Jr., and David G. Moore

2001   The Burke Phase: Mississippian Chiefdoms in the North Carolina Foothills. Ms. on file, Department of Anthropology, Northwestern University, Chicago.

Blakely, Robert L., and Bettina Detweiler-Blakely

1989   The Impact of European Diseases in the Sixteenth-Century Southeast: A Case Study. *Midcontinental Journal of Archaeology* 14(1):62–89.

Blitz, J. H.

1993   *Ancient Chiefdoms of the Tombigbee.* University of Alabama Press, Tuscaloosa.

1999   Mississippian Chiefdoms and the Fission-Fusion Process. *American Antiquity* 64(4): 577–592.

Bohanan, E. R., Jr.

1975   A Petrographic and Spectrographic Analysis of Several Soapstone Artifacts from Tennessee and Soapstone Deposits in North Carolina and South Carolina in an Attempt to Determine the Source of the Artifacts. Unpublished Master's thesis, Department of Geology, University of Tennessee, Knoxville.

Booker, Karen M., Charles M. Hudson, and Robert L. Rankin

1992   Place Name Identification and Multilingualism in the Sixteenth-Century Southeast. *Ethnohistory* 39:399–451.

Boyd, Clifford

1986a   An Evolutionary Perspective on the Prehistory of Upper East Tennessee. Unpublished Ph.D. dissertation, Department of Anthropology, University of Tennessee, Knoxville.

1986b   *Archaeological Investigations in the Watauga Reservoir, Carter and Johnson Counties, Tennessee.* University of Tennessee, Department of Anthropology, Report of Investigations No. 44, Tennessee Valley Authority, Publications in Anthropology, No. 46. Knoxville.

Boyd, C. Clifford, Jr., and Gerald F. Schroedl

1987   In Search of Coosa. *American Antiquity* 52:840–844.

Brain, Jeffrey

1985   Introduction: Update of De Soto Studies Since the United States De Soto Expedition Commission Report. In *Final Report of the United States De Soto Expedition Commission.* Originally published 1939, reprinted by Smithsonian Institution Press, Washington, D.C.

Brown, Douglas Summers

1966   *The Catawba Indians: The People of the River.* University of South Carolina Press, Columbia.

Bushnell, D. I., Jr.
1939   The Use of Soapstone by the Indians of the Eastern United States. *Annual Report of the Smithsonian Institution*, pp. 471–489. Washington, D.C.

Cambron, James W., and D. C. Hulse
1969   *Handbook of Alabama Archaeology, Part 1: Point Types.* Archaeological Research Association of Alabama, Birmingham.

Carneiro, Robert
1981   The Chiefdom: Precursor of the State. In *The Transition to Statehood in the New World*, edited by G. D. Jones and R. R. Kautz. Cambridge University Press, Cambridge.

Clark, Larry R.
1976   *An Archaeological Survey of Burke County, North Carolina.* Pioneer Press, Morganton, North Carolina.

Coe, Joffre L.
1952a   Cultural Sequence of the Carolina Piedmont. In *Archaeology of Eastern United States*, edited by James B. Griffin. University of Chicago Press, Chicago.

1952b   Certain Eastern Siouan Pottery Types. In *Prehistoric Pottery of the Eastern United States*, edited by James B. Griffin. Museum of Anthropology, University of Michigan, Ann Arbor.

1964   Formative Cultures of the Carolina Piedmont. *Transactions of the American Philosophical Society* 54(5). Philadelphia.

1983   Through a Glass Darkly: An Archaeological View of North Carolina's More Distant Past. In *The Prehistory of North Carolina, An Archaeological Symposium*, edited by Mark A. Mathis and Jeffrey J. Crow, pp. 161–177. North Carolina Division of Archives and History, Raleigh.

1995   *Town Creek Indian Mound: A Native American Legacy.* University of North Carolina Press, Chapel Hill.

Coe, Joffre L., and Earnest Lewis
1952   Dan River Series Statement. In *Prehistoric Pottery of the Eastern United States*, edited by James B. Griffin. Museum of Anthropology, University of Michigan, Ann Arbor.

Davis, R. P. Stephen, Jr.
1987   Pottery from the Fredricks, Wall, and Mitchum Sites. In *The Siouan Project: Seasons I and II*, edited by Roy S. Dickens, Jr., H. Trawick Ward, and R. P. Stephen Davis, Jr., pp. 185–216. Monograph Series 1, Research Laboratories of Anthropology. University of North Carolina, Chapel Hill.

1988   Pottery. In Archaeology of the Historic Occaneechi Indians, edited by H. Trawick Ward and R. P. Stephen Davis, Jr. *Southern Indian Studies* 36-37:31–63.

1990a   *Aboriginal Settlement Patterns in the Little Tennessee River Valley.* University of Tennessee Department of Anthropology Report of Investigations No. 50, Tennessee Valley Authority Publications in Anthropology No. 54. Knoxville.

1990b The Travels of James Needham and Gabriel Arthur Through Virginia, North Carolina, and Beyond, 1673–1674. *Southern Indian Studies* 39:31–55.

Davis, R. P. Stephen, Jr., and H. Trawick Ward

1989 The Evolution of Siouan Communities in Piedmont North Carolina. Paper presented at the 46th Annual Meeting of the Southeastern Archaeological Conference, Tampa.

1991 The Evolution of Siouan Communities in Piedmont North Carolina. *Southeastern Archaeology* 10(1):40–53.

Deagan, Kathleen

1987 *Artifacts of the Spanish Colonies of Florida and the Caribbean 1500–1800.* Vol.1, *Ceramics, Glassware, and Beads.* Smithsonian Institution Press, Washington, D.C.

Decker, Deena S.

1988 Origin(s), Evolution and Systematics of *Cucurbita pepo* (Cucurbitaceae). *Economic Botany* 42:4–15.

Delpino, Irene

1992 The Pearson Memoir and Prehistory in Piedmont Carolina. *Carolina Backcountry Studies* 1:80–105.

DeMarrais, E. L., J. Castillo, and T. K. Earle

1996 Ideology, Materialization, and Power Strategies. *Current Anthropology* 37:15–31.

DePratter, Chester B.

1983 *Late Prehistoric and Early Historic Chiefdoms in the Southeastern United States.* Ph.D. dissertation, University of Georgia. University Microfilms, Ann Arbor.

1989 Cofitachequi: Ethnohistorical and Archaeological Evidence. In *Studies in South Carolina Archaeology, Essays in Honor of Robert L. Stephenson,* edited by Albert C. Goodyear III and Glen T. Hanson, pp. 133–156. Anthropological Studies 9, Occasional Papers of the South Carolina Institute of Archaeology and Anthropology. University of South Carolina, Columbia.

1994 The Chiefdom of Cofitachequi. In *The Forgotten Centuries: Indians and Europeans in the American South 1521–1704,* edited by Charles Hudson and Carmen Chaves Tesser, pp. 197–226. University of Georgia Press, Athens.

DePratter, Chester, Charles Hudson, and Marvin Smith

1983 Juan Pardo's Explorations in the Interior Southeast, 1566–1568. *Florida Historical Quarterly* 62:125–158.

1990 The Juan Pardo Expeditions: North from Santa Elena. *Southeastern Archaeology* 9(2):140–146.

DePratter, Chester B., and Christopher Judge

1990   Phase Characteristics: Wateree River. In *Lamar Archaeology: Mississippian Chiefdoms in the Deep South,* edited by Mark Williams and Gary Shapiro, pp. 56–58. University of Alabama Press, Tuscaloosa.

DePratter, Chester, and Marvin T. Smith

1980   Sixteenth-Century European Trade in the Southeastern United States: Evidence from the Juan Pardo Expeditions (1566–1568). In *Spanish Colonial Frontier Research,* edited by Henry F. Dobyns, pp. 66–77. Center for Anthropological Studies, Albuquerque.

Dickens, Roy S., Jr.

1967   The Route of Rutherford's Expedition Against the North Carolina Cherokees. *Southern Indian Studies* 19:3–24.

1970   The Pisgah Culture and Its Place in the Prehistory of the Southern Appalachians. Unpublished Ph.D. dissertation, Department of Anthropology, University of North Carolina, Chapel Hill.

1976   *Cherokee Prehistory: The Pisgah Phase in the Appalachian Summit Region.* University of Tennessee Press, Knoxville.

Dickens, Roy S., Jr., and Linda F. Carnes

1977   Preliminary Investigations at Soapstone Ridge, DeKalb County, Georgia. In *Proceedings of the Southeastern Archaeological Conference* Bulletin 20.

Dobyns, Henry F.

1983   *Their Number Become Thinned.* University of Tennessee Press, Knoxville.

Dorwin, John T., Robert N. Tiger III, and Marian Bistline

1975   Upper Hiwassee River Survey: 1974–1975. Ms. on file, Department of Sociology and Anthropology, Western Carolina University, Cullowhee.

Drennan, R. D.

1991   Pre-Hispanic Chiefdom Trajectories in Mesoamerica, Central America, and Northern South America. In *Chiefdoms: Power, Economy, and Ideology,* edited by T. K. Earle, pp. 263–287. Cambridge University Press, Cambridge.

Earle, Timothy K.

1987   Chiefdoms in Archaeological and Ethnohistorical Perspective. *Annual Review of Anthropology* 16:279–308.

1991   The Evolution of Chiefdoms. In *Chiefdoms: Power, Economy, and Ideology,* edited by T. K. Earle, pp. 1–15. Cambridge University Press, Cambridge.

1997   *How Chiefs Come to Power: The Political Economy in Prehistory.* Stanford University Press, Stanford.

Eastman, Jane M.

1994a   The North Carolina Radiocarbon Date Study (Part 1). *Southern Indian Studies* 42. North Carolina Archaeological Society, Raleigh, Research

Laboratories of Anthropology, University of North Carolina, Chapel Hill.

1994b   The North Carolina Radiocarbon Date Study (Part 2). *Southern Indian Studies* 43. North Carolina Archaeological Society, Raleigh, Research Laboratories of Anthropology, University of North Carolina, Chapel Hill.

Eblen, Martha
1981   *Summary Report of Testing at 31Mc41.* Ms. on file, Research Laboratories of Anthropology, University of North Carolina, Chapel Hill.

Egloff, Brian J.
1967   An Analysis of Ceramics from Cherokee Towns. Unpublished Master's thesis, Department of Anthropology, University of North Carolina, Chapel Hill.

Egloff, Keith T.
1971   Methods and Problems of Mound Exploration in the Southern Appalachian Area. Unpublished Master's thesis, Department of Anthropology, University of North Carolina, Chapel Hill.

Emerson, T. E.
1997   *Cahokia and the Archaeology of Power.* University of Alabama Press, Tuscaloosa.

Eubanks, W. S., Jr.
1989   Studying De Soto's Route: A Georgian House of Cards. *Florida Anthropologist* 42:369–80.

Evans, Clifford
1955   *A Ceramic Study of Virginia Archaeology.* Bulletin No. 160. Bureau of American Ethnology, Smithsonian Institution, Washington, D.C.

Ewen, Charles
1988   *The Discovery of de Soto's First Winter Encampment in Florida.* De Soto Working Paper 7. Alabama De Soto Commission, University of Alabama, State Museum of Natural History. Tuscaloosa.

1989   Anhaica: Discovery of Hernando de Soto's 1539–1540 Winter Camp. In *First Encounters, Spanish Explorations in the Caribbean and the United States, 1492–1570,* edited by Jerald T. Milanich and Susan Milbrath, pp. 110–118. University of Florida Press, Gainesville.

1990   Soldier of Fortune: Hernando de Soto in the Territory of the Apalachee, 1539–1540. In *Columbian Consequences,* edited by David Hurst Thomas, pp. 83–91. Smithsonian Institution Press, Washington, D.C.

Feinman, G.
1991   Demography, Surplus, and Inequality: Early Political Formations in Highland Mesoamerica. In *Chiefdoms: Power, Economy, and Ideology,* edited by T. K. Earle, pp. 229–262. Cambridge University Press, Cambridge.

Ferguson, Leland G.
1971   South Appalachian Mississippian. Unpublished Ph.D. dissertation,

Department of Anthropology, University of North Carolina, Chapel Hill.

1989   Lowcountry Plantations, the Catawba Nation, and River Burnished Pottery. In *Studies in South Carolina Archaeology, Essays in Honor of Robert L. Stephenson,* edited by Albert C. Goodyear III and Glen T. Hanson, pp. 185–191. Anthropological Studies 9, Occasional Papers of the South Carolina Institute of Archaeology and Anthropology. University of South Carolina, Columbia.

Ferguson, Terry A.
1980   Prehistoric Soapstone Procurement in Northwestern South Carolina. Unpublished Master's thesis, Department of Anthropology, University of Tennessee, Knoxville.

Fewkes, Vladimir J.
1944   Catawba Pottery-Making, with Notes on Pamunkey Pottery Making, Cherokee Pottery-Making, and Coiling. *Proceedings of the American Philosophical Society* 88. Philadelphia.

Fried, Morton
1967   *The Evolution of Political Society.* Random House, New York.

Galloway, Patricia
1995   *Choctaw Genesis: 1500–1700.* University of Nebraska Press, Lincoln.

Goggin, John
1960   The Spanish Olive Jar: An Introductory Study. *Yale University Publications in Anthropology* 62. Yale University Press, New Haven.

1968   Spanish Majolica in the New World. *Yale University Publications in Anthropology* 72. Yale University Press, New Hartford.

Gremillion, K. J.
1993   The Development of a Mutualistic Relationship Between Humans and Maypops (*Passiflora incarnata* L.) in the Southeastern United States. *Journal of Ethnobiology* 13:149–169.

Griffin, James B.
1967   Eastern North American Archaeology: A Summary. *Science* 156(3772): 175–191.

Hagerty, Gilbert
1963   The Iron Trade-Knife in Oneida Territory. *Pennsylvania Archaeologist* 33(1&2):93–104.

Hally, David J.
1975   *Archaeological Investigation of the King Site, Floyd County, Georgia.* Submitted to the National Endowment for the Humanities, Grant No. 20561-74-441.

1979   *Archaeological Investigation of the Little Egypt Site (9Mu102), Murray County, Georgia, 1969 Season.* Laboratory of Archaeology Series, Report No. 18. University of Georgia, Athens.

1986   An Overview of Lamar Culture. Paper presented at the Ocmulgee National Monument 50th Anniversary Conference, Macon, Georgia.

1990   Phase Characteristics: Upper Coosa River. In *Lamar Archaeology: Mississippian Chiefdoms in the Deep South,* edited by Mark Williams and Gary Shapiro, pp. 43–44, 52–55. University of Alabama Press, Tuscaloosa.

1993   The Territorial Size of Mississippian Chiefdoms. In *Archaeology of Eastern North America: Papers in Honor of Stephen Williams,* edited by J. B. Stoltman, pp. 143–168. Mississippi Department of Archives and History, Jackson.

1994   An Overview of Lamar Culture. In *Ocmulgee Archaeology 1936–1986,* edited by David J. Hally, pp. 144–174. University of Georgia Press, Athens and London.

1996   Platform Mound Construction and the Instability of Mississippian Chiefdoms. In *Political Structure and Change in the Prehistoric Southeastern United States,* edited by J. F. Scarry, pp. 92–127. University of Florida Press, Gainesville.

Hally, David J., and James L. Rudolph

1986   *Mississippi Period Archaeology of the Georgia Piedmont.* Laboratory of Archaeology Series, Report No. 24. University of Georgia, Athens.

Hann, John H.

1986   Translation of the Ecija Voyages of 1605 and 1609 and the Gonzalez Derrotero of 1609. *Florida Archaeology* 2:1–80.

Hargrove, Thomas H.

1997   Magnetometer Survey at the Berry Site (31BK22): A Study of Sixteenth-Century Spanish and Native American Contact in the Carolina Piedmont. Ms. on file, Office of State Archaeology, Raleigh.

Hargrove, Thomas H., and Robin A. Beck, Jr.

2001   Magnetometer and Auger Testing at the Berry Site (31BK22), Burke County, North Carolina. Paper presented at the 58th Annual Meeting of the Southeastern Archaeological Conference, Chattanooga.

Harrington, M. R.

1908   Catawba Potters and Their Work. *American Anthropologist* 10(3).

Hatch, James W.

1975   Social Dimensions of Dallas Burials. *Southeastern Archaeological Conference Bulletin* 18:132–138.

Hogue, Susan Homes

1988   A Bioarchaeological Study of Mortuary Practice and Change Among the Piedmont Siouan Indians. Unpublished Ph.D. dissertation, Department of Anthropology, University of North Carolina, Chapel Hill.

Holland, C. G.

1970   *An Archaeological Survey of Southwest Virginia.* Smithsonian Contributions to Anthropology No. 12. Smithsonian Institution Press, Washington, D.C.

Holmes, William H.

1890   Excavations in an Ancient Soapstone Quarry in the District of Columbia. *American Anthropologist* 3:321–330.

1903   Aboriginal Pottery of the Eastern United States. *Bureau of American Ethnology Annual Report* 20. Washington, D.C.

Hudson, Charles

1965   The Catawba Nation: A Social History. Unpublished Ph.D. dissertation, Department of Anthropology, University of North Carolina, Chapel Hill.

1970   *The Catawba Nation.* University of Georgia Press, Athens.

1976   *The Southeastern Indians.* University of Tennessee Press, Knoxville.

1986   Some Thoughts on the Early Social History of the Cherokee. In *The Conference on Cherokee Prehistory,* assembled by David G. Moore, pp. 139–147. Warren Wilson College, Swannanoa.

1987   An Unknown South: Spanish Explorers and Southeastern Chiefdoms. In *Visions and Revisions: Ethnohistoric Perspectives on Southern Cultures,* edited by George Sabo III and William M. Schneider, pp. 6–24. University of Georgia Press, Athens.

1990   *The Juan Pardo Expeditions.* Smithsonian Institution Press, Washington, D.C.

1997   *Knights of Spain, Warriors of the Sun: Hernando de Soto and the South's Ancient Chiefdoms.* University of Georgia Press, Athens and London.

Hudson, Charles, and Marvin T. Smith

1990   Reply to Eubanks. *Florida Anthropologist* 43(1): 36–42.

Hudson, Charles, Marvin T. Smith, and Chester DePratter

1984   The Hernando DeSoto Expedition: From Apalachee to Chiaha. *Southeastern Archaeology* 3:65–77.

Hudson, Charles, Marvin T. Smith, David J. Hally, Richard Polhemus, and Chester B. DePratter

1985   Coosa: A Chiefdom in the Sixteenth Century United States. *American Antiquity* 50:723–737.

1987   Reply to Boyd and Schroedl. *American Antiquity* 52:845–846.

Hudson, Charles, and Carmen Tesser

1994   *The Forgotten Centuries: Indians and Europeans in the American South 1521–1704.* University of Georgia Press, Athens.

Idol, Bruce

1995   The Yadkin River Headwater Region in the Late Prehistoric Period. Paper presented at the 52nd Annual Southeastern Archaeological Conference, Knoxville.

1996   Reconstructing Social Contexts in the Upper Yadkin River Headwater Region. Paper presented at the 61st Annual Meeting of the Society for American Archaeology, New Orleans.

Johnson, Allen W., and Timothy Earle

1987   *The Evolution of Human Societies.* Stanford University Press, Stanford.

Keel, Bennie C.

1972   Woodland Phases of the Appalachian Summit Area. Ph.D. disserta-
        tion, Department of Anthropology, Washington State University,
        Pullman.

1976   *Cherokee Archaeology.* University of Tennessee Press, Knoxville.

1990   Salvage Archaeology at the Hardins Site, 31Gs29, Gaston County,
        North Carolina. *Southern Indian Studies* 39:1–18.

Keeler, Robert W.

1971   An Archaeological Survey of the Upper Catawba River Valley. Un-
        published B.A. honors thesis, Department of Anthropology, Univer-
        sity of North Carolina, Chapel Hill.

Kidd, Kenneth E., and Martha A. Kidd

1970   *A Classification System for Glass Beads for the Use of Field Archaeologists.*
        Occasional Papers in Archaeology and History, Canadian Historic
        Sites, Ottawa.

Kimball, Larry R.

1985   *The 1977 Archaeological Reconnaissance: An Overall Assessment of the Ar-
        chaeological Resources of Tellico Reservoir.* Report of Investigations No.
        40. Department of Anthropology, University of Tennessee, Knox-
        ville.

Kimball, Larry R., Patti J. Evans-Shumate, and M. Scott Shumate

1996   *Nelson Mound Group Archaeological Project, Caldwell County, North Caro-
        lina.* Appalachian State University Laboratories of Archaeological
        Science. Submitted to the State Historic Preservation Office, North
        Carolina Division of Archives and History, Raleigh.

Knight, V. J.

1990   Social Organization and the Evolution of Hierarchy in Southeastern
        Chiefdoms. *Journal of Anthropological Research* 46:1–23.

Knight, V. J., and V. P. Steponaitis

1998   A New History of Moundville. In *Archaeology of the Moundville Chief-
        dom,* edited by V. J. Knight and V. P. Steponaitis, pp. 1–25. Smith-
        sonian Institution Press, Washington, D.C.

Larson, Lewis

1971   Settlement Distribution During the Mississippian Period. *Southeast-
        ern Archaeological Conference Bulletin* 13:19–25.

1990   The Pardo Expedition: What Was the Direction at Departure? *South-
        eastern Archaeology* 9(2):124–139.

Lefler, Hugh (editor)

1967   *A New Voyage to Carolina by John Lawson* [1709]. University of North
        Carolina Press, Chapel Hill.

Levy, Janet E., and J. Alan May

1987   Archaeological Investigations at 31Gs30, Gaston County, North Caro-
        lina. Paper presented at the 44th Annual Southeastern Archaeologi-
        cal Conference, Charleston.

Levy, Janet E., J. Alan May, and David G. Moore
1990   From Ysa to Joara: Cultural Diversity in the Catawba Valley from the Fourteenth to Sixteenth Century. In *Columbian Consequences*, vol. 2, edited by David Hurst Thomas, pp. 153–168. Smithsonian Institution Press, Washington, D.C.

Lewis, Thomas M. N., and Madeline Kneberg
1946   *Hiwassee Island: An Archaeological Account of Four Tennessee Indian Peoples.* University of Tennessee Press, Knoxville.

Lister, Florence C., and Robert H. Lister
1982   *Sixteenth Century Maiolica Pottery in the Valley of Mexico.* Anthropological Papers of the University of Arizona, No. 39. University of Arizona Press, Tucson.

Little, Keith J., and Caleb Curren
1990   Conquest Archaeology of Alabama. In *Columbian Consequences*, vol. 2, edited by David Hurst Thomas, pp. 169–196. Smithsonian Institution Press, Washington, D.C.

Lopinot, Neal H.
1983   Analysis of Flotation Sample Materials from the Late Archaic Horizon. Chapter 7 in *The 1983 Excavations at the Cahokia Interpretive Center Tract, St. Clair County, Illinois,* edited by Michael S. Nassaney, Neal H. Lopinot, Brian M. Butler, and Richard W. Jefferies, pp. 77–108. Research Paper No. 37. Center for Archaeological Investigations, Southern Illinois University, Carbondale.

Loucks, L. Jill
1982   General Report on 1982 Excavations at the Ward Site (31WT22), Watauga County, North Carolina. Ms. on file, Department of Anthropology, Appalachian State University, Boone, North Carolina.

McCabe, J. Terrence, Thomas H. Hargrove, and Jerry L. Cross (edited by Mark A. Mathis)
1978   U.S. 321: A Cultural Resource Reconnaissance Survey of the Proposed U.S. 321 Relocation: Gaston, Lincoln, and Catawba Counties, North Carolina. Ms. on file, North Carolina Office of State Archaeology, Raleigh.

Marshall, Rhea Rogers
1988   Intrasite Settlement Patterns at the Hardy Site, 31SR50. Unpublished Master's thesis, Department of Anthropology, Wake Forest University, Winston-Salem.

Martin, Alexander C., and William D. Barkley
1961   *Seed Identification Manual.* University of California Press, Berkeley.

Mathis, Mark A.
1979   Shuford Site National Register Nomination. Ms. on file, Office of State Archaeology, North Carolina Division of Archives and History, Raleigh.
1980   31Bk56. Memorandum on file, Research Laboratories of Archaeology, University of North Carolina, Chapel Hill.

1981   The Blue Rock Soapstone Quarry (31YC7), Yancey County, North Carolina. In *Collected Papers on the Archaeology of North Carolina,* edited by Joseph B. Mountjoy, pp. 81–103. North Carolina Archaeological Council Publication No. 19. Raleigh.

Mathis, Mark A., and David G. Moore

1984   Some Thoughts on Woodland Period Ceramics from Northwestern North Carolina and Adjacent Areas. In *Upland Archaeology in the East: Symposium 2,* edited by Michael B. Barber. Cultural Resources Report No. 5. USDA Forest Service, Southern Region.

May, J. Alan

1985   *An Archaeological Reconnaissance of Selected Portions of Gaston County, North Carolina.* Submitted to North Carolina Division of Archives and History, Archaeology and Historic Preservation Section, Raleigh.

1987   Archaeological Investigations at 31GS55, Gaston County, N.C. Paper presented at the 44th Annual Southeastern Archaeological Conference, Charleston.

1988   Public Archaeology at the Schiele Museum: The Carolina Piedmont Archaeology Project. *South Carolina Antiquities* 20(1&2):21–28.

1989   Archaeological Excavations at the Crowders Creek Site (31Gs55): A Late Woodland Farmstead in the Catawba River Valley, Gaston County, North Carolina. *Southern Indian Studies* 38:23–48. Archaeological Society of North Carolina, Chapel Hill.

May, J. Alan, and Robert A. Pace

n.d.   Archaeological Investigations at the Crowders Creek Site, 31GS55, Gaston County. Ms. on file, Office of State Archaeology, Raleigh.

May, J. Alan, and V. Ann Tippett

2000   Early Historic Catawba Nation Archaeology. Paper presented at the 57th Annual Meeting of the Southeastern Archaeological Conference, Macon, Georgia.

Merrell, James H.

1982   *Natives in a New World: The Catawba Indians of Carolina, 1650–1800.* Ph.D. dissertation, Johns Hopkins University. University Microfilms, Ann Arbor.

1989   *The Indians' New World: Catawbas and Their Neighbors from European Contact Through the Era of Removal.* University of North Carolina Press, Chapel Hill.

Meyers, M. S.

1995   Natural Factors Affecting the Settlement of Chiefdoms in Northwest Georgia. Unpublished Master's thesis, Department of Anthropology, University of Georgia, Athens.

Milner, George R.

1980   Epidemic Disease in the Postcontact South: A Reappraisal. *Midcontinental Journal of Archaeology* 5:39–56.

1998   *The Cahokia Chiefdom: The Archaeology of a Mississippian Society.* Smithsonian Institution Press, Washington, D.C.

Milner, G. R., and S. Schroeder
  1999   Mississippian Sociopolitical Systems. In *Great Towns and Regional Polities in the Prehistoric American Southwest and Southeast*, edited by J. E. Neitzel, pp. 95–108. University of New Mexico Press, Albuquerque.

Misra, K. C., and F. B. Keller
  1978   Ultramafic Bodies in the Southern Appalachians: A Review. *American Journal of Science* 278:389–418.

Mitchem, Jeffrey M.
  1989   Redefining Safety Harbor: Late Prehistoric/Protohistoric Archaeology in West Peninsular Florida. Unpublished Ph.D. dissertation, University of Florida, Gainesville.

Montgomery, F. H.
  1977   *Seeds and Fruits of Plants of Eastern Canada and Northeastern United States*. University of Toronto Press, Toronto.

Mooney, James
  1894   *The Siouan Tribes of the East*. Bulletin No. 22. Bureau of American Ethnology, Smithsonian Institution, Washington, D.C.

  1982   *Myths of the Cherokee*. Reprinted, Charles and Randy Elder, Nashville. Originally published 1900, Nineteenth Annual Report of the Bureau of American Ethnology, Washington, D.C.

Moore, David G.
  1981   A Comparison of Two Pisgah Ceramic Assemblages. Unpublished Master's thesis, Department of Anthropology, University of North Carolina, Chapel Hill.

  1983   Report on the Excavation of a Burial at Gaston County Site W055. Ms. on file, North Carolina Office of State Archaeology, Raleigh.

  1986   The Pisgah Phase: Cultural Continuity in the Appalachian Summit. In *The Conference on Cherokee Prehistory*, assembled by David G. Moore. Warren Wilson College, Swannanoa, North Carolina.

  1987   Archaeological Investigations in the Upper Catawba Valley. Paper presented at the 44th Annual Southeastern Archaeological Conference, Charleston.

  1999   Late Prehistoric and Early Historic Period Aboriginal Settlement in the Catawba Valley, North Carolina. Ph.D. dissertation, Department of Anthropology, University of North Carolina, Chapel Hill.

Moore, David G., and Robin A. Beck, Jr.
  1994   New Evidence of Sixteenth Century Spanish Artifacts in the Catawba River Valley, North Carolina. Paper presented at the 51st Annual Southeastern Archaeological Conference, Lexington, Kentucky.

Moore, David G., and Christopher B. Rodning
  2001   In Search of Burned Buildings at the Berry Site. Paper presented at the 58th Annual Meeting of the Southeastern Archaeological Society, Chattanooga.

Mountjoy, Joseph B.
  1989   Early Radiocarbon Dates from a Site on the Pee Dee–Siouan Frontier

in the Piedmont of Central North Carolina. *Southern Indian Studies* 38:7–21.

Muller, Jon D.

1997 *Mississippian Political Economy.* Plenum Press, New York.

Myer, William E.

1928 Indian Trails of the Southeast. *Forty-second Annual Report of the Bureau of American Ethnology.* Washington, D.C.

Navey, Liane

1982 An Introduction to Mortuary Practices of the Historic Sara. Unpublished Master's thesis, Department of Anthropology, University of North Carolina, Chapel Hill.

Oberg, K.

1955 Types of Social Structure Among the Lowland Tribes of South and Central America. *American Anthropologist* 57(3): 472–487.

Oliver, Billy L.

1981 The Piedmont Tradition: Refinement of the Savannah River Stemmed Point Type. Unpublished Master's thesis, Department of Anthropology, University of North Carolina, Chapel Hill.

1992 Settlements of the Pee Dee Culture. Unpublished Ph.D. dissertation, Department of Anthropology, University of North Carolina, Chapel Hill.

Pace, Robert A.

1986 1985 Testing at the Crowders Creek Site, 31GS55, Gaston County, North Carolina. Ms. on file, North Carolina Office of State Archaeology, Raleigh.

Pauketat, T. R.

1994 *The Ascent of Chiefs.* University of Alabama Press, Tuscaloosa.

Peebles, Christopher, and Susan M. Kus

1977 Some Archaeological Correlates of Ranked Societies. *American Antiquity* 42:421–448.

Phillips, Philip

1970 *Archaeological Survey in the Lower Yazoo Basin, Mississippi, 1949–1955.* Papers of the Peabody Museum of American Archaeology and Ethnology Vol. 60. Harvard University, Cambridge.

Polhemus, Richard R.

1987 *The Toqua Site: A Late Mississippian, Dallas Phase Town.* Report of Investigations No. 41. Department of Anthropology, University of Tennessee, Knoxville.

1988 Bead Analysis. Appendix XV in *Spanish Artifacts from Santa Elena,* by Stanley South, Russell Skowronek, and Richard Johnson, pp. 425–452. Anthropological Studies 7. South Carolina Institute of Archaeology and Anthropology, University of South Carolina, Columbia.

n.d. Caldwell County Field Notes. Ms. on file, Research Laboratories of Archaeology, University of North Carolina, Chapel Hill.

Radford, A. W., H. E. Ahles, and C. R. Bell
1968   *A Manual of the Vascular Flora of the Carolinas.* University of North Carolina Press, Chapel Hill.

Ramenofsky, Ann F.
1987   *Vectors of Death: The Archaeology of European Contact.* University of New Mexico Press, Albuquerque.

Reid, J. Jefferson
1965   A Comparative Statement on Ceramics from the Hollywood and Town Creek Mounds. *Southern Indian Studies* 17:12–25.
1967   Pee Dee Pottery from the Mound at Town Creek. Unpublished Master's thesis, Department of Anthropology, University of North Carolina, Chapel Hill.

Rights, Douglas L.
1931   The Trading Path to the Indians. *North Carolina Historical Review* 8(4):403–426. Reprinted 1989, *Southern Indian Studies* 38:49–73.
1957   *The American Indian in North Carolina.* John F. Blair, Winston-Salem.

Rivers, William J. (editor)
1874   *An exact account of ye Number and Strength of all the Indian Nations that were subject to the Government of South Carolina, and solely traded with them in ye beginning of ye year 1715 . . .* British Public Record Office, Colonial Office Series 5 (BPRO, C05:1265, Q201). Walker, Evans & Cogswell, Charleston.

Robinson, Kenneth W.
1990   Archaeological Survey and Deep Testing of a Corridor Along the Catawba River in Morganton, Burke County, North Carolina. Ms. on file, Office of State Archaeology, Raleigh.
1996   Archaeological Investigations in McDowell County, North Carolina, 1988–1990. Ms. on file, Office of State Archaeology, Raleigh.

Robinson, Kenneth W., David G. Moore, and Ruth Y. Wetmore
1996   Advances in Understanding Woodland Chronology and Settlement in the Appalachian Summit Region of Western North Carolina. Paper presented at the Integrating Appalachian Highlands Archaeology Symposium, Albany, New York.

Rodning, Christopher B.
1996   Gender and Social Institutions of Native Communities of the Appalachian Summit. Paper presented at the 53rd Annual Southeastern Archaeological Conference, Birmingham, Alabama.

Rogers, Anne Frazier, and Jane Brown
1994   Artifacts from the Hiwassee River Valley in North Carolina. Paper presented at the 51st Annual Southeastern Archaeological Conference, Lexington, Kentucky.

Rogers, Rhea J.
1993   A Re-examination of the Concept of the Tribe: A Case Study from the Upper Yadkin Valley, North Carolina. Unpublished Ph.D. disser-

tation, Department of Anthropology, University of North Carolina, Chapel Hill.

Rudolph, James L.

1984   Earthlodges and Platform Mounds: Changing Public Architecture in the Southeastern United States. *Southeastern Archaeology* 3(1):33–45.

1986   Lamar Period Exploitation of Aquatic Resources in the Middle Oconee River Valley. *Early Georgia* 11(1-2):86–103.

Saunders, William L. (editor)

1886   *The Colonial Records of North Carolina,* vol. 5. Raleigh.

Scarry, J. F.

1996   Stability and Change in the Apalachee Chiefdom: Centralization, Decentralization, and Social Reproduction. In *Political Structure and Change in the Prehistoric Southeastern United States,* edited by J. F. Scarry, pp. 192–227. University of Florida Press, Gainesville.

1999   How Great Were the Southeastern Polities? In *Great Towns and Regional Polities in the Prehistoric American Southwest and Southeast,* edited by J. E. Neitzel, pp. 59–74. University of New Mexico Press, Albuquerque.

Schoolcraft, Henry

1853   *Historical and Statistical Information Respecting the History, Conditions, and Prospects of the Indian Tribes of the United States,* vol. 3. Bureau of Indian Affairs, Philadelphia.

Senior, Christopher D.

1981   A Preliminary Analysis of Pisgah Phase Ceramics from the Ward Site, Northwestern North Carolina. Ms. on file, Office of State Archaeology, Raleigh.

Service, Elman

1962   *Primitive Social Organization: An Evolutionary Perspective.* Random House, New York.

Setzler, Frank M., and Jesse D. Jennings

1941   *Peachtree Mound and Village Site.* Bulletin No. 131. Bureau of American Ethnology, Washington, D.C.

Simpkins, Daniel L.

1985   First Phase Investigations of Late Aboriginal Settlement Systems in the Eno, Haw, and Dan River Drainages, North Carolina. Research Laboratories of Anthropology, University of North Carolina, Chapel Hill.

Skowronek, Russell K.

1991   Return to Peachtree: A Catalogue of Amateur Surface Collections from Cherokee and Clay Counties, North Carolina. Ms. on file, Office of State Archaeology, Raleigh.

Smith, Bruce D.

1984   Mississippian Expansion: Tracing the Historical Development of an Explanatory Model. *Southeastern Archaeology* 3:13–32.

1985   The Role of Chenopodium as a Domesticate in Pre-maize Garden Systems of the Eastern United States. *Southeastern Archaeology* 4:51–72.

Smith, Marvin T.
1981   *Archaeological Investigations at the Dyer Site, 9GE5.* Wallace Reservoir Project, Contribution No. 11. Department of Anthropology, University of Georgia, Athens.
1987   *Archaeology of Aboriginal Culture Change in the Interior Southeast: Depopulation During the Early Historic Period.* University of Florida Press, Florida State Museum, Gainesville.

Smith, Marvin, and Steven Kowalewski
1981   Tentative Identification of a Prehistoric "Province" in Piedmont Georgia. *Early Georgia* 8:1–13.

Smith, Marvin T., and Mark Williams
1990   Phase Characteristics: Piedmont Oconee River. In *Lamar Archaeology: Mississippian Chiefdoms in the Deep South,* edited by Mark Williams and Gary Shapiro, pp. 60–63. University of Alabama Press, Tuscaloosa.

Snow, Dean R., and Kim M. Lanphear
1988   European Contact and Indian Depopulation in the Northeast: The Timing of the First Epidemics. *Ethnohistory* 35(1): 15–33.

South, Stanley A.
1959   A Study of the Prehistory of the Roanoke Rapids Basin. Unpublished Master's thesis, Department of Anthropology, University of North Carolina, Chapel Hill.
1973   Indian Pottery Taxonomy for the South Carolina Coast. *The Notebook* 5:54–55.

South, Stanley, Russell Skowronek, and Richard Johnson
1988   *Spanish Artifacts from Santa Elena.* Anthropological Studies 7. South Carolina Institute of Archaeology and Anthropology, University of South Carolina, Columbia.

Spainhour, James Mason
1873   Antiquities in Lenoir County, North Carolina. *Annual Report of the Board of Regents of the Smithsonian Institution* (1871), pp. 404–406. Government Printing Office, Washington, D.C.
1897   Speech delivered July 2, 1897. Copy of manuscript from Charles Carey.
1899   Speech before Chester Lodge No. 18, South Carolina, April 14, 1899. Copy of manuscript from Charles Carey.

Speck, Frank G.
1935   Siouan Tribes of the Carolinas as Known from Catawba, Tutelo, and Documentary Sources. *American Anthropologist* 37(2):201–225.
1939   The Catawba Nation and Its Neighbors. *North Carolina Historical Review* 16(4):404–417.

Spencer, C. S.
1987   Rethinking the Chiefdom. In *Chiefdoms in the Americas,* edited by

R. D. Drennan and C. A. Uribe, pp. 369–389. University Press of America, Lanham, Maryland.

1990   On the Tempo and Mode of State Formation: Neoevolutionism Reconsidered. *Journal of Anthropological Archaeology* 9(1): 1–30.

1994   Factional Ascendance, Dimensions of Leadership, and the Development of Centralized Authority. In *Factional Competition and Political Development in the New World,* edited by E. M. Brumfiel and J. W. Fox, pp. 31–43. University of Cambridge Press, Cambridge.

Steponaitis, Vincas P.

1978   Location Theory and Complex Chiefdoms: A Mississippian Example. In *Mississippian Settlement Patterns,* edited by Bruce D. Smith, pp. 417–453. Academic Press, New York.

1991   Contrasting Patterns of Mississippian Development. In *Chiefdoms: Power, Economy, and Ideology,* edited by T. K. Earle, pp. 193–228. Cambridge University Press, Cambridge.

Storey, Rebecca

1985   Review of *Their Number Become Thinned:* Native American Population Dynamics in Eastern North America. *American Anthropologist* 87:455.

Stuckey, Jasper L.

1965   *North Carolina: Its Geology and Mineral Resources.* Department of Conservation and Development, Raleigh.

Stuiver, M., and B. Becker

1986   High-Precision Decadal Calibration of the Radiocarbon Time Scale, A.D. 1950–2500 B.C. *Radiocarbon* 28:863–910.

Swanton, John R.

1936   Early History of the Eastern Siouan Tribes. In *Essays in Anthropology Presented to A. L. Kroeber.* University of California Press, Berkeley.

1939   *Final Report of the United States DeSoto Expedition Commission.* House Document 71, 76th Congress, 1st session, Washington, D.C.

1946   *The Indians of the Southeastern United States.* Bulletin No. 137. Bureau of American Ethnology, Smithsonian Institution, Washington, D.C.

Thomas, Cyrus

1887   Burial Mounds of the Northern Sections of the United States. *Fifth Annual Report of the Bureau of American Ethnology, 1883–1884,* pp. 1–119. Washington, D.C.

1891   *Catalogue of Prehistoric Works East of the Rocky Mountains.* Bulletin No. 12. Bureau of American Ethnology, Smithsonian Institution, Washington, D.C.

1894   Report on the Mound Explorations of the Bureau of American Ethnology. *Twelfth Annual Report of the Bureau of American Ethnology, 1890–1891,* pp. 3–730. Washington, D.C.

Thomas, David Hurst (editor)

1990   *Columbian Consequences.* Vol. 2, *Archaeological and Historical Perspectives on the Spanish Borderlands East.* Smithsonian Institution Press, Washington, D.C.

Tippitt, V. Ann, and I. Randolph Daniel, Jr.
1987   Lithic Artifacts from the Fredricks, Wall, and Mitchum Sites. In *The Siouan Project: Seasons I and II,* edited by Roy S. Dickens, Jr., H. Trawick Ward, and R. P. Stephen Davis, Jr., pp. 217–236. Monograph Series 1. Research Laboratories of Anthropology, University of North Carolina, Chapel Hill.

Ward, H. Trawick
1965   Correlation of Mississippian Soil Types. *Southeastern Archaeological Conference Bulletin* 3:42–48.
1977   A Summary Report of Excavations at 31Mc41. Ms. on file, Research Laboratories of Archaeology, University of North Carolina, Chapel Hill.
1980a   Assessment of the Status of Bk56. Ms. on file, Research Laboratories of Archaeology, University of North Carolina, Chapel Hill.
1980b   Recent Disturbance at Bk56. Ms. on file, Research Laboratories of Archaeology, University of North Carolina, Chapel Hill.
1983   A Review of Archaeology in the North Carolina Piedmont: A Study of Change. In *The Prehistory of North Carolina, An Archaeological Symposium,* edited by Mark A. Mathis and Jeffrey J. Crow, pp. 53–82, North Carolina Division of Archives and History, Raleigh.

Ward, H. Trawick, and R. P. Stephen Davis, Jr.
1989   The Impact of Old World Diseases on the Native Inhabitants of the North Carolina Piedmont. Paper presented at the 46th Annual Southeastern Archaeological Conference, Tampa.
1993   *Indian Communities on the North Carolina Piedmont* A.D. *1000 to 1700.* Monograph No. 2. Research Laboratories of Anthropology, University of North Carolina, Chapel Hill.
1999   *Time Before History: The Archaeology of North Carolina.* University of North Carolina Press, Chapel Hill.

Waselkov, Gregory A.
1989   Indian Maps of the Colonial Southeast. In *Powhatan's Mantle: Indians in the Colonial Southeast,* edited by Peter H. Wood, Gregory A. Waselkov, and M. Thomas Hatley, pp. 292–343. University of Nebraska Press, Lincoln.

Watson, Patty Jo
1976   In Pursuit of Prehistoric Subsistence: A Comparative Account of Some Contemporary Flotation Techniques. *Midcontinental Journal of Archaeology* 12:77–100.

Wauchope, Robert
1966   *Archaeological Survey of Northern Georgia with a Test of Some Cultural Hypotheses.* Society for American Archaeology Memoir 21, Salt Lake City, Utah.

Weaver, David S.
1988   Report on the Human Skeletal Remains from the Berry Site (31BK22). Report submitted to the North Carolina Office of State Archaeology, Raleigh.

Welch, P. D.
1991   *Moundville's Economy.* University of Alabama Press, Tuscaloosa.

Wheaton, Thomas R., Amy Friedlander, and Patrick H. Garrow
1983   *Yaughan and Curriboo Plantations: Studies in Afro-American Archaeology.* Submitted to the National Park Service, Southeast Regional Office, Atlanta.

Widmer, R. J.
1988   *The Evolution of the Calusa.* University of Alabama Press, Tuscaloosa.

Willey, Gordon R., and Philip Phillips
1958   *Method and Theory in American Archaeology.* University of Chicago Press, Chicago and London.

Williams, Mark
1984   *Archaeological Excavations, Scull Shoals Mounds, Georgia.* Cultural Resources Report No. 6. USDA Forest Service, Southern Region.
1990   Middle Ocmulgee River. In *Lamar Archaeology: Mississippian Chiefdoms in the Deep South,* edited by Mark Williams and Gary Shapiro, pp. 63–64. University of Alabama Press, Tuscaloosa.

Williams, Mark, and Gary Shapiro (editors)
1990   *Lamar Archaeology: Mississippian Chiefdoms in the Deep South.* University of Alabama Press, Tuscaloosa.

Wilson, Jack H., Jr.
1983   A Study of Late Prehistoric, Protohistoric, and Historic Indians of the Carolina and Virginia Piedmont: Structure, Process, and Ecology. Unpublished Ph.D. dissertation, Department of Anthropology, University of North Carolina, Chapel Hill.
1985   Mundane Matters, Missive #1—Ceramics of the Late Prehistoric, Protohistoric, and Historic Periods from the Carolina and Virginia Piedmont: The Lower Catawba River Drainage. *South Carolina Antiquities* 17:18–34.

Woodall, J. Ned
1984   *The Donnaha Site: 1973, 1975 Excavations.* North Carolina Archaeological Council Publication No. 22. Raleigh.

Worth, John R.
1994a   Exploration and Trade in the Deep Frontier of Spanish Florida: Possible Sources for Sixteenth-Century Spanish Artifacts in Western North Carolina. Paper presented at the 51st Annual Southeastern Archaeological Conference, Lexington, Kentucky.
1994b   Recollections of the Juan Pardo Expeditions: The 1584 Domingo de Leon Account. Ms. on file, Fernbank Museum of Natural History, Atlanta.

Wright, Henry T.
  1984   Prestate Political Formations. In *On the Evolution of Complex Societies: Essays in Honor of Harry Hojier 1982*, edited by Timothy K. Earle, pp. 43–77. Undena Publications, Malibu.

Wright, J. Leitch, Jr.
  1981   *The Only Land They Knew: The Tragic Story of the American Indians in the Old South.* Free Press, New York.

Yarnell, Richard A.
  1982   Problems of Interpretation of Archaeological Plant Remains of the Eastern Woodlands. *Southeastern Archaeology* 1:1–17.

  1986   A Survey of Prehistoric Crop Plants in Eastern North America. In *New World Paleoethnobotany: Collected Papers in Honor of Leonard Blake. Missouri Archaeologist* 47:47–59.

Yarnell, Richard A., and M. Jean Black
  1985   Temporal Trends Indicated by a Survey of Archaic and Woodland Plant Food Remains from Southeastern North America. *Southeastern Archaeology* 4:93–106.

Index